D The Best of

WASHINGTON, D.C.

REVISED EDITION

Editors
Colleen Dunn Bates
Robert C. Fisher

Contributing Editors
Ellen Brown, Michael Dulan,
Rob Kasper, Nina Killham, Phyllis Richman

Associate Editor
Catherine Jordan

Additional editorial assistance
Nicky J. Leach, Roland Leiser

Prentice Hall Travel Editor
Amit Shah

Operations
Alain Gayot

Directed by
André Gayot

PRENTICE HALL

New York ■ London ■ Toronto ■ Sydney ■ Tokyo ■ Singapore

Other Gault Millau Guides Available
from Prentice Hall Trade Division

The Best of Chicago
The Best of France
The Best of Hong Kong
The Best of Italy
The Best of London
The Best of Los Angeles
The Best of New England
The Best of New York
The Best of Paris
The Best of San Francisco

Published by Prentice Hall Trade Division
A Division of Simon & Schuster Inc.
15 Columbus Circle
New York, NY 10023

Please address all comments regarding
The Best of Washington, D.C. to:
Gault Millau, Inc.
P.O. Box 361144
Los Angeles, CA 90036
(213) 965-3529

Please address all advertising queries to:
Mr. Geoffrey Gropp, Vice President
Welsh Publishing Group, Inc.
300 Madison Avenue
New York, NY 10017
(212) 687-0680

Library of Congress Cataloging-in-Publication Data

The Best of Washington, D.C. / contributing editors, Ellen Brown . . .
[et. al.].—Rev. ed.
    p.   c.m.
  ISBN 0-13-068230-6: $16.95
  1. Washington (D.C.)—Description—1981—Guide-books.
I. Brown, Ellen.
F192.3.B48   1990
917.53'044—dc20   89-26492

Special thanks to the staff of Prentice Hall Travel for their invaluable
aid in producing these Gault Millau guides.

Manufactured in the United States of America

CONTENTS

OUT OF WASHINGTON

Had enough of politics? Spend a refreshing day in Annapolis or Baltimore. Go for a sail on the Chesapeake Bay, salute the cadets at the U.S. Naval Academy, or wander the stalls of the Lexington Market. Includes suggestions for pleasant Sunday drives.

CITYLORE

A collection of offbeat, amusing stories that offer a look at D.C.'s colorful—and sordid—past.

BASICS

Everything you need to know about getting around Washington like a true native. Includes useful phone numbers, a calendar of interesting events and loads of transportation tips.

MAPS

Finding your way around the capital.

INDEX

INTRODUCTION

POTOMAC FEVER

Washington is such a glorious city these days, it's hard to believe that a mere 200 years ago it was scoffed at as crude, undeveloped and uninspired. Unlike other great capitals of the world, Washington was not chosen because of its vital role in trade and commerce or because of its rich history. Rather, America's first leaders set about to create a new form of government in the world, and as its seat they planned a city from the ground up—or, more precisely, from the swamp up. The early years were rocky. The city was so unpopular and unpleasant that congressmen stayed as briefly as their legislative duties allowed, and most left their families at home. For foreign ambassadors, early Washington was considered a hardship post.

The year 1814 was a turning point. Official Washington was literally burned to the ground by the British, and the spirit of city residents was nearly broken. But in the darkest moments, the citizens of this capital city met the challenge, and Washington finally began its rise to its hoped-for splendor. Three years after the fire, James Monroe moved back into the official residence of the Chief Executive, until then called simply "The President's House." But the repainting of the smoke-stained sandstone walls of the mansion lent it a sparkling new look and gave it the name it has been known by ever since: The White House. Congress, too, received a revitalized home, and Washington finally began to take pride in itself and realize the potential that George Washington had seen when he picked the undeveloped site.

The city grew with the republic, as each national crisis and victory left its mark and helped build its character. From the earliest days, when Native Americans came here to seek redress for broken treaties and broken promises, Washington has attraced petitioners who travel to the capital in the name of a cause. The largest gathering in history was in 1969 in protest of the Vietnam War, when an estimated 600,000 people filled the streets and brought the city to a virtual standstill. The most eloquent and inspiring demonstration was in August 1963, when more than 200,000 people marched for civil rights and gathered at the foot of the Lincoln Memorial to hear Dr. Martin Luther King, Jr. deliver his famous "I have a dream" speech. The tradition continues as new issues arise. In October 1987, hundreds of thousands of gays, lesbians, AIDS victims and friends of AIDS victims gathered on the Mall to demand equal rights for homosexuals, pay tribute to fallen comrades and request greater government efforts to combat the deadly disease. In November 1989, the Capitol lawn filled with a massive crowd demonstrating against restrictive abortion legislation.

Washington is one of the most political cities in the world. It is the home of politicians who make the decisions that shape history, the lobbyists and lawyers who attempt to influence the course of events in a direction acceptable to their clients, a mass of government bureaucrats who keep the huge governmental machine oiled and running, no matter who is in charge, and thousands of journalists who seek, with varying degrees of success, to keep the other groups honest.

It is a city that keeps up with the news of the world on a minute-by-minute basis, a city with an all-consuming need for information that can't wait for the nightly news. Television sets all over town are turned to the Cable News Network or C-SPAN to catch the latest news developments or a critical House or Senate debate. Countless teletype machines clatter away in offices and corridors of government buildings, spewing out the latest news from around the globe, courtesy of AP, UPI and Reuters.

Amid all the spectacular monuments, museums and galleries, the business of the city goes on, day and night. Visitors can witness history inadvertently, as a presidential motorcade ties up traffic on a city street, or deliberately, by sitting in the audience when Congress investigates the latest government scandal or considers a new Supreme Court nominee. Official business can be conducted any time, over breakfast, lunch, cocktails or dinner. After-work receptions are a way of life in Washington, and more than a few young political aides and reporters have survived their early years on low salaries with the free food and drink of the reception circuit.

In his Pulitzer Prize–winning novel *Advice and Consent*, Allen Drury wrote of Washington,"It is a city of temporaries, a city of just-arrived and only-visitings, built on the shifting sands of politics, filled with people just passing through." This seems especially true in the spring, when tourist buses clog the major traffic arteries and lines of sightseers make passage from the House to the Senate side of the Capitol, an exercise in survival of the fittest. Drury's words also hit home in the difficult shake-out times after national elections, when old faces are replaced by new, and political trends wax or wane according to the will of the electorate.

But increasingly, Washington is becoming less of a city of transients and more a permanent place for those touched by the force of political power. More and more, those who lose their previous positions of power choose to stay on, biding their time until the pendulum swings back and their views and counsel are once again in vogue. This captivating quality of the city, coupled with the feeling that there's nothing going on anywhere that is as important as what's happening here, is known as "Potomac Fever." By the time you realize you've caught it, it's too late for a cure.

A DISCLAIMER

RESTAURANTS

THE POLITICS OF CUISINE

Washington was once a city where visitors would want to get out of town before dinner. In the last decade the tide has turned, so that one could readily believe that the pressure for scheduling airline flights even later at night than regulations now permit has been the work of tourists who want just one more meal in Washington. The city has French restaurants to rival some of the best in France, Chinese restaurants as glamorous as any in the world and adventurous American restaurants that are providing leadership in the movement to develop New American cuisine. What's more, Washington has such a variety of ethnic restaurants as to make its range among the broadest of any city in the world. At least 50 nationalities are represented on the menus of Washington. In the suburbs, entire shopping malls are devoted to the food of Vietnam, for example. It may seem odd that with all this diversity, there are few restaurants with Central or Eastern European cuisine, and none from Scandinavia. Instead, most of the foreign restaurants outside the familiar French, Italian and Chinese, are Vietnamese, Thai, Korean, Salvadoran and Ethiopian. They constitute the gastronomic bonus a world capital reaps from the trouble spots of the planet, as upheavals and strife elsewhere bring immigrants to this city, entering the work force through the kitchen.

The immigrants' restaurants sink or swim, and the most stable eventually join the mainstream. With this process of elimination, culinary space is then left for another new wave of immigration. Along the way, these immigrant cuisines have affected the restaurants already here. Vietnamese spring rolls have begun to appear on American menus, as did burritos and pizza before them. More subtly, lemon grass has become a staple ingredient in even the grand kitchens, just as soy sauce and fresh ginger became culinary necessities before.

In politics, as in cuisine, one thing you can count on is change. Every four years, the style of the city is subject to shifts or total reversals as administrations change or enter their lame-duck periods. It matters greatly whether the president is a Republican, Democrat, Californian, Southerner, New Englander, populist or brahmin. Sometimes in the wake of this, the top restaurants sink or even disappear, and others change to cater to the tastes of the new ruling elite. It is a city of newcomers; anyone born here is the object of amazement, an entity whose rarity is upstaged only by Washington's famous pandas. In restaurants, the faddishness is evident in inconsistency. An excellent restaurant today might be dreadful next year—or next month. Service swings from suave to awkward. It is a particular irony in Washington to see in a restaurant window the reviews from ten years ago, since only the stock market is considered more volatile than the capital's restaurant scene.

Nevertheless, eating places are crowded. Reservations are often necessary, particularly among the newer, highly rated restaurants. Sometimes, you can't even get a reservation within a week or two (in which case, you should try at the last minute, since there are likely to be cancellations). This is, after all, a city where tables are often likely to be held for members of the power elite. While Washington only recently has developed ethnic neighborhoods, mostly in the suburbs, it has restaurant neighborhoods that reflect the structure of the city. Capitol Hill has few fine restaurants for its size; instead, the focus is on convivial bars and efficient eateries, reflecting the working neighborhood. (Few senators admit to eating lunch at all.) As the residential character of Capitol Hill has been revived, however, some delightful restaurants have accompanied the change. Downtown is the eating center for business, for the executive branch of the government and for tourists. The full gamut is there, from stellar expense-account dining rooms to fast food, and more than 50 nationalities represented in between.

Recently, downtown dining is edging into new territory, around the convention center, along Pennsylvania Avenue east and west, and up into Adams Morgan. Adams Morgan is the closest the city has to an ethnic neighborhood, with its lively combination of Latin and Ethiopian eateries, interspersed with French bistros and casual American eating places. In recent years, it has overtaken Georgetown as the most vibrant restaurant neighborhood and the most difficult place to park. Georgetown, too, has a strong ethnic mix, from Afghan to Vietnamese, and some of Washington's oldest restaurants and traditional pubs. Washingtonians, though, dread the traffic of Georgetown, and tend to leave it to the young and the tourists. The traffic problem is further complicated by the lack of a subway line into the area. Then there are the more residential neighborhoods, where restaurants are thinly scattered, though developing somewhat densely along Wisconsin and Connecticut avenues. As a rule, downtown restaurants are more crowded at lunch, the more outlying ones at dinner. You should sample the best of a chef's art at lunch, when prices are lower, then do the same thing in the evening, with a different venue, and price your meal according to the thickness of your wallet.

Washington is also a city where the daily specials reflect the best in the market, and where the chef's newest creations are offered, rather than second-rate items the kitchen wants to sell fast. Be sure to look for local specialties and products of the season first when you order. Unlike other world capitals, Washington does not linger at dinner. While there are restaurants where dinner might stretch to three or four hours, at most restaurants you are expected to make way for the next round of diners after 90 minutes or two hours. A frequent complaint among diners is that they are rushed to vacate a table or that they have to wait for someone else to vacate a table. These restaurants are reserved to the hilt, keeping to a very tight schedule.

As in all Gault Millau guidebooks, we have assigned ratings to restaurants, although it was a difficult task due to their volatility and diversity. Gault Millau is known for its precise numerical ratings of restaurants: one, two, three or four toques indicate a restaurant's standing. But we plead that the numbers be taken with a grain of salt. Read carefully. As in all Gault Millau guides, the text is essential and rounds off the rating. If you go only by the numbers, you might miss some of the best dishes in town, those from uneven kitchens or from chefs who do a few things superbly, but don't know where to stop. Washington is a city for the intelligent diner, one who keeps up with the news and who tests the culinary winds as carefully as pundits do the political ones. Even for such simple facts as days and hours of operation, it is best to check ahead, rather than depend on past history.

ABOUT THE REVIEWS

R estaurants are ranked in the same manner that French students are graded, on a scale of one to twenty. The rankings reflect *only* the quality of the cooking; decor, service, welcome and atmosphere are explicitly commented on within the reviews. Restaurants that are ranked 13/20 and above are distinguished with toques (chef's hats), according to the following table:

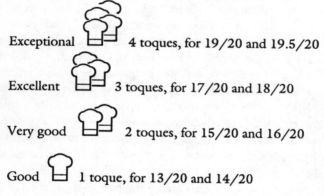

Exceptional   4 toques, for 19/20 and 19.5/20

Excellent   3 toques, for 17/20 and 18/20

Very good   2 toques, for 15/20 and 16/20

Good   1 toque, for 13/20 and 14/20

Keep in mind that we are comparing Washington's restaurants to the very best in the world. Also, these ranks are *relative*. One toque for 13/20 is not a very good ranking for a highly reputed (and very expensive) restaurant, but it is quite complimentary for a small place without much culinary pretension. Unless otherwise noted, the prices given are for a complete dinner for two, including an appetizer, main course and dessert per person, along with tax, tip and a bottle of wine. It is, naturally, hard to estimate the cost of wine; for our purposes we assume a modest bottle at a modest restaurant and a good California wine (usually $20 to $30) at a more serious place. Lovers of the great Burgundies, Bordeaux or Champagnes will find their tabs higher than our estimations; conversely, those who like to eat lightly, sharing appetizers and desserts, will spend less. However, prices continue to creep up, so forgive us if a restaurant becomes more expensive by the time you visit it. In many Washington restaurants, chefs barely stay long enough to collect their first paychecks. This can—and frequently does—wreak havoc on a restaurant, which can go from good to bad overnight when the chef leaves. Menus are also subject to the winds of change, and the dishes we've described may no longer be available when you visit. We ask your forgiveness if a restaurant is somewhat different when you visit—we've done everything we can to keep up with the always-changing Washington dining scene.

TOQUE TALLY

19/20

Jean Louis

17/20

Galileo
Inn at Little Washington
21 Federal

16/20

Obelisk
I Ricchi
The River Club

15/20

La Colline
McPherson Grill
Morrison-Clark Inn
Nora
Occidental

Le Pavillon
Taberna del Alabardero
Vincenzo

14/20

Jockey Club
Le Lion d'Or
Tiberio

13/20

Adirondacks
L'Auberge Chez François
Bacchus
Aux Beaux Champs
Bistro Bistro
The Bombay Club
La Brasserie
City Café
Dar Es Salam
Duangrat's
Enriqueta
Germaine's
The Guards
Jean Pierre
Morton's of Chicago
Saigonnais

THE WORLD'S CUISINES

AFGHAN

Bamiyan
Khyber Pass

AMERICAN

Adirondacks
America
Austin Grill
Aux Beaux Champs
Belmont Kitchen
Bistro
Bistro Bistro
Brickskeller
City Café
Clyde's
Flutes
Foggy Bottom Café
Georgetown Bar & Grill
The Guards
Hazel's
Herb's
Houston's
Inn at Little Washington
J. Paul
Kalorama Café
McPherson Grill
Morrison-Clark Inn
Morton's of Chicago
Mrs. Simpson's
New Heights
New Orleans Café
Nicholas
Nora
Occidental
Old Angler's Inn
Old Ebbitt

Palm
Prime Rib
The River Club
1789
Suzanne's
Tabard Inn
Tila's
21 Federal
Union Street Public House
Willard Room
Duke Zeibert's

AMERICAN/BARBECUE

Red Hot & Blue

AMERICAN/CAJUN

Louisiana Express Company

AMERICAN/DELI

Carnegie Deli

AMERICAN/SEAFOOD

Crisfield
Dancing Crab
Georgetown Seafood Grill
R.T.'s

ASIAN

Pan Asian Noodles & Grill

BRAZILIAN

Dona Flor

CHINESE

Big Wong
Tony Cheng's Mongolian Barbecue
Tony Cheng's Seafood Restaurant
China Coral
City Lights of China
Fortune Chinese Seafood Restaurant
Mr. K's
Peking Gourmet Inn
Szechuan
Szechuan Gallery

CUBAN

Omega

ETHIOPIAN

Meskerem
Red Sea

FRENCH

L'Auberge
Chez François
Bistro Français
La Brasserie
Le Caprice
La Chaumière
Chez Grand Mère
La Colline
Dominique's
La Ferme
La Fourchette
Le Gaulois
Jean Louis
Jean Pierre
Jockey Club
Le Lion d'Or
Maison Blanche

La Marée
La Miche
Le Pavillon
Au Pied de Cochon

GERMAN

Café Berlin

GREEK

Taverna Cretekou

INDIAN

The Bombay Club
Bombay Palace

INDONESIAN

Sarinah Satay House

INTERNATIONAL

Cities

ITALIAN

Amalfi
AV Ristorante
Café Petitto
Cantina d'Italia
Galileo
Obelisk
Paper Moon
Primi Patti
I Ricchi
Tiberio
Panevino

ITALIAN/SEAFOOD

The Daily Catch
Vincenzo

JAMAICAN

Fish, Wings & Tings

JAPANESE

Hisago
Perry's
Sushi-Ko
Takesushi
Tako Grill

LATIN AMERICAN

El Caribe

LEBANESE

Bacchus

MEXICAN

Enriqueta
Lauriol Plaza

MIDDLE EASTERN

Iron Gate Inn

MOROCCAN

Dar Es Salam
Marrakesh

PERSIAN

Caspian Tea Room
Kolbeh

RUMANIAN

Vagabond

SEAFOOD

Sea Catch
Tony & Joes's Seafood Place

SPANISH

El Bodegon
Taberna Del Alabardero

SPANISH/MEXICAN

La Plaza

SWISS

Broker

THAI

Bangkok Gourmet
Duangrat's
Sala Thai
Thai Taste

VIETNAMESE

Saigonnais
Vietnam Georgetown

VIETNAMESE/FRENCH

Nam's River

VIETNAMESE/PAN-ASIAN

Germaine's

ADAMS MORGAN

Belmont Kitchen
2400 18th St. NW
• 667-1200
AMERICAN

11/20

It is just a little slip of a restaurant, and just the kind of place you feel like popping into for a casual supper or a sunny-day brunch on the patio. The Belmont is spiffy and appealing, its menu fresh and its ingredients equally so, right down to freshly squeezed juices. The hit of this kitchen is its pizza, the most unusual in town, with a big puff of a crust baked over a bowl of filling. The waiter turns it over on your plate and carefully trims the crust away from the bowl to reveal a thick ooze of very good ingredients—eggplant and cheese or pungent lean sausage with cheese or just plain cheese. On the lighter side, Belmont Kitchen turns out particularly good salads, including one of the last remaining great Caesar salads. The service is friendly, and attentive enough that you are always made to feel welcome. Lunch can be under $20, while a full meal with wine or beer can run as high as $60.

Open Mon. 5:30 p.m.-midnight, Tues.-Thurs. 11:30 a.m.-2:30 p.m. & 5:30 p.m.-11 p.m., Fri. 11:30 a.m.-2:30 p.m. & 5:30 p.m.-midnight, Sat. 11:30 a.m.-3:30 p.m. & 5:30 p.m.-midnight, Sun. 11:30 a.m.-3:30 p.m. & 5:30 p.m.-11 p.m. All major cards.

El Caribe
1828 Columbia Rd. NW
• 234-6969
LATIN AMERICAN

11/20

There are three El Caribe restaurants, and though they take on some of the character of the neighborhood (the one in Adams Morgan has an outdoor café that perfumes the block with garlic), they are very much alike. Their look is soothing white with bright Latin decorative touches. The service is mature with experience, yet friendly and energetic. And the menu spans Latin America. Appetizers are top-notch, from the fried squid to the empanadas to the garlicky shrimp. The black beans are fragrant; the rice is glistening and flavorful from its touch of oil. The stews and casseroles are hefty—order pork, and you won't go wrong. Nothing on the menu beats the tender, densely flavored tongue; other dishes taste too similar or are not as good as in restaurants that specialize in their regions. Once you find a couple of favorites, you can depend on them at any of the three locations. A full dinner with wine is about $55 for two.

Open Mon.-Fri. 11:30 a.m.-11 p.m., Sat.-Sun. 11:30 a.m.-midnight. All major cards.

Cities

2424 18th St. NW
• 328-7194I
INTERNATIONAL

12/20

Once the hottest restaurant in Washington, Cities has slowed down to a chic, but quiet, restaurant, with a popular bar room in front and a nightclub upstairs, each element distinct. In the restaurant itself, the shtick is that each few months, the menu and decor change to reflect a new city—Rio, Bangkok, Leningrad, Madrid and Paris in the past. But the basic style of *faux* decay and designer chaos remains to soften the blow of the new decorations. Thus, Cities has settled into being a trendy restaurant with a solid base. The cooking is good, with a wood-burning oven churning out pizzas and breads of whatever type. Salads are sophisticated and soups are particularly fine, as are a few pastas. Some of the ethnic dishes are modernized, adapted to current fashion. Finally, the desserts run to American home-style—don't miss the fresh fruit cobblers. Unlike many hot-spot restaurants that run their course and fizzle out, Cities has learned lessons from the roller-coaster ride. It now serves moderately priced food—dinner runs about $60 with wine, but bar food, pizzas and light meals can be under $20. The cooking still shows flair and quality; the dining room is cunning; and the service has a kind of funky charm that typifies the best of Adams Morgan.
Open Sun.-Thurs. 6 p.m.-11 p.m., Fri.-Sat. 6 p.m.-11:30 p.m. All major cards.

Fish, Wings & Tings

2418 18th St. NW
• 234-0322
JAMAICAN

12/20

Jamaican cooking has been polished up for urban diners at Fish, Wings & Tings, a casual and lively little restaurant decorated in dramatic black, with accents in primary colors. The kitchen plays with an abundance of curry, hot sauce, coconut milk and ginger to season its menu, which appears on the blackboard and concentrates on chicken and fish. In fact, the only red meat is likely to be oxtail or goat. This is a restaurant that takes no reservations, serves no coffee or liquor, and often requires a wait for a table. But its popularity is warranted by the brilliant flavors and low prices. And even with such a small menu, it is hard to choose among the jerk chicken thighs, pineapple wings, curry-ginger wings or fish soup. Don't miss the fresh and fiery pineade, pineapple juice well spiked with ginger. Side dishes include Jamaican rice and peas alongside an American grated-carrot-and-raisin salad, and desserts mix the two cultures to sweet advantage. A meal is not likely to cost more than $20 or $30 at Fish, Wings & Tings, and it comes with the local chatter of a homey Adams Morgan crowd.
Open Mon.-Thurs. noon-10 p.m., Fri.-Sat. noon-11 p.m. No reservations, no liquor. Cards: AE.

La Fourchette
2429 18th St. NW
• 332-3077
FRENCH

12/20

Over the years, the popularity of this little French restaurant has waxed and waned, probably having more to do with dining trends or even the weather than changes in the restaurant itself. Just now, it looks good again to a public growing tired of fussy cooking. This is a traditional kitchen, where lamb shanks are still braised, and seafoods are still stewed into a bouillabaisse rather than slivered and braided and sent on a blind date with papayas or kiwis. The service is of the fresh, cheerful type that you expect in a small French country inn. The tables are small and close, for it is a friendly room, a place where you would exchange more than nods with the neighbors who happen along. The food is highly professional, but far from pretentious, and certainly not priced pretentiously. You can find the haughty French cocktail Kir Royale (Champagne with blackcurrant liqueur), but at half the price you might find farther downtown. And a "petite entrée" such as onion tart, ham and cheese in puff pastry, or herbed zucchini tourte, is priced as an appetizer might be elsewhere. Full meals rarely surpass $50. The best dishes are probably those listed on the blackboard outside and handwritten on the daily sheet. You might find a leek salad to start with, or ripe tomatoes vinaigrette. Main dishes include some rarely found in Washington's French restaurants: tongue, perhaps with an intense garlic sauce, or filet of pork with mustard sauce. There also might be salmon, perfectly cooked so that it is crisp at the edges, yet utterly juicy, and it might even be bedded on old-fashioned creamed spinach. The printed menu leans to hearty dishes such as chicken breast en croute, liver with shallots, braised veal or lamb shanks and sweetbreads with cream and mushrooms; and there are seafoods such as casseroles or brochettes, mussels, lobster and filet of sole stuffed with scallop mousse. Appetizers are the usual onion soup, pâtés and snails, plus a wonderful aïoli served with warm shrimp in the shell. This is the kind of family-run, hospitable restaurant that we imagine exists in every French neighborhood and we wish existed in ours. *Open Mon.-Thurs. 11:30 a.m.-10:30 p.m., Fri. 11:30 a.m.-midnight, Sat. 4 p.m.-midnight, Sun. 4 p.m.-10 p.m. All major cards.*

Hazel's
1834 Columbia Rd. NW
• 462-0415
AMERICAN

6/20

There ought to be much to love about Hazel's. It's one of our few soul food restaurants, certainly the only one in Adams Morgan's bustling restaurant strip. Add to that its live jazz, and it is singular. With the downstairs bar and the upstairs dining room—and its two very private tables overlooking Columbia Road—Hazel's is homey and entertain-

ing. Its prices are moderate, and it has on its menu the soul food standbys: fried chicken, catfish, ribs, pork chops, blackeyed peas, cooked greens and banana pudding. Where's the warm and friendly service, though? In fact, where is the service at all? The staff stands around while the customers sit and wait. The food, moreover, is hit-or-miss. The Cajun blackened catfish, accompanied by blackeyed peas and greens, is worth celebrating. Crabcakes are creamy and rich, with good, fresh-tasting crab and careful, crisp frying. Cornbread is crunchy. Potato salad and banana pudding taste like the best of an old-fashioned church social (if you scrape off the "whipped cream" from the banana pudding). So why is the chicken soggy and tasteless? Why are the ribs so fatty under their candy-sweet barbecue glaze? Is factory fluff a reasonable topping for strawberry short-cake? Hazel's has the idea, and it makes a start in the right direction, but it's not home yet.
Open Mon.-Thurs. 11 a.m.-2 a.m., Fri. 11 a.m.-3 a.m., Sat. 11 a.m.-3 a.m. All major cards.

Kalorama Café
2228 18th St. NW
• 667-1022
AMERICAN

8/20

This is the last remaining '60s-style restaurant, earthy and wholesome, committed as much to a philosophy as a cooking style. The menu is largely vegetarian, with a few chicken and fish entrées, and the ingredients emphasize naturalness and purity. That means a whole-grain heartiness in the baked goods and a rusticity in the cooking overall. In sum, it is reminiscent of the cooking in college cooper-ative houses, sometimes good and sometimes not, but always providing a lot of nutrients for the money. This mix is occasionally leavened by guest chefs and sometimes by guitar music. Dinner is unlikely to reach $40 for two.
Open Tues.-Thurs. 11:30 a.m.-3 p.m. & 6 p.m.-10 p.m., Fri.-Sat. 11:30 a.m.-3 p.m. & 6 p.m.-11 p.m., Sun. 11 a.m.-3 p.m. No cards.

Lauriol Plaza
1801 18th St. NW
• 387-0035
MEXICAN

12/20

The ownership is the same as La Plaza and some of the dishes overlap, but Lauriol Plaza emphasizes the Mexican dishes on the menu, and serves them in simpler surround-ings at less hefty prices. The room is white from head to toe; the decoration in this case is the neighborhood itself, seen through the window walls or from the sidewalk café. Lauriol Plaza serves as café as well as restaurant, for a casual snack or a full meal. In either case, ceviche is a good choice, one of the most deftly seasoned, generous and fresh ver-sions in town. Shrimps in garlic sauce are an impeccable rendition of this appetizer. Among Spanish main dishes, duck, particularly with olives, is outstanding. Roast chicken is juicy and aromatic. Latin America is well represented by masitas de puerco ("morsels of pork," marinated in a bitter orange sauce and roasted with garlic). Look to the Mexican dishes for knockout flavors with a touch of refinement. The margaritas and pisco sours—by the pitcher—are enough reason for many to make this a regular haunt, and even the strong black coffee is unusually good. You could have a light snack for under $20 for two, or up to $50, a numbingly full meal.

Open Mon.-Thurs. noon-11 p.m., Fri.-Sun. noon-midnight
All major cards.

Meskerem
2434 18th St. NW
• 462-4100
ETHIOPIAN

8/20

Washington has become a major outpost of Ethiopian cooking, with about a dozen restaurants serving this unusual cuisine. The first thing to know about Ethiopian meals is that they require no utensils. You eat by scooping up thick stews with pieces of large, floppy, tangy, fermented pancakes called injera. The menus are simple. Watts, the more peppery stews, and alichas, less fiery, are made from beef, lamb, or chicken and a hard-boiled egg. Tibbs is diced beef or lamb sautéed with onions and hot peppers; and kitfo is raw chopped beef fired with hot peppers and mellowed with butter. Then there are the vegetable side dishes, of lentils, chickpeas, cauliflower, potatoes, greens and such. It is simple and fragrant food, best washed down with beer, though an Ethiopian sweet honey wine is also available. Meskerem may not be the most adept of the Ethiopian kitchens, but it is the most attractive of the dining rooms. The cooking is an edge below, say, the Red Sea across the street: the tibbs not as crustily browned, the doro watt a little less intricate in taste, the injera not quite as even or supple. But Meskerem's top-floor dining area is a delightful, skylit room with a ceiling reminiscent of a tent, and serving as tables there are the covered baskets traditional used for injera. The first and lower floors are also attractive, bright with Ethiopian designs, but more like lunchrooms than dining rooms. The food is served with a warm welcome and, if necessary, a quick lesson in scooping with injera. Meskerem is one of the few Ethiopian restaurants with a menu so elaborate as to offer appetizers and desserts, but basically this is a one-course meal that lends itself to lingering for one last bite and then another. A couple need not spend more than $30.

Open Mon.-Thurs. 5 p.m.-midnight, Fri.-Sun. noon-1 a.m.
All major cards.

New Orleans Café
1790 Columbia Rd. NW
• 234-5111
AMERICAN

8/20

While the craze has calmed down, Cajun food is bound to stick around for a long time more, because, beyond its trendiness, it is solid, satisfying food with exciting tastes. And New Orleans Café is also bound to stay around a long time, because not only is its food good but it is a casual, friendly and very inexpensive gathering place. You have to be prepared to wait in line at peak hours, and to sit close enough to get to know your neighbors; the long, narrow dining room is sometimes reminiscent of Bourbon Street at Mardi Gras. But the list of traditional New Orleans drinks smooths the way. As for what to eat, start by considering breakfast—particularly the eggs Creole, teamed with garlicky sausage and fried grits, then blanketed with Creole sauce. With a change in management, New Orleans Café lost its brilliance, but it remains worthwhile as the only casual in-town source for New Orleans cooking: gumbo, po' boys and muffalettas. For snacks, there are beignets and milky, chicory-scented New Orleans coffee. A full dinner can escalate to $50.
Open Sun.-Thurs. 8:30 a.m.-10 p.m., Fri.-Sat. 8:30 a.m.-11 p.m. All major cards.

Omega
1858 Columbia Rd. NW
• 462-1732
CUBAN

9/20

Omega has been part of Adams Morgan as long as nearly anybody can remember, and this Cuban restaurant is still, for many, the introduction to ethnic cooking. Prices are minimal; portions are maximal; and the cooking is authentic. The atmosphere is also minimal, which means that you are paying—little though it may be—for food, not for frills. Start out with fried squid—plain and perfect, with a wedge of lemon to squeeze on it—or a soup hearty enough to see you through the day. Main dishes to remember are pork—crusty masitas or shredded ropa vieja. There are also rustic versions of paellas and the soupy Puerto Rican alternatives, asopaos. Dinner with beer costs less than $40.
Open Tues.-Thurs. & Sun. 11:30 a.m.-10 p.m., Fri.-Sat. 11:30 a.m.-11 p.m. All major cards.

Perry's
1811 Columbia Rd. NW
• 234-6218
JAPANESE

6/20

On a balmy evening in Adams Morgan, thoughts have long turned to Perry's and its rooftop sushi menu. But nowadays they are beginning to turn elsewhere. There was a time that Perry's was adored, even when the weather dictated indoor dining. Its cavernous new wave dining room was almost as much fun as its open roof, and its long list of Japanese-style appetizers was a strong attraction unto itself. Now its menu has expanded and changed, downplaying appetizers and emphasizing Japanese-western main dishes. The problem is that the cooking has been just awful lately. The sushi is all right, though the tuna has an odd plastic look. Beyond sushi, however, only the fried oysters are bearable among the appetizers, and they grow soggy in their sauce. Sautéed wild mushrooms have a mere trace of flavor, and the other appetizers are worse. As for main dishes, tempura squid is rubbery and limp, on a bed of cellophane noodles with a particularly disagreeable sauce. And that is the best of the main dishes of late. Perry's is far outreaching itself in the kitchen, and has neither the service nor the prices to compensate, costing as much as $90 for two, with saké. Nowadays, it is just a pretty rooftop.

Open Sun.-Thurs. 6 p.m.-midnight, Fri.-Sat. 6 p.m.-1 a.m. All major cards.

La Plaza
1847 Columbia Rd. NW
• 667-1900
SPANISH/MEXICAN

12/20

La Plaza has developed into one of the few uptown restaurants with downtown style. The dining room provides a sparkling white background that heightens the impact of lavish flowers and curtains of greenery on the windows. Thus, the seasons themselves become the decoration. The menu is a nice mix of Spanish and Mexican dishes, the latter served with an upscale flair that the decor deserves. This is not original or exquisite cooking; it is standard dishes carefully prepared and moderately priced. The emphasis is on seafood, from the very garlicky—and plentiful—shrimps as an appetizer to the seafood enchiladas with supple shellfish in an admirably delicate tortilla. There are also plainer preparations—grilled and stuffed fish as well as paella and zarzuela. The meat dishes include Americanized steaks and more Spanish recipes such as lamb stew, pork, or duck with bitter orange juice. Tongue illustrates the balance of this kitchen: it is bathed in a homey stew with flour-thickened sauce, yet with sweet nuances of Madeira in the subtle flavor. As for the wine list, it could serve as a travelogue of Latin America. La Plaza has showed that the restaurant mix of Adams Morgan can support elegance as well as ethnicity. Dinner, with beer or a modest wine, will cost about $60 to $80 for two.

Open daily 6 p.m.-11 p.m. Cards: AE, MC, V.

Red Sea
2463 18th St. NW
• 483-5000
ETHIOPIAN

9/20

As crowded as a holiday train, with tables leaving little space for waiting or serving, Red Sea concentrates on food, inexpensive Ethiopian food to eat with your hands, with the assistance of floppy, fermented pancakes called injera as plates and scoops. Like the dozen other Ethiopian restaurants, Red Sea has a menu limited to a few thick peppery stews (watts or alichas), an even more fiery tartar steak (kitfo), and a wonderful sauté of diced meat with onions and peppers (tibbs). With injera overlapping as the communal platter, these dishes are spooned into mounds, with stewed vegetables as condiments. Then you tear off bits of injera and swipe up a bit of everything, one dish at a time or in combination. With beer, of course, or a sweet honey wine called tej. The differences between most Ethiopian restaurants are subtle, but Red Sea's kitchen has the edge of a little more fire and flavor in the stews, a little more tenderness and suppleness to the pancakes, a little more savor overall. Dinner will cost no more than $40 for two, with a carafe of the sweet honey wine.

Open Sun.-Thurs. 11:30 a.m.-midnight, Fri.-Sat. 11:30 a.m.-1 a.m. All major cards.

Saigonnais
2307 18th St. NW
• 232-5300
VIETNAMESE

Vietnamese restaurants have been established in Washington for nearly two decades now, and in recent years they have been moving upscale. One of the best is Saigonnais, an Adams Morgan townhouse with pale peach walls, decorated with paintings of Saigon city life. Not only is the cooking skilled and careful, but the service is gracious and personal, as well as dignified. Best in this kitchen are the grilled foods, from appetizers of skewered meats or shrimp paste wrapped around sugar cane, to the main dishes of pork, beef, spice-rubbed chicken, or large and succulent shrimp and scallops. What's more, many of these grilled dishes are meant to be wrapped in translucent rice paper, with slices of cucumber and carrot, leaves of fresh mint or basil, then dipped into a faintly sweet and lightly fiery sauce. This is participatory cooking at its best. In addition, the soups are exceptionally flavored broths, whether your choice be the beef-topped pho with its Chinese five-spice aroma, or the sweet-hot fish soup with pineapple. Whole fish are beautifully fried, or equally well steamed when the fish are fresh enough to benefit from such delicacy. For dessert, ice creams are laced with ginger, lichees or jackfruit. With wine from a small but carefully culled list that is bargain-priced, a very attractive dinner will cost $40 to $50 for two.

Open Mon.-Thurs. 11:30 a.m.-2:30 p.m. & 5:30 p.m.-10:30 p.m., Fri. 11:30 a.m.-2:30 p.m. & 5:30 p.m.-11 p.m., Sat. 5:30 p.m.-11 p.m., Sun.5:30 p.m.-10:30 p.m. All major cards.

CAPITOL HILL

Adirondacks

Union Station
50 Massachusetts Ave. NE
• 682-1840
AMERICAN

It took awhile, but Adirondacks has found the magic formula. Against the backdrop of one of Washington's most elaborate dining rooms, it serves some of the simplest expense-account food in the city. Adirondacks is the work of California restaurateur Michael McCarty, and is a branch of Denver's Adirondacks (formerly the Rattlesnake Club), so the menu is Californian-inspired (though without California's extraordinary ingredients). A few simple salads and pastas are starters, and main dishes are grilled foods—chicken, superb lamb chops, thick pork chops and the usual glamour fish—with particularly good vegetables, in honest portions, not just garnishes. It is all quite correct, and rather good, with gooey chocolate desserts to reward restrained appetites. The dining room, once the presidential waiting room and now sumptuously restored, and the lounge, ringed by a breathtaking collection of modern paintings, are the stars. The wine list needs improvement, and given its high prices, you aren't likely to finish dinner with less than a $120 tab.

Open daily noon-2 p.m. & 6 p.m.-10 p.m. All major cards.

America

Union Station
50 Massachusetts Ave. NE
• 682-9555
AMERICAN

7/20

This is the kind of restaurant that gives American exuberance a bad name. Hundreds of tables are set on several levels. The balconies offer dazzling vistas of this Union Station grand restoration. The design is a charmer—murals of working America and of space exploration stretch from floor to floor, an elegant rendition of a working-class theme. But the real stunner is the menu, a one-page encyclopedia of America's favorite foods from coast to coast—New Orleans's po' boy sandwiches and blackened beef, New England's seafood chowders and lobster rolls, the Southwest's tortilla-wrapped hot stuff, dishes from the Midwest and the Northwest, the Deep South, and even the peanut-butter sandwiches of childhood. You could close your eyes and point, and come up with something that sounds thrilling. The problem is that some disaster hits between the prose and the plate. The kitchen clearly cannot handle the heroic task that this huge menu demands, nor the volume of business these hundreds of seats imply. The

food is soggy, overcooked, reheated, gummy, insipid—with a few exceptions. Southwestern dishes are safest, ice cream desserts are fun, and potatoes are great stuff here. Prices are moderate and portions are enormous, so the easily impressed are, indeed, impressed. Two can eat for $30, with good boutique beers, but don't insist on anything more complex than a peanut-butter-and-jelly sandwich.
Open daily 11:30 a.m.-midnight. All major cards.

La Brasserie
239 Massachusetts Ave. NE
• 546-9154
FRENCH

Chef Gaby Aubouin is a technician and a talent. For diners with special needs, he has invented fat-free sauces based on corn, and dressings with no oil; and for special occasions, he has designed stunning menus. Diners can always expect an interesting array of specials, as modern as belon oysters with raspberry vinegar and as old-fashioned as rabbit Dijon. This is a restaurant that smokes its own salmon and prepares its own foie gras terrines. It serves a sumptuous bourride and is likely to dip into the least-known regional French repertoires for such specials as vegetable soup with bacon and Beaujolais. This is a small, two-story French restaurant of quiet attributes rather than grandeur: the kind of restaurant you might expect to find as the best in a small French town, rather than a contender for big-city honors. The service is gently efficient and most hospitable. In spring and fall, its popularity intensifies, for it has one of the most comfortable of the city's outdoor terraces. But modernization is catching up with this old favorite. The dinner menu is much abbreviated, and fish dishes are nowadays likely to be less succulent than the other seafood or lamb. Try lobster, particularly if it is teamed with peaches for a gloriously perfumed dish. Rack of lamb is generous and dependable. Among the garnishes of latticework carrots and potato rosettes, there are some deliciously inventive bits. As for appetizers, the house-smoked salmon and soups are standouts, along with a beautiful and delicate scallop ceviche. For dessert, it's painful to have to choose between fruit in a velvety hot caramel sauce and crème brûlée, cold or hot, with seasonal fruit. The prices have escalated, so that dinner is at least $100 for two, even with one of the most reasonably priced wine lists of any ambitious restaurant. While the consistency has lapsed lately, La Brasserie has the personal charm of a country inn "worth a detour," as the French would say, despite its Capitol Hill location.
Open Mon.-Sat. 11:30 a.m.-11:30 p.m., Sun. 11 a.m.-10 p.m. All major cards.

Broker
713 8th St. SE
• 546-8300
SWISS

12/20

Capitol Hill is largely a neighborhood of bars, rather than fullblown restaurants, and even the few restaurants tend to be crowded. So the Broker is unique in its serenity. Its walls are old-brick, decorated only by draperies and the glow from skylights. It doesn't look bare, it looks lovely. The menu is what used to be called Continental, but concentrates on a few Swiss touches such as fondue, veal and crusty rösti potatoes, with some particularly good homemade bread available à la carte. The Broker does not make a big splash among Washington restaurants, but remains as a steadily good outpost of quiet pleasure, at about $60 to $80 for two with wine, tax and tip.
Open Mon.-Thurs. 11:30 a.m.-2:30 p.m. & 6 p.m.-10 p.m., Fri. 11:30 a.m.-2:30 p.m. & 6 p.m.-11 p.m., Sat. 6 p.m.-11 p.m. All major cards.

Café Berlin
322 Massachusetts Ave. NE
• 543-7656
GERMAN

10/20

Washington has only a few German restaurants, and only Café Berlin has German food that escapes stodginess. It's a Capitol Hill version of a German country inn dining room, pink and pretty, primarily decorated by a table of home-style desserts—crumb cakes and strudels, Kugelhopfs and tortes. Be guided by the seasonal delicacies, particularly if it is asparagus season. And seek the veal dishes, the paprikás, and the perfectly executed Wiener Schnitzel. Sauerbraten is fine, and anything made with ham is well made. Even better than the main dishes themselves are the accompaniments—the Sauerkraut, Spätzle, red cabbage and potato salad. Prices are middling, and a rather simple meal could climb to $60 or $80; but the warmth of the dining room, the outdoor terrace and the personal attention of the staff count for a lot.
Open Mon.-Thurs. 11:30 a.m.-10 p.m., Fri. 11:30 a.m.-11 p.m., Sat. 4 p.m.-11 p.m., Sun. 4 p.m.-10 p.m. All major cards.

La Colline
400 N. Capitol St. NW
• 737-0400
FRENCH

At half the price of other equivalent French restaurants, La Colline consistently turns out some of the best French food in Washington. Robert Greault was one of the early superstar chefs in the city's most expensive restaurants, and now prepares food that is no less sublime—maybe even more so—at astonishingly modest prices. The restaurant is large, and about as charming as an office-building restaurant is likely to get; let's say that it is comfortable and provides quiet privacy, and leave it at that. Service is suave, the wine list is as professionally adept as the cooking. The food is continually superb. Fine pâtés, outstanding smoked salmon and elegant chicken-liver mousse are regulars among the appetizers, along with such main dishes as duck breast with cassis, bouillabaisse and old-fashioned pleasures like jambon persille and tripe stew. Then there are daily specials as modern as blackened fish or beef, soft-shell crabs with Southwestern seasonings or seafood ravioli with roasted-red-pepper sauce. The accompanying vegetables are individually prepared to match each dish; there is no one-vegetable-for-all offhandedness here. La Colline has over the years become the model for expensive restaurants, as well as for other sensibly priced ones. $70 to $100 for two, with wine, tax and tip.

Open Mon.-Fri. 7 a.m.-10 a.m., 11:30 a.m.-3 p.m. & 6 p.m.-10 p.m., Sat. 6 p.m.-10 p.m. All major cards.

DOWNTOWN

AV Ristorante
607 New York Ave. NW
• 737-0550
ITALIAN

12/20

One look at the bare and scruffy waiting room, and the dining rooms with their vinyl tablecloths, the strange assortment of decorations (from beer steins to a suit of armor), and you may wonder why the crowd is waiting for tables at AV. The fact is, this big and clattery Italian restaurant has been drawing crowds for decades. One reason is the pizza, among the best in town. The long menu is irrelevant; most of the dishes don't exist. Most people using the menu order the huge, tomato-sauced mixed-meat or seafood assortments. Otherwise, they order from the list of daily specials at the entrance: the sometimes-juicy veal or pork roasts, the sausages with lentils, the pasta with mussels, the stews or organ meats rarely found in other Italian restaurants. They wouldn't miss ordering a pizza—or the wonderful white pizza as a side dish. The cooking at AV can be trattoria great. The wine list is bare-bones and cheap; the service is rough-hewn and friendly (if the evening isn't too frantic). And the prices—rarely over $40 for a gargantuan meal—allow forgiveness for the occasional disappointments.

Open Mon.-Thurs. 11:30 a.m.-11 p.m., Fri. 11:30 a.m.-midnight, Sat. 5 p.m.-midnight. All major cards.

Bacchus

1827 Jefferson Pl. NW
• 785-0734
LEBANESE

The best way to enjoy Bacchus is to gather a group for an evening of mezes, the Middle Eastern answer to smörgåsbord. This Lebanese restaurant may look small, but its appetizer list is enormous, and even if you fill your table with two dozen of them, you will have missed some good ones. The hummus special—topped with ground meat and pine nuts—is as good as hummus gets. The sausages are piquant and homemade. Phyllo dough filled with cheese, meat or whatever is flaky and buttery. The menu stretches from the familiar stuffed grape leaves to eggplant dishes with accompaniments such as pomegranates and sesame paste. A table crowded with these little dishes and a basket of warm pita, with pickled turnips and radishes to crunch, needs only wine, beer or some Middle Eastern fire water to complete the feast. You may, however, want to go on to main dishes; they are no less exceptional. The lamb kebabs are lean and juicy, the chicken imbued with a lemony tang, and there is a succulent casserole of lamb layered with crisp, toasted pita drenched in yogurt. This inviting food is served in two small dining rooms, by waiters who are brisk and efficient as well as personable. For a meal of tantalizing little dishes, with wine, you'll spend $60 for two.

Open Mon.-Thurs. noon-2:30 p.m. & 6 p.m.-10 p.m., Fri. noon-2:30 p.m. & 6 p.m.-10:30 p.m., Sat. 6 p.m.-10:30 p.m. All major cards.

Big Wong

610 H St. NW
• 638-0116
CHINESE

8/20

A full array of Cantonese cooking is to be found in this rather unkempt restaurant down a few steps from the center of Chinatown. Don't expect amenities. The waitresses rush you to order, throw the food at the table and then disappear, even if you need something. The tables are too small for much more than snacking. The room is noisy, and you don't want to look too closely at the sanitation standards. Big Wong's kitchen is a good source, though, for Canton's stir-fried, steamed and salt-baked dishes, for noodles fat and thin, for barbecued meats or dim sum. And its seafoods range from abalone and conch to lobster. Try the fat and crunchy crystal shrimp with walnuts, crispy duck stuffed with shrimp paste, or stir-fried combinations with Chinese vegetables. Prices are low enough that, even at lunch, you should order from the full dinner menu rather than the bargain-priced lunch combinations, unless you want dim sum, a rice bowl or congee. Big Wong is culturally, as well as geographically, in the center of Chinatown, and it dishes out a lot of authentic Cantonese cooking for hardly more than $30 for two.

Open daily 11 a.m.-3 a.m. All major cards.

Bistro
The Westin Hotel,
2401 M St. NW
• 457-5020
AMERICAN

9/20

You would expect the Colonnade restaurant to be the attraction at the Westin Hotel, and indeed it is a luscious dining room, a kind of gazebo writ large, with delicious soft colors and skylights galore. But the word has gone around that the Bistro is *the* place to eat in this sumptuous hotel (with the exception of the Colonnade's lavish Sunday brunch buffet). The Bistro is also a sunny space which looks nearly like outdoors, because it has more windows than walls. Like the Colonnade, it has servers of great enthusiasm. It also has a more realistic kitchen, which emphasizes homey French dishes and specializes in bouillabaisse. It is a good bouillabaisse, thicker and more heavy on the tomato than most, well-spiked with rouille and very generous for the price. Most of the cooking is straightforward: nicely garlicky mussels in snail butter, crisp asparagus in a too-sharp pepper purée, competently cooked liver and agreeable fish dishes. What is most refreshing about the Bistro, besides its marble-and-tile, wood-accented decor, is that this professional French cooking comes at a modest price for a hotel dining room, at most about $70 for two.
Open daily 6:30 a.m.-10:30 p.m.; lighter fare 3 p.m.-11 p.m. All major cards.

El Bodegon
1637 R St. NW
• 667-1710
SPANISH

10/20

El Bodegon is hokey, no doubt about it. Its small rooms are decorated with folksy Spanish stuff and the menu hits every Spanish cliché. Generations of youths have been inducted into wine-drinking by chugging it from El Bodegon's pourrons (special jugs—you don't touch the spout with your mouth). But they continue to come back, even when they are educated drinkers of first-growth Bordeaux, because El Bodegon is also friendly, homey and a good value. The food is good—not great, mind you, but good. The paella is aromatic with saffron and seafood; the casseroles are pungent with sausage and peppers. Appetizers such as steamed mussels, fried squid, baby octopus and empanaditas are highlights. This kitchen does more than most with pork, from pork tenderloin simmered in red wine to suckling pig, which must be ordered 48 hours in advance. With this reasonably priced, hearty food comes such entertainment as Spanish guitar music and, if you are lucky, an introduction to the pourron. With wine, dinner averages $60.
Open Mon.-Thurs. 11 a.m.-2:30 p.m. & 5:30 p.m.-10:30 p.m., Fri. 11 a.m.-2:30 p.m. & 5:30 p.m.-11 p.m., Sat. 5:30 p.m.-11 p.m. All major cards.

The Bombay Club

815 Connecticut Ave. NW
• 659-3727
INDIAN

From India by way of England comes one of the most beautiful of Washington's restaurants, the Bombay Club. The deeply cushioned chairs and spacious table, the ceiling fans and luxurious decorative details are intended to represent the era of the Raj. The chairs are oh, so comfortable, the ceiling fans are oh, so lazily swirling. And the service is oh, so eager to please. As for the food, it has the true flavors of India, but without fiery challenge to Western tastebuds. More care is taken than in most Indian restaurants here with the texture, the color, the shape of the food. One is tempted to make a meal of just the appetizers, so pretty and aromatic are the poppy-seed-coated filets of Bombay Fish masala, the smoky skewers of scallops, chicken or minced lamb. Main dishes offer a range of curries, and also include many items from the tandoor oven, spice-rubbed grilled meats and fish in tune with the fashion of light eating. Accompany them with wheaty flat breads and some unusual vegetable side dishes, and the modern diet is fulfilled, with more intricate flavor and aroma than the habitual American grilled-fish dinner. The Bombay Club brings new insights to Washington's otherwise narrow vision of Indian cooking. Dinner averages $50 to $70 for two.

Open Mon.-Thurs. 11:30 a.m.-2:30 p.m. & 6 p.m.-10:30 p.m., Fri. 11:30 a.m.-2:30 p.m. & 6 p.m.-11 p.m., Sat. 6 p.m.-11 p.m., Sun. 11:30 a.m.-2:30 p.m. All major cards.

Bombay Palace

1835 K St. NW
• 331-0111
INDIAN

11/20

The pale aqua walls are softly lit. The decorative details are in an art deco mode. Elaborate brass animals are displayed as if the dining room were a museum. The Bombay Palace is accurately named. What's more, not only is it handsome, its service is courtly. While obviously this is an Indian restaurant, it clearly is an Americanized one, or at least Europeanized. The seasoning is intricate but also moderate—not much is likely to challenge a fire-eater. Some of the cooking is outstanding; samosas, for instance, are far lighter and more generously filled than is typical of these meat- or vegetable-stuffed fried pastries, and they are served with a delightfully tart yogurt sauce. Curries are each perfumed with their own signature seasonings. Breads are well made, from the puffiest and most fragile puri to the dense and chewy naan blistered from the tandoori oven. The quality of the meats is high; the homemade cheese is supple; the vegetables are not cooked to shriveling; all of which mark this as an Indian restaurant above the standard. Choosing among the tandoor-cooked meats requires some caution; lamb and shrimp are more intensely flavored than the ground-meat kufta, which is, to be polite, delicate.

Tandoori chicken, which at its best is a revelation in day-glo red, is at Bombay Palace likely to be much more brilliant-looking than it tastes, having been underseasoned and left in the oven too long. Bombay Palace has a capable kitchen and beautiful surroundings. As part of an international chain, it has developed less as an ethnic restaurant than as a Continental version of an Indian restaurant. Expect to pay upward of $60 for two to sample this genre.

Open Sun.-Thurs. noon-2:30 p.m. & 5:30 p.m.-10 p.m., Fri.-Sat. noon-2:30 p.m. & 5:30 p.m.-10:30 p.m. All major cards.

Brickskeller
1523 22nd St. NW
• 293-1885
AMERICAN

7/20

You won't find the Brickskeller on any list of the great restaurants of Washington, but it is one of the great drinking places. This dim basement houses the largest collection of beers you might find anywhere. The list goes on for pages, and within any one category, there might be dozens. German Weissbier? Which brand? Christmas beers? Sure, several. There are beers from countries you probably didn't know had beer at all. And some of the Belgian beers are bottled more like wines. What's more, the waiters are aficionados and love to discuss their favorites or make suggestions for you to try. By the end of the evening, they may have led you on a tasting tour of Eastern Bloc beers or beers of the Pacific. And if you need to nibble while you drink, the Brickskeller serves a great hamburger (don't be seduced into trying the buffalo burger, which tastes like compacted frozen meat), and even the trout is perfectly fine. Or at least good enough to accompany your exploration of malts and porters and ales and the rest of these wonderful brews. You could eat for as little as $20 if it weren't for all those tempting, expensive beers.

Open Mon.-Thurs. 11:30 a.m.-2 a.m., Fri. 11:30 a.m.-3 a.m., Sat. 6 p.m.-3 a.m., Sun. 6 p.m.-2 a.m. All major cards.

Café Petitto
1724 Connecticut Ave. NW
• 462-8771
ITALIAN

8/20

Look in the window and you will know what makes Café Petitto so popular. The array of antipasti vies with any salad bar in town (a plateful makes a light and compelling lunch). Washington has few such assortments of marinated vegetables and fish; antipasto in this city usually means cold cuts and cheese. So for that alone Café Petitto stands out. What's more, its pizzas are both original and very good. The dough is fried, thin and crisp. And the toppings—concoctions of seafoods and vegetables, as well as the usual Italian meats and cheeses—are high quality. The refreshing antipasti, savory pizzas and a charming little dining room are sufficient assets to overcome some indifferent pastas.

Add reasonable prices—about $40 to $50 for dinner—to the equation and Café Petitto stays perennially popular. *Open daily 11:30 a.m.-midnight. All major cards.*

Cantina d'Italia
1214-A 18th St. NW
• 659-1830
ITALIAN

12/20

Washington had never seen an authentic and ambitious Italian kitchen before Cantina arrived, decades ago. Over the years, this city has willingly weathered its ups and downs. At its best, Cantina serves superlative ingredients cooked simply; its tomato and mozzarella salad is impeccable, and such main dishes as fish cooked in parchment can be extraordinary. Its pastas tend to be complex and intense; sometimes they soar and sometimes they are overwhelming. Such dishes as duck and rabbit require a cold winter day—maybe even a blizzard—to warrant their heaviness. But the main complaint about Cantina is that its plasticized, handwritten menu has remained unreadable through the decades, and even though its warren of basement dining rooms was redecorated, it still looks like the Italian restaurant of a grade-B movie. Cantina has not retained its leadership among Italian restaurants; it has gone through some hard times, during which the food has suffered. Measured at the moment, it still seems uncertain. Its wine list remains extensive but high priced; with even a modest choice, dinner will run at least $120 for two.
Open Mon.-Fri. noon-2 p.m. & 6 p.m.-10:30 p.m., Sat. 6 p.m.-10:30 p.m. All major cards.

Tony Cheng's Mongolian Barbecue
619 H St. NW
• 842-8669
CHINESE

10/20

If you like salad bars and you find steak subs irresistible, Tony Cheng's will seem not only familiar, but wonderful. It is a big, splashy dining room with Asian glitter updated and Americanized. In the center is the floor show: chefs wielding long chopsticks over huge cast-iron grills to whip your ingredients into dinner. You choose your own mix of raw vegetables and paper-thin slices of meat from the lineup around the grill, and ladle on the sauces and seasonings of your choice. Then the chef does his quick-stir magic over the grill and hands you back your finished product. At your table, you stuff your barbecued mixture into delicious, flaky sesame-seed rolls. And that's it, unless you choose to cook at your own table in a charcoal-fired hot pot. Mongolian barbecue makes a savory lunch or a filling all-you-can-eat dinner at about $40 for two. Varying your choice and proportion of vegetables and meats, as well as experimenting with the seasonings, keeps the format from being too routine.
Open Sun.-Thurs. 11 a.m.-11 p.m., Fri.-Sat. 11 a.m.-midnight. All major cards.

Tony Cheng's Seafood Restaurant
619 H St. NW
• 371-8669
CHINESE

11/20

Behind shiny, gilded arches is what amounts to a Chinese restaurant complex: downstairs a Mongolian barbecue, and upstairs, a huge, elegant seafood restaurant, with under-populated fish tanks and a battalion of rolling dim sum carts at lunch. Tony Cheng's can be outstanding when the staff is attentive and the chef is sending out his most exotic seafood preparations. The menu is extensive—with the full range of Cantonese meat dishes as well as seafood—and the dim sum assortment vast. The waiters can be forgetful or indifferent when you need help deciphering all the confusing choices. If in doubt, choose a steamed fish; it is likely to be just-from-the-tank fresh, and cooked so that the flesh is barely firm. If the maître d' lends a hand to your ordering, you might be guided to some extraordinary oyster or shrimp invention, or unfamiliar seafood adventure. Much is ordinary, however, and the clattery room can make conversation difficult. Tony Cheng's has the potential for excellence, but only intermittently achieves it. While prices range widely, you could dine for as little as $40 for two. *Open Sun.-Thurs. 11 a.m.-midnight, Fri.-Sat. 11 a.m.-1 a.m. Cards: AE, MC, V.*

City Café
2213 M St. NW
• 797-4860
AMERICAN

Nora Pouillon has had many "firsts" in Washington: She turned the Tabard Inn into the first small hotel to become known primarily for its restaurant, and Restaurant Nora into the first upscale restaurant to emphasize the wholesomeness, as well as the deliciousness, of its food. Now in City Café, she serves the same additive-free meats and vegetables, in the first of the city's post-modern cafés. City Café is two floors of delightful geometry, which turns triangular tables and balcony into squares by way of mirror tricks. And though the menu is quite circumscribed, it seems large because of the changing array of specials. Seasonings are borrowed from everywhere—from the Southwest as well as Asia, to multiply a few pizzas, pastas, grilled fish and chicken into something to pique your appetite by day, evening or late at night. Pasta primavera is a new dish under Nora's direction, not the tired cliché found elsewhere. Roast chicken is often worthy of a Bresse grandmother. It is a restaurant that suggests concentrating on appetizers: mussels with caper mustard, grilled shiitake mushrooms with tomato salsa, roasted peppers with goat cheese or squid salad. Soups are uniquely good; so are the wines by the glass. City Café is small, lively and convivial, and dinner for two won't be more than $50. *Open Mon.-Thurs. noon-10:30 p.m., Fri. noon-11 p.m., Sat. 6 p.m.-11 p.m. No cards.*

City Lights of China

1731 Connecticut Ave. NW
• 265-6688
CHINESE

12/20

While Chinatown restaurants play musical chairs with their chefs, so that you need a monthly update on which are good, City Lights of China keeps on an even keel. This is a pretty and serene Chinese restaurant, softly lit and appointed with sophistication, and it continually serves food that is carefully contrived. Peking duck is a proud bird here, exactingly cooked, and carved at the table, bargain-priced as well. Lobster comes live from tanks. Vegetable dishes—garlic-spiked spinach and eggplant—are highlights. Some of the trickiest Chinese dishes are this kitchen's most reliable: try crisp fried shredded beef, with its matchstick-cut beef and vegetables in a faintly sweet-hot glaze. Or try flounder duet, the glistening, stir-fried, boneless flounder and vegetables served on its whole crisply fried frame of bones. Among appetizers, the sesame noodles are arranged with artistry, and the vegetable curl is almost too lovely to eat. With generally fine food, solicitous service and a dining room of such gentle assets, it is surprising to finish with a bill of only about $40 for two.
Open Mon.-Thurs. 11:30 a.m.-10:30 p.m., Fri. 11:30 a.m.-11 p.m., Sat. noon to 11 p.m., Sun. noon-10:30 p.m. All major cards.

Dominique's

1900 Pennsylvania Ave. NW
• 452-1126
FRENCH

9/20

Food is only incidental to Dominique's success, though the menu weighs enough to satisfy your weight-lifting requirements for the day. What makes Dominique's enormously successful is that every guest is treated like an important member of the party in power—and indeed Dominique's is always a party. In a city where French restaurants tend to be stiff, Dominique's is unbent. The greetings are effusive, the waiters are friendly and attentive, the decor is—well, there is lots of it. And the menu includes among the duck à l'orange and filet mignon such exotica as rattlesnake salad. But what about the food? Some is good, some is bad, and if you have missed the bargain-priced pre-theater dinner ($16.95 a person), prices are high—in the $100-plus range for two. Best bets are cream of crab soup, farm-raised duck from Dominique's own farm and, sometimes, the fish dishes. It serves as a kind of community center after the theater or on such occasions as Bastille Day. Some go to Dominique's in order to see celebrities; others go in order to be treated as celebrities.
Open Mon.-Thurs. 5:30 p.m.-midnight, Fri.-Sat. 5:30 p.m.-1 a.m., Sun. 5 p.m.-9:30 p.m. All major cards.

Foggy Bottom Café

River Inn Hotel,
924 25th St. NW
• 338-8707
AMERICAN

9/20

Dining well before or after performances at the Kennedy Center is no small feat, so as long as you aren't looking for grandeur, this restaurant is important to know. The menu has been New American since before we even called it that, and the range is from hamburgers to haute inventions. Foggy Bottom Café is a pert little dining room, with welcome sunlight by day and charming flower prints to brighten the evenings. Dinner is a short but eclectic list; tempura, spareribs and the perennial favorite, calf's liver with watercress-mustard sauce. This is also a favorite spot for dessert after the theater, for delights such as its very homey sour-cream-chocolate cake and its original pecan dessert of the day. With dinner in the $50 range for two, Foggy Bottom Café has become a neighborhood restaurant as well as a Kennedy Center outpost.
Open Mon. 7 a.m.-10 a.m. & 5 p.m.-10:30 p.m., Tues.-Fri. 7 a.m.-10 a.m. & 5 p.m.-11:30 p.m., Sat. 8 a.m.-2 p.m. & 5 p.m.-11:30 p.m., Sun. 8 a.m.-2 p.m. & 5 p.m.-10:30 p.m. All major cards.

Galileo

2014 P St. NW
• 293-7191
ITALIAN

The city breathed a big sigh of relief when chef Roberto Donna became full owner, as well as chef, at Galileo. He was one of the first to establish a real Italian restaurant, one where the menu went beyond veal marsala and fettuccine Alfredo. This chef understands the deceptive simplicity of Italian cooking. Galileo was matched only by the all-seafood Italian restaurant, Vincenzo, and it was immediately and overwhelmingly popular. Now, with I Ricchi and Obelisk competing in kind, it is one of the four stellar Italian kitchens. A diner does have to put up with a small, stuffy and sometimes uncomfortable dining room; all the romance is in the cooking. But it can be such superb cooking! Carefully marinated vegetables and seafoods as antipasti, cunningly sauced pastas and wonderful rissottos come as first courses, while wild game and Donna's new inventions, as well as plain, grilled seafoods, are the main courses. All this is accompanied by homemade bread sticks and a changing array of homemade breads with herbs or olives. Such are the glories of Galileo, you must remember not to bother with the ordinary scallopine or whatever else you would find in an ordinary restaurant; choose the unusual dishes from this menu, which changes not once, but twice, a day. Dinner with wine is likely to cost more than $120 for two.
Open Mon.-Fri. 11:45 a.m.-2 p.m. & 5:30 p.m.-10:30 p.m., Sat. 5:30 p.m.-10:30 p.m., Sun. 5:30 p.m.-8:30 p.m. All major cards.

Le Gaulois

2133 Pennsylvania Ave. NW
• 466-3232
FRENCH

11/20

The printed menu hasn't changed for years in this small, crowded, modestly priced French restaurant, and now it is pretty much duplicated in a larger, more handsome, Alexandria branch. The menu still includes what was the city's first *cuisine minceur* (light, healthful cuisine), the best of which is trout with the same ingredients that would be used in ratatouille, but baked in sealed foil. What does change— every day—is the long list of specials. Le Gaulois still offers some bargains, though there is more competition now in its price range. People go here not for the atmosphere— which is about as exciting as a that of a hotel coffee shop—or for the service, which is rushed. People go to Le Gaulois strictly for the food. You can still find such traditional dishes as brains ravigote or beef bourguignon made very well. In summer, the cold plates are outstanding. Every day, the seafoods, served on shredded zucchini "spaghetti," and the lobster with beurre blanc, are not only the product of a highly professional kitchen, but very modestly priced. Nowadays, there are lunch specials the likes of braised tongue with mustard, seafood crêpes and tian farci au poulet (chicken in a mold). Dinner can run upward of $80. *Open Mon.-Thurs. 11:30 a.m.-2:30 p.m. & 5:30 p.m.-11 p.m., Fri. 11:30 a.m.-2:30 p.m. & 5:30 p.m.-midnight, Sat. 5:30 p.m.-midnight. All major cards.*

Herb's

1615 Rhode Island Ave. NW
• 333-4372
AMERICAN

10/20

The unexpected is the norm at Herb's. The menu is New American, which means a little bit from everywhere, prettily dressed and inventively combined. The food is light and fresh, and after numerous ups and downs, Herb's is becoming very good for the price. In summer, the center of action moves outside to the large terrace. In winter, it spreads throughout the dining room, which is divided into several sections, ranging from booths to bar stools. It is a casual lunch room and after-work gathering place. Instead of pretensions, it serves very good food, with a wide array of choices, at modest prices: dinner for two is about $40. *Open daily 7 a.m.-11 a.m., noon-2:30 p.m. (sandwiches 2:30 p.m.-5 p.m.) & 5:30 p.m.-11:30 p.m.. All major cards.*

Iron Gate Inn

1734 N St. NW
• 737-1370
MIDDLE EASTERN

6/20

Iron Gate Inn comes into its own in spring, when, suddenly, everyone remembers that it has one of the most appealing gardens in town. Otherwise, the restaurant would not be worth mentioning. Its Arabic food is of indifferent quality and its service matches, with middling prices as well. But how bad can hummus and shish kebab be? They are certainly good enough here to warrant a sun-dappled afternoon in this quiet, walled garden, shaded by trees. If the waiters are too busy to notice that you are ready to leave, all the better to while away another quarter-hour. Dinner these days climbs to $70 with wine.

Open daily 11:30 a.m.-3 p.m. & 5:30 p.m.-10 p.m. All major cards.

Jean Louis

2650 Virginia Ave. NW
• 298-4488
FRENCH

Is there a restaurant better than Jean Louis? Not in Washington, and perhaps not in New York, Chicago or San Francisco. Even Paris would have to make room among its top ranks for the cooking of this Gascon artist. Jean Louis Palladin is always inventing; last year, it was lobster or langoustine on a bed of diced pigs' feet and ears, salmon cooked rare under a wrapper of straw potatoes, rare tuna teamed with collard greens and mild curry sauce and noodles of coral lobster roe and black squid ink. Jean Louis has had his fritter period, his corn period, his beet period. Yet simple veal noisettes with an olive purée or baby lamb stuffed with wild mushroom are no less dazzling, if less startling. Whatever he invents is likely to become familiar, not just in his restaurant, but in those of others who follow his lead. Along with these inventions, Jean Louis has improved the restaurant's wine list so that it is a connoisseur's fantasy and a budget-watcher's delight. His staff has developed the sureness that too often distinguishes European restaurants from American ones. Dinner at Jean Louis is fixed-price and runs well into three figures. While there is a pre-theater menu, astonishingly reasonable at under $80, this is a restaurant worth an evening of its own. The ingredients are the most luxurious you will find, from the foie gras and caviar to the privately supplied game, lamb, rabbit and duck. Whenever some new rarity becomes available, Jean Louis seems to get it first. Jean Louis has become the city's most notable restaurant—and the one most notables visit. Such fame has also drawn him from his kitchen far too often, to show his art in Napa Valley or at Atlanta banquets. But these days, you might not even see a difference, so mature has this operation become. This is art, and even his failures can be interesting, instructive, influential. For someone who cares deeply about cuisine to miss Jean Louis would be akin to an art student visiting Paris and skipping the Musée d'Orsay.

Open Mon.-Sat. 5:30 p.m.-9:30 p.m. All major cards.

Jean Pierre
1835 K St. NW
• 466-2022
FRENCH

From its opening day, the city's first French restaurant, Jean Pierre, has had to race hard to keep up with the pack. Its strength is in the expertise of its dining room staff: headed by owner Jean Michel Farrat, the team here is suave and experienced. Farrat has redecorated the dining room so that a dreary space has become spiffy. He has also hired a chef—Larbi Dahrouch, formerly sous chef at Jean Louis—who is capable, ambitious and energetic enough to produce very complex dishes at lunch as well as dinner. Dahrouch has added some hints of North Africa to the menu, with his lamb-topped couscous and duck with dates, honey and cumin. Also a master with vegetables, he can turn a simple side dish of asparagus—one or two stalks, sliced and fanned out—into a remarkable treat. Having worked with Jean Louis Palladin for more than a decade, Dahrouch belongs to the former's school of cooking, but he doesn't quite exhibit the same finesse: his flavors are often too mild or his sweetenings too strong, and he doesn't cook fish quite as lightly. Thus, some of the straightforward, old-fashioned French cooking emerges as the best, particularly the Dover sole. Dahrouch needs to develop a surer touch, but his hot apple tart needs no improvement. A thin, crusty base wears a layer of even thinner slices of tart apple, and served with it are exceptional caramel and chocolate ice creams. Service in this small and quiet restaurant shows its many years of experience, and the dining room is soft and soothing, with suede cloth panels, and mirrors to enlarge the space. Farrat has long been recognized for his expertise in wines, and he puts together a list for aficionados as well as ordinary diners to enjoy. In all, he has maintained a good restaurant, albeit an expensive one, about $140 for two at dinner. He is the last of the top French restaurants to remain on K Street, which was once French Restaurant Row.
Open Mon.-Fri. noon-2 p.m. & 6 p.m.-10 p.m., Sat.-Sun. 6 p.m.-10 p.m. All major cards.

Jockey Club
2100 Massachusetts Ave. NW
• 659-8000
FRENCH

No matter what else changes in Washington, the Jockey Club stays the same. What's more, no matter what happens at the Jockey Club—new ownership, new hotel name, even new chef—the Jockey Club stays the same. It is a grand, solid, reliable, expensive (around $140 at dinner) and stolid French restaurant, where not much newfangled intrudes, despite the chef's experiments with intermingling his Asian heritage and his French training. The clubby dining room of wine-red leather and dark wood is carved into cozy dining areas, and the staff pay plenty of attention, along with their carving and flaming and saucing and serving. It is the kind of restaurant where most people are eating rack of lamb (though the crabcakes are justifiably famous), and with good reason. It is where rock-ribbed Republicans with type A personalities hold court with a business deal in mind or with a guest they want to impress. It is one of the few restaurants with a serious kitchen where the apéritif is as likely to be bourbon as white wine, and where Champagne probably outsells Bordeaux.

Open daily 6:30 a.m.-11 a.m., noon-2:30 p.m. & 6 p.m.-10 p.m. All major cards.

Le Lion d'Or

1150 Connecticut Ave. NW
• 296-7972
FRENCH

Le Lion d'Or is not the star it was, but that is not because it has changed for the worse; it is that competition is much stiffer among Washington's French restaurants. Excellence has become commonplace. Even so, Le Lion d'Or can sometimes thrill those who have turned their attention to Jean Louis or Le Pavillon. Chef Jean Pierre Goyenvalle can produce wondrous ravioli filled with slabs of foie gras. He can turn a simple rack of lamb or squab into lifelong memories. His kitchen's soufflés are so light in texture and intense in flavor that they revived soufflé art in this city. The menu is long, however, and retains some duds—a dry and insipid pheasant, perhaps, or perfectly ordinary veal or fish fillet. Goyenvalle's fans have learned what to order: fresh shrimp when they are available, or hot rabbit pâté or salmon in a beautiful puff pastry crust, gossamer pasta with wild mushrooms or lobster. The captains whisper in your ears when something special is in the kitchen. This is a grand, old-fashioned restaurant, with a handsome and serious look to the gold-striped room and lots of flourishes in the service. It is a well-established fixture in Washington, and those who know it love it, while newcomers may have a hard time learning what all this affection is about. Dinner with wine, tax and tip costs at least $140 if you have done justice to the excellent wine list.

Open Mon.-Fri. noon-2 p.m. & 6 p.m.-10 p.m., Sat. 6 p.m.-10 p.m. All major cards.

Maison Blanche

1725 F St. NW
• 842-0070
FRENCH

11/20

As the restaurant closest to the White House, Maison Blanche is known for catering to diners close to power in its spacious dining room of traditional grandeur. The expense-account crowd conducts the business of seeing and being seen—as well as the more direct sort of business. The waiters discreetly and expertly see to their needs. And the work of feeding stomachs and egos goes on. But with expense accounts trimmed, and French cachet being transferred to newer American and Italian restaurants, Maison

Blanche is not at the head of the pack anymore. Shifts in the kitchen have left the food showy but disappointing. The best dishes these days are pastas, particularly a lobster lasagne that is to ordinary lasagne what a Dove Bar is to a popsickle. Otherwise, the food is better photographed than eaten; flavor doesn't seem to be a prime consideration. So, fish soup is pastry-topped, fish steaks are wrapped in vapid mushroom duxelles, and sweetbreads are smoked and sauced, but not seasoned. While this grand restaurant show goes on, the kitchen performs as if it were cast with understudies.

Open Mon.-Fri. 11:45 a.m.-2:30 p.m. (smaller menu 2:30 p.m.-6 p.m.) & 6 p.m.-10 p.m., Sat. 6 p.m.-10 p.m. All major cards.

La Marée
1919 I St. NW
• 659-4447
FRENCH

11/20

La Marée is the kind of restaurant that serves as a backbone of French dining. It is reliable, comfortable, efficient and skilled. If the food doesn't dazzle, neither does it disappoint or frustrate. It exemplifies competent cooking and service. An old reliable. The two dining rooms, upstairs and downstairs, are dressed for success and for businesslike comfort. The menu reflects the seasons, but not the fashions; the only nod to trendiness found lately has been julienned ginger with the soft-shell crabs. Otherwise, La Marée is where you look for a classical fish with mustard sauce, the whole-grain mustard in cream turned nut-brown under the salamander, or a lobster with beurre blanc, or a new-world bouillabaisse. This is not food to talk about for days, but it is food to satisfy, showing traditional French training in the carefully trimmed fresh artichoke stuffed with duxelles and creamed oysters and clams just lightly cooked, or in fish carefully bought and competently braised. This is a professional restaurant, through and through. Dinner is in the $80 to $100 range.

Open Mon.-Thurs. 11:30 a.m.-2:30 p.m. & 5:30 p.m.-10 p.m., Fri. 11:30 a.m.-2:30 p.m. & 5:30 p.m.-10:30 p.m., Sat. 5:30 p.m.-10:30 p.m. All major cards.

Marrakesh
617 New York Ave. NW
• 393-9393
MOROCCAN

10/20

This is a new kind of dinner theater for Washington. An auto body shop on a drab industrial street has been turned into a Moroccan wonderland, with tiles and fountains and waiters in robes serving on their knees. Diners sit on low cushions and eat with their hands from central platters, and everything is done for them, from the choice of wine (there is only one) to the washing of hands to the selection of dinner (only a few choices are available). Dinner starts with an array of salads and ends several hours later with honeyed pastries and minted tea. In between, there have been chicken and lamb and couscous and belly dancers and audience participation in the floorshow. If some of the dishes are second-rate stews in exotic dress, nobody really remembers the specifics by the end of the evening. Prices are moderate (about $70), though even an anonymous jug wine can add significantly to the bill over such a long evening.

Open Mon.-Sat. 6 p.m.-11 p.m., Sun. 5 p.m.-11 p.m. No cards.

McPherson Grill
950 15th St. NW
• 638-0950
AMERICAN

Simple is chic these days, and McPherson Grill is certainly both. The large, sunny dining room is crisply art deco, all black and white, punctuated with etched glass. The menu concentrates on glamourous grills—thick veal and pork chops and fish steaks, with lavish sandwiches at lunch. But plainness is sidestepped with homemade and sparkling relishes and chutneys, with a basket of herbed biscuits and rolls made in-house and with vivid salads. Appetizers are more complex than main dishes, and the leek-strewn, bacon-flavored, creamy oyster stew reaches greatness. Charred rare tuna is accompanied by red onion marmalade, daikon radish and arugula, adding up to another compelling appetizer. The menu changes often, and new fish inventions, new sausages, new flavor combinations suggest you keep an open mind. Side dishes are also worth considering, particularly potato and leek pancakes. This is an urban gathering place, a welcome addition to a neighborhood where few other restaurants compete. Dinner, given the interesting wine list and the irresistible side dishes, is likely to run $100 for two.

Open Mon.-Fri. 11:30 a.m.-2:30 p.m. & 5:30 p.m.-10 p.m., Sat. 5:30 p.m.-10 p.m. All major cards.

Morrison Clark Inn
Mass Ave. & 11th St. NW
• 898-1200
AMERICAN

In this restored, turn-of-the-century inn, Morrison Clark deftly combines tradition and modernity, and presents food of such character as to have been a force in upgrading the neighborhood. The dining rooms are reminiscent of a Victorian parlor, with chinoiserie exhibiting the worldliness of that era. Tall windows and identically framed mirrors sweep the dining room with light. A well-trained and committeed staff creates a comfortable ambience. The cooking is regional American, updated classics and recent inventions. Start with the likes of smothered wild mushrooms on brioche, or parsley salad with fried bread and sesame seeds. Then move to the chicken in cream gravy with a contemporary zest of toasted garlic and mustard. As

with the best of contemporary restaurants, the menu changes with the market, so look for the freshest daily specials. Chef David Frye does well with fish, and sets himself apart from most of the moderns by risking heavier, heartier and longer-cooking dishes as well. For dessert, the summer pudding or strawberry shortcake are worth seeking in warm weather, the pecan squares will certainly suffice in winter. Dinner will cost around $80 for two.
Open Mon.-Thurs. 11:30 a.m.-2:30 p.m. & 6 p.m.-10 p.m., Fri. 11:30 a.m.-2:30 p.m. & 6 p.m.-10:30 p.m., Sat. 6 p.m.-10:30 p.m., Sun. 11 a.m.-3 p.m. All major cards.

Mr. K's

2121 K St. NW
• 331-8868
CHINESE

12/20

Forget all the clichés about Chinese restaurants. Mr. K's sumptuous dining room could as easily house a grand Italian or French restaurant, except for the chopsticks and etched, covered soup bowls and rice bowls. This is a most elegant restaurant, the tables spaced for privacy and the waiters dressed for evening. The food matches: beautiful, elegant, luxurious and comfortable. The problem is not that the food is less than good, but that much of it tastes the same, from the lamb to the beef to the venison. It all emerges as beautifully julienned meat, stir-fried to a juicy tenderness and lightly washed with a glistening of well-seasoned brown sauce. Tender seafood in a translucent gloss looks the same. The other, more serious, problem is that the waiters hustle to increase your bill, pressing you to let them order for you, and bringing double portions without being asked. Mr. K's is a handsome place to eat sophisticated Chinese food, but it is not for adventurous diners. You might get away with $100 for two, but $200 dinners are not unkown.
Open Mon.-Thurs. 11:30 a.m.-11 p.m., Fri. 11 a.m.-11:30 p.m., Sat. 12:30 p.m.-11:30 p.m., Sun. 12:30 p.m.-10 p.m. All major cards.

Nicholas

The Mayflower,
1127 Connecticut Ave. NW
• 347-8900
AMERICAN

11/20

A luxury-hotel restaurant of utter sumptuousness, this is the lunchtime choice of lawyers, lobbyists and groups of shy Japanese ladies, thin as rails, who take photos of each other and barely pick at their food. The dining room is so quiet, so gracious, with its neutral tones and old-world art. The service, though, is erratic, sometimes oozing European polish, other times amateurish. The regulars know this chef's secret strengths. His appetizer of black bean pâté, for instance, is a stunning dish, a small, crusty round filled with soft and zesty bean purée and whole beans, plus luscious shredded duck, the whole wrapped in pancetta and floated in a pale-green, mild garlic cream. Those who don't know the menu well might stumble onto a heavyweight seafood turnover, with a dreary bland filling, or a too-gamy frilled squab in a nondescript brown sauce. This is a chef who takes risks—and often the diner is on the receiving end of a mistake. The adventurer, however, might appreciate a kind of smoked-seafood choucroute, its mild, fresh and sweetly tart cabbage topped with barely warmed smoked salmon, an odd but tasty combination. And even a misstep of grilled quail might come with a marvelously explosive Cajun-hot fruit compote or a lively tomato relish. Desserts continue in the same vein, with sorbets such as pear-mint, which create intriguing matches. For a hotel restaurant, Nicholas is adventurous. For an experimental restaurant, it's exceptionally comfortable. Dinner for two cost s well over $100. *Open Mon.-Fri. 11:45 a.m.-2:30 p.m. & 6 p.m.-10:30 p.m., Sat. 6 p.m.-10:30 p.m. All major cards.*

Nora

2132 Florida Ave. NW
• 462-5143
AMERICAN

Nora is in its prime. There seems to be new enthusiasm in the kitchen. This is a restaurant that respects simplicity. The dining room is lightly decorated with museum-quality American folk arts. And the menu is not long, though it draws from around the world for inspiration. Its ingredients are not only seasonal and fresh, they are chosen from the most wholesome available: meats grown without hormones, vegetables without pesticides whenever possible. Moreover, Nora smokes its own bacon and fish—without nitrates, of course. Nora's serves beautiful food; the plates could compete with the decorations for museum space. It goes to great lengths, making its vinaigrette with goat cheese and sherry, its pastas with fresh parsley, its ice creams in exotic combinations. Its simple tomato and mozzarella salad is made with ripe tomatoes and buffalo mozzarella—perfect. And its soft-shell crabs with pesto or with corn and smoked tomatoes are a necessary part of summer. It risks serving lamb liver and unfashionable veal stew. Its flavors are more vivid than ever, to match the brilliant colors. Ravioli might be stuffed with ham, cheddar and mustard greens; peppers with grilled fresh tuna, peppered cheese and pepitas in a lime-spiked tomato sauce. The Middle East now contributes honey to a glazed lamb and black olives to swordfish with saffron aïoli, and the Southwest donates black beans to veal stew. Despite Nora's having its attention diverted by opening City Café, the food is better than ever, but it will cost about $120 for two after a serious sampling of the well-chosen wine list.
Open Mon.-Thurs. 6 p.m.-10 p.m., Fri.-Sat. 6 p.m.-10:30 p.m. No cards.

Obelisk

2029 P St. NW
• 872-1180
ITALIAN

So pure and personal is this small Italian restaurant that there are only two options for each course (three for the entrée); the menu is fixed-price, with antipasto, pasta, entrée, cheese and dessert for $60. Even so, it can be hard to choose—it all sounds so good. Before dinner, it is enticing to start with an apéritif of sparkling prosecco with house-made cassis, accompanied by a canapé, perhaps of country bread, also house-made, with roasted peppers. First courses might be caponata of extraordinary flavor, or a game bird, perhaps a rolled rabbit pâté or a tiny seafood concotion. Portions are small; this multi-course dinner is not over-filling. Pasta courses are light, just a toss of home-made noodles with some aromatic bit of meat with vegetables, a thick soup or stew, occasionally risotto. Main dishes include one fish, often game, and a red meat. The best dessert might be hard almond cookies to dip in sweet wine (ask for Vin Santo). Obelisk, as you can see, goes to great lengths to make everything in-house. The chef has a delicate touch with textures, a sure boldness with flavors. The wine list is as intelligently constructed as the procession of dishes. The small dining room is spare and plain, attractive, but not plush. Service is efficient and matter-of-fact. This is a restaurant where the food is intended to star.
Open Mon.-Sat. 6 p.m.-10 p.m. Cards: MC, V.

Occidental

1475 Pennsylvania Ave. NW
• 783-1475
AMERICAN

Adjacent to the recently restored Willard Hotel is another revived favorite of Washington's earlier days, the Occidental. Actually, this old standby is two restaurants in one: the more formal dining room upstairs, and the clubby Occidental Grill downstairs, with its collection of photo portraits reaching to the ceiling. In the upstairs room, the sedate atmosphere borders on sterile. Its menu, however, is highly experimental—which means, unfortunately, that the quality isn't always consistent. Chef Jeff Bubens's creations can be exceptional, particularly the soups, but sometimes they flop, when he combines ingredients that don't quite work together, or when the kitchen has paid more attention to presentation than to the basics of cooking. Downstairs, the food is more predictable—both in conception and in preparation. The Grill's prices are lower, too, which makes us more forgiving. Even so, don't assume that the food is uneventful. There's always a steak—a terrific steak—served with varying sauces and garnishes. We love the excellent fried onion rings and burgers, and we're never afraid to try new offerings: a grilled seafood salad, perhaps, or an interestingly garnished grilled chicken breast. For starters, the best bet is homemade sausage, and for a perfectly satisfying finish, try one of the American old-favorite desserts, which always surprise with a slight twist on the original recipe. The Occidental has put together a decent collection of American wines, but the tempting list of beers might divert you from it. Try the Occidental Grill's own label on draft; it's one of America's best micro-brewed beers. Downstairs, dinner will cost around $80 for two; upstairs could be twice that.

Grill: open Mon.-Sat. 11:30 a.m.-11:30 p.m. Formal Dining Room: open Mon.-Thurs. 11:30 a.m.-2 p.m. & 6 p.m.-10:30 p.m., Fri. 11:30 a.m.-2 p.m. & 6 p.m.-11 p.m., Sat. 6 p.m.-11 p.m. All major cards.

Old Ebbitt Grill
675 15th St. NW
• 347-4800
AMERICAN

9/20

Once a lonely outpost, and now the gateway to the downtown resurgence, Old Ebbitt is a branch of Clyde's. Clyde's has always known how to bring in the crowds. Much of the attraction at Old Ebbitt is the bar, which takes up about half the space on its own. The menu is more ambitious than that would suggest, though; this is a kitchen given to experimentation in the New American mode. In addition to Clyde's traditional big, fat, juicy hamburgers, Old Ebbitt serves fancy grills and even its own house-made pastas and ice creams. It really comes into its own at Sunday brunch. A casual dinner is likely to cost $70 for two.

Open Mon.-Fri. 7:30 a.m.-1 a.m., Sat. 8 a.m.-1 a.m., Sun. 9:30 a.m.-1 a.m. All major cards.

Palm
1225 19th St. NW
• 293-9091
AMERICAN

11/20

Nothing ever changes at the Palm, except the diners—they grow older, become partners in their law firms, develop paunches and switch from steak to fish. Or at least lobster—four-and-a-half-pound lobsters, in the Palm style. In the meantime, the Palm still has its walls lined with caricatures of Washington's power elite and it still serves big, fat, juicy steaks with mountains of thick, homemade potato chips (Palm Fries) or hash browns. At lunch, the menu lightens up to include seafood salad or maybe a sauté or casserole, and very good soup. But stick to the middle-of-the-road. This kitchen does plain food well; the green salad with roquefort should be a required course for all those young chefs who try to dazzle with raspberry vinegar and unheard-of oils. The Palm is dependable, for good solid food and no-nonsense service. Just keep in mind that one order of anything is probably too much; find someone to share with. Don't save room for dessert. $120 to $140 for two should do it for dinner, unless you like eight-pound lobsters. *Open Mon.-Fri. noon-10:30 p.m., Sat. 6 p.m.-10:30 p.m. All major cards.*

Pan Asian Noodles & Grill
2020 P St. NW
• 872-8889
ASIAN

10/20

In winter, Pan Asian is most appreciated for its noodle soups, huge bowls of chicken or beef broth, with the noodles and meat or seafood toppings of your choice, the kind of home-style fare to chase away the faintest thought of cold. Then there are the plates of noodles—thin or wide, rice or wheat—topped with an array of meats or seafood cooked in the styles of China, Thailand or other parts of Southeast Asia. Finally, there are the grills: from tiny quail to giant shrimp, from little skewered appetizers to main dish portions, they are also a mix-and-match of Asian styles. Pan-Asian is a conglomeration of Asian flavors, but pared down to a rather small menu, served at rock-bottom prices. The dining room is stylish and utterly casual, its matte-black furniture accented with a splash of color here and there. It's fun; it's easygoing; it's a friendly place for just a bowl of soup or a full meal, ending with a superb Asian-style crème caramel and the sweet, creamy Asian iced coffee that tastes like a dessert in itself. Dinner for two costs as little as $25. *Open Mon.-Thurs. 11:30 a.m.-3 p.m. & 5 p.m.-10:30 p.m., Fri. 11:30 a.m.-3 p.m. & 5 p.m.-11 p.m., Sat. noon-3 p.m. & 5 p.m.-11 p.m., Sun. noon-3 p.m. & 5 p.m.-10 p.m. All major cards.*

Panevino
Embassy Suites Hotel,
1250 22nd St. NW
• 223-0747
ITALIAN

10/20

This breezy and stylish Italian café in the Embassy Suites hotel breaks the mold of hotel restaurants. First, it is modestly priced; you could eat for as little as $20 or spend in the $50 range. Second, it is personal and friendly, with ever-cheerful and eager-to-please waiters. The dining room is a charmer, with walls covered with whimsical original artworks depicting fruits and vegetables. Far from institutional, this kitchen even makes its own breads and breadsticks, and serves them with a bottle of deep-green olive oil. The menu is informal, divided among carpaccios in pleasant variations, pastas in fashionable renditions, modernized pizzas and daily specials of grilled fish. There are a few meat dishes, but fish—very fresh and simply grilled—is the highlight among entrées. You can eat ever so lightly, with carpaccio under shaved parmesan cheese and a bright, crisp salad. For dessert, strawberries are embellished with mascarpone and bittersweet chocolate. *Open daily 11 a.m.-11 p.m. All major cards.*

Le Pavillon

1050 Connecticut Ave. NW
• 833-3846
FRENCH

Chef Yannick Cam is capable of being one of Washington's premier chefs. When he is at top form, he can turn a single scallop into a haunting memory. His tiny, pink beet ravioli flecked with green chives have been widely applauded—and copied. After traveling to Thailand, he has added Asian adaptations with extraordinary results, as in a kind of spring roll (called a wild salmon pancake on the menu) with a silken slice of salmon and zucchini in a buttery sauce of curry and herbs. Cam creates wondrous miniatures: a tiny salad of duck or lobster, a crusty miniature filet of beef, a witty little version of liver and onions (foie gras and shallots)—and serves them in a parade of a tasting menu to make your senses reel. But this is a very subtle and personal art. So when his imagination flags, it shows on the plate. Ordinarily, Cam can produce six courses with never a repetition in style or flavor; sometimes, though, dinner has seemed to be variations on just a couple of themes. Two beurre blancs in a row, or bacon flavoring in two successive courses—these show an absentminded chef. While there are always some dishes that are revelations, such as lobster with ruby-colored beet-and-shiitake sauce, others can be merely ordinary (asparagus vinaigrette with garnish of red peppers and quail egg), and some shockingly inferior—rubbery and flavorless swordfish steak. Much as his bitter chocolate terrine and lemon-curd galette are delectable, the dessert selection needs more frequent freshening. Le Pavillon has always had a stunning wine list. In its early days, the prices were stunningly low; now they have reached astonishing heights, though some good values can be found. As for the environment at Le Pavillon: soft colors and spare decoration seem restful to some, cold to others, even with the magnificent Lalique table as centerpiece. Service is correct, if tense, perhaps reflecting the forbidding prices. Small portions and an intellectual style cause some to complain, while others feel that $250 or more per couple is not too much to pay for the possibility of culinary genius.
Open Mon.-Fri. 11:45 a.m.-2 p.m. & 6:45 p.m.-9:45 p.m., Sat. 6:45 p.m.-9:45 p.m. All major cards.

Prime Rib

2020 K St. NW
• 466-8811
AMERICAN

11/20

Steakhouses used to be bare, plain places where you washed down your beef with bourbon. Prime Rib couldn't be further from that old truth. The dining room is glamorous black, with brass trim and a lucite-topped grand piano, and the wine list shows the pride of California in full force. Otherwise, it is an old-fashioned steakhouse. The waiters blatantly play favorites, so your service can be the best or the worst. The food is good honest stuff, with nice touches, such as fresh horseradish with the prime rib. While steaks, lamb chops and the namesake prime rib are fine, crab imperial is probably the best bet. Dinner checks are likely to run $120 or more for two.

Open Mon.-Thurs. 11:45 a.m.-3 p.m. & 5 p.m.-11 p.m., Fri. 11:45 a..m.-3 p.m. & 5 p.m.-11:30 p.m., Sat. 5 p.m.-11:30 p.m. All major cards.

Primi Piatti
2013 I St. NW
• 223-3600
ITALIAN

11/20

Primi Piatti is a huge, bustling trattoria with a wood-burning pizza oven, rotisserie and grill, and on warm days the dining spills out onto the sidewalk. Noisy as the dining room is, many prefer to watch the kitchen in action from the tables in the back, amid streams of waiters dashing around, refilling bread baskets (the homemade bread sticks and country loaves are highlights here). Primi Piatti's is a simple menu, limited to antipasti displayed on the buffet in the front, a few pizzas, some very interesting pastas, some grilled fish and meats and a couple of rotisserie specialties. It is simple food, presented with little adornment, and can be wonderful, or—as is often the case with the roasted meats—drab. The pizzas are authentically blistered and chewy—good, homey stuff. The pastas are skillfully made, and likely to be the best part of the meal. Grilled fish are fine, and meats or birds, when they haven't been cooked dry, are generally good. Dinner will cost about $80 for two.

Open Mon.-Thurs. 11:30 a.m.-2:30 p.m. & 5:30 p.m.-10:30 p.m., Fri. 11:30 a.m.-2:30 p.m. & 5:30 p.m.-11:30 p.m., Sat. 5:30 p.m.-11:30 p.m. All major cards.

I Ricchi
1220 19th St. NW
• 835-0459
ITALIAN

Even Italy has few such authentic and traditional trattorias as I Ricchi anymore, or so it seems. I Ricchi is a branch of a rustic restaurant in the hills north of Florence, having duplicated its wood-burning stove and grill, and reproduced its cooking with remarkable faithfulness. The Washington branch is far more elegant than the original in its simply chic whitewashed and frescoed dining room, its downtown location, its intelligent wine list and its urban prices. Grilled meats are the highlight, particularly leg of rabbit and thin, herbed goat chops. Steaks remind one of Florence's famous T-bones. The fried mixtures of seafood or of vegetables—each in its own unique batter—are outstanding. Then there are grand, aromatic risottos, rustic homemade pastas in sauces of simple glory, delicate seasonal antipasti and perfect, uncomplicated salads. The ingredients are exceptional, from tiny, whole artichokes to real prosciutto. The breads, baked in those wood-burning ovens, not only decorate the counter of the open kitchen, but taste as one would expect in Italy. I Ricchi is bright, bustling and crowded, one of the most popular of Washington's restaurants. And you can buy a stomach-numbing feast of hearty food for about $70 to $90 for two. *Open Mon.-Thurs. 11:30 a.m.-2:30 p.m. & 5:30 p.m.-10:30 p.m., Fri. 11:30 a.m.-2:30 p.m. & 5:30 p.m.-11:30 p.m., Sat. 5:30 p.m.-11:30 p.m. Cards: AE, MC, V.*

Sala Thai
2016 P St. NW
• 872-1144
THAI

11/20

A tiny restaurant downstairs from the P Street restaurant row, Sala Thai is a chic little spot. The food is dressed up with carved vegetable garnishes, but the disco-snazzy room of laminate and lucite invites dressed-down dining. Concentrate on appetizers—the chili-hot meat salads, the small skewers of beef or pork saté, the fried tofu or shrimp fried in egg-roll wrappers. Main dishes range from curries to sweet-and-tart noodle combinations to myriad seafood and fish dishes. These Thai curries are particularly aromatic, and fish is usually a good bet. Sala Thai invites lingering over a daiquiri made from seasonal fresh fruit, an imported beer or a glass of well-chosen wine. It's a full restaurant, with some glamourous dishes, but equally a place for light eating to accompany drinking and talking. Either way, it won't cost much more than $40 to $50 for two.
Open Mon.-Thurs. 11:30 a.m.-2:30 p.m. & 5 p.m.-10:20 p.m., Fri. 11:30 a.m.-2:30 p.m. & 5 p.m.-11 p.m., Sat. noon-11 p.m., Sun. 5 p.m.-10:20 p.m. All major cards.

Suzanne's
1735 Connecticut Ave. NW
• 483-4633
AMERICAN

10/20

Suzanne's doesn't stop at being a very good casual restaurant. It is also a wine bar, a carry-out and a market. On the first floor, the market displays interesting, packaged fancy foods and exquisite, often exotic, produce. In the deli cases are some of the best home-style take-out foods in the city, including salads, main dishes, pizzas and tortes; and in the back are outrageously good baked goods, from breads to chocolate chestnut torte. Upstairs, the dining room is homey, a close and crowded gathering place, and the menu changes daily to suit the season and a variety of moods. The repertoire is drawn from around the world, with hummus and pâtés, quiches and Mexican-style stews. Always experimental, the kitchen falters, but with its high-quality ingredients, doesn't slip too far. Food and service are exuberant, sometimes amateurish. Keep in mind those terrific pastries downstairs to round out your dinner upstairs. Dinner can range from $60 to $100 for two.
Open Mon.-Thurs. 11 a.m.-2:30 p.m. & 6 p.m.-11:30 p.m., Fri. 11 a.m.-2:30 p.m., Sat. 11:30 a.m.-3 p.m. & 6 p.m.-10:30 p.m. (desserts 6 p.m.-1 a.m.). Cards: Choice, MC, V.

Szechuan
615 I St. NW
• 393-0130
CHINESE

11/20

Not only is Szechuan the oldest of Chinatown's Szechuan and Hunan restaurants, its long menu can vie with the breadth of the local Cantonese menus, and seasonal vegetables show up to vary the fare. Check with the kitchen for spring asparagus or maybe baby bok choy, and ask what the kitchen can do specially on a given night. Otherwise, explore the less-familiar Szechuan dishes, though the sweet-hot crispy beef and whole fish are likely to be excellent, even if familiar from every other Szechuan menu. Szechuan has its ups and downs, particularly as the chain of restaurants expands. But even at its nadir, Szechuan serves an interesting and competently made variety of dim sum for weekend brunches. In recent years, the service has improved even as the kitchen has grown occasionally erratic. Dinner is likely to cost $50 for two.
Open Mon.-Thurs. 11 a.m.-11 p.m., Fri.-Sat. 11 a.m.-midnight, Sun. 11 a.m.-10 p.m. All major cards.

Szechuan Gallery
617 H St. NW
• 898-1180
CHINESE

11/20

What is most interesting at this misnamed Chinatown restaurant is not the Szechuan food at all, but the Taiwanese food, most of which is on a separate menu. Put yourself in the hands of your waiter if you are adventurous, and while duck-blood dishes may not delight you, duck tongues or some other exotica might; the menu has all the standbys as well. The dining room is more comfortably furnished than most; prices are low; and the staff are as eager as tour guides to show you what makes Taiwanese food special. Dinner will cost less than $40.
Open Sun.-Thurs. 11 a.m.-3 a.m., Fri.-Sat. 11 a.m.-4 a.m. All major cards.

Tabard Inn
1739 N St. NW
• 833-2668
AMERICAN

12/20

A homey little hotel dining room with tile floors and primitive art, Tabard Inn has a long, friendly bar for waiting or for cocktails, and a lounge packed with so many sofas you would think they were waiting for a clearance sale. Behind the dining room is a marvelous outdoor garden, brick-walled, with umbrellas, hanging plants and attention-grabbing sculpture. The food is homey, too, all fresh, and changing daily at lunch and dinner. In summer, there will be fresh crab salad, perhaps with fresh corn, or blackberry brûlée tart. In winter, the menu turns heartier. But, always, there are fish specials, such as grilled swordfish with mango relish or tuna stuffed with gingered shrimp and topped with fresh pineapple relish. Steaks and prime rib and chicken fill out the menu, along with more complex pasta dishes. Herbs are grown on the inn's own farm, and meats are raised additive-free whenever possible. The cooking is good, if a bit rustic. Soups are intense; french fries are mellow and grease-free; fish is gently cooked. As for the flaws, they are the other side of the homeyness: a too-sweet and timid chili, though made with chunks of beef and freshly cooked beans. Tabard Inn is not a place in which to seek cuisine with finesse; it's a place to go for a refreshing outdoor lunch or casual dinner. The menu offers everything from a good hamburger or a freshly barbecued chicken, to an invention with Middle Eastern flavor or a properly grilled fish filet. Lunch is in the $40 range, dinner will cost more than $60.

Open Mon.-Fri. 7 a.m.-10 a.m., 11:30 a.m.-2:45 p.m. & 6 p.m.-10:30 p.m., Sat. 8 a.m.-10 a.m., 11 a.m.-2:45 p.m. & 6 p.m.-11 p.m., Sun. 8 a.m.-10 a.m., 11 a.m.-2:45 p.m. & 6 p.m.-10 p.m. Cards: MC, V.

Taberna del Alabardero

1776 I St. NW (entrance on 18th St.)
• 429-2200
SPANISH

Imported directly from Spain, from the chef to the sherry glasses, this is perhaps the most authentic upscale Spanish restaurant in the country. The proprietor is a Spanish priest who founded the chain of restaurants in Spain to employ the downtrodden, and produced a series of highly reputed restaurants along the way. Washington's branch is a beauty, with soft, velvety colors and textures, and intricately carved wood and lace in the several dining areas. At lunchtime, the menu is more obviously Spanish; at dinner, it tends toward generalized Continental cooking, with Spanish accents. In both cases, it is ambitious cuisine, from the simple roast peppers raised to high art, to the thick filet mignon, topped with bone marrow and red wine sauce. The sherry list, as expected, is enough to please aficionados. The wine list teaches us something about Spain's best. Taberna is a distinguished restaurant, with formal service and cooking that emphasizes beauty as well as technical expertese. It has become a second home to the Spanish diplomatic community, and a change of pace for Washingtonians who frequent the usual fine French and Italian restaurants, but were ready for something new. Dinner will cost about $120, and definitely should include one of the kitchen's glorious desserts.

Open Mon.-Thurs. 11:30 a.m.-2:30 p.m. & 6 p.m.-10:30 p.m., Fri. 11:30 a.m.-2:30 p.m., Sat. 6 p.m.-11 p.m. All major cards.

Takesushi

1010 20th St. NW
• 466-3798
JAPANESE

12/20

From the outside, you can easily pass by this tiny-looking Japanese restaurant, which is upstairs from a Chinese luncheonette. Inside, it is indeed tiny, and its tables are packed—mainly with Japanese. The reason is that it has a very sophisticated sushi bar, with a steady stock of seasonal delicacies and the resources to produce spectacular (and spectacularly expensive) platters, if you are willing to leave yourself in the chef's hands. There is not much else on the menu besides a few tempura and teppanyaki dishes; raw fish is the focus here. Unless you are with a group and looking for elaborate sushi or sashimi arrangements, sit at the sushi bar and point to what you want. The chefs are communicative enough to help you along in your ordering, and their art is fascinating entertainment. Takesushi can be counted on for fresh, supple tuna and yellowtail, a full range of clams and other shellfish and handsomely constructed sushi rolls and hand rolls. Dinner can be as low as $50, but ordering freely among the sushi choices can increase it to $100.
Open Mon.-Fri. noon-2:30 p.m. & 5:30 p.m.-10 p.m., Sat. 5 p.m.-10 p.m. All major cards.

Tiberio

1915 K St. NW
• 452-1915
ITALIAN

While the superstar French restaurants up and down K Street have disappeared into history, Tiberio, the city's first sedately elegant northern Italian restaurant, just goes on and on. It is dignified—white, white, white, with long-stem red roses the main decoration. It is predictable—conservatively dressed homemade pastas and a menu that seems French, except for the accent and the number of veal dishes. It is expensive—outrageously so. The wine list is so overpriced that one wants to order water in protest. The cooking is refined and correct, but nothing more (agnolotti are the highlight and have been for years). Tiberio showed what it could do when its partners opened Terrazza in Alexandria with similar decor, better food and much lower prices. Did Terrazza reform Tiberio? No, it was the other way around. Terrazza has grown more snobbish, more expensive and less gastronomically reliable. And Tragara, the third sibling, opened in Bethesda with more acceptable prices and service, but it, too, is maturing in the family mold. Dinner for two at Tiberio costs $150 or more.
Open Mon.-Fri. 11:45 a.m.-2:30 p.m. & 6 p.m.-11 p.m., Sat. 6 p.m.-11 p.m. All major cards.

21 Federal

1736 L St. NW
• 331-9771
AMERICAN

From the day it opened, 21 Federal settled amid the top of Washington's restaurant hierarchy and stayed there. A branch of a Nantucket restaurant, run by chef Bob Kinkead, who first made his mark in Boston, 21 Federal is professional in every nuance. The dining room is large and grand, its walls paneled in exotic wood, its massive open space softened by lavish flowers. While the dining room is noisy, the tone is utterly dignified. The menu is full of New American adventures. Kinkead's emphasis is on seafood, and his style is updated New England, though he adds touches of every region, from the Southwest—with chipotle peppers seasoning the pork loin and ancho chilies flavoring the seafood fritto misto and his soft-shell crabs—to nouveau Southern crabcakes, made with lobster as well as crab, and accompanied by okra and corn relish. Each dish is a complexity of sauces, garnishes and accompaniments that make it a full palette of colors, textures and flavors. There is, for example, a trio of lamb, rosemary and sweet garlic in which each flavor is distinct, yet complements the others. Kinkead's appetizer salads are complex and intriguing; his main dishes are so wide-ranging that choice becomes difficult. And 21 Federal's seasonal dessert fantasies, such as blueberry, lime and bourbon pie with blueberry ice cream, are enough reason to return. Prices here are ever climbing; dinner is likely to top $120 for two, particularly given the compelling wine list. But that is to be expected in such a showcase of American culinary invention.
Open Mon.-Thurs. 11:30 a.m.-2:30 p.m. & 6 p.m.-10 p.m., Fri. 11:30 a.m.-2:30 p.m. & 6 p.m.-10:30 p.m., Sat. 6 p.m.-10:30 p.m. All major cards.

Vincenzo

1606 20th St. NW
• 667-0047
ITALIAN/ SEAFOOD

The mystery of what makes Italian food unique may not be totally explainable, but it is there to be observed at Vincenzo. This is a set of simple dining rooms—tile floors and whitewashed walls with arches between them—and a menu that is both short and almost totally focused on seafoods. Those seem no limitations at all, once you have explored the menu for yourself. You start with antipasti—simply delicious marinated vegetables and a couple of lightly dressed seafood salads. The accompanying breads are homemade. Supple al dente noodles are tossed with crab and just a tinge of tomato, tiny clams, mixed seafoods or no seafood at all—and they are wonderful. Next comes a seafood stew or maybe fritto misto or, best of all, a whole fish with the barest of seasonings, just lemon and oil with perhaps a touch of fresh herb, grilled so that the skin has crunch and the flesh is moistly steamy. Part of the secret at

Vincenzo is superb ingredients, from the seafood to the deep-green olive oil. Another part is the reliance on those ingredients and on careful cooking, rather than on invention and experimentation that attempts to dazzle. Vincenzo has an instinct for the appropriate, whether it be the small list of well-chosen wines or the few simple desserts. Such simplicity does not come cheap; Vincenzo's prices vie with the top-priced Italian restaurants, with dinner checks easily $120 or more for two. For those prices, you not only get fine food, but also smoothly professional service without a smidgen of pomposity.

Open Mon.-Fri. noon-2 p.m. & 6 p.m.-10 p.m., Sat. 6 p.m.-10 p.m. All major cards.

Willard Room

**The Willard
Inter-Continental,
1401 Pennsylvania Ave. NW
• 637-7440**
AMERICAN

12/20

This ornate ceiling and glowing wood paneling, these velvet banquettes and monumental chandeliers create such an opulent dining room that the Willard wouldn't really need to serve food in order to be a success. No room in Washington is more beautiful. It does, however, go to great lengths for its food. The ingredients are top class, and the constructions are elaborate. The menu walks a careful line between mainstream and fanciful. American inventiveness is tempered by tradition. If the cooking has its faults, they are quiet ones: this is good food. It is often, however, food that doesn't quite live up to its promise. The menu promises strong and bold combinations, and the plates promise great artistry in their bright colors and ingenious composition. The crabcakes are on a sea of muted gold, a few vivid green spears of asparagus branching across one side, and a small dab of caviar at their base. But the crabcakes are too bready and the sauce is more aroma than flavor. Swordfish-and-tomato salad is a stunner of an appetizer, the tiny slabs of swordfish sandwiched beteen lacy potato pancakes. But the bed of greens doesn't meld. Fried oysters are cleverly linked with a delicate sauce of poblano chiles, but the oysters are upstaged by their breading. And if the rolls are homemade, they need a better home. The food is artistically matched with the setting, but judged in the tasting rather than in the conception, the Willard is still a hotel dining room rather than a great restaurant that happens to be in a hotel. Prices are $100 for lunch, and $125 or more for dinner, with wine.

Open Mon.-Fri. 7:30 a.m.-10 a.m., 11:30 a.m.-2:30 p.m. & 6 p.m.-10:30 p.m., Sat.-Sun. 8 a.m.-10:30 a.m. & 6 p.m.- 10:30 p.m. All major cards.

Duke Zeibert's
1050 Connecticut Ave. NW
• 466-3730
AMERICAN

9/20

Newcomers see Duke's as a vast, modern dining room in sedate gray and burgundy, with a large terrace overlooking Connecticut Avenue. Oldtimers see it as a kind of public men's club for jocks and politicos, and they probably don't even notice that the food is, at best, ordinary, that the roast beef tastes of a steam table, the fish is big but bland, the matzoh-ball soup anemic. Or that the prices are right up there with the top dogs. They are still looking for big portions (although now probably low-cholesterol big portions). And if the salads are dreary, they know that eventually, winter will come, and it will be time to order the good, homey beef-in-a-pot. They really come to see, be seen and catch up on the gossip with Duke himself. And they'll pay upward of $100 (for two) at dinner for the possibility. *Open Mon.-Sat. 11:30 a.m.-11:30 p.m., Sun. 5 p.m.-10 p.m. All major cards.*

GEORGETOWN

Austin Grill
2404 Wisconsin Ave. NW
• 337-8080
AMERICAN

11/20

Texas has been invading Washington full force in recent years, with restaurants galore. The one that strikes the most authentic note is Austin Grill, a bright little hole-in-the-wall that resounds with country music and the yelping of city kids who have a hankering for the plains. Yes, it's young and brassy, and the staff seems on a break from classes. The walls are painted with cartoon renditions of Texas symbols; the booths are plastic; and anything upscale from jeans might seem out of place. The food is serious, however, with three different home-style hot sauces at the table. Quesadillas might be packed with homemade chorizo as well as fresh crab meat and green chiles. Fajitas are made from real skirt steak, properly marinated and grilled so it is crusty and rare, rather than gray and chewy, and there are plenty of accompaniments to roll with them in the flour tortillas. The guacamole, the refried beans and the red rice are standouts. There are more elegant dishes—grilled fish, steak, barbecued shrimp. The mood is right, though, for a margarita or a Texas beer and something chile-spiked, tortilla-rolled, Texas-accented. Whatever it is, it is not likely

123 4538

to cost you more than $30 to $40 for dinner.
Open Mon. 5:30 p.m.-11 p.m., Tues.-Thurs. 11:30 a.m.-11 p.m., Fri.-Sat. 11:30 a.m.-midnight, Sun. 11:30 a.m.-10:30 p.m. (Sun. brunch 11:30 a.m.-3 p.m.). Cards: AE, MC, V.

Bamiyan
3320 M St. NW
• 338-1896
AFGHAN

12/20

Washington's first Afghan restaurant, this upstairs dining room now has plenty of competition, but still is among the best. It has a welcoming warmth, with artifacts and rugs creating an impression of an exotic culture, and a serving staff slightly shy, but still gracious. The menu is inexpensive—and justifiably short. After all, once you have tasted Bamiyan's aushak (homemade noodles stuffed with scallions or leeks and topped with yogurt, mint and tomato-meat sauce) and its chicken kebabs, you'd probably want to order the same thing on your next visit, anyway. Aushak also comes in a fried version and as a soup. And kebabs could be lamb rather than chicken. Then there is a highly fragrant dark rice studded with meat, raisins and carrots which is well worth sampling; the side dishes of eggplant and pumpkin are equally delicious. The bread is homemade, washboard-shaped and lightly seeded. For dessert there is a giant, thin, fried pastry to nibble. Bamiyan illustrates why Afghan food has become one of the most popular in Washington. Dinner is less than $50 for two, with wine.
Open Mon.-Sat. 5:30 p.m.-11 p.m. All major cards.

Aux Beaux Champs
Four Seasons Hotel,
2800 Pennsylvania Ave. NW
• 342-0810
AMERICAN

If you are planning a banquet, the Four Seasons Hotel can't be beat. Its rooms are sumptuous; its staff is polished; and its chef can produce food as impeccable and imaginative for 200 as for 25. Maybe better. The restaurant, Aux Beaux Champs, has these same assets, but seems to suffer from the banquets' success. One feels that the best is siphoned off too often. The dining room itself is as spacious, comfortable and sedately beautiful as one could wish. And between the wine list and menu, you could spend an evening in indecision, so compelling are they. This cooking in the New American style is clever and handsome. The garnishes—chutneys, relishes, bits of vegetable creations—are more elaborate than many restaurants' main dishes. Truly, this restaurant begins in excellence, with top-notch ingredients, the best of the season. There are, often enough, raves, say, over a perfect grilled salmon or a delicately sauced duck breast. Then there is the carelessness of oversalting or underseasoning or mistiming that makes you wonder who's getting the good stuff. The best of Aux Beaux Champs is

51

brunch, when the sumptuous comes cheaper and the cooking is less a high-wire act. Also, tea in the lobby is one of Washington's favorite respites. Expect to spend close to $200 for dinner.
Open Mon.-Fri. 7 a.m.-11 a.m., noon-2:30 p.m. & 6:30 p.m.-10:30 p.m., Sat.-Sun. 10 a.m.-2:30 p.m. & 6:30 p.m.-10:30 p.m. All major cards.

Bistro Français
3124-28 M St. NW
• 338-3830
FRENCH

11/20

It is not only the fixtures—pressed-tin ceiling and etched glass against dark wood—that identify this as a very French bistro, the menu is enough to make a grown Frenchman weep with nostalgia: salade gasconne, studded with giblet confit and served warm, keeps company with moules niçoise, coq au vin and entrecôte marchand de vin à la moelle. The bistro also nods to modern fashions in its veal chop with dates and juniper berry sauce, scallops with ginger and sweet red pepper sauce, and even blackened grouper New Orleans–style on occasion. In all, Bistro Français is a cozy and bustling restaurant where the French chefs gather late at night, tourists come for the very inexpensive early-bird special, and the faithful return year after year, knowing that if the food has only a 50/50 chance of being better than ordinary, it has a 100-percent chance of being a good value. There are such bargain-priced specials as T-bone steak and lobster, and in fact, the best dish we have had at Bistro Français, salmon on a lobster mousse. The cooking has its ups and downs: the restaurant's signature dish, rotisserie roasted chicken, can be juicy or dry; sauces sometimes are vague; steaks can be overcooked; and the pastries are a glittery array of supersweet tortes and fruit tarts with brick-hard crusts. Keep in mind that this is a bistro, and order the simple, the hearty and the endearingly old-fashioned. In all, dinner costs about $70 to $80 for two.
Open Sun.-Thurs. 11 a.m.-3 a.m., Fri.-Sat. 11 a.m.-4 a.m. All major cards.

Le Caprice
2348 Wisconsin Ave. NW
• 337-3394
FRENCH

10/20

The assets and pitfalls of the new French cooking are laid out on your plate at Le Caprice. This is a small and simple dining room, dressed in blue cloth, with blue walls. The menu is far more ambitious than the decor. To start with are a dozen appetizer choices, ranging from terrines of sweetbreads or liver to ballotine of duck and chicken, from two-salmon quenelles with anise and avocado sauce on the cold side to seafoods in puff pastry and Provençal fish soup on the hot side. Main dishes are fewer, but no less elaborate:

scallops of salmon with mussel velouté and salmon caviar, two brochettes of seafood wrapped with smoked salmon or ham and flavored with anise, duck breast with glazed fruit and veal with fresh chanterelles, for example. The emphasis is not only on offbeat combinations but on elaborate presentations: fish brochettes float on tiny eggplant boats with sprays of vegetable batons propelling them; soups are paved with sauce squiggles. A little tortured? Definitely. But the real pity is that the cooking is erratic. A ballotine as pretty as a pinwheel tastes of pleasant ingredients but is disagreeably damp, yet it is surrounded with the most tantalizing little clumps of marinated vegetables. A fish soup is robustly seasoned; a watercress soup tastes of little more than slightly rancid cream. Salmon is beautifully sautéed, and tastes as if it were bathed in sea breezes, while brochettes are too firm and too salty from their ham or salmon wraps. Such ups and downs have divided Le Caprice's audience into those who adore it and those who can't understand why anyone would return. Furthermore, since prices are identical at lunch and dinner, and you could spend more than $80 easily, there are camps who consider it expensive, others who find it a good value. It strikes me as the work of a talented amateur—an interesting mind without the experience or judgment to develop consistent excellence.

Open Tues.-Fri. 11:45 a.m.-2 p.m. & 6 p.m.-10 p.m., Sat. 6 p.m.-10:30 p.m., Sun. 6 p.m.-9:30 p.m. All major cards.

El Caribe
3288 M St. NW
• 338-3121
LATIN AMERICAN

See review in "Adams Morgan" section, page 11.
Open Mon.-Fri. 11:30 a.m.-11 p.m., Sat. 11:30 a.m.-11:30 p.m., Sun. 11:30 a.m.-10 p.m. All major cards.

Chez Grand Mère
3057 M St. NW
• 337-2436
FRENCH

10/20

The chef in this kitchen respects the tradition implied in the restaurant's name, but also speaks to modern trends. Here is a place where you will find routinely such homey dishes as sweetbreads, brains, liver, kidneys and pork roasts or stews. There are simple family-style dishes and also game in season, plus lighter composed salads that grandmother never knew. Finally, the assets of Chez Grand Mère include a darling of a dining room, dressed with grandmotherly lace and partitioned with etched glass. It is a dear of a place, with dinners at $60 to $80 for two.

Open Mon.-Thurs. 11:30 a.m.-3 p.m. & 5:30 p.m.-10:30 p.m., Fri. 11:30 a.m.-3 p.m. & 5:30 p.m.-11 p.m., Sat.-Sun. 5:30 p.m.-10:30 p.m. All major cards.

Clyde's Georgetown
3236 M St. NW
• 333-9180
AMERICAN

7/20

Clyde's, like its early saloon customers, has grown up and moved out to the suburbs. In fact, it has expanded even more than that: the Old Ebbitt, 1789, F. Scott's and The Tombs are affiliated, as well as branches in Tyson's Corner and Columbia. The original still has undeniable character in its long, cozy bar room, its sunny atrium and the glitzy omelet room. It still has its famous hamburgers, though the dinner menu is far more extensive than that, and the bar menu has interesting—if not always delicious—tidbits to accompany a beer. But food is not the focus at Clyde's. It's as much an historic sight as some of the monuments. Dinner costs between $30 and $60 for two, with wine. *Open Mon.-Thurs. 7:30 a.m.-1 a.m., Fri.-Sat. 7:30 a.m.-2 a.m., Sun. 9 a.m.-1 a.m. All major cards.*

Dar Es Salam
3056 M St. NW
• 342-1925
MOROCCAN

Behind its small facade is the most exotic interior in Georgetown, if not the city, for Dar Es Salam is the arduous work of twenty Moroccan craftsmen. The walls are tile mosaics; the ceilings are carved-and-painted plaster; the windows are stained glass; and the seating is at low tables. If it looks straight out of *The Arabian Nights*, a dinner lives up to every fancy it inspires. Start with tiny dishes of the most tinglingly savory salads, to be slathered onto bits of home-made bread. Go on to pigeon pie in phyllo, flavored with raisins and almonds as well as egg and parsley. Then there are roasted or steamed haunches of lamb, kebabs or stews of chicken with olives and preserved lemons or of organ meats. There might be fish in paprika sauces or sweet-tart spice combinations. All this is meant to be eaten with your hands, which are washed before and after with perfumed waters from intricately chased metal ewers. This is the closest Washington comes to real Moroccan cuisine, and it makes for a gloriously exotic evening, which can finish downstairs in the nightclub with a belly-dancing show. Dinner will cost about $80 to $100 for two. *Open Sun.-Tues. 5 p.m.-11 p.m., Wed.-Sat. 5 p.m.-3 a.m. All major cards.*

Enriqueta
2811 M St. NW
• 338-7772
MEXICAN

Enriqueta is small and cramped, but compensates by being bright and festive, decorated with colorful paper cutouts, tin lamps and dazzlingly painted chairs. The cooking is head and shoulders above almost every other local Mexican restaurant. Enriqueta was the first to establish that Mexican food need not be the one-sauced mush that passes for Mexican cooking at fast-food restaurants. Enriqueta's green sauce has the tang of fresh tomatillos; its mole sauce tastes of myriad seeds and spices with the catalyst of bitter chocolate; and its seafoods are not overwhelmed by seasoning. The menu is long, and ranges from the clichés of enchiladas to elegant beef fillets (which are among the best entrées). The mood is often like a party. Thus, despite the uncomfortable high-backed chairs and the overcrowded tables, Enriqueta is still a favorite. Dinner is $60 for two. *Open Mon.-Thurs. 11:30 a.m.-2:30 p.m. & 5 p.m.-10 p.m., Fri. 11:30 a.m.-2:30 p.m. & 5 p.m.-11 p.m., Sat. 5 p.m.-11 p.m., Sun. 5 p.m.-10 p.m. All major cards.*

Flutes

1025 Thomas Jefferson St. NW
• 333-7333
AMERICAN

11/20

Flutes surrounds champagne with its proper accoutrements in a two-story dining room. The walls are sumptuous woods, fabrics and *faux* marble, lit by chandeliers that add a giant diamond sparkle to the room. The theme is champagne, the wine list displays a fine selection, and the staff knows its bubbles. While Flutes once was a sipping-and-nibbling kind of place, it now concentrates on full meals. The food is more visual dazzle than follow-through on the palate, but it is good enough to serve as background for a great bottle. Or you can just concentrate on caviar. The menu runs to supper-club standbys, such as steak tartare, smoked salmon and prime rib—good, but not stunning. If ravioli is on the menu, it is the standout. Steamed fish, wrapped in scales of zucchini or the like, can be interesting. If it is atmosphere you seek, rather than gastronomic epiphany, Flutes is the place. Dinner for two is $100 plus . *Open Mon.-Thurs. 5 p.m.-2 a.m., Fri. 5 p.m.-3 a.m., Sat. 6 p.m.-3 a.m. All major cards.*

Georgetown Bar & Grill

1310 Wisconsin Ave. NW
• 337-7777
AMERICAN

9/20

Seldom do you choose a neighborhood bar for its beauty, but you can when the neighborhood is Georgetown. The Georgetown Bar & Grill is green marble, dark wood and brass, woven through a spacious room to create a stunning pub. It is at the same time bright and airy, warm and intimate; you feel part of the large mainstream even as you have some privacy. The large wood-trimmed bar in the middle of the room leaves plenty of space for a proper dining room. As for the menu, it is tavern food sauced with American innovation. Most successful are the salads, which combine smoky grilled meats, such as chicken or shrimp, with an everything-but-the-kitchen-sink mix of romaine, Roquefort, bacon and such. Grilled meats are also made into upscale club sandwiches. But several changes of chefs have left us with doubts; from time to time, the kitchen's ambition overreaches its skill. Dinner is about $75 for two. *Open daily 7 a.m.-10:30 a.m., 11 a.m.-3 p.m. & 5 p.m.-1 a.m. All major cards.*

Georgetown Seafood Grill

3063 M St. NW
• 333-7038
AMERICAN/SEAFOOD

10/20

This is the seafood-theme restaurant of the savvy group that runs the River Club, J. Paul's and Paolo's. To get the best of it, you need to be a savvy diner. Some of the food is just fine, but price is no guide to quality here. The priciest entrées are formulaic dishes with fancy-sounding ingredients. Skip the mixed-seafood stews and pastas: the shellfish taste like long-frozen clones, the sauces are wan and the pasta is heavy. Choose among the oysters on the half-shell, or something utterly simple like the steamed mussels. For main dishes, the homier the better: catfish fried in cornmeal is crunchy and moist, though the fish hasn't much flavor, soft-shell crabs in season are wisely just sautéed plain. Otherwise, this is a bustling and pleasant seafood house that tries to be imaginative and only succeeds at showing its amateurishness. The sauces are insignificant, the fish are rarely local, but more likely to be glamour species that taste interchangeable, and the cooking is merely satisfactory. You can, however, finish with a properly tangy and creamy key lime pie. Service is cheery, and the wine list has reasonable and refreshing choices. If you order from the low end, you'll spend closer to $50 than to $80 for two.
Open Sun.-Thurs. 11:30 a.m.-11:30 p.m., Fri.-Sat. 11:30 a.m.-midnight. All major cards.

Germaine's

2400 Wisconsin Ave. NW
• 965-1185
VIETNAMESE/PAN-ASIAN

The first modernized, upscale Asian restaurant, Germaine's has kept pace with its intense competition, for the kitchen is innovative and flexible, as well as talented. This second-floor dining room has a quiet elegance without much adornment, except for the large grill where the satés are prepared. It also offers a fine wine list and service that is so quietly efficient one hardly notices it. The menu is Pan-Asian, but since Germaine herself is Vietnamese, those dishes are the ones with the greatest depth. Highlights, as you might expect, are grilled meats and seafoods. Also pay attention to the daily specials, which include seasonal ingredients and Germaine's newest inventions. The best of those become regulars, and some of those—scallop salad in a pale-green sauce with pine nuts, for instance—are copied elsewhere until they have become Washington classics. About $100 for two should take care of dinner.
Open Mon.-Thurs. 11:30 a.m.-2:30 p.m. & 5:30 p.m.-10 p.m., Fri. 11:30 a.m.-2:30 p.m. & 5:30 p.m.-11 p.m., Sat. 5:30 p.m.-11 p.m., Sun. 5:30 p.m.-10 p.m. All major cards.

The Guards
2915 M St. NW
• 965-2350
AMERICAN

This is the grownup, clubby side of Georgetown: a dark-wood-paneled dining room with a fireplace for winter and back garden for summer. While the service is sometimes clumsy, the cooking is generally skilled. There are clever modern dishes and contemporary touches such as sun-dried tomatoes in the seafood salad or roasted corn in the soup, but the strength of this kitchen is in meat-and-pota-toes fare. Start with smoked trout or with sausage and peppers in a buttery bagna cauda. Go on to red meat—steaks, rack of lamb or the stellar veal chop. At lunch, the black-and-blue burger, well crusted and very rare, is an American classic, with unpeeled French fries worthy of it. The Guards is an oasis of quiet in Georgetown, and a cozy place for a sturdy steakhouse dinner for $80 or so for two. *Open Sun.-Thurs. 11:30 a.m.-11 p.m., Fri.-Sat. 11:30 a.m.-midnight. All major cards.*

Hisago
3050 K St. NW
• 944-4181
JAPANESE

12/20

This is the most Japanese of Washington's restaurants, not just in its menu and environment, but in its prices. So it is to be addressed with caution. For diners who know enough about how to deal with a Japanese restaurant and get the best of it, or who are known by this particular restaurant, the food can be exquisite. The tempura menu includes extraordinary seaweed-wrapped shrimp; the sushi list offers some varieties not easily found elsewhere; and the tableside cooking is of a very high order. Your best bet is to sit at the sushi or tempura bar or to order carefully at a table, after finding someone who speaks enough English to explain the differences between the various kinds of menus. There is at Hisago much ordinary food at outlandish prices (well over $100 for two at dinner), though the management has seen the light and offered more reasonable lunch prices. You may have to be very much aware of Japanese cuisine's capabili-ties for Hisago's expensive subtleties to be worthwhile. *Open Mon.-Thurs. noon-2:30 p.m. & 6 p.m.-10:30 p.m., Fri. noon-2:30 p.m. & 6 p..m.-11 p.m., Sat. 6 p.m.-11 p.m., Sun. 6 p.m.-10:30 p.m. All major cards.*

Houston's
1065 Wisconsin Ave. NW
• 338-7760
AMERICAN

10/20

The menu is so very familiar, just the usual burgers and ribs and onion rings and grilled meats to be found at every other modern-day saloon. But Houston's pays enough special attention that it rises above the crowd. It obviously cares about what it serves: the burgers are hickory-scented, fat and juicy, the French fries and onion rings light and crisp and the grill cooking accurate. This is not the place you would go for great food, but certainly for all-American stuff like French fries and hamburgers, knowing that they will be good enough to keep the tradition alive. Dinner averages $50 for two, with beers .

Open Sun.-Wed. 11:15 a.m.-11 p.m., Thurs. 11:15 a.m.-midnight, Fri.-Sat. 11:15 a.m.-1 a.m. All major cards.

J. Paul's
3218 M St. NW
• 333-3450
AMERICAN

10/20

Men who consider themselves hunks and like their food by the pound will feel comfortable at J. Paul's. Slightly overstating the case, this is the young man's version of what used to be the big brawny saloon. It is a handsome version, to be sure, with a long carved-wood bar of magnificent proportions and a nice clubby dining room. The waiters are friendly, bustling steakhouse guys. The menu leans heavily on meat and potatoes. In fact, potatoes are a highlight here, from the potato skins—crisp and nongreasy—to the chunky French fries to the French-fried sweet potatoes. The emphasis is on freshness and large servings. A half-portion of nachos, for instance—great gooey ones, with plenty of sweet-hot chili and beans and swamps of cheese—is sufficient to accompany an evening's worth of drinks. Don't count on finesse: the burger is likely to be overcooked, the Caesar salad to be tossed with gritty, prepacked cheese and the chicken to taste more of marinade than of meat. But the crabcakes are all crab; the corned beef is imported from Baltimore (though lean corned beef just doesn't have the impact of juicy, fatty cuts of brisket); and the onion rings are a marvelous mountain of crisp strands. The talent here is in the purchasing—from the real dill pickles to the dark, moist devil's food cake. Keep in mind, though, that this is a drinking pub, where the bar scene is more important than the table scene. Dinner is about $40 to $60 for two.

Open Mon.-Thurs. 11:30 a.m.-11:30 p.m., Fri.-Sat. 11:30 a.m.-midnight, Sun. 10:30 a.m.-11:30 p.m. All major cards.

Kolbeh
1645 Wisconsin Ave. NW
• 342-2000
PERSIAN

7/20

Washington's Persian restaurants are far more than eating places: they are a shifting set of community centers, where Iranians come to talk long into the night or day, entertain their friends, show off their country's cooking. The enduring favorite is Kolbeh, perhaps as much for its mirrored walls and ceiling, and hospitable service, as for the food. The menu is easy for the uninitiated, as it shows color photos of each dish. The waitresses readily offer advice, though the recommendation of stuffed peppers as an appetizer was not the most astute suggestion. You can start with small nibbles—feta cheese with raw vegetables, or an assortment of pickles. More hefty are an eggplant dip called kash-e bademjan, the earthy and exotically spiced ash-e reshteh soup or more familiar hummus and big, soft meatballs. Main dishes are kebabs or stews, the former more tame choices for newcomers. Persian kebabs are thin slabs of meat, cooked over wood, but not particularly spicy or juicy, and are best combined with the buttered rice, heavily sprinkled with tangy powdered sumac at the table. Among the stews, the most fascinating is fessenjan, slices of chicken in a thick, sweet and compelling sauce of pomegranate juice and walnuts. Kolbeh is an adventure, from the herbed and spiced yogurt drink called doogh, to the pretzel-shaped dessert fritters. Glorious cooking? No. A bargain? Not at $40 to $60 for dinner for two (including wine). An interesting cultural investigation? Certainly.

Open Sun.-Thurs. 11 a.m.-11 p.m., Fri.-Sat. 11 a.m.-4 a.m. Cards: AE, MC, V.

Morton's of Chicago
3251 Prospect St. NW • 342-6258
AMERICAN

Steak still reigns, no matter what the American Heart Association says. The moneyed masses continue to line up for tables at Morton's. And if you are going to eat steak, Morton's is the place to do it. Its sirloins and porterhouses are simply the best in town, and some of the best you will find anywhere. Not much is wasted on words in this no-nonsense, noisy dining room. The menu is on a blackboard and the food is brought to your table in the raw—the beef, the lobster (live), the chicken, the veal chop. While the veal and chicken are terrific, you wouldn't want to pass up a thick, black-and-blue steak from a kitchen that knows how to buy and cook it as well as this one does. And the potatoes and onion rings are its equal, far better than the clumsy tomato salad or dessert. Plan on $140 for two for dinner, with wine.

Open Mon.-Sat. 5:30 p.m.-11 p.m., Sun. 5 p.m.-10 p.m. All major cards.

Paper Moon
1073 31st St. NW • 965-6666
ITALIAN

9/20

Chalk one up for youthful vigor. Paper Moon is a big, gray display case for the Georgetown crowd, decorated with great bunches of fabric and neon, but mostly with the fashions of punk youth. It is noisy fun: an entertainment of boy-meets-girl filling the bar, with the audience dining at surrounding tables. The real surprise is that the food is good. Big tureen-sized bowls of pasta, pizzas draped with sun-dried tomatoes and wild mushrooms, a few more serious meat and seafood dishes. Grilled fish can be fine; meats are less reliable; pizzas are middling; and among the pastas are some zesty and wonderful combinations that add to the fun. You can dine for about $50 here.

Open Mon.-Wed. 5:30 p.m.-11 p.m., Thurs.-Sat. 5:30 p.m.-1 a.m., Sun. 5:30 p.m.-10 p.m. All major cards.

Au Pied de Cochon

1335 Wisconsin Ave. NW
• 333-5440
FRENCH

Au Pied de Cochon represents France to its fans. The long bar, the aging dark dining room, the tough, sneering waiters are the American image of a Paris bistro. Given its low prices, the youth of Washington can pretend they are expatriates, arguing the fate of American capitalism late into the night over a bowl of watery onion soup. If they haven't actually been to Paris, maybe they don't know what the food is supposed to taste like. Certainly not what it tastes like here. Au Pied de Cochon has a menu that reads like an authentic French bistro, but serves food no better than the grub at a Midwestern roadhouse. Dinner costs less than $40 for two, with wine.
Open daily 24 hours. All major cards.

The River Club

3223 K St. NW
• 333-8118
AMERICAN

If you have a yen to wear your dancing shoes and sip champagne, and you seek glorious food to accompany a full-dress evening, The River Club is what you want. A dim and yet sparkling art deco space with etched glass and waterfalls, it is carved into dining, drinking, dancing and private party areas, with all the glitter of the supper clubs of the forties. The food, however, is the work of a very talented and very modern chef, Jeff Tunks, who is at home with Asian ingredients as well as American. He stuffs spring rolls with seafood, marinates squid in Thai spices, coats salmon with sesame seeds, tosses lobster with Asian hot chilis and serves it on a bed of fried spinach leaves. Intermingled are the likes of European-style veal with wild mushrooms and venison medallions. In all, Tunks picks up flavors from here, techniques from there, garnishes from elsewhere, for a personal style that often tastes dazzling and always looks stunning. He also makes choices easier by offering half portions of most entrées, so you can fashion a gastronomic sampler to your own taste. Dessert, too, borrows from several continents, fashioning spring rolls with bananas, enlivening bread pudding with macadamia nuts. The River Club is altogether dramatic, with a scintillating wine list, a staff that is suave and far from stiff, and food that is a constantly changing show from a versatile talent.
Open Mon.-Sat. 6 p.m.-midnight. All major cards.

Sarinah Satay House

1338 Wisconsin Ave. NW
• 337-2955
INDONESIAN

10/20

Indonesian food is rare to come by in Washington, and good Indonesian food was nearly impossible to find until Sarinah took over this pretty, slate-floored and glass-walled dining room. Now, the modern French indoor garden has been transformed into a hint of tropical jungle, and rijstaffels replace beurre blancs. If you don't want your dinner chosen for you as a rijstaffel (buffet selection), you can order an array of spicy little main dishes (note the emphasis on *little* and order more than you might otherwise) and build your own combination. But don't miss peanut-sauced skewers of grilled meat, to start. Other good appetizers are reminiscent of Chinese dim sum or European croquettes. And an Indonesian meal would not be complete without gado-gado, the peanut-sauced salad of cooked vegetables. From then on, there are dozens of choices. Just take note that "spicy" is a term taken seriously here. So mix and match, with plenty of Holland's Brand beer, for a very exotic and delightfully inexpensive meal, perhaps $40 for two.

Open Tues.-Sat. noon-3 p.m. & 6 p.m.-10:30 p.m., Sun. 6 p.m.-11 p.m. All major cards.

Sea Catch

Canal Square,
1054 31st St. NW
• 337-8855
SEAFOOD

8/20

On a sunny Sunday afternoon, Sea Catch becomes one of Georgetown's favorite restaurants, at least for its balcony that hangs over the towpath. No Washington experience makes one more appreciate this city than sitting on this wooden balcony, shaded by a canvas awning, the old stone and brick facade on one side, the canal on the other. The waiter pours champagne and brings a basket of croissants, muffins and breads, then a homey, buttery seafood and vegetable soup or a respectable pâté with fresh-tasting ratatouille. You can watch the strollers and joggers, the children feeding the ducks. Bicycles zoom by, and the canal boat floats under the bridge, to be hitched up to horses for a trip down the canal. The gloriousness is reflected in the plate when the order is eggs benedict with smoked salmon and mustard-dill hollandaise—oozy pink and gold, fragrant and buttery-tart. The other dishes bring reality back with a jolt, though—second-rate cooking is commonplace here, in the likes of an overcooked omelet and a boring thicket of heavy noodles with ordinary cream-sauced seafood. Then comes a tray of desserts, heavy but agreeable ones, perhaps including cream-puff swans to reflect the canal scene, or strawberry shortcake, to evoke summer. Inside are two separate dining rooms, one formal and one casual, both handsome with stone and brick, fireplaces and a long, white marble bar. The array of dishes is a marvel, a tribute to the versatility of seafood. Yet, at dinner as well as brunch, there are some high notes, but much pedestrian food. The Sea Catch offers a wide range of prices, from the $40 range to upward of $100, and a range of quality that is every bit as wide and unpredictable—not particularly related to price, but more to just plain luck.

Open daily 11:30 a.m.-11 p.m. All major cards.

1789

1226 36th St. NW
• 965-1789
AMERICAN

10/20

In a one-block restaurant complex owned by Clyde's, the crowd divides: Students hit the downstairs pub known as The Tombs; glitter-seekers spend late nights at the supper club with dancing that is called F. Scott's; and 1789 draws sedate Georgetowners, visiting parents, gray eminences and dowagers. The dining rooms are traditional at 1789, one of Georgetown's most beautiful restaurants. Dining is in several rooms: one has Colonial formality; another is a cozy bar; a third is rustic, in the hunting-lodge mode. Service is comfortably efficient, except for the pileups at the valet parking station and the front door. The menu, while updated, doesn't stray too far from steak, rack of lamb, duck, grilled fish and seafood. This is modern American cooking with the restraint of tradition. While it is ambitious cooking, using classy ingredients such as wild greens and fresh berries, it shows more honest work than talent. Pasta with smoked salmon is heavy and rich, more like a nantua sauce than one would expect, but it tastes fine. Grilled quail is perfectly done, bedded on nice greens. Rack of lamb is carefully timed, though the mustard coating is a little pasty, and the ratatouille accompanying it is murky. Other dishes are disappointing—chewy pork medallion, a fish that is tough and bouncy, bitter eggplant flan. Dessert perks up the meal, and the wine list, while priced on the outrageous end, offers far more than predictable choices. Dinner for two, with wine, will average $125.
Open Sun.-Thurs. 6 p.m.-11 p.m., Fri.-Sat. 6 p.m.-11:30 p.m. All major cards.

Sushi-Ko

2309 Wisconsin Ave. NW
• 333-4187
JAPANESE

11/20

First among the city's sushi bars, Sushi-Ko still retains its consistent quality. It is an unassuming, two-story restaurant, with a menu that extends very little beyond sushi, tempura and teriyaki (though the meat-stuffed dumplings are a delicious departure). There are no flourishes of decor—it is spare, simple and very Japanese—or of cuisine, beyond the straightforward and traditional. Sushi is clearly the specialty, and you can do no better than to put yourself in the sushi chef's hands for impeccable tuna, yellowtail, eel, clams, raw shrimp, or whatever else is available fresh at the time, and ask what he might concoct among seaweed-wrapped rolls. Expect to spend at least $50—or, more likely, $75—for dinner for two, with wine.
Open Tues.-Fri. noon-2:30 p.m. & 6 p.m.-10:30 p.m., Sat. 5 p.m.-10:30 p.m., Sun. 5 p.m.-10 p.m. All major cards.

Thai Taste

3287 1/2 M St. NW
• 965-7988
THAI

See review in the "Uptown" section, page 67.
Open Sun.-Thurs. noon-10 p.m., Fri.-Sat. noon-11 p.m.
Cards: AE, MC, V.

Tony & Joe's Seafood Place

3000 K St. NW
(Washington Harbour)
• 944-4545
SEAFOOD

11/20

Washington has hardly any consistently reliable seafood restaurants, and even fewer restaurants with a view, so Tony & Joe's started with points in its favor. Right on the waterfront, with tables set outside in good weather, it provides one of the most scintillating settings in Washington. Its menu emphasizes fresh fish in season, and local crab dishes. For the most local meal of all, come in jeans and order a pile of spiced steamed crabs, with mallets and picks, served on brown-paper tablecloths. It's the only place downtown that serves this Chesapeake Bay favorite. You can appreciate Washington's history as a seafood town if you stick to local ingredients such as oysters, crabs and Mid-Atlantic fish. Don't bother with shrimp dishes, salmon, swordfish or other regions' seafood. Fried seafood is better than most, and grilled fish is usually good. With the accompanying peppered corn muffins, onion rings and French fries, you'll get a $60 dinner for two. To end on a sweet note, try one of the sensational home-style puddings. *Open Sun.-Thurs. 11 a.m.-11 p.m., Fri.-Sat. 11 a.m.-midnight. All major cards.*

Vietnam Georgetown

2934 M St. NW
• 337-4536
VIETNAMESE

8/20

On a balmy evening when Georgetown is crowded, you might wonder at the empty tables in the Vietnam Georgetown's dining room. Especially since you can stand and watch people streaming in the door. Where they are headed is the back garden, one of the nicest in town, brick-walled and shaded, and a major reason for this restaurant's enduring popularity. Otherwise, it is a pleasant, but plain, eatery that serves all the now-familiar Vietnamese dishes: fat pork-stuffed cha gio (the Vietnamese version of spring rolls), beef-noodle soup flavored with anise, stir-fried dishes moistened with a thin caramel-darkened sauce, sweet-and-sour sauce or ginger. From the grill come sugar cane wrapped with shrimp paste, or meats seasoned with lemon grass and lightly sweetened. And there are stuffed crêpes, stuffed crabs and meat-shrimp-vegetable mélanges fried with noodles or rice. It is not glorious cooking: oversweetening and oversalting are typical. But the combination of large portions and low prices with efficient service make it a Georgetown standby. Two will spend $30 to $40. *Open Mon.-Fri. 11 a.m.-11 p.m., Sat. noon-midnight, Sun. noon-11 p.m. No cards.*

UPTOWN

Caspian Tea Room
4801 Massachusetts Ave. NW
• 244-6363
PERSIAN

8/20

In a nondescript, modern office building is this most surprisingly charming of restaurants. The Caspian Tea Room is furnished with family heirlooms—from a diplomatic family who stayed in America after the Iranian revolution. And the cooking is partly French, partly Persian, about what you would expect in a sophisticated Iranian home. The dining room has tearoom prettiness, with pink tablecloths and brass samovars. But it also has some extraordinarily elegant mirrors and sideboards. It would suit Paris or Vienna, as would the lush pastries brought from Patrick Musel's superb pastry shop. As for the menu, the European dishes range from veal piccata to "pasta of the day." The cooking can be good, but sometimes is bland. More interesting (though lately not as carefully prepared as in Caspian's earlier days) are the Persian dishes: the soup called aush, the fried eggplant with kashk, the kebabs and the vegetable-lamb stews. The most scintillating of Persian dishes, fesenjan, is pieces of chicken in a thick, dark sweet-and-sour sauce of walnuts and pomegranate juice. The intensely sweet sauce is irresistible, though the chicken can be stringy. The Caspian Tea Room was once a mecca, now it is merely an oasis in a neighborhood short on good eating places. It remains, however, a very civilized environment for a $50 dinner.
Open Mon.-Sat. 10 a.m.-3 p.m. & 6 p.m.-9:30 p.m. All major cards.

Dancing Crab
4611 Wisconsin Ave. NW
• 244-1882
AMERICAN/ SEAFOOD

7/20

This area's soul food is crabs—fat blue crabs coated with red pepper and Old Bay seasoning, and steamed until they turn red. They are eaten on tablecloths of brown paper, accompanied by a roll of paper towels to serve as napkins, a wooden mallet for breaking through the shells and a pitcher of beer to cool the red-pepper fire. One of the few places to witness this ritual within the city is the Dancing Crab, and the best time to observe it is on an all-you-can-eat night, when crabs are downed by the bushel. The dress code, as you might guess, is as casual as is imaginable. And though the Dancing Crab serves a few other seafood dishes, ignore them all. Crabs are the reason for this restaurant's success. Dinner costs about $50 for two.
Open Mon.-Fri. 11 a.m.-10:30 p.m., Sat. noon-11 p.m., Sun. 3 p.m.-11 p.m. All major cards.

Dona Flor
4615 41st St. NW
• 537-0404
BRAZILIAN

11/20

This small Brazilian restaurant hits the middle ground between casual and elegant. It has enough decorative flourishes that you wouldn't feel out of place dressed up, but its comfortable conviviality is just as suited to Sunday-evening casualness. The menu covers the regions of Brazil, but centers on feijoada, its well-spiced black beans burying chunks of sausage, pork and seemingly whatever the kitchen happens to have. It is different every time you try it, but always accompanied by starchy grains of manioc and wedges of orange. Another winner at Dona Flor is chicken passarinha: bite-size pieces of chicken on the bone, highly seasoned with garlic and fried to a crisp seal for the juiciest of meat. The menu is far more extensive than that, though, with several interesting fish dishes and more of shrimp, and appetizers are worth exploring. Whatever the choice to eat, though, the drink choice should be caipirinhas, a mixture of Brazilian firewater and lots of lime wedges over ice. Dinner costs about $60 for two.

Open Mon.-Thurs. 11:30 a.m.-3 p.m. & 5 p.m.-11 p.m., Fri. 11:30 a.m.-11 p.m., Sat. noon-11 p.m., Sun. noon-10 p.m. All major cards.

Khyber Pass
2309 Calvert St. NW
• 234-4632
AFGHAN

9/20

Afghan food strikes a happy medium between Middle Eastern and Indian, and offers some extraordinarily delicious combinations of tastes. Khyber Pass is a good place to be introduced to those tastes, for the small, second-floor dining room is pleasant, and the cooking is competent. Any Afghan meal should start with aushak, homemade noodles stuffed with leeks or scallions, topped with yogurt, mint and a light touch of tomato-meat sauce. Then go on to kebabs of chicken or lamb, tangy and fragrant, and accompany them with eggplant or squash awash in that wonderful yogurt-mint-tomato-meat sauce. Or order rice, spiced and tossed with meat and faintly sweetened carrot shreds. In any case, these are exotic and luxurious tastes at low prices, under $50 for two.

Open daily 5:30 p.m.-11 p.m. All major cards.

New Heights
2317 Calvert St. NW
• 234-4110
AMERICAN

10/20

The most controversial restaurant to open in recent years, New Heights seems to inspire everyone to love it—or hate it. First, it deserves credit for having turned a nondescript second-floor Italian restaurant into a stunning, sunny dining room, simply decorated with handcrafted furnishings right down to the tables. The food is also beautifully handcrafted, though perhaps New Heights went too far when it started braiding fish and forming cookies into a garden fence with a fruit purée pond. Through several changes of chefs, there has always been imagination at work here: innovation that teams crab, pork and peanuts, then rolls them in eggplant slices, or tosses fettuccine with almonds, radicchio and dill, or tops foie gras with lentils and spinach. When it works, the results are sensational. But some dishes taste misguided, and the cooking can take second place to the construction. New Heights dazzles more than satisfies, and it has not yet settled into graceful middle age. Dinner is in the neighborhood of $90 for two. *Open Mon.-Fri. 11:30 a.m.-2:30 p.m. & 5:30 p.m.-11:30 p.m., Sat. 5:30 p.m.-11:30 p.m., Sun. 11 a.m.-3 p.m. & 5:30 p.m.-11:30 p.m. All major cards.*

Mrs. Simpson's
2915 Connecticut Ave. NW
• 332-8300
AMERICAN

11/20

The name might suggest a homey English tea room, but actually Mrs. Simpson's is a tribute to Wallis Simpson—and to romance. Far from being cozy, it is a bright and snazzy-looking dining room, one wall mirrored and the others vaguely mauve. The tables are blond wood, and well placed so that you need not overhear your neighbors' conversation. The decorations satisfy both the voyeur and the romantic, with souvenirs of the Duke and Duchess of Windsor in display cases, on the walls, even hung in the bathrooms. The food is modern, all-American, inventive, but not ludicrous. An Americanized pu-pu platter has Chinese forms—fried ravioli, spring rolls, barbecued spareribs—but with westernized seasonings, such as roquefort with the ravioli and bourbon glaze on the ribs. The best of the starters, though, are a big, crisp green salad with warm roquefort and bacon dressing, and lightly curried seafood soup. Main courses run the range from parchment-baked fish to Chinese-style duck with mandarin pancakes, and a few "light entrées," such as grilled chicken breast, tempura, an eclectic tostada and a spiced shrimp salad. The light entrées are certainly enough for a normal eater, and the grilled chicken is worth keeping in mind, particularly with its vegetable fritters. But the star of Mrs. Simpson's has always been its calf's liver: a thick and delicate slab, carefully cooked and sauced imaginatively. Accompaniments are often charming flourishes, whether herbed butter with very crisp-crusted rolls, or bright, crunchy brussels sprouts. The wine list has a good selection of armagnacs and eaux de vie. In all, this is a magnetic, fresh restaurant with service that is a little pompous, but unfailingly pleasant. Prices are moderate enough that two can dine easily for under $80. *Open Sun.-Thurs. 5:30 p.m.-10 p.m., Fri.-Sat. 5:30 p.m.-11 p.m., Sun. 10:30 a.m.-2:15 p.m. & 5:30 p.m.-10 p.m. All major cards.*

Thai Taste
2606 Connecticut Ave. NW
• 387-8876
THAI

10/20

Washington has dozens of Thai restaurants by now, and even Thai Taste has three branches, the others in Georgetown and Rockville Pike. But this restaurant, even when its food is not a challenge to the best, remains the most appealing within the city. It is housed in a former rib house, and the art deco design has been made even more delightful by a careful renovation, starting with the neon marquee at the entrance. It is a whimsical and witty dining room. The menu goes beyond most Thai lists to include such daily specials as charcoal-grilled, marinated chicken or fish, both of which are wonderful. If the list of satays and fish cakes and basil-scented or curried dishes becomes bewildering, ask the staff's suggestions. Dinners are about $50 for two. *Open Mon.-Thurs. 11:30 a.m.-10:30 p.m., Fri.-Sat. 11:30 a.m.-11 p.m., Sun. 5 p.m.-10:30 p.m. All major cards.*

MARYLAND

Amalfi
12307 Wilkins Ave.,
Rockville
• (301) 770-7888
ITALIAN

10/20

In most major cities, Amalfi would be one of a dozen good, homey, down-to-earth, southern Italian restaurants. But Washington, for all its Afghan, Ethiopian and Vietnamese restaurants (you could pick any of a dozen and find it delightful), has very few southern Italian restaurants that are solid rather than stolid. Thus the lines form at Amalfi—and to its credit, the restaurant is likely to hand out glasses of wine to ease the mood, if not the flow of the line. Once you are inside, it is like an Italian house party, full of bustle and redolent of garlic, the service both brusque and cheerful. The pizzas are fine, both red and white, and the pastas are pleasantly earthy. Don't go for the refined foodstuffs. Keep in mind that such low prices—less than $50 for two—bring lusty satisfactions rather than subtlety and delicacy. This is an old-fashioned, red-checked-cloth eating place, where the carbohydrates and the jug wine flow freely. *Open Tues.-Thurs. 11:30 a.m.-10 p.m., Fri. 11:30 a.m.-11 p.m., Sat. 1:30 p.m.-11 p.m., Sun. 1:30 p.m.-9 p.m. All major cards.*

Bacchus
7945 Norfolk Ave.,
Bethesda
• (301) 657-1722
LEBANESE

See review in "Downtown Washington" section, page 23. *Open Mon.-Thurs. 11:30 a.m.-2 p.m. & 6 p.m.-10 p.m., Fri. 11:30 a.m.-2 p.m. & 6 p.m.-10:30 p.m., Sat. 6 p.m.-10:30 p.m. All major cards.*

China Coral
6900 Wisconsin Ave.
Chevy Chase
• (301) 656-1203
CHINESE

11/20

Several Washington-area Chinese restaurants now boast tanks full of live fish for cooking to order, but China Coral was one of the first, and it has maintained a steady preeminence for years. Until one of the new ones proves itself, this is the safest bet. In season, crabs are king; out of season, try whole fish done many different ways, the best of them steamed with a simple seasoning of soy sauce and scallions. Whole flounder, with its frame fried to a crisp platter for the stir-fried flesh, is beautifully done here. Shellfish are excellent. On Sundays, China Coral has become a mainstay for dim sum. Also, banquet food, such as whole duck layered with shrimp paste and fried, or fried stuffed fish rolls, is available on the regular menu, but cooked with celebration quality. China Coral imports a steady stream of ideas from Hong Kong and serves the most simple of meals well, in addition to arranging extravagances for as little as $40 for two, with wine.
Open Mon.-Thurs. 11:30 a.m.-10:30 p.m., Fri.-Sat. 11:30 a.m.-11:30 p.m., Sun. 11 a.m.-10 p.m. All major cards.

El Caribe
8130 Wisconsin Ave.,
Bethesda
• (301) 656-0888
LATIN AMERICAN

See review in the "Adams Morgan" section, page 11.
Open Mon.-Thurs. noon-10 p.m., Fri.-Sat. noon-11 p.m., Sun. noon-9 p.m. All major cards.

Crisfield
8012 Georgia Ave.,
Silver Spring
• (301) 589-1306

Crisfield at Lee Plaza
8606 Colesville Rd.,
Silver Spring
• (301) 588-1572
AMERICAN/ SEAFOOD

12/20

You either love or hate Crisfield, and everybody has an opinion on it. The old Georgia Avenue branch looks like a standard luncheonette, with booths lining a narrow aisle, and a big square oyster bar for catching a quick meal. Most of the time, you have to wait in line for one of those noisy, uncomfortable tables. The newer Colesville Road branch is larger, with a bright, shiny, art deco look, and it takes reservations. The reason for the crowds is that Crisfield has long been the best, most reliable Eastern Shore fish house around. It is still often good, sometimes stellar, but its prices are high for a slam-bang eating house, and in recent years, the quality has been known to slip. The meal to have is oysters or clams on the half shell (the clam chowder is thick and starchy), followed by rockfish or flounder topped with crab meat, which is the most delectable, creamy lump crab-meat stuffing you can find. Stuffed shrimp runs the fish a second best, and this is a good place to try Norfolk-style seafoods, which are simply sautéed in butter. The menu isn't long, but does include some mistakes, such as seafood creole or lobster-and-meat dishes. Fried seafoods are too heavily breaded, even the otherwise impeccable soft-shell crabs. Keep in mind that plainest is best here, accompanied by fresh, homey coleslaw and finely made French fries. Dinner can easily cost $70 for two, with wine. *Georgia Ave. branch: open Tues.-Thurs. 11 a.m.-10 p.m., Fri.-Sat. 11 a.m.-11 p.m., Sun. noon-9:30 p.m. No cards. Colesville Rd. branch: open Mon.-Thurs. 11 a.m.-10 p.m., Fri. 11 a.m.-11 p.m., Sat. 4 p.m.-11 p.m. Cards: MC, V.*

La Ferme

7101 Brookville Rd.,
Chevy Chase
• (3010 986-5255
FRENCH

11/20

The environment alone is a balm for city folk: La Ferme (a French "farmhouse") is a pretty barn of a building, brought to human scale with unpolished woods, white and gray fabrics and baskets full of enchanting things. The food, too, is a balm—traditional, yet fresh, down-to-earth and competent. The pastry wrappers are light, the pâté is from farm-raised duck, the onion soup tastes fresh from the kitchen rather than a can. The menu has a Sunday-dinner quality, with touches of foie gras and crayfish for glamour and well-puffed soufflés for dessert. It is not a single quality that stands out; rather it's the totally soothing and warm environment, just off the commuter hustle of Connecticut Avenue. Expect to spend $80 for two, with a bottle of wine. *Open Tues.-Fri. noon-2 p.m. & 6 p.m.-10 p.m., Sat. 6 p.m.-10 p.m., Sun. 5 p.m.-9 p.m. All major cards.*

Louisiana Express Co.

4921 Bethesda Ave.,
Bethesda
• (301) 652-6945
AMERICAN/CAJUN

12/20

The best Cajun food in town was in Adams Morgan's New Orleans Emporium and New Orleans Café until Peter Finkhauser left them to open the Louisiana Express Company. The express part refers to take-out and delivery, which is a big part of this enterprise. But the sit-down restaurant, in which you order at the counter and have your meal served on disposable plates, is a pleasant trellised space. With the carefully chosen list of wines and beers or fresh lemonade, the food tastes all the better. The menu is mix-and-match gumbos, creoles, étouffees and the like, made with seafood, sausage or chicken. Spice-rubbed chickens revolve on a rotisserie, and if they are removed to your order, rather than left sitting around, they are sensational. So are the fried things—crab or shrimp balls, chunks of catfish or redfish. Daily specials range from Cajun pizza to blackened fish. Even the biscuits and muffins—spiced and chile-spiked, of course—are house-made. Sandwiches are gargantuan. Some of the desserts, particularly pecan pie or pralines, are models of New Orleans confectionery. Prices are rock-bottom, so this is some of the best food you'll ever find for under $20 for two (including beers). *Open Mon.-Thurs. 11 a.m.-10 p.m., Fri.-Sat. 11 a.m.-11 p.m., Sun. 10:30 a.m.-10 p.m. No cards.*

La Miche

7905 Norfolk Ave.,
Bethesda
• (301) 986-0707
FRENCH

11/20

Bethesda had hardly seen a serious French restaurant before La Miche opened, and this restaurant probably sparked the town's restaurant renaissance. La Miche has been an admirable model. Its dining room is charming, hung with baskets, and decorated in a countrified, but still sophisticated, manner. Its service has been professional and personable—though not necessarily so in the crush of a Saturday night. And the food has been interesting, its quality high. From the beginning, La Miche's most popular dishes have been appetizers, particularly seafoods with beurre blanc in a croissant shell (long before croissants became fast-food clichés). In between, ups and downs, generally up. This is a highly professional restaurant with a well-trained chef who has imagination and the restraint not to let it run wild. La Miche has become a steady asset to Bethesda. Dinner for two, with wine, costs $100.

Open Mon.-Fri. 11:30 a.m.-2:30 p.m. & 6 p.m.-10 p.m., Sat. 6 p.m.-10 p.m. Cards: Choice, MV, V.

Old Angler's Inn

10801 MacArthur Blvd.,
Potomac
• (301) 365-2425
AMERICAN

11/20

The love-hate relationship with Old Angler's continues. Nearly everyone in Washington dreams of taking over this beautiful spot and making more of it. The management keeps trying, but never quite makes it. Still, much as we hate it when we have to wait interminably for indifferent food served by a surly waiter, we love it on a spring afternoon, when the music of the birds wipes out the surliness, and we adore it on a winter evening, when the fireplace is lit and we can sip our overpriced wine on a sofa before we go upstairs for dinner. Old Angler's is all environment, a country rest stop just up the hill from the canal, its space carved out of the woods, so that you would hardly know it was right off a highway and just fifteen minutes from downtown Washington. Sunday brunch on the terrace becomes the reward for a long bike ride, and there has to be some reason this restaurant has served as a trysting place in several Washington novels. At last, an outside entrance has been opened to the upstairs dining room, which means you can avoid the narrow ship's-hold, winding staircase. There is also a new chef, formerly sous chef at Jean Louis, serving such high-wire acts as timbale of duck breast, lobster with smoked tomato sauce and red snapper with orange butter sauce. But then, there is always a new chef. The food isn't the point, and people who understand that just order the rack of lamb and take it easy. Dinner averages $110 for two.

Open Tues.-Sun. noon-2:30 p.m. & 6 p.m.-10 p.m. All major cards.

Tako Grill
7756 Wisconsin Ave. NW,
Bethesda
• (301) 652-7030
JAPANESE/ SEAFOOD

12/20

Fish lovers have two ideologies to follow in this pristine, little Japanese restaurant: raw or cooked. The sushi bar is a good one, the fish as fresh as you are likely to find around town, and the choices include a few more exotic specialties than most. There is a Japanese grill for robata-yaki, appetizer-size portions of crisp-skinned, moist-fleshed grilled fish, and unusual vegetables such as mushrooms or eggplant with ginger, or crusty rice cakes (also cooked on the grill). Portions are small and prices are low, so that for $50 to $60, two could sample a wide array of both raw and cooked fish, with beer or saké to lubricate your dinner. Try the small, fresh smelts, for example, and the large whole baby red snapper or redfish. Add some shrimp, clams or scallops. Venture into a bony, succulent jaw of yellowtail. This is the simplest sort of cooking, which is, of course, the vehicle for Japanese virtuosity.
Open Mon.-Thurs. 11:30 a.m.-2 p.m. & 5:30 p.m.-10 p.m., Fri. 11:30 a.m.-2 p.m. & 5:30 p.m.-10:30 p.m., Sat. 5:30 p.m.-10:30 p.m. Cards: AE, MC, V.

Tila's
2 Wisconsin Circle,
Chevy Chase
• (301) 652-8452
AMERICAN

10/20

The sun rises and sets in Tila's, on murals and in the subtle shadings of colored light. It is a blazing neon beauty, this stage-set restaurant, which meanders from one of the world's longest bars to several dining rooms, from sunny, vague colors to vibrating tropical hues. The menu, too, covers a gamut of emotions. It is somewhat southwestern, with touches of Caribbean and Asian—Tex-Mex food for the jaded. Sometimes it makes sense, other times it seems a hodgepodge. After an awkward start, Tila's has settled down, and the kitchen seems to have improved. While the enchiladas were once a grab-bag of disconnected ingredients, they're now a harmonious blend. Beef enchilada, for instance, eclipses almost any in town, with its blue corn tortilla and its rare and crusty grilled shards of beef, tangy from marinade and smoky from the grilling. Equally competent is the empanada, a large fried turnover, luxuriously stuffed with crab, cheese and spinach. Even better is its accompanying tomatillo sauce, boldly acid and spicy with a faint sweetness. Tila's has always used ingredients of high quality for a Tex-Mex (or Asian/Caribbean/Tex-Mex) place. The chiles are fresh, the corn is likely to be as well, and the avocados are ripe. Its salsas are explosively good. The familiar southwestern dishes, such as nachos, stuffed chiles and taquitos, benefit from that. Grilled fish and meats are reasonably reliable. Just watch out for the flights of fancy. Save the fantasies for dessert, for this kitchen knows how to please a sophisticated sweet tooth, with its key lime pie and coconut flan. Prices range widely, so dinner could run a mere $30, or three times that.

Open Mon.-Fri. 11:30 a.m.-10:30 p.m., Sat. noon-11 p.m., Sun. noon-10 p.m. Cards: AE, MC, V.

Vagabond
7315 Wisconsin Ave., Bethesda
• (301) 654-2575
RUMANIAN

9/20

Washington is overrun with French and Italian restaurants, heavily populated with Chinese and Southeast Asian restaurants, and has its fair share of American and Central American restaurants. There are very few restaurants from central Europe, however. A few German, a Hungarian or two—that's about it. So Vagabond stands alone as a Rumanian restaurant and keeps the flame alive for nearly all of eastern Europe. Its charm lies mostly in its owners' expansiveness. Host and hostess roam among the tables, greeting, suggesting dishes and encouraging the diners. With Vagabond's pleasant little wine list and particularly good selection of European and American beers, conviviality is the order of the day here. The setting is traditional and European. But it is the menu that really sets the tone. Among first courses are crisp-edged, fried cascaval cheese, pirozki, two kinds of sausages, and tangy eggplant salad, which together make up a compelling hors d'oeuvres plate for two or more. Among main dishes are the familiar goulash, Wiener Schnitzel and chicken paprikas, plus a homey stuffed cabbage, and duck prepared two ways—skewered pieces with smoked sausage or wine-glazed roasted halves. Few restaurants serve organ meats these days, but Vagabond lists brains and sweetbreads, as well as liver. This is agreeable, low-key, home-style cooking, with few flourishes. The sausages are not the most pungent; the stuffed cabbage has as much rice as meat; the duck is a bit chewy; the accompaniments are middling. Vegetables, however, are intriguing, from spicy, long-stewed cabbage to gravy-drenched cornmeal mush, a kind of Rumanian polenta. Vagabond, which costs about $60 to $70 for two for a full dinner with wine, is not for grand dining. Rather, it is a friendly cave of a restaurant, where long-lost favorites from old Europe are prepared well enough to keep memories satisfied.

Open Mon.-Thurs. 11:30 a.m.-2:30 p.m. & 5:30 p.m.-10:30 p.m., Fri. 11:30 a.m.-2:30 p.m., Sat. 6:30 p.m.-10:30 p.m. All major cards.

VIRGINIA

L'Auberge Chez François

332 Springvale Rd.,
Great Falls
• (703) 759-3800
FRENCH

What makes this restaurant a perennial hit is that it fits everyone's idea of a French country inn. It requires a ride over hills and dales to reach it; it looks darling and Alsatian; and its waiters and waitresses play their roles with seeming effortlessness. The menu is fixed price and moderate, about $80 to $100 for two for dinner with wine. The choices, which elsewhere might sound clichéd (hors d'oeuvres variés, quiche, pâté to start), here ring true. L'Auberge Chez François feels like a trip to France at a bargain price. Thus, not many people seem to mind the flaws. The cooking is pedestrian, with some highlights (quiche, salmon soufflé, kugelhopf and plum tart, for a start), and the familial warmth compensates for the ordinary. The wine list is indeed outstanding in its choice of Alsatian bottles. And in the summer, dining in the garden raises the pleasure to a higher pitch.
Open Tues.-Thurs. 5:30 p.m.-9:15 p.m., Fri.-Sat. 5:30 p.m.-9:30 p.m., Sun. 2 p.m.-8 p.m. All major cards.

Bangkok Gourmet

523 S. 23rd St.,
Crystal City
• (703) 521-1305
THAI

11/20

A Thai restaurant in Crystal City is perhaps the last place in which you would expect to find nouvelle cuisine, but there it is, Asian-style. The main part of the menu lists the usual curries and satays, along with some surprises, such as sweet-and-sour pheasant and stuffed quails with crab meat. The long list of Thai nouvelle cuisine includes a stellar appetizer of mussel salad marinated with slivered ginger, garlic, hot chilis and myriad intense seasonings. The menu changes, but is likely to include some appetizer variation on a sashimi theme—perhaps with raspberry vinegar dressing, in the nouvelle style—and soups such as wonton, with feathery lobster-filled noodles. Main dishes emphasize grilled fish, prettily arranged and brightly seasoned. Swordfish, for instance, might be thinly sliced and topped with barely cooked prawns and a mushroom-scented, light-textured sauce. Or seafood might be ground into an airy sausage, grilled, sliced and arranged on a bed of thin noodles, tantalizing you even more with an interplay of peppery sweet-and-sour seasonings. The forms are Western—veal chops, fish filets, cornish hen—but the flavorings are such Asian intricacies as mustard, leeks, lime, oyster

sauce, garlic and ginger. The wine list has French sensibilities and careful pricing, with a range from Haut Brion to a hefty selection of $10 bottles. Desserts are definitely European, with such things as puff pastries, tarts, flans and ice creams. Coffee or lychee ice creams keep company with blueberries in a very light and flaky puff pastry, or hazelnut-caramel-flavored custard is crowned with raspberries and whipped cream plus a superior chocolate sauce. This is a simple, closely packed and friendly little restaurant, with most of its charms on the menu and prices somewhere between bargain-basement and new-French elevation. Bangkok Gourmet is an original and well worth the cost of an exploration. Expect to spend about $60 for two.
Open Mon.5:30 p.m.-10 p.m., Tues.-Fri. 1 a.m.-3 p.m. & 5:30 p.m.-10 p.m., Sat.-Sun. 3 p.m.-10:45 p.m. Cards: DC, MC, V.

Bistro Bistro

4021 S. 28th St.,
Arlington
• (703) 379-0300
AMERICAN

The French bistro translates well to an American style, and this large, casual and efficient restaurant has captured the spirit. The style is breezy and easygoing, but behind it, there is a computerlike efficiency. White paper, bistro-style tablecloths play against a dashing mural and some seriously beautiful decorative details. Similar seriousness attends the ingredients and the cooking. The changing menu emphasizes fresh fish, plus meaty American classics with new, but never irrelevant, twists. Even vegetarian tastes are honored, particularly with a sweet potato tart that is a revelation—the sweetness underplayed as few sweet potato dishes manage. To start—or to have as a light meal—the oyster stew is exceptional, the barely cooked oysters in a peppery cream afloat with green chard. The array to follow encompasses interesting sandwiches and salads as well as more formal meals. The emphasis is on freshness and seasonality, simple cooking with a touch of inventiveness. As much care is taken with the wine list and the in-house baked goods as with the main dishes. For such quality, the prices are modest if your dine modestly: two can dine for $30 to $60.
Open Sun.-Thurs. 11 a.m.-10 p.m., Fri.-Sat. 11 a.m.-11 p.m. Cards: AE, MC, V.

The Daily Catch

1118 King St.,
Alexandria
• (703) 683-4989
ITALIAN/ SEAFOOD

9/20

American life is so specialized that we can support a whole chain of Italian squid restaurants: that's the premise of The Daily Catch, which branched out from Boston to Washington and is now about to spread into more Washington locations. In reality, it works only in part: the squid part and the Italian part. The menu is filled out with fish dishes and pastas made of squid ink and lobster, with soups and salads, but keep your eye on the squid and the tomato sauces. Fried squid is fine, with just enough chewiness along with the crispness. Squid salad is a little oily, but zesty. Stuffed squid unexpectedly combines raisins with the seafood and breadcrumbs, to good effect. And squid meatballs are tender and fluffy under a blanket of bright-flavored tomato sauce. Otherwise, heaviness and creaminess override the seafood theme and cold dishes can taste as if they left all their flavor in the refrigerator. Moreover, the Daily Catch has the distinction of serving the world's worst fried potatoes. Lacy, paper-thin, waffle-cut potatoes are limp, gray and greasy, and taste as though they were bathed and warmed in oil rather than fried. Well, as the waiter insisted when asked about this disaster, "That's the way they're supposed to be." In all, this is a whimsical-looking, casual restaurant with gray laminated tables and squid memorabilia, with absent-minded but agreeable service, and with moderate prices for large servings—$40 could get two through at dinner. It's a pleasantly funky place to eat squid, tomatoes and olive oil every which way.

Open Mon.-Sat. 11:30 a.m.-3 p.m. & 5:30 p.m.-10:30 p.m., Sun. 4 p.m.-9 p.m. Cards: AE, MC, V.

Duangrat's
5878 Leesburg Pike, Falls Church
• (703) 820-5775
THAI

Now that Washington is awash in Thai restaurants, they are moving upscale and broadening their repertoires. Duangrat's has gone furthest—its dining room a beauty of soft, but vivid, colors and Thai treasures displayed in niches; its staff wearing long Thai dresses in luscious colors; and its menu including the chef's inventions as well as Thai classics. This is one of the most gracious and charming of Asian dining rooms, and the food lives up to its setting. Those classics—mee krob, pad Thai, satés, beef with basil—are seasoned with delicacy and balance. Seafood fishes are made with luxurious shell fish. Beyond the usual sautés and grills, there are such exotic preparations as seafood sausage, fish wrapped in banana leaves, and steamed fish with pickled plums. Panang chicken, seasoned with chili paste and coconut milk, is one of the favorites, and the more poetically named dishes—Fried Shrimp Mermaid, Chicken Debutante, Gold Sachet, and Abalone Rendezvous—are worth trying. Dinner, teamed well with Thai beer, is likely to cost about $50 to $60 for two.

Open Sun.-Thurs. 11:30 a.m.-10:30 p.m., Fri.-Sat. 11:30 a.m.-11 p.m. All major cards.

Fortune Chinese Seafood Restaurant

5900 Leesburg Pike,
Falls Church
• (703) 998-8888
CHINESE

10/20

Suburban shopping center Chinese restaurants have changed their image from chow mein houses to Hong Kong in America, and Fortune is one of the most ambitious. It is an enormous restaurant, decorated with dignity, and shows its specials in fish tanks just inside the entrance. There certainly will be lobster, and probably eel, alive until the moment they are cooked. As you can learn from signs outside the entrance—or from the waiter, if he speaks English—the specials vary with the season, including soft-shell or hard-shell crabs in summer, whole fish, such as grouper or red snapper, and fresh shrimp with the heads on. At midday, the specialty is dim sum, an extensive variety that is served from rolling carts on weekends. Even at dinner the pan-fried dumplings are the star, with a filling lighter and more boldy seasoned than most. Appetizers made with shrimp paste—shrimp-stuffed crab claws, shrimp toast—are also unusually good, with a mousse-light and full-flavored layer of shrimp paste raising them above the norm. But while the ingredients are good, the cooking is generally pedestrian at Fortune. Fish is fried with a heavy hand; salt-baked seafood is timidly seasoned; steamed fresh shrimp with garlic only whispers of garlic; and duck has been drab and chewy. Fortune has assets that could verify its name, but it needs to add more skill to its luck. Dinner costs about $50 for two.

Open Sun.-Thurs. 11 a.m.-11:30 p.m., Fri.-Sat. 11 a.m.-midnight. All major cards.

Le Gaulois

1106 King St.,
Alexandria
(703) 739-9494
FRENCH

See review in the "Downtown" section, page 31.
Open Mon.-Thurs. 11:30 a.m.-5:15 p.m. & 5:30 p.m.-10:30 p.m., Fri. 11:30 a.m.-2:30 p.m. & 5:30 p.m.-11 p.m., Sat. 5:30 p.m.-11 p.m. Cards: AE, MC, V.

Inn at Little Washington

Middle & Main Sts.,
Washington, Va.
• (703) 675-3800
AMERICAN

Boasting a home-grown chef and maître d' with a by-now-international recognition, Patrick O'Connell and Reinhardt Lynch have developed their young inn into a showplace that has put little Washington, Virginia on the map. O'Connell seeks the best ingredients of the region, and arranges to have grown, hunted or made-to-order those ingredients he doesn't find. In the cooking of these, he displays the distinctiveness and maturity he has developed as a chef in the Inn's half-dozen years. Local crab he turns into a fragile timbale layered with spinach. Local raspberries garnish salads or duck, as well as dessert. Local corn becomes a soup, a flan or bread sticks. Local country ham teams with melon or figs or even seafood. No wonder connoisseurs beat a path to his door, even when that path is an hour and a half out of their way from big Washington. Those who plan ahead now can stay overnight in the exquisite one- and two-story guest rooms. Or they can stay at one of the dozen bed-and-breakfasts that have opened in nearby towns because of the Inn's popularity. That allows time for lingering over coffee in the handsomely landscaped garden, complete with a tiny canal and frogs. Nowadays, the menu is fixed price, slightly more expensive and elaborate on weekends. Whatever its format of the moment, its tastefulness and imagination warrant the price, the trouble and the necessity to reserve well in advance for this world-class restaurant. Dinner with wine costs about $200 for two weekdays and Sunday, $240 on Saturday.

Open Mon. & Wed.-Fri. 6 p.m.-9:30 p.m., Sat. 5:30 p.m.-9:30 p.m., Sun. 4 p.m.-8 p.m. Cards: MC, V.

Nam's River

715 King St.,
Alexandria
• (703) 836-5910
VIETNAMESE/FRENCH

12/20

This small and charming dining room, with tiny vases of flowers, and napkins folded into blossom shapes, is the first in the area to intermingle French and Vietnamese food. It not only serves purely Vietnamese dishes such as cha gio (spring rolls) and such French dishes as calf's liver with raspberry vinegar, but blends the cuisines deliciously. Filet mignon and chicken are sauced with Asian perfumery; mussels are steamed with French herbs and Asian coconut milk; cornish hen is glazed with garlic, wine and honey. Sweetness and pepperiness—always with a light hand—frequently seesaw in the same dish. Spices are so complex and subtle as to form a mysterious whole. Sometimes, the cooking is pedestrian (more likely with the European dishes than the Asian), but when it comes together it is memorable. Always, the staff is as hospitable as if you'd been invited home for dinner. Dinner is moderately priced—$60 should suffice, even with the compelling wine list diverting you from the usual Asian beer.

Open Mon.-Thurs. 11:30 a.m.-2:30 p.m. & 5:30 p.m.-10 p.m. Fri. 11:30 a.m.-2:30 p.m. & 5 p.m.-10:30 p.m., Sat.-Sun. 5 p.m.-10:30 p.m. Cards: AE, MC, V.

Peking Gourmet Inn

6029 Leesburg Pike,
Falls Church
• (703) 671-8088
CHINESE

9/20

Peking Gourmet Inn started as a small, cramped, bargain-priced Chinese restaurant specializing in duck; a dozen years later, it is a rambling set of dining rooms, the newer ones spacious and grandly decorated. Its prices, particularly for the Peking duck, have increased equally. Certainly, this has something to do with its recent fame as the favorite restaurant of George Bush and his family. Still, the duck is irresistible. It arrives golden, crisp and juicy, to be carved at the table so skillfully and so carefully that every scintilla of fat is scraped off the skin. It is accompanied by a dozen pancakes, which means that half a dozen diners can share it satisfactorily. The restaurant also specializes in home-grown garlic sprouts, a rather nice vegetable to stir-fry with shrimp, pork or chicken. But not only are available tables scarce nowadays, the specialties run out some evenings. Peking Gourmet Inn has friendly and attentive waiters, and its menu is interesting. But its cooking has slipped. Hot-and-sour soup is still a bargain at $1.75, and still thick with good ingredients, but its seasoning has been tamed. Duck bone soup is watery, Szechuan beef oily and insufficiently crisped, and the previously wonderful Peking Gourmet chicken has grown soggy, greasy and only faintly flavored with garlic and pepper. Vegetables can be limp and their sauces cloying. The restaurant's recent celebrity has added an air of fun—the waiters love talking about the effect of its newsworthiness. But it has put a strain on the kitchen, and now, a $70 dinner for two is not necessarily worth it. *Open Sun.-Thurs. 11 a.m.-10:30 p.m., Fri.-Sat. 11:30 a.m.-midnight. Cards: MC, V.*

R. T.'s
3804 Mount Vernon Ave., Alexandria
• (703) 684-6010
AMERICAN/ SEAFOOD

10/20

For a city near a river, bay and ocean, Washington is remarkably deficient in reliable seafood restaurants. R. T.'s fills the gap. It is an unprepossessing restaurant, somewhere between a tavern and a fancy-dress dining room, and certainly it has a down-home charm. While the menu is not exclusively seafood, it might as well be. The fish are fresh; the cooking is very competent; and the choice of seafoods is interesting. Best are those dishes with a Cajun touch: the fish have enough flavor to stand up to the spicing. In fact, any kind of grilled fish is a good bet. In downtown Washington, or even in downtown Alexandria, a seafood restaurant of this caliber would fetch a high price, but R. T.'s has kept its prices modest—about $60 for two for dinner—in line with its out-of-the-way location, rather than as a reflection of the quality of its food. *Open Mon.-Thurs. 11 a.m.-10:30 p.m., Fri.-Sat. 11 a.m.-11 p.m., Sun. 4 p.m.-9 p.m. All major cards.*

Taverna Cretekou
818 King St., Alexandria
• (703) 548-8688
GREEK

10/20

On a spring or summer afternoon, no better celebration of a sunny Sunday could there be than brunch in the garden of Taverna Cretekou. It is a beautifully planted brick-walled space, and the dashing waiters add to the dazzle. But summer or winter, Taverna is the most consistently appealing Greek restaurant in the area. The indoor dining room is arched and whitewashed in a replication of Greek sim-

plicity. The menu is broad; the cooking is very good; and the prices are moderate. There are some disappointments—the phyllo-wrapped lamb has always been a steamy, soggy main dish, for instance. Phyllo-wrapped appetizers are better; in fact, the appetizer assortments, cold or hot, are excellent bits of things in generous combination. Kebabs are fine as main dishes, or look for fresh fish. Add a bottle of retsina and Taverna Cretekou is as refreshing as a stop at Mykonos. Dinner for two, with retsina, is about $60.
Open Tues.-Fri. 11:30 a.m.-2:30 p.m. & 5 p.m.-10:30 p.m., Sat. noon-11 p.m., Sun. 11 a.m.-3 p.m. & 5 p.m.-9:30 p.m. All major cards.

Union Street Public House

121 S. Union St.,
Alexandria
• (703) 548-1785
AMERICAN

12/20

American pubs used to be culinary abominations. Union Street Public House shows what a long way they have come. The menu is inventive, but keeps plain old hamburgers, crabcakes, turkey pot pies, steaks, club sandwiches, fried oysters and spareribs among the lobster fritters, grilled smoked meats and seafood-and-ham pastas. For a noisy, busy, casual, families-and-singles pub, the quality is remarkably high. Sandwiches, from a plain burger to fried oysters with smoked sirloin, are wonderful, even a plain old filet mignon is excellent. Then there are such side dishes as apple fritters, sweet potato pancakes and onion rings. Portions are very large, and prices are modest. Skip the lobster dishes and pastas. While the wine list is impressive, it would be a shame to pass up the beers at Union Street, particularly the dark, full-flavored Virginia Native, brewed exclusively for the restaurant. Service is friendly and energetic, and while the choice of rooms includes fairly private upstairs nooks, the overall mood is convivial—in fact, noisy. A complete dinner need not cost more than $100 for two, with wine.
Open Mon.-Thurs. 11:30 a.m.-10:30 p.m., Fri.-Sat. 11:30 a.m.-11:30 p.m., Sun. 11 a.m.-10:30 p.m. All major cards.

QUICK BITES

INTRODUCTION

L ike most large cities, Washington's restaurant scene is a combination of dining genres. Sure, there are the pricey expense-account restaurants where the bill for a dinner for two could seem to match the budget of a Third World nation. These are the places where lobbyists take legislators in order to have the latter as a captive audience for a three-hour, if not three-martini, lunch. But Washington is also a city with some innovative, more casual, fare, and offers a number of places where you can go for a quick bite. These are places that are not on very many hotel concierge's lists, but are highly recommended for their price/value ratio. While some are the best of their category, they are all spots to which you would feel comfortable going on a limited budget and casually dressed.

This is where you may spot the same congressmen and senators who are wined and dined on the "K Street Strip" at lunchtime, eating on weekends with their friends. Many of the better ethnic spots are in the Washington suburbs, such as the Clarendon section of Arlington, known for its Vietnamese restaurants. Good ethnic fare and downtown rents don't seem to mix, and many of these spots are worth a Metrorail ride to Silver Spring, for instance.

DOWNTOWN & ADAMS MORGAN

Afterwords Café
1517 Connecticut Ave. NW
• 387-1462

Even for the Dupont Circle area—the closest Washington gets to New York's funky SoHo—Afterwords is unique. The café, serving the best cappuccino in town (in addition to light meals), is located at the back of Kramerbooks, one of the city's more serious bookstores. You can browse on your way to order, or talk with people entering the bookstore while you sip or sup at the tables on the sidewalk. It can be a bit congested if both businesses are busy, but it's fun. It's about the most sophisticated place to get a snack at 3 a.m. Around $15 for two.
Open Mon.-Thurs. 7:30 a.m.-1 a.m., Fri.-Sat. 24 hours, Sun.7:30 a.m.-1 a.m . Cards: AE, MC, V.

**Bread &
Chocolate**
2301 M St. NW
• 833-8360

The crusty breads and pastries are why Bread & Chocolate is famous, but if you order correctly, a light lunch here can be very good. That means you should stick with the salads and sandwiches, which are all served with the heavenly

bread and pastries. The soups are another good bet, but stay away from the hot items, as they frequently have the earmarks of having been heated in a microwave. Drop in for breakfast, lunch or an afternoon break. Spending more than $7 a person is almost impossible.
Open Mon.-Fri. 7 a.m.-6 p.m., Sat. 7 a.m.-8 p.m. All major cards.

Café Splendide
1521 Connecticut Ave. NW
• 328-1503

You should always leave room for dessert when eating at any good Austrian restaurant. Café Splendide is no exception. The Black Forest cake and crème brûlée are unbeatable, especially when either is consumed on a lovely spring day at one of the outdoor tables of this Dupont Circle café. Don't forego the starters, such as goulash or garlic soup. All entrées are under $10, including excellent schnitzels. About $15 per person.
Open Mon.-Thurs. 9 a.m.-11:30 p.m., Fri. 9 a.m.-1 a.m., Sat. 8 a.m.-1 a.m., Sun. 8 a.m.-11:30 p.m. Cards: MC, V..

C. F. Folks
1225 19th St. NW
• 293-0515

You look at the hours—open only for lunch five days a week—and assume this cannot be a serious business. Art Carlson cooks such eclectic serious food for such incredibly low prices (relative to the quality), that you wish more restaurateurs had his schedule. One day, the specials are excellent fiery Cajun, while the next, they are provençal French, or perhaps Middle Eastern. The dining room is as small as the schedule, expanded during good weather by tables outdoors. You'll know you're there by the sight of the trademark penguin, and it's less than $10 for lunch, ending with a slice of homemade pie in a flaky crust.
Open Mon.-Fri. 11:45 a.m.-3 p.m. No cards.

Cone E. Island
2000 Pennsylvania Ave. NW
• 822-8460

The main attraction of Cone E. Island, which has another branch tucked into a Georgetown store front, is the homemade, butter-rich ice creams, with which one should end any meal. There are also Kosher hot dogs and good sandwiches, if you cannot live by ice cream alone. About $5 per person, including a double dip.
Open daily noon to midnight. No cards.

Fio's
3636 16th St. NW
• 667-3040

With all of the northern Italian restaurants now eclipsing the great culinary triumphs of the southern part of that country, a trip to Fio's makes one recall why Americans fell in love with Italian food. The pastas, pizza, parmigiana dishes (including fennel) and osso buco are fantastic, as are the prices. Nothing on the menu is more than $10, with a

huge portion of chicken cacciatore with pasta and vegetables for $8. With a starter and beverage, it costs about $15 per person for a true Italian feast.
Open Tues.-Sun. 5 p.m.-11 p.m. All major cards.

Fitch, Fox & Brown
1100 Pennsylvania Ave. NW
• 289-1100

Even though this sounds like a quintessential Washington law firm in the days of WASP dominance, it is really the ultimate fern bar, replete with hanging plants. The location, on the main floor of the Pavilion at the Old Post Office, makes it convenient to the museums on the Mall, and the food is well prepared. The "Holy Mackerel" is an excellent smoked fish salad, and the "Santa Barbara" contains smoked duck. Burgers, sandwiches and salads are the best options. About $15 per person, including a glass of wine or a beer.
Open Mon.-Fri. 7:30 a.m.-10:30 a.m. & 11:30 a.m.-10 p.m., Sat.-Sun. 11:30 a.m.-10 p.m. All major cards.

Food & Co. Café
1200 New Hampshire Ave. NW
• 223-8070

It looks just like any Yuppie carry-out when you walk in the door of this shop, located at the corner of M Street in the West End. The display case is a gourmet's delight of salads and cold entrées, cheeses and some sublime desserts. Upstairs on the balcony is a café that serves the same foods, plus some of the chilled dishes heated up on cold winter days. Stop in and try a salad sampler, and then take some home with you for later. About $7 per person.
Open Mon.-Fri. 8 a.m.-9 p.m., Sat. 10 a.m.-7 p.m., Sun. 10 a.m.-5 p.m. Cards: MC, V.

Hogs on the Hill
732 Maryland Ave. NE
• 547-4553

The controversy about the way to cook ribs properly is only surpassed by the battles over barbecue. At this Capitol Hill joint, with the sort of minimal decor that everyone associates with this finger-lickin' food, customers can have it their own way. The sauce comes hot, mild or mixed, the ribs are meaty and falling-off-the-bone tender, the beef brisket can sometimes be wonderful (but at other times be too fatty), and the chicken is great. Each dinner comes with two side dishes and real corn bread. About $15 per person.
Open Tues.-Thurs. 11 a.m.-10:30 p.m., Fri. 11 a.m.-11:30 p.m., Sun. 12:30 p.m.-9:30 p.m. Cards: AE, MC, V.

International Square Food Court
1850 K St. NW
• No phone

This group of eating places is located in the basement of an office complex, but the atrium (complete with gurgling fountain) gives the space a sense of light and openness. In addition to perhaps two dozen stalls selling everything from fried chicken wings, burgers, Chinese and Greek offerings, pizzas and the usual panoply of junk food, you'll find La Prima, with excellent prepackaged salad plates and sandwiches made to order, or Quigley's, a fern-filled restaurant and bar, in case you want an aperitif before your junk food. *Open Mon.-Fri. 11 a.m.-7 p.m. No cards.*

The Irish Times
14 F St. NW
• 543-5433

Across from the Union Station, this is basically a bar, which has probably been around since the time Prohibition was repealed, but they also serve inexpensive and excellent hamburgers. There are some specials that really count, such as the blue plate (the hot turkey is served with real mashed potatoes, and the corn beef and cabbage transports you to Dublin). The bar is full of Washington memorabilia, and there's a bit of poetic musing from Yeats on the menu. About $5 per person for food, and what you select from the huge bar list is additional.
Open Mon.-Thurs. 11 a.m.-2 a.m., Fri.-Sat. 11 a.m.-3 a.m. All major cards.

Marché
1810 K St. NW
• 293-3000

It's easy to miss this café, located in a narrow store front on K Street. All you see from the street is a carry-out counter, but if you enter, there is a spacious and lovely dining room, decorated with huge, old, black-and-white photographs of Paris. The food is primarily salads, sandwiches and the specialties of croque monsieur and croque madame (glorified grilled cheese sandwiches with either ham or turkey). There is a happy hour with discount drinks from 4 p.m. to 6 p.m. Count on $6 per person for a meal.
Open Mon.-Fri. 11 a.m.-8 p.m. All major cards.

Marshall's
2525 Pennsylvania Ave. NW
• 659-6886

There is a crowd of regulars (lawyers from local firms and some *USA Today* staffers taking refuge from the newsroom) who frequent the bar and even have their parties in the upstairs room. The food is basic burgers, with specials such as meatloaf with real mashed potatoes on Wednesdays. During warm weather, there are tables out on the sidewalk, if you don't mind the bus fumes. About $10 per person.
Open Mon.-Thurs. 11:30 a.m.-2 a.m., Fri.-Sat. 11:30 a.m.-3 a.m., Sun. 11 a.m.-2 p.m. Cards: AE, MC, V.

I Matti
2436 18th St. NW
• 462-8844

Washington rarely begins food trends; here is another case in point. This time, it's the trend of the second restaurant being a casual cousin of a famous, richer place. Roberto Donna, the talented chef-owner of Galileo, has recently opened this offspring in the funky Adams Morgan area of town. The menu is primarily pastas and pizzas, with some

wonderful antipasti and a few entrées. The menu is the same downstairs, with a bustling bar and wood tables, or upstairs, where it is slightly quieter and where tablecloths are used. The food is great, and you can wear faded jeans or black tie and feel comfortable. About $15 per person.
Open Mon.-Thurs. & Sun. noon-4:30 p.m. & 6 p.m.-11 p.m., Fri.-Sat. noon-4:30 p.m. & 6 p.m.-4 a.m.). All major cards.

Mixtec
1792 Columbia Rd. NW
• 332-1011

This tiny Adams Morgan restaurant began life as a grocery, and some Hispanic staples are still sold at the counter facing the door. The mainstay of the menu is the soft tacos, which make those cardboard things filled with overly chile-powdered beef sold elsewhere seem even more like junk food. The tacos here are filled with tender strips of beef and a choice of savory salsas. The other highlights of the menu are burritos and enchiladas. Expatriate Texans who moved east to join the Bush administration can get a bowl of menudo on Sunday mornings, in a town where tripe stew is still uncommon. About $10 per person.
Open Sun.-Thurs. 11 a.m.-10 p.m., Fri.-Sat. 11 a.m.-10 p.m. No cards.

Pavilion at the Old Post Office
1100 Pennsylvania Ave. NW
• No phone

When this building was converted to a few levels of fairly boring and touristy shops, a food court was added to the basement. The Indian and Greek are the only vaguely interesting options in the panoply of domestic and international options. More interesting is the cafeteria on the upper level. While it is a yawn to a New Yorker, this is new for the capital. You select what you want from the salad bar and hot Asian and Western food bar, and then pay by the pound. Less than $5 per person, no matter where you eat.
Open Mon.-Sat. 10 a.m.-7 p.m., Sun. noon-5 p.m. No cards.

Royal Frontier
1823 L St. NW
• 785-0785

Either for an introduction to Indian food, or for a fairly inexpensive meal downtown, the $8.95 buffet lunch is one of the best deals in Washington, both for quality and quantity of food. There is a blending of northern tandoori cooking and fiery southern curries, served in an attractive Indian dining room that looks as if it were decorated from the duty-free shop at the New Delhi airport. Dinner includes even more choices, and is about $15 per person.
Open Mon.-Thurs. 11:30 a.m.-2:30 p.m. & 5:30 p.m.-10 p.m., Fri. 11:30 a.m.-2:30 p.m. & 5:30 p.m.-10:30 p.m., Sat. noon-3 p.m. & 5:30 p.m.-10:30 p.m., Sun. noon-3 p.m. & 5:30 p.m.-10 p.m. Cards: AE, MC, V.

The Shops at National Place Food Court
1331 Pennsylvania Ave. NW
• No phone

This was one of the first junk-food paradises built in the city. Natives still refer to the building as the National Press Club, so don't be confused if you hear that name. There is everything from sushi and tacos to cookies and ice cream, served in pleasant, if dark, surroundings. If you are shopping or taking in museums on the Mall, this is convenient and cheap. Less than $5 per person.
Open Mon.-Sat. 10 a.m.-7 p.m., Sun. noon-5 p.m. No cards.

Thai Kingdom
2021 K St. NW
• 835-1700

Washington has really "Thai-d" one on in the past few years, restaurants with the name of Thai This or Thai That having opened in almost every space where a sushi bar once stood. Few of them, alas, are very good, so when this one opened, it was greeted with great enthusiasm, both for the quality of the food and the exceptionally low prices, especially for a restaurant smack in the middle of the expense account "K Street Strip." The fried squid and homemade sausage are wonderful starters, and the grilled chicken and smoked fish served in a banana leaf cannot be beaten for entrées. The room is delightful, in tones of mauve. Less than $10 per person.
Open Mon.-Fri. 11:30 a.m.-10:30 p.m., Sat. noon-10:30 p.m., Sun. 5 p.m.-10 p.m. All major cards.

Union Jack Pub
Canterbury Hotel,
1733 N St. NW
• 393-3000

Not only does it look like a real pub, with London street signs around the walls and laminated Union Jacks as placemats, but it even serves authentic pub food at real pub hours. The half dozen tables are set in what was the lobby bar of the Canterbury Hotel, and the bangers and mash, English pork pies with chutney, ploughman's platter of meats and cheeses, and fish and chips with malt vinegar are fantastic. Wash lunch down with a Watney's or Ram Rod ale. Less than $10 per person, including a few pints.
Open Mon.-Fri. 11 a.m.-2:30 p.m. & 5 p.m.-10 p.m., Sat. 5:30 p.m.-10:30 p.m. All major cards.

Union Station
50 Massachusetts Ave. NE
• No phone

This is the newest, largest and nicest of the city's food courts, the walls and pillars covered in cheerful ceramic tiles with a Mexican tree motif. You will find every type of junk food, from pizza and burgers to chicken wings and Chinese, but also look for a sushi bar, the Georgetown Seafood Grill's raw seafood bar, and a moderately good deli. There is barbecue, Mexican food and a fresh-juice stand, too. The multi-screen movie theaters are also on this lower level, so get your tickets and then enjoy a meal. About $5 per person.
Open daily 10 a.m.-9 p.m. No cards.

Vie de France Café

1615 M St. NW
• 659-0992

Vie de France made its mark on the city by popularizing authentic croissants. This light and bright café in the middle of the downtown business district not only serves the best in baked goods, with delicious coffee, but also very good chicken salads, roasted chicken platters, sandwiches and hamburgers. Sit upstairs, away from the carry-out lines. About $7 per person, with a luscious croissant or pastry. *Open Mon.-Fri. 7:30 a.m.-6 p.m., Sat. 9 a.m.-3 p.m. No cards.*

Wolensky's

2000 Pennsylvania Ave. NW
• 463-0050

Wolensky's is a bastion of "Cute Cuisine." Cute Cuisine is casual American food given quaint names on the menu. While names like "Chicago saté" (skewers of Polish kielbasa on sauerkraut), "Kosher guacamole" (served with bagel chips) and "American sushi" (such as smoked salmon, cream cheese and cucumber rolls) are enough to make one turn as green as lime jello, the food itself is delicious. Lots of salads, burgers and sandwiches are available in this hip, two-story dining room. About $10 per person. *Open Tues.-Sat. 11:30 a.m.-11 p.m., Sun.-Mon. 11:30 a.m.-11 p.m. All major cards.*

GEORGETOWN

Artie's Harbour Deli & Café

3000 K St. NW (in the Washington Harbour complex)
• 944-4350

As Nora Ephron wrote in *Heartburn*, "You can't get a decent bagel in Washington," and that, unfortunately, remains true. Artie's, at least, has lean corned beef and real pastrami, and it's a most pleasant place to sit out on the plaza and look at the bizarre fountains and the Potomac River. Sandwiches and a drink will run about $12 for two. *Open Mon.-Fri. 7 a.m.-6 p.m., Sat.-Sun. 11 a.m.-6 p.m. Cards: AE, MC, V.*

Bill's of Beverly Hills

3340 M St. NW
• 333-4063

It's a good bet, from his accent, that Bill is not from Beverly Hills, but that doesn't matter. This is a delightful, hip spot, with a sense of humor, that makes some good and authentic "Yuppie" pizzas. Two favorites: the "Maxwell," with baby clams and garlic (named for Bill's first-born), and the "Jesse," with feta cheese and walnuts on a whole wheat crust (named for the second son). Bill also delivers—even to your hotel room. A pizza for two will be about $10. *Open Mon.-Thurs. noon-midnight, Fri.-Sat. noon-3 a.m., Sun. noon-10 p.m. Cards: AE, DC.*

Furin's

2805 M St. NW
• 965-1000

Washington has not been blessed with the great array of gourmet carry-out places to be found in New York, but Furin's is one of the best in the capital. In the display case, you'll find a few dozen salads—such as an excellent tabouli, tomatoes and mozzarella, and pasta primavera, soups and entrées such as chicken parmesan or London broil, not to mention some rich tarts to tempt you for dessert. You can eat at one of a dozen tables, covered with brightly colored tablecloths, in the bay windows of the store. In case you lack reading material, there's a bookcase filled with cookbooks to peruse. Even better than dining in, take advantage of the carry-out service and walk to the Old House or to the C&O Canal, just a few blocks away, after creating your own picnic, weather permitting. About $10 for two.
Open Mon.-Sat. 11 a.m.-7 p.m. No cards.

Garrett's

3003 M St. NW
• 333-1033

It seems that all burger joints have to have a theme, and the railroad is the one at Garrett's, a bustling bar as well as casual restaurant, featuring everything you've come to expect from the genre. During the winter, it's just like most spots along the "M Street Strip," but during the summer, you can sit in the magical garden in the back, if it's one of the rare days that the heat and humidity of Washington are under control. The appetizers are excellent, and the greaseless potato skins, nachos and pastas are good. Look at the blackboard in the front window for the specials; they are usually well priced, and you can't go wrong with a burger. About $20 for two.
Open Mon.-Thurs. 11:30 a.m.-2 a.m., Fri.-Sat. 11 a.m.-3 a.m. All major cards.

Geppetto

2917 M St. NW
• 333-2602

Despite all the burger and pizza joints in Georgetown that may have tables open immediately, it's still worth standing in line for Geppetto's pizza (although if you arrive before the crowd coming from the Biograph theater down the block arrives, you can frequently avoid the wait). The pizzas come with either a toothsome, crispy, thin crust or a thicker crust, as you prefer, and the highlight of the menu is the pizza blanca. There are also huge sandwiches, and some classic, if boring, pasta and entrée items. Most of the people are lined up for the pizzas.
Open Mon.-Thurs. noon-11:30 p.m., Fri.-Sat. noon-1:30 a.m., Sun. 4 p.m.-11:30 p.m. All major cards.

Hamburger Hamlet

3125 M St. NW
• 965-6970

5225 Wisconsin Ave. NW
• 244-2037

10400 Old Georgetown Rd.,
Bethesda, Md.
• (301) 897-5350

Washington and Los Angeles are the two cities where this chain has outposts, and they have one of the best burgers in town. The three branches here are pleasant and reliable places for dining at any time of the day or night. There are more than twenty permutations of grilled burgers; one of the more unusual is the Henry IV, with melted cheese, ham, tomato, bacon and Russian dressing. The breakfast huevos rancheros and frittatas are excellent, as is the Brie-and-mushroom omelet served from the Sunday brunch menu. Hamburger Hamlet is also a great place to "graze," with a bunch of appetizers—from quesadillas and Buffalo wings to impeccably fresh oysters and clams. The space is large, but it is broken into smaller areas around a grand staircase. At the Bethesda location, eat in the greenhouse bar area instead of the dimly lit and cavernous main room. About $20 for two.
Open Sun.-Thurs. 11 a.m.-midnight, Fri.-Sat. 11 a.m.-1 a.m. Cards: AE, MC, V.

Hunan Garden

1201 28th St. NW
• 965-6800

In a previous incarnation, this was a fancy French restaurant, hence the gold-foil wallpaper in the main dining room of what is one of the few Chinese restaurants in Georgetown. The clientele at Hunan Garden is mainly people from the neighborhood who shy away from the touristy burger joints farther up M Street. The food is solid and reliable, if not totally inspired. There is a good selection of dim sum at lunch, as well as a special lunch menu, with soup and entrée, for a very reasonable price. At dinner, the beef with spicy black bean sauce, scallops wrapped in ground pork, pan-fried noodles, orange chicken and Peking duck are all excellent.
Open daily 11:30 a.m.-10 p.m. Cards: AE, MC, V.

Madurai

3318 M St. NW
• 333-0997

While Georgetown has always boasted a number of fine Indian restaurants, Madurai, which also has a carry-out for some of its specialties, is the only restaurant serving the spicy, vegetarian cuisine of Southern India. Their specialties include a good array of breads, such as puffed pooris and crêpelike dosas. The best bargain is the Sunday buffet, available at lunch and dinner for $6.95. Try the kofta curry of vegetable "meatballs," dosas filled with spiced potatoes, various lentil preparations and the curried cauliflower. Dinner for two will be about $20.
Open Mon.-Thurs. 11 a.m.-2:30 p.m. & 5 p.m.-10 p.m., Fri.-Sat. noon-2:30 p.m. & 5 p.m.-11 p.m., Sun. noon-4 p.m. & 5 p.m.-10 p.m. Cards: AE, MC, V.

Manhattan Bar & Grill
3116 M St. NW
• **333-4733**

This is a small café, with hanging art-deco lamps and marble tables. The menu has practically nothing to do with New York City, despite the name. There is fresh, raw seafood for starters, a good selection of burgers and salads, and some extremely well-prepared vegetarian entrées, such as eggplant parmigiana or vegetarian lasagna. About $20 for two. *Open daily noon-midnight. Cards: AE, MC, V.*

Pâtisserie Café Didier
3206 Grace St. NW
• **342-9083**

When the cavernous Potomac restaurant closed in 1988, pastry chef Dieter Schorner, who had moved from New York's Tavern on the Green, decided to remain in Washington. His bakery and ten-table café, tucked away in an alley off chaotic Wisconsin Avenue, offer light fare, but the best reason to visit is for breakfast or dessert. The array of fruit tarts and luscious butter-cream tortes, crispy nut cookies and meringues and creamy miniature tarts, is exceptional. You can start with soup and a slice of quiche or a chicken-walnut salad for lunch or a light supper, but save a lot of room for dessert. About $15 for two. *Open Tues.-Sat. 8 a.m.-7 p.m., Sun. 8 a.m.-7 p.m. No cards.*

Mr. Smith's
3104 M St. NW
• **333-3104**

Most of the burger joints on M Street in Georgetown have almost interchangeable menus, so pick your place for the atmosphere. The front room of this casual restaurant, with hanging stained-glass lamps, can feel like some foreboding, dark den of iniquity. But just keep walking: there is a bright and incredibly cheerful greenhouse garden in the back, and during good weather, an outdoor garden is open as well. The menu of this burger place is amusing: it's inscribed on newsprint paper. Start with one of the fruit daiquiris, and then enjoy a burger, a Philly cheese sandwiches or a fajita. There's music on weekends, and a meal for two is just $20. *Open Sun.-Thurs. 11:30 a.m.-2 a.m., Fri.-Sat. 11:30 a.m.-3 a.m. All major cards.*

The Tombs
1228 36th St. NW
• **337-6668**

This pizzeria, located near the Georgetown University campus, is bustling at all times, so expect to wait. Not only is the pizza consistently good, but The Tombs shares a kitchen with F. Scott's and 1789, so the quality of salad dressings and desserts is always high, too. The place attracts a combination of Georgetown students and Gucci-type Washington lawyers who live in the neighborhood, so whatever you wear is appropriate. A pizza and beers will be $20 for two. *Open Mon.-Sat. 11 a.m.-midnight, Sun. 10 a.m-11 p.m. All major cards.*

UPTOWN

American City Diner
5532 Connecticut Ave. NW
• 244-1949

Washington is never in the vanguard of food trends; in fact, many food fads are on Social Security by the time they strike the banks of the Potomac. So it was no surprise that the nostalgia craze for diner food—complete with blue plate specials of meat loaf and mashed potatoes—was a few years late in arriving. The American City Diner is a facsimile of the real thing. The Coke machine is an antique, but the remainder of the setting was re-created for the site. Most of the food is classic coffee-shop sandwiches, grilled burgers and hot dogs, with just enough touches like the brown-and-serve rolls and '50s outfits on the waitresses to pull off the act. About $20 for two.
Open Sun.-Thurs. 6:30 a.m.-2 a.m., Fri.-Sat. 24 hours. All major cards.

Armand's
4231 Wisconsin Ave. NW
• 686-9450

Armand's brought the deep-dish Chicago-style pizzas to the Washington area a decade before Pizzeria Uno opened its doors, and natives are addicted to the chewy, yeasty crust and overflowing toppings. The menu is limited to a few salads and sandwiches, but pizza is definitely the name of the game. There is delivery to most of the northwest area, and to Chevy Chase and Bethesda. Tip: if part of your group wants a thinner-crust pizza, go to Maggie's, two doors down. Count on $14 for pizza and drinks for two.
Open Mon. 11:30 a.m.-10 p.m., Sun.-Thurs. 11:30 a.m.-11 p.m., Fri.-Sat. 11:30 a.m.-1 a.m. Cards: AE, MC, V.

Austin Grill
2404 Wisconsin Ave. NW
• 337-8080

With the entire country hotter for Southwestern food than a fire of aged mesquite wood, there are still relatively few outposts with really good chili in Washington. This narrow restaurant is easy to pass by, partly because it looks from the street like a bar. The interior, done in Santa Fe turquoise and pink with a thin band of crude drawing across the top of the walls, is the authentic stuff. The quesadillas are great; the chili would make a Texan homesick; the fajitas and burritos are done with fine-quality meat; and the chocolate cake uses real Mexican Ibarra chocolate. Start with a margarita, and you're all set. About $25 for two.
Open Mon. 5:30 p.m.-11 p.m., Tues.-Thurs. 11:30 a.m.-11 p.m., Fri.-Sat. 11:30 a.m.-midnight, Sun. 11:30 a.m.-10 p.m. Cards: AE, MC, V.

CHAMPAGNE

Veuve Clicquot Ponsardin

MAISON FONDÉE EN 1772

REIMS
FRANCE

*"Une seule qualité:
la toute première"*

*"One quality...
the very finest"*

Madame Veuve Clicquot Ponsardin

The Booeymonger

5252 Wisconsin Ave. NW
• 686-5805

3265 Prospect St. NW
• 333-4810

While the Georgetown location is a bit off the main drag, the Uptown spot is right across from that temple of conspicuous consumption, Mazza Gallerie. No matter what time of the day or night you drop by, this small shop, with tables on a covered porch or inside, will be bustling. It's one of the few places that offers breakfast while you wait for the stores to open, and it's convenient to the Friendship Heights Metrorail stop. Good, honest sandwiches at a fair price is a winning combination for the Booeymonger.
Open Sun.-Thurs. 8 a.m.-1 a.m., Fri.-Sat. 8 a.m.-2 a.m. No cards.

Chadwick's

5247 Wisconsin Ave. NW
• 362-8040

3205 K St. NW
• 333-2565

203 Strand St.,
Alexandria, Va.
• (703) 836-4442

Chadwick's, across from the Mazza Gallerie near the Maryland border and also under the Whitehurst Freeway in Georgetown, has all the standard items of a yuppie watering hole—potato skins, nachos and fried calamari. But, hold on. There are also some of the best crabcakes in town, a credible New England clam chowder, and such delicious Sunday brunch items as eggs Omar (served with a large filet of beef and Bernaise sauce) and eggs Idaho (on potato skins with sour cream and cheese). Don't scoff at the fiesta salad with grilled flank steak. There's also a repertoire of standard salads, sandwiches and burgers. About $20 for two.
Open Mon.-Thurs. 11:30 a.m.-2 a.m., Fri.-Sat. 11:30 a.m.-3 a.m., Sun. 10 a.m.-2 a.m. All major cards.

Faccia Luna

2400 Wisconsin Ave. NW
• 337-3132

Did the world need yet another pizzaria? In the case of Faccia Luna (the name means "moon face"), the answer is yes. This little restaurant, with glass-brick tiles and light-toned wooden booths, is located one level below Germaine's in Upper Georgetown. It offers some of the best-quality pizza crust and toppings in the area. The crust is chewy and yeasty, and the toppings fresh and deftly prepared, not canned. Of the oven-baked sandwiches, the charcoal-broiled chicken breast has an aromatic and delightfully pungent walnut-garlic pesto topping. The wines-by-the-glass list is far better than one would expect from a pizza parlor. About $15 for two.
Open Mon.-Thurs. 11:30 a.m.-11 p.m., Fri.-Sat. 11:30 a.m.-midnight, Sun. 4 p.m.-11 p.m. Cards: AE, MC, V.

Ivy's Place

3520 Connecticut Ave. NW
• 363-7802

When you see the line down the sidewalk, it's not for the movie theater. They queue up for the satés and other Indonesian favorites served behind the striped canopy, which marks this small street-front restaurant. Ivy's was "discovered" by the chic about five years ago, but far from being overwhelmed, this tiny place has maintained its

high-quality eats. The decor is basic, which allows one to concentrate even more on the food. With drinks, $20 for two is all you'll spend.
Open Mon.-Sat. noon-11:30 p.m., Sun. 4 p.m.-11 p.m. Cards: AE, MC, V.

Maggie's
4237 Wisconsin Ave. NW
• 363-1447

Traditional thin and crispy New York–style pizzas here are some of the best in town, with a sauce that is house made, not from a can. What makes Maggie's even more interesting are the white pizzas bursting with garlic and whole-milk mozzarella, and the taco pizza that mixes metaphors with beef and spicy salsa on top of mozzarella and cheddar. The calzone and the pastas are excellent, as is the homemade minestrone. Bargain hunters ought to try the $6 buffet lunch that includes entreés, such as fried chicken, as well as pizza and salad. With drinks, two will escape for $16.
Open Sun.-Thurs. 11 a.m.-1 a.m., Fri.-Sat. 11 a.m.-2 a.m. Cards: AE, MC, V.

MARYLAND

Bethesda Crab House
4958 Bethesda Ave.,
Bethesda
• (301) 652-9754

Usually, you have to travel to the shores of the Chesapeake or to Baltimore to find crabs served in the proper environment. Real crab houses don't have cute, checked tablecloths; there is newspaper on the tables and pitchers of beer coming from the bar. This crab house has been around since Bethesda was a sleepy little village rather than the urban sprawl it has become. Natives call up and order their prized crustaceans in advance, to insure that both the number and size requested are reserved. During the summer, they cover the cement front patio with a tent; during the winter, it's first come, first served. Diners rid themselves of anxiety by pounding away with wooden mallets and then picking the crab from its body with small paring knives. For visitors: Crab is one of the only indigenous foods, so enjoy! About $30 for two, depending on where the crabs come from.
Open daily 9 a.m.-midnight. No cards.

Il Forno
4926 Cordell Ave.,
Bethesda
• (301) 652-7757

Every neighborhood has its favorite pizza parlor, but in the case of Il Forno, you should seek out the neighborhood, as the pizza is worth a drive from the city. First of all, it's cooked in a gleaming copper-and-steel, wood-burning

oven, so the smell of the wood and the yeasty crust greets diners about a block away. The pizza crust is crispy and hearty, and the toppings are nicely handled. During the summer, you can sit at umbrella-topped tables outside. You'll spend about $15 for two, with a few beers.
Open Mon.-Thurs. 11 a.m.-10 p.m., Fri.-Sat. 11 a.m.-11 p.m. Cards: MC, V.

House of Chinese Chicken

12710 Twinbrook Pkwy.,
Rockville
• (301) 881-4500

While many Chinese restaurants try to produce menus the thickness of the phone book, Pat Chao is a specialist. Her China Coral in Bethesda is really a seafood restaurant, preparing finny food in an Asian fashion, and this restaurant, located along an urban-sprawl road in Rockville, has little on its menu that didn't cluck when alive. Chicken is one of the foods usually done best in Chinese restaurants, and this is clearly the case here. From fiery Szechuan to subtle Cantonese, the dishes are well-seasoned and perfectly cooked. Count on about $15 to $20 per person.
Open Mon.-Thurs. noon-10:30 p.m., Fri.-Sat. noon-11 p.m., Sun. noon-10 p.m. Cards: AE, MC, V.

House of Chinese Gourmet

1485 Rockville Pike,
Rockville
• (301) 984-9440

The interior design is plastic tables with phony stained-glass lamps, but the food is real. You can easily miss this restaurant; it's located in a small strip shopping center about five minutes from Ikea and the other bargain attractions of suburban Rockville. Not only does the menu include some unusual options—homemade Chinese sausage, fried longfish with a garlicky sauce—but it also contains an entire page of vegetarian dishes, many of which substitute tofu for other forms of protein. The mock fried duck skin, using bean curd skin, is stellar. About $30 for two.
Open Mon.-Thurs. 11:30 a.m.-10 p.m., Fri.-Sat. 11:30 a.m.-11 p.m., Sun. 11:30 a.m.-10 p.m. Cards: AE, MC, V.

Matuba

4918 Cordell Ave.,
Bethesda
• (301) 652-7449

Start with a few rounds of sushi, and then move on to the cooked food, and rarely will you be disappointed in a dish. The serene grasscloth walls and multiple levels of this restaurant, in what has become the "restaurant row" of Bethesda, are far more elegant than the prices on the menu would dictate. The tempuras are light and greaseless, and the grilled fish is always fresh and perfectly cooked. Also try one of the teriyaki preparations, including a rather unusual squid dish. About $30 for two.
Open Mon.-Thurs. 11:30 a.m.-2 p.m. & 5:30 p.m.-10 p.m., Fri. 11:30 a.m.-2 p.m. & 5:30 p.m.-10:30 p.m., Sat. 5:30 p.m.-10:30 p.m., Sun. 5:30 p.m.-10 p.m. All major cards.

Maxim

640 University Blvd. East,
Silver Spring
• (301) 439-0110

Maxim is an Asian village under a roof, with everything from the best Asian market in the region to a dentist and tailor. So it is only fitting that it would have a café. The restaurant is in the center of the complex, with a window that sells succulent barbecued pork and dim sum specialties to customers pushing carts through the market. The soups are made with a rich, intensely flavored chicken stock, and the dim sum are superb. No alcohol is served, but there is a large selection of chilled Chinese fruit drinks in the display case. About $3 per person for a filling bowl of soup, up to $10 for an outrageously large feast.
Open Mon.-Sat. 9:30 a.m.-8 p.m., Sun. 9:30 a.m.-7 p.m. No cards.

O'Brien's Pit Barbecue

387 E. Gude Dr.,
Rockville
• (301) 569-7801

6820 Commerce St.,
Springfield
• (301) 569-7802

7305 Waverly St.,
Bethesda
• (301) 654-9004

This is Texas-style barbecue, so don't expect it to be too spicy. It does depart from its geographic parentage in the variety of foods that are placed in the low-temperature hickory pit. Beef, of course, is used, but there is also pork, ribs and chicken—all foods that would be heresy to cook in the Lone Star state. The slowly smoked foods are incredibly tender, and then they are slathered with a sauce that is sweet and savory, but not particularly hot. Good coleslaw, baked beans and potato salad follow, and you can get the food to go if you're not crazy about the suburban plastic decor. About $8 per person.
Open Sun.-Thurs. 11 a.m.-10 p.m., Fri.-Sat. 11 a.m.-11 p.m. Cards: MC, V.

Rio Grande Café

4919 Fairmont Ave.,
Bethesda
• (301) 656-2981

When former Texan George Bush wants to recapture his culinary past, the Secret Service swoops in to secure him a table behind one of the stacks of Corona beer crates serving as room dividers so the President can munch on tostadas and salsa or anticipate a dish of the sizzling fajitas approaching the table. Rio Grande Café was a popular hit long before it gained presidential approval, however. The interior is intentionally funky, with a detailed paint job to replicate peeling paint, and a tortilla press serving as a kinetic sculpture behind the bar. The tamales are wonderful and spicy, the cabrito is a huge portion of roasted kid goat, and the chiles rellenos are some of the best east of the Rio Grande. That's why the spot is always crowded, so plan on some waiting time, and spend it in the bar, sipping margaritas. From $10 to $20 per person.
Open Mon.-Thurs. 11:30 a.m.-10:30 p.m., Fri. 11:30 a.m.-11:30 p.m., Sat. noon-11:30 p.m., Sun. noon-10:30 p.m. All major cards.

Tastee Diner

7731 Woodmont Ave.,
 Bethesda
• (301) 652-3970

8516 Georgia Ave.,
Silver Spring
• (301) 589-8171

118 Washington Blvd.,
Laurel
• (301) 953-7567

Long before Ed Debevic's and the diner nostalgia swept the country, there were places like the Tastee Diner that didn't know that chipped beef on toast ever went out of fashion, and where you can get eggs for lunch or a burger at 3 in the morning. Not only do the dark wooden booths and tiny tiles on the floor look the same as they did in the 1930s when the diners were opened, but the prices are almost the same. The most expensive meal is $7.95, and that's for a steak with two vegetables. Otherwise, it's a challenge to spend more than $5 a head. The food isn't haute cuisine, but real diner food never was.
Open daily 24 hours. No cards.

Thai Place

4828 Cordell Ave.,
Bethesda
• (301) 951-0535

Real Thai food, redolent of lemon grass and spicy basil, was available in the suburbs long before it reached downtown. This spot has been around for more than a decade, and its food is still fiery-hot and well prepared. Start with chicken wings stuffed with crab and mushrooms (dubbed, unfortunately, " wings of angels"), and then a bowl of tom yom goong (shrimp in a hot-and-sour soup, fragrant with lemon grass). The list of entrées is seemingly endless, but as is true with so many Chinese restaurants, most of the dishes are repetitive preparations, only the form of protein changing from page to page. About $20 for two.
Open Mon.-Fri. 11 a.m.-3:30 p.m. & 5 p.m.-10 p.m., Sat. 11 a.m.-10:30 p.m., Sun.11 a.m.-10 p.m. Cards: AE, MC, V.

VIRGINIA

Bilbo Baggins

208 Queen St.,
Alexandria
• (703) 683-0300

This popular Old Town restaurant is the perfect place to finish a walking tour of the historic district. The kitchen does a good job with veal, chicken and pasta dishes, and the price is reasonable. About $12 per person.
Open Mon.-Fri. 11:30 a.m.-2:30 p.m. &5:30 p.m.-10:30 p.m., Sat. 11:30 a.m.-3 p.m. & 5:30 p.m.-10:30 p.m., Sun. 11 a.m.-2:30 p.m. & 4:30 p.m.-9:30 p.m. All major cards.

Carnegie Deli

8517 Leesburg Pike,
Vienna
• (703) 790-5001

Yes, Virginia, there is a Carnegie Deli. It's right there, in the shadow of Carnegie Hall, where they know pastrami from corned beef, and no one would dare ask for Swiss cheese on a salami sandwich. But here in the vast consumer country near Tysons Corner, the Carnegie Deli pales by comparison to the original. However, it does serve sky-scraper-size portions of everything, and the cheescake fulfills our dreams of this huge, dense, impossibly rich dessert. Carnegie is still the best deli the city has to offer, and that's all that can be said for it.

Open Sun.-Thurs. 11 a.m.-10 p.m., Fri.-Sat. 11 a.m.-midnight. Cards: AE, MC, V.

Ecco
220 North Lee St., Alexandria
• (703) 684-0321

The high-tech interior is only matched by the high-tech pizzas and pastas served. Ecco is the brainchild of one of Washington's most innovative restaurateurs, Mark Carraluzzi, who began the American Café chain. He now also runs Bistro Bistro, in nearby Shirlington. This was the first of the fun, innovative pizza and lighthearted pasta restaurants, and remains one of the best. It's located near the river in Old Town; the best place to sit is in the back room. About $10 per person.

Open Sun.-Thurs. 11 a.m.-midnight, Fri.-Sat. 11 a.m.-2 a.m. All major cards.

Hard Times Café
140 King St., Alexandria
• (703) 683-5340

When times were hard during the Depression, even a bowl of chili and a plate of onion rings would have been considered haute cuisine, and those are the stars at this Old Town chili parlor, with a great juke box and funky memorabilia on the walls. The offerings are both Texas- and Cincinnati-style chilis, and you should start with a plate of the best onion rings in town. About $8 per person.

Open Mon.-Thurs. 11 a.m.-10 p.m., Fri.-Sat. 11 a.m.-11 p.m., Sun. 4 p.m.-10 p.m. Cards: MC, V.

Pho 75
1711 Wilson Blvd., Arlington
• (703) 525-7355

The Pho is hardly *faux* at this small, strip-mall restaurant in the Vietnamese section of Arlington. The broth for the noodle soup is rich and intensely flavored, and all soups are served with rice noodles, bean sprouts, slices of hot pepper, lemon and mint. You choose from a selection of cuts of beef for your topping, from eye of round to tripe and meat balls. The choice of beverages includes fresh lemonade and salty plum soda. About $5 per person.

Open daily 9 a.m.-8 p.m. No cards.

Queen Bee
3181 Wilson Blvd., Arlington
• (703) 527-3444

Located in the heart of "Little Saigon," also called the Clarendon section of Arlington, Queen Bee's frequently packed dining room is a place to try such delicacies as spicy-and-sour fish or shrimp soup, some of the best cha gio in the region and succulent roast pork with a soy-based barbecue sauce. The whole fried fish, roast quail and beef skewers grilled and placed on vermicelli are all excellent. About $10 per person.

Open daily 11 a.m.-10 p.m. Cards: MC, V.

Red, Hot & Blue
1600 Wilson Blvd.,
Arlington
• (703) 276-7430

The "blue" might refer to the musical preferences of Lee Atwater, Republican national chairman and one of the owners of this Memphis-style barbecue restaurant. It is just across the Key Bridge in Rosslyn, on the ground floor of a new office building. The dry ribs in a spicy crust are wonderful, but if you must have sauce, then it is an excellent sweet-and-spicy one. The "pulled pig" sandwiches are so moist and tender, no further saucing is needed. Although it would be heresy in Tennessee, beef and chicken are also served. About $15 per person.

Open Mon.-Thurs..11 a.m.-10 p.m., Fri.-Sat. 11 a.m.-11 p.m., Sun. 3 p.m.-9 p.m. Cards: MC, V.

P. J. Skidoo's
9908 Lee Hwy.,
Fairfax
• (703) 591-4515

While, unfortunately, the red wine to accompany your beef here has probably never seen a cork, beef is the name of the game at this restaurant with a split personality. At times, it looks like Beaver Cleaver's family was cloned and flown here; the place seems to be filled, at times, with perfect American families eating the $8 roast-beef and $10 steak dinners. But on other nights, from the number of well-dressed people jammed into the bar, it looks like the River Club crowd of chic singles decided to hit the suburbs all at once. The kitchen knows how to cook beef, and it also knows how to grill chicken. About $10 per person.

Open Mon.-Sat. 11:30 a.m.-11 p.m., Sun. 4 p.m.-10 p.m. Cards: AE, MC, V.

Skyline Chili
8102 Arlington Blvd.,
Falls Church
• (703) 698-5669

Transplanted Midwesterners flocked to this chili parlor when it opened in 1988, nostalgic for the culinary curiosity of their youths called "Cincinnati chili." Once described as "Alpo marinated in kerosene, with a touch of cinnamon added," this soupy and mild chili is served atop limp spaghetti, with a sprinkling of onions, cheese, beans and oyster crackers. As odd as it sounds, it tastes even odder, at first. Once you have acquired the taste, however, you can't get enough of it. About $5 per person.

Open Mon.-Thurs. 11 a.m.-9 p.m., Fri.-Sat. 11 a.m.-9 p.m., Sun. noon-8 p.m. No cards.

HOTELS

INTRODUCTION

L ike its restaurants, Washington's hotels are on a par with those in New York or Los Angeles. There are just fewer of them, and they cost less than in other cities. The recent boom in hotel construction and the renovation of many existing establishments have blessed the District with a broad spectrum of lodging options, not all of which require an enormous vacation budget (or expense account). Outside of downtown's high-rent district, a traveler of modest means can find agreeable accommodations at rates that are moderate or, indeed, downright cheap. The following is not a complete listing; it is, however, a representative mix in terms of price and location. Nearly all the establishments mentioned accept major credit cards. The hotels in metropolitan Washington are divided into three categories: Expensive, Moderate and Budget. In addition, we have reviewed a number of hotels in nearby Maryland and Virginia for those who prefer to base their operations outside the city. Count on adding a 5-percent state tax to your bill in Maryland, and 4.5 percent in Virginia—plus an additional 5-percent county tax in most areas. In Washington, the hotel tax is a hefty 10 percent. Here are a few hints to keep in mind when selecting your hotel:

- Try to avoid the peak tourist or convention periods, and don't even think of coming during a presidential inaugural. Rates are frequently lower and availability is greater in July and August, for example, because it's a prime vacation time for bureaucrats and members of Congress, so the hotels are not crowded with lobbyists courting their favors. Similarly, the city empties out around Christmas and Thanksgiving, and hotels often drop rates to lure customers. January is also a slow period. The month to avoid is April, when conventioneers descend en masse and tourists flock to the capital for the annual Cherry Blossom Festival.
- Always ask for special deals. It's sometimes best to call the hotel's direct number, because the reservations clerks on the toll-free 800 numbers may not be familiar with special rates and packages.
- Check to see if you belong to a group or organization that can get a special rate. Members of the Smithsonian Institute and similar organizations are accorded discounts at many hotels, for example.
- Take advantage of Washington's clean, safe and efficient Metrorail subway system. If you're bringing the kids, chances are that you'll all be happier in a suburban hotel close to a Metrorail stop. You won't have to hassle with downtown parking, which is scarce and expensive (how does $18 a day sound?), and the room rates outside the District will be cheaper, except for some of the new luxury hotels.
- Do a little homework. For example, if you're coming to visit the pandas at the National Zoo and you're on a shoestring budget, scout the listings for the inexpensive guest houses within walking distance (there are several).
- Ask questions in advance. What does it cost if you need an extra roll-away bed?

SYMBOLS & ABBREVIATIONS

Our opinion of the comfort level and appeal of each hotel is expressed in the following ranking system:

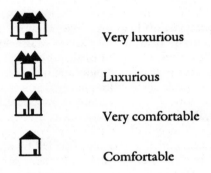

Very luxurious

Luxurious

Very comfortable

Comfortable

Symbols in red denote charm.

EXPENSIVE

The Capital Hilton
16th & K Sts. NW,
Wash., D.C. 20036
• 393-1000, (800) HILTONS
Fax 393-7992

Not so many years ago, The Capital Hilton was slipping into uninspiring banality—just another downtown Hilton, blessed with a better-than-average location. But recently, perhaps spurred by the opening of a number of new luxury hotels, it has spent a good deal of time and money to regain its former luster. Long-time guests say the hotel seems rejuvenated. Every March, The Capital Hilton hosts the star-studded spring dinner of the Gridiron Club, a group of journalistic high-brows who stage a song-and-dance attack on the news and newsmakers of the day. Smack in the heart of Washington's business district, The Capital Hilton is just a two-block walk to either the White House or the Farragut North Metrorail station. The Twigs restaurant is serviceable, if not distinguished, and for those who fancy exotic cocktails and Polynesian fare, take note that this is the site of Trader Vic's restaurant, that goodies place for adults. Children of any age stay free in the same room as their parents.

Singles: $160-$225; doubles: $185-$260; suites: from $450; weekends: $75-$95.

Embassy Row Hotel

2015 Massachusetts Ave. NW,
Wash, D.C. 20036
• 265-1600, (800) 424-2400
Fax 328-7526

The Embassy Row Hotel is often overlooked on lists of Washington's better hotels, but it clearly belongs there. Located just off Dupont Circle, at about the midway point of Embassy Row, it looks across Massachusetts Avenue to the beautiful, old Indonesian Embassy. The decor vies for glitz with that of its diplomatic neighbors, and the bar is full of locals since it frequently features some of the best jazz in town. The restaurant is now ascending since the new chef, Daniel Voinovich, arrived from Alexandria's Morrison House. Once you're settled into your room, you'll find all the usual amenity goodies provided by most pricey hotels. The staff is multilingual, and there are complimentary coffee and pastries for guests who must head off before dawn. The hotel is a favorite with European businessmen and the diplomatic crowd. Children under 18 stay free, except on a package rate. Charge of $12 per day for parking. Rooftop swimming pool. Only a half block from the Dupont Circle Metrorail station.

Singles: $155-$175; doubles: $175-$195; suites: $335-$640; weekends: $99-$139.

Four Seasons Hotel

2800 Pennsylvania Ave. NW,
Wash., D.C. 20007
• 342-0444, (800) 268-6282
Fax 342-1673

It's no wonder that in recent years the Four Seasons has chalked up the highest occupancy rate among Washington's luxury hotels. The serene lobby, furnished with antiques, radiates an unmistakeable aura of wealth, and no doubt many Washingtonians have fantasized about meeting a millionaire in the Garden Terrace, a lushly planted, sunlit room which is one of the city's most popular spots for a late evening tête-à-tête or an afternoon tea. Aux Beaux Champs, the dining room, is perhaps the best restaurant housed in a Washington hotel, with tables placed far enough apart for discrete conversations. Desirée, an on-site private nightclub, is open to hotel guests. The maids do their thing twice a day, and the hotel even offers jogging attire to fitness-minded guests who want to work out in the newly constructed health club. The Four Seasons is located at the entrance to Georgetown, on the edge of Rock Creek Park, within easy walking distance of varied shopping and dining opportunities. Children under 16 stay free. There is a $14-per-day charge for parking. Amenities include cable TV, nonsmoking rooms, accommodations for the handicapped. Animals the size of Fifi, the Poodle, may stay in the rooms if prior arrangements are made. Georgetown has no Metrorail subway service, and the closest station is a ten-minute walk. But there are buses right at the front door. *Singles: $205-$245; doubles: $235-$275; suites: $425-$1,500; weekends: $175 (including parking).*

The Georgetown Inn

1310 Wisconsin Ave. NW, Wash., D.C. 20007
• 333-8900, (800) 424-2979
Fax 337-6317

You can't get any closer to Georgetown, Washington's fashionable neighborhood for shopping and nightlife, than The Georgetown Inn. You're just a few minutes from some of the city's liveliest bars and most exclusive shops. Or you can soak up the charm of old Georgetown by simply strolling along its tree-lined streets, occasionally peeking in the windows of the sleek and costly rowhouses. The downside of being in the center of the action, unfortunately, is that the rooms can be somewhat noisy, especially on Saturday nights. The lobby is small but tasteful, as are the rooms. A bonus at The Georgetown Inn is the Georgetown Bar & Grill it houses, featuring New American cuisine and a champagne Sunday brunch. There is a $12-per-night charge for parking. All rooms offer in-house movies, and there is a nonsmoking floor. There are no Metrorail subway stations near Georgetown, but buses stop at the front door, and it's easy to get cabs.
Singles: $145-$275; doubles: $145-$160; suites: $185-$275; weekends: $120-$200.

The Grand Hotel

2350 M St. NW, Wash., D.C. 20037
• 429-0100, (800) 848-0016
Fax 429-9759

There's an aura of quiet serenity about The Grand, and the hotel maintains a very high standard of service. The Grand boasts a scenic corner location in the West End, the city's law district, on what is the fringe of the downtown area. The White House is a good mile away, but the best Georgetown shopping is about a 10-15 minute walk. The lobby is elegant, if a bit sterile, and the guest rooms are small. But the fantastic, gigantic bathrooms are reason enough to stay here. In addition to stunning marble fixtures, the bathrooms feature freestanding showers with memory temperature controls and European tubs that fill within a minute. Expecting calls? Each room has three telephones, one with two incoming lines. If you can't afford the rooms but want a bit of the atmosphere, visit the Promenade Lounge, which often features a pianist, for a quiet drink or afternoon tea. Children under 12 stay free. There is a $12-per-day charge for parking. Other amenities include a swimming pool, a fitness center and accommodations for the handicapped. The Foggy Bottom Metrorail stop is about a ten-minute walk.

Singles: $200-$210; doubles: $220-$230; suites: $350-$1,700; weekends: $155 (single or double), $185 (including parking and champagne breakfast).

Grand Hyatt Washington

1000 H St. NW,
Wash., D.C. 20001
• 582-1234, (800) 228-9000
Fax 637-4781

What can you do to top the usual Hyatt soaring atrium, considering there are already a pack of them in Washington? Add a waterfall and lagoon at the bottom to one-better the usual fountains, of course. The best thing that can be said for this 900-room hotel with a post-modern facade is that it is right across the street from Convention Center. So if a convention is the reason for your trip to the capital, this would be a good option. The rooms are reached from the walkways around the twelve-story atrium, and all are fitted with small seating areas decorated in peaceful pink-and-gray tones. When you're at a Hyatt, you know exactly what you're getting into, down to the piano player in the lobby (whose tinkling of the ivories will probably drive you crazy in your room). The restaurants are hardly of note, though the Grand Café on the swirling lagoon level is pleasant enough for a quick meal. One of the best features of this Hyatt is the suites, all of which have wet bars. The presidential suites have saunas, and the grand suites offer marble whirlpool baths. The Metro Center Metrorail stop is right here, and there is a $14 charge for parking.

Singles: $155-$200; doubles: $180-$225; suites: $350-$900; weekends: $89-$126.

Guest Quarters Hotel

801 New Hampshire
Ave. NW,
Wash, D.C. 20037
• 785-2000, (800) 424-2900
Fax 785-9485

2500 Pennsylvania
Ave. NW,
Wash., D.C. 20037
• 333-8060, (800) 424-2900
Fax 338-3818

Since our concept of the perfect vacation involves a quest for a bigger and better bathroom, a kitchen is absolutely the last thing we want to find in a hotel room. But if you're looking for a place that's just like home—if your house is furnished like a hotel—except that you don't have to clean it, consider either of these Guest Quarters hotels. The units in both "all-suite" hotels feature a combination living room–dining room, a separate bedroom and a fully equipped kitchen (but don't expect a food processor, as you get cheap dishes and flatware for four, plus a few miserable pots). You don't even have to find a supermarket if you avail yourself of the hotel's grocery delivery service. And for dessert, you're temptingly close to the Watergate Pastry Shop, which sells some of the best sweets in the city. The New Hampshire Avenue location is on a tree-lined street of rowhouses in Washington's Foggy Bottom section, just a short walk from the Kennedy Center. The Pennsylvania

Avenue Guest Quarters is nearby, a little larger and a little closer to Georgetown, but on a far busier street. The New Hampshire Avenue location has a swimming pool. Children do not stay free. Guest parking is available at a daily $8 charge. Other amenities include in-house movies, pet facilities, nonsmoking rooms, babysitting and accommodations for the handicapped. The closest Metrorail stop is the Foggy Bottom station, about a block from both locations. *Rates $99-$185 (all suites).*

The Hay–Adams Hotel

One Lafayette Square NW, Wash., D.C. 20006
• 638-6600, (800) 424-5054
Fax 638-2716

Didn't get that long-awaited invitation to stay at the White House? Never mind, you can stay, practically next door, in one of Washington's finest hotels. For elegance and location, it's hard to beat The Hay-Adams, the bright yellow building directly across Lafayette Park from the White House. Many of the hotel's rooms—all furnished in a Federal-period look—offer a magnificent view of Washington's most famous address. Staying in the Hay-Adams is like visiting someone's very expensive house. Its quiet, opulent bar and restaurant were the staging areas of choice for Ollie North and Company as they stroked wealthy "patriots" to seek private funding for the Contra forces in Nicaragua. A century ago, novelist and presidential descendant Henry Adams and his friend, statesman John Hay, built adjoining residences on this prime piece of real estate. The houses were razed in 1927, and the present hotel took their place. California financier David Murdock purchased the run-down hotel in 1983 and entrusted its restoration to his wife, Gabriele. The result rated a major spread in *Architectural Digest* and is well worth your consideration today. Parking is $15 a night. It is just a two-block walk to two Metrorail subway stops—the Farragut North and McPherson Square stations.
Singles: $155-$315; doubles: $205-$340; suites: $450-$1,550; weekend: $189-$235 (includes fruit-and-wine basket, parking, breakfast and afternoon tea).

Holiday Inn Crowne Plaza at Metro Center

775 12th St. NW, Wash., D.C. 20005
• 737-2200, Fax 347-0860

This blocklike building, surrounded by construction sites, has more crystal and plants than the average Holiday Inn, and the dining room, The Metro Center Grille, has a real, honest-to-goodness chef—Melissa Balinger of New Heights fame—in charge. But it's still a Holiday Inn, and compared with its neighbors around Convention Center, it just doesn't stack up. The rooms are moderately large, but nothing out of the ordinary, and the lobby is pleasant, if not inspired. There is a first-rate health club with a pool for swimming laps, and if shopping is your primary form of recreation, there is Woodie's across the street, although this is not a neighborhood for strolling. Of course, you couldn't be more convenient to the Metrorail system. In fact, you're right at a stop. Parking is $12 a night, babysitting can be arranged, and eleven rooms are equipped for the handicapped.

Singles & doubles: $125-$195; suites: $250-$700; weekends: $59.50-$125.

Hyatt Regency on Capitol Hill

400 New Jersey Ave. NW,
Wash., D.C. 20001
• 737-1234, (800) 228-9000
Fax 737-5773

This Hyatt, with its razzle-dazzle atrium, glass elevator, indoor fountain and high-tech architecture, is just like every other modern-day Hyatt. It was quite an attraction when it opened a decade ago, but it has since lost some of its appeal as other expensive hotels have moved into the area. Still, its proximity to the Capitol, the Mall and the newly renovated historic Union Station (now filled with shops, restaurants and movie theaters) is a big plus. The hotel remains a favorite with convention-goers and reception-throwers because of its huge ballroom, multiple meeting rooms and extensive banquet facilities. While the restaurants are hardly of note, the Hyatt Sunday Brunch, served in a delightful forest of plants to the quiet strains of a harp, is a paradise of plenty, complete with all the champagne you can drink. There's not much in the way of nightlife here, but the rooms are quite nice, and the Hyatt has a health club and a glass-enclosed, stainless-steel, heated swimming pool. Children under 18 stay free. There is a $12-per-night charge for guest parking. Amenities include in-house movies, nonsmoking rooms, accommodations for the handicapped, limo and babysitting services. The nearest Metrorail stop is at Union Station, about four blocks away, and, of course, you can catch Amtrak there, too.

Singles: $155-$195; doubles: $180-$220; suites: $350-$1,025; weekends: $119-$139.

The Jefferson

1200 16th St. NW,
Wash., D.C. 20036
• 347-2200, (800) 368-5966
Fax 331-7982

The Jefferson is a very private place, loaded with personalized services. Built in the 1920s as an apartment house for Washington's political and social elite, the Jefferson became a hotel in 1941, and has been catering to elite travellers ever since. Washingtonian or not, The Jefferson's clientele cherishes the hotel's warmth and intimacy, which has appealed to such members of the Republican WASP nobility as former Defense Secretary Caspar Weinberger and former Texas Senator John Tower. Its 69 guest rooms and 35 suites underwent a complete redecoration in 1986, when the hotel was owned by the famous lawyer, Edward Bennett Williams, resulting in a variety of decors ranging from Louis XV to Oriental to eighteenth-century English. Now that the Lancaster Group from Houston has bought it, the public areas are being spruced up in a similar manner, and the food in the dining room has been transformed from country club nondescript to exciting New American. The hotel is situated just four blocks from the White House and within walking distance of Metrorail subway stations. There is a $25-per-night charge for a roll-away cot for children, and a $20-per-night charge for car parking.

Singles: $175-$260; doubles: $195-$285; suites: $275-$1,000; weekends: $160 (includes parking, fruit basket and brunch if you stay two nights).

J. W. Marriott Hotel at National Place
1331 Pennsylvania Ave. NW, Wash., D.C. 20004
• 626-6900, (800) 228-9290
Fax 626-6991

The name "Marriott" in Washington is synonymous with mass appeal, from fast food joints to predictable hotels, but add the initials "J. W." and you enter another world entirely. This hotel is regarded by the Marriott empire as the jewel in its crown, but, in fact, it's more glitter than class. The interior of glass and brass sparkles like a diamond and is just as cold. The lobby is so huge that we had trouble finding the main desk, to say nothing of locating the elevator bank. And we had the uncomfortable feeling that we might never find our way out of the lower-level conference areas. To make things even more confusing, the hotel lobby melds into a colonnade of shops and restaurants known as The Shops of National Place, which in turn connects with the recently renovated National Press Building. We would note that this was once the site of Bassin's, a wonderful, sleazy watering hole where you could drink all month for the price of one night's stay at the J. W. Marriott. What price progress? Location, it is said, is everything, and in that regard, this hotel can't be beaten: it's within easy walking distance of the White House, the Smithsonian museums, the National Theater and the central business district. Children under 18 stay free. There is limited guest parking (no vans) at $11 per day. The hotel has a health club, indoor pool, in-house movies, nonsmoking rooms and accommodations for the handicapped. The Metro Center Metrorail Station is a block away.

Singles: $189-$209; doubles: $209-$235; suites: $1,500; weekends: $125.

The Madison Hotel

15th & M Sts. NW,
Wash., D.C. 20005
• 862-1600, (800) 424-8577
Fax 785-1255

Washington has recently seen the birth of several new luxury hotels, but most look a bit gauche when compared to the stately elegance and charm of the Madison, privately owned and managed by well-known hotelier Marshall Coyne. The hotel caters to the international community as well as to business people, and the Madison is worth a look if only to gasp at the stunning collection of fine antiques that adorn the lobby, behind what is a very banal facade. The hotel is across the street from *The Washington Post*, and the owners of some of the city's best-known bylines regularly dine at the hotel's pricey coffee shop and restaurants. They eat here for the convenience, since the food at both is nothing a critic would want to review. The Madison is also near the heart of the downtown business district and less than three blocks from the McPherson Square Metrorail stop. But walking in the other direction is not recommended; the neighborhood borders on a rough zone. The charge for each additional room occupant is $30 per night; parking is $14 a night. The hotel permits small pets in rooms, and guests can use a nearby fitness center. *Singles: $195-$265; doubles: $225-$285; suites: $395-$2,500; weekend packages: $270-$390 (two nights, including parking and breakfast).*

The Mayflower

1127 Connecticut Ave. NW,
Wash., D.C. 20036
• 347-3000, (800) HOTELS-1
Fax 466-9082

This superb old hotel has been a Washington landmark for more than 60 years. Its ballroom and meeting rooms, which open off a monumental hallway that runs a full city block, have hosted a rich mixture of society and political events. By the late 1970s, this grand old lady was becoming shabby, but an extensive renovation program has returned much of her original splendor. The formal, stylish lobby, with its lush fabrics and carpets, provides one of the city's more elegant settings for people-watching. The hotel itself is so huge, that unless you score a room near the elevators, you'll get an aerobic workout just going back and forth through the hallways. The Mayflower, a Stouffer hotel, is in the heart of Washington's business district and only a short walk from the White House. While the main restaurant's food tastes like Stouffer's frozen, Nicholas, a gem of a New American restaurant, is located off the lobby. Children under 18 stay free. There is a $12-a-day charge for guest parking. Small, arm-carried pets are permitted. Amenities include in-house movies, nonsmoking rooms, accommodations for the handicapped, babysitting and limo service. Metrorail's Farragut North station is on the same block. *Singles: $139-$199; doubles: $159-$219; suites: $250-$350; weekend package: $79-$130.*

Morrison Clark Inn

Massachusetts Ave. & 11th St. NW,
Wash., D.C. 20001
• 898-1200, (800) 332-7898
Fax 289-8576

When the original house now converted into the Morrison Clark Inn was constructed in 1864, the area around Logan Circle was a millionaire's row. Now, unfortunately, it borders on one of Washington's slums (although it is very convenient to the Convention Center), which is why this gem of a hotel is so reasonably priced. If it were on Lafayette Park, it could probably triple the rates. While most of the 54 unique rooms and suites are newly constructed in an adjoining space, they all have the feel of the original Victorian mansion. Many rooms have bay windows and porches, all are elegantly furnished, and the hotel does offer complimentary limousine service to the downtown business district and Capitol Hill. While the Morrison Clark is one of the most romantic hotels in the region, it is also prepared to meet the needs of the business traveler—two phone lines with modem hookups, notary public on call, and some small conference rooms. Parking is $10 per night, there is babysitting and limo service, and complimentary continental breakfast. The dining room, features excellently prepared New American cuisine. The Metro Center Metrorail stop is just four blocks away, but walking in the neighborhood is not suggested.

Singles: $115-$195; doubles: $135-$215; suites: $195; weekends: $85-$115.

Omni Shoreham Hotel

2500 Calvert St. NW,
Wash., D.C. 20008
• 234-0700,
(800) THE-OMNI
Fax 332-1373

This is one of Washington's original big hotels. It probably holds the local record for hosting conventions and association meetings. Set on eleven acres at the edge of Rock Creek Park, it is within easy walking distance of the National Zoo and the lively Adams Morgan area. It seems as if the rooms of the old Shoreham are constantly being renovated with each new owner, and unfortunately, never very well. But the handsome, elegant lobby remains the same; its marble floors and giant glass chandelier have a 1930s air, conjuring visions of ladies and gentlemen taking tea on the terrace. Joggers, hikers and bikers should take note of the pleasant trail that passes just below the hotel in Rock Creek Park and winds along the Potomac River to the Mall. Also behind the hotel is an exclusive neighborhood filled with expensive residences, many of which house members of the diplomatic corps. Children under 17 stay free. Guest parking is $7 per day. Amenities include in-house movies, nonsmoking rooms, accommodations for the handicapped, limousine and babysitting services, an outdoor pool and tennis courts.

Singles: $110-$170; doubles: $130-$190; suites: $300-$850; weekends: $79.

The Park Hyatt

24th & M Sts. NW,
Wash., D.C. 20037
• 789-1234, (800) 922-PARK
Fax 457-8823

We've finally figured out what the two miniature stone horses, both wearing startled expressions, are doing in the entry of the new Park Hyatt. Clearly, the steeds trotted into the lobby and were so appalled by what they saw that they froze in place. The postmodern interior design of this hotel, the newest of a trio of first-class hotels clustered in the West End, is surely the work of a rampaging schizophrenic. The long, cramped lobby is a mixture of concrete, marble and carpet that clash and distract. Large modern paintings, some quite impressive, seem to have been thrown on the walls without regard for context or mood. Still, the Park Hyatt's guest rooms are spacious, and the main dining room, Melrose, deserves its respectable reviews; service is excellent. The hotel is a bit distant from the historic areas of Washington, and is probably better suited for visitors interested in the shops and restaurants of Georgetown or proximity to the business district. Children under 18 stay free in the same room, or there is a 50-percent reduction for an adjoining room. There's a $14-per-day parking charge. Amenities include a health club with indoor pool, nonsmoking rooms and accommodations for the handicapped. The nearest Metrorail stop is the Foggy Bottom station, three blocks away.
Singles: $235; doubles: $265; suites: $300-$850; weekends: $159-$179.

The Ramada Renaissance Techworld

999 9th St. NW,
Wash., D.C. 20001
• 898-9000, (800) 228-9898
Fax 789-4213

The promoters have had the audacity to compare Techworld, a sales and marketing center for information technology, to Rockefeller Center. This block-large, blocklike structure is hardly an architectural monument, but this is a convenient location if you're in Washington attending a convention, since Convention Center is directly across the street. The lobby of this 800-room hotel looks as if it were built on the back lot of MGM, with a giant pseudo-Oriental pagoda, as well as the usual fountains and forest of trees that are intended to soften new, uninspired spaces. If you want true Oriental, Chinatown is almost that, and just a few blocks away. There is a complimentary fitness club and swimming pool, and bars galore. Or, everything you would expect from a convention hotel. The rooms are small and sterile, but clean. Parking is $12 per day, and the Metro Center Metrorail stop is a few short blocks away. There are facilites for the handicapped.
Singles: $115-$175; doubles: $170-$195; suites: $250-$1,500.

The Ritz-Carlton

2100 Massachusetts Ave. NW,
Wash., D.C. 20008
• 835-2100, (800) 424-8008
Fax 293-0641

Washingtonians still call it The Fairfax, and it almost had to become so again in 1986, when Ritz-Carlton sued then-owner John Coleman for using their glittering Ritz-Carlton name in Washington. Coleman was accused of allowing the hotel to become dirty and its employees surly—allegations he denied. The case remained unsettled pending resolution of Coleman's subsequent petition for bankruptcy when the hotel was sold to a local real estate developer last year. If all the resulting publicity has hurt business, it isn't readily apparent. The hotel continues to attract a loyal, upper-crust clientele. The lobby is small but grand, with huge urns of flowers enlivening the white marble, and the rooms are large with the sort of quiet and excellent service the clientele expects. The hotel's expensive and excellent restaurant, the Jockey Club, with red-checked tablecloths and $24 crabcakes, is still the place for the elite to eat and greet, including, on occasion, former First Lady Nancy Reagan and her chums. The Fairfax Bar, with its hunting scenes, is a favorite watering hole for the well heeled. The Ritz-Carlton is smack dab in the middle of old and staid Embassy Row, so it's a particular favorite of the diplomatic corps. You're within a quick two-block walk to Dupont Circle, convenient if you're looking for a livelier atmosphere or the subway. Children under 16 stay free. Guest parking is $10 per day. Accommodations available for the handicapped. *Singles & doubles: $190-$320; suites: $400-$1,000; weekend package: $125-$190.*

The Sheraton Carlton

923 16th St. NW,
Wash., D.C. 20006
• 638-2626, (800) 325-3535
Fax 638-4231

Take a seat in the ornate lobby of the Sheraton Carlton just before 8 on a weekday morning, and you're likely to see a political luminary—a senator, perhaps, or a cabinet secretary—heading to the Crystal Room for a one-hour breakfast grilling by some of Washington's best-known journalists. These so-called "Sperling Breakfasts" (named for *Christian Science Monitor* reporter Godfrey Sperling) have become a local institution, and so has the Sheraton Carlton as a gathering spot for the politically powerful. Its downtown location is just two blocks from the White House and the Executive Office Buildings, which makes it a convenient spot for administration officials to gather for receptions or to trade gossip over lunch, tea or drinks. The hotel was designed and built in 1926 by Harry Wardman, one of Washington's most innovative and controversial builders, and its lobby features elaborately carved ceilings, Palladian windows and Louis XIV furnishings. The hotel has been recently renovated, both upstairs and down, but the restaurant menu needs the next overhaul. Children under 18 stay free, but there's a $25-a-night charge for a roll-away. The hotel offers valet parking for $16.80 a day. Amenities include in-house movies and a babysitting service. Small pets are accepted.

Singles: $210-245; doubles: $235-270; suites: $310-$625; weekends: $150.

Sheraton Washington Hotel

2660 Woodley Rd. NW,
Wash., D.C. 20008
• 328-2000, (800) 325-3535
Fax 232-2571

There's enough glistening chrome and plastic in this mammoth hotel to make a naturalist wince. It's convention city here, so be prepared to run into hundreds of folks wearing name tags, all looking for a good time. The skylit, multi-level atrium has a roof that looks as if it was put together with an Erector Set. The hotel itself is a monument to urban sprawl. There's no guarantee that you'll ever find anyone you're supposed to be meeting once you pass through the hotel entrances. And who knows how many people have been lost trying to find their way from the parking garage into the hotel? Still, the hotel is away from the downtown hurly-burly and on the edge of a comfortable northwest Washington neighborhood. For history buffs, the Sheraton Washington connects with the Wardman Tower, an old apartment building where numerous Washington notables, including the late Supreme Court Chief Justice Earl Warren, once lived. The National Zoo is just two blocks away (best to check the twice-daily feeding times for the pandas, otherwise they might not be out when you visit), and you can be whisked to the downtown area or the Mall by jumping on the subway at the Woodley Park Metrorail station, located in the same block. Children under 17 stay free. There is an $8-per-day charge for guest parking. Amenities include in-house movies, nonsmoking rooms, accommodations for the handicapped, an exercise room, two outdoor swimming pools, limo and babysitting services. Small pets are permitted.

Singles: $165-$210; doubles: $195-$240; suites: $230-$1,600; weekends: $79-$129.

Vista International Hotel

1400 M St. NW,
Wash., D.C. 20005
• 429-1700, (800) HILTONS
Fax 785-0786

The Vista isn't one of those loud, brassy hotels that shout for attention. In fact, you could easily miss its set-back facade on M Street near the downtown business district and just around the corner from The Madison Hotel. At the Vista, the action is indoors. Step inside and you are in the hotel's atrium lobby, which soars up fourteen stories. Many of the rooms have balconies that look out onto the glass-enclosed courtyard. It is not a small hotel—it has 413 rooms and suites—but it offers a sense of intimacy that belies its size. A string quartet occasionally plays in the afternoons below the large courtyard clock. When you leave the front door, walk to the left and not to the right, however. The neighborhood to the right gets more than a little rough. The American Harvest restaurant is very good. Children stay free, although there is a limit of three people to a room. There is a $12-per-day charge for guest parking at a nearby public lot. Amenities include in-house movies, accommodations for the handicapped and babysitting service. The hotel has a floor reserved for nonsmokers. Small pets are permitted, but guests must sign a liability agreement to cover the cost of any damage they might cause. *Singles & doubles: $138-$185; weekends: $116 (including parking).*

Washington Court Hotel

525 New Jersey Ave. NW,
Wash., D.C. 20001
• 628-2100, (800) 325-3535
Fax 879-7918

Don't be surprised if you see a congressman or senator wandering through the lobby of this hotel, formerly called the Sheraton, and now home to Mel Krupin's restaurant. Located a few blocks from the Capitol and the congressional office buildings, it is the site of numerous breakfasts, dinners and other events that attract government notables and their staffs. The large lobby is nicely decorated in contemporary pastels, and the lobby bar on the open mezzanine provides a good lookout for well-known political figures who are dining at Mel's, a bastion of basic food presided over by one of the true characters of Washington. The Capitol Hill location is a quick cab ride or a pleasant walk from the national museums on the Mall, and is just two blocks from elegant, old Union Station. The station, which serves Metrorail's Red Line and Amtrak, is now filled with shops, restaurants and movie theaters. There is not much nightlife in the neighborhood, but several good restaurants have opened in the area. Children stay free. There is a $13 charge for guest parking. Amenities include in-house movies, nonsmoking rooms, accommodations for the handicapped and babysitting and limo services. *Singles & doubles: $150-$205; suites: $320-$1,500; weekends: $95 (including parking and Continental breakfast).*

The Washington Hilton and Towers

1919 Connecticut Ave. NW,
Wash., D.C. 20009
• 483-3000, (800) HILTONS
Fax 265-8221

This hotel is destined to be forever remembered as the place where John Hinckley shot Ronald Reagan as the latter headed toward his car following a speech. Infamy aside, this huge hotel—upward of 1,200 rooms and suites—is a favorite with conventioneers. The gigantic ballroom seats 3,000, so on any given night there is a steady flow of people wearing black ties and formal gowns as the Washington social set arrives for this or that charity ball or association dinner. The hotel's Olympic-size swimming pool, workout facilities and lighted tennis courts are considered so spectacular that Washington residents pay top dollar for a coveted health club membership here. The Washington Hilton is close to downtown and only a short walk down Connecticut Avenue to the bohemian charms of Dupont Circle. You're also only blocks away from the nightspots and fine ethnic restaurants of the Adams Morgan area. Children stay free. There is a $10 charge per day for guest parking. Other amenities include nonsmoking rooms, in-house movie rental and accommodations for the handicapped. Pets are accepted. The closest Metrorail station is three blocks away at the Dupont Circle stop.

Singles: $140-$210; doubles: $160-$230; suites: $320-$850; weekends: $85 (including breakfast).

The Watergate Hotel

2650 Virginia Ave. NW, Wash., D.C. 20037
• 965-2300, (800) 424-2736
Fax 337-7915

Now, where have we heard this name before? Indeed, so inextricably is the name "Watergate" tied to the Nixon administration scandals, out-of-towners are often unaware that the hotel is a prime D.C. accommodation and provides condominium homes to luminaries such as Senator Robert Dole and his wife, Secretary of Labor Elizabeth Dole. The hotel is the centerpiece of the luxury Watergate complex perched on the banks of the Potomac River, next door to the Kennedy Center for the Performing Arts, and including some elegant shops at the lower levels. The premier restaurant in the complex, and one of the finest in the country, is Jean Louis, located in the bowels of the hotel. Purchased by Cunard from businessman Nicholas Salgo, the hotel has undergone a complete renovation program, and the lobby areas and rooms are glistening, although not much can be said for the fare in the hotel's own restaurant. The hotel features a spectacular view of the river, and its fine location, a short cab ride from Georgetown and some of Washington's monuments, is a plus. Hotel guests are offered free use of its health club, including a pool and exercise rooms—a magnet for the Washington social set. Children under 14 stay free. There is a $14-per-night charge for parking. Amenities include in-house movies, the health club, limo and babysitting services, nonsmoking rooms and accommodations for the handicapped. Small pets are permitted. The Foggy Bottom Metrorail stop is about five blocks away. Call for weekend rates.

Singles: $195-$265; doubles: $220-$290; suites: $335-$750.

Westin Hotel

2401 M St. NW,
Wash., D.C. 20037
• 429-2400, (800) 228-3000
Fax 457-5010

One cocktail too many in the Westin's main lounge and you may fear you're in yet another remake of *Little Shop of Horrors*. The multitude of potted plants, ferns and palms clustered around the couches and chairs make one suspect that innocent guests could be swallowed up without a trace. Still, the abundant plant life is a cool and pleasant break from the concrete jungle of office buildings and construction in the West End. Just off the lobby is a lovely, formal courtyard with still more greenery. The Westin staff is pleasant and helpful. The rooms here are large and elegantly decorated: Each has an oversize writing desk, three telephones and a minibar with refrigerator. Down on the mezzanine level is one of Washington's most complete fitness centers, where more iron is pumped than in Pittsburgh. Other facilities include a lap pool and squash and racquetball courts. The Bistro is excellent for light meals, while The Colonnade, with its chartreuse velvet banquettes and central atrium, needs some help in the kitchen. Children under 18 stay free. Guest parking is available at a $14 fee, and the nearest Metrorail stop is the Foggy Bottom station, a three-block hike.
Singles: $195-$305; doubles: $225-$335; suites: $525-$1,350; weekends: 50-percent discount.

The Willard Inter-Continental Hotel

1401 Pennsylvania Ave. NW,
Wash., D.C. 20004
• 628-9100, (800) 327-0200
Fax 637-7326 $300

When they closed the Willard after Richard Nixon's 1968 inauguration, it looked as if the old hotel would slowly crumble and be replaced with yet another ugly, modern building. But amazingly, this majestic and historically important structure has not only been saved, but has been painstakingly restored to the beautiful hotel it was when it opened in 1901. The original front desk—a lovely petal-shaped structure of ochre marble, glass and polished wood—now serves as the concierge desk. The hotel's main promenade, Peacock Alley, is again the place to see and be seen in Washington. Workers used early photographs of the interior and even the memories of former guests to duplicate every detail of the original hotel, itself a new building replacing an earlier incarnation. Looking for history? The Willard was known as the "residence of the presidents," having hosted every president from Franklin Pierce to Woodrow Wilson in the transition period between their elections and inaugurations. Julia Ward Howe was staying at the Willard when she penned the "Battle Hymn of the Republic." The location is superb, with the White House, the Mall and its museums, the National Theater, the monuments and the Capitol all within walking distance. But be forewarned: this is one expensive place. Even a casual lunch for two in the coffee shop can top $50, and a few drinks in the Round Robin Bar will bring a heart-stopping tab. The Willard Room's food is excellent, and attached in the new shopping complex are the Occidental and the Occidental Grill for superb fare. Also check out the shopping in the courtyard. Parking is $13.50 a night, and children under 12 stay free.

Singles: $220-$275; doubles: $245-$300; suites: $450-$2,300; weekends: $145.

Wyndham Bristol

2430 Pennsylvania Ave. NW,
Wash., D.C. 20037
• 955-6400, (800) 822-4200
Fax 955-5765

If your idea of celebrity-watching involves actors and actresses of theatrical, rather than political, renown, consider staying at the Wyndham Bristol. Its proximity to the Kennedy Center (three blocks away) makes it a favorite with performing artists. There's nothing exceptional about the outside of the Wyndham. But inside its lobby, the marble floors, glistening chandeliers and comfortable chairs and sofas create the crisp but welcoming atmosphere of a fine European hotel. The rooms are of ample size for a modern hotel and very quiet. Both the Bristol Grill, where American cuisine and a wonderful Sunday brunch are served, and the Bristol Bar are pleasant spots to wine and dine. Georgetown's trendy shops and restaurants are only four blocks down Pennsylvania Avenue, and Washington's central business district is about a five-minute cab ride in the other direction. Children under 17 stay free. There is a $12 overnight charge for parking. Amenities include in-house movies and nonsmoking rooms.

Singles: $140-$160; doubles: $160-$180; suites: $215-$875; weekends: $80-$90.

MODERATE

The Canterbury

1733 N St. NW,
Wash., D.C. 20036
• 393-3000, (800) 424-2950
Fax 785-9581

The Canterbury is a 99-room gem that is unfortunately fading, snuggled amid old Victorian houses in the area between Dupont Circle and the central business district. A European atmosphere pervades this functional, but pleasant, hotel, from its English pub off the lobby to its modest, but fine, French restaurant. The hotel is built on the site of "The Little White House"—the turn-of-the-century residence of Teddy Roosevelt while he was vice-president and in the early days of his presidency. The Canterbury is relatively modern and more elegant—if less brimming with personality—than its less expensive neighbor, the Tabard Inn. Up to two children under 14 can stay free in the same room with their parents. Parking is $6.75 per day. The Dupont Circle Metrorail station is only a few blocks away. *Singles: $140-$200; doubles: $160-$220; suites: $280-$350; weekend package: $88-$98.*

Dupont Plaza Hotel

1500 New Hampshire Ave. NW,
Wash., D.C. 20009
• 483-6000, (800) 421-6662
Fax 328-3265

The Dupont Plaza Hotel is located in one of the city's most action-filled neighborhoods. Dupont Circle is the closest Washington comes to a bohemian ambience. You'll find here a broad array of little boutiques, art galleries and international restaurants, as well as some of the city's most elegant shops. The Dupont Circle Metrorail station is a short walk (and one of the world's longest escalator rides) from the hotel; museums and major government buildings are only minutes away. The hotel has recently undergone some remodeling and has a contemporary urban feel, with an airy lobby and large rooms. Children under 12 stay free. Guest parking is $9.
Singles: $125-$175; doubles: $145-$195; suites: $350-$495; weekends: $70.

Georgetown Marbury Hotel

3000 M St. NW,
Wash., D.C. 20007
• 726-5000, (800) 368-5922
Fax 337-4250

The Marbury Hotel is right in the middle of Georgetown in an architecturally confusing building that tries (but fails) to blend into the surrounding historic structures. The same could be said for the sparsely furnished lobby, which attempts to achieve the air of a garden room but doesn't come close. Garden lovers should not despair, however, because the spectacular public gardens of Dumbarton Oaks are only a few charming residential blocks away. Again, the hotel's main attraction is its location, which is, literally, in the middle of some of Washington's best-known elegant boutiques, cafés and restaurants. Children under 16 stay free with parents. Guest parking is available at a daily rate of $6—a good deal in Georgetown, where on-street parking is very hard to find and local lots charge top rates. Amenities include an outdoor swimming pool, nonsmoking rooms and accommodations for the handicapped. Some rooms have videotape decks, and movies may be rented from the front desk. There's no Metro in Georgetown, and the Foggy Bottom stop is a fifteen-minute walk away.
Singles: $139-$179; doubles: $149-$189; suites: $219-$229; weekends: $99.

The Henley Park Hotel

926 Massachusetts Ave. NW,
Wash., D.C. 20001
• 638-5200, (800) 222-8474
Fax 638-6740

If it were not for the neighborhood, the Henley Park would be one of the most coveted hotels in Washington. Entering the Henley Park is a little bit like walking into a cozy French country inn. The small hotel is a nicely restored and appointed little gem in an out-of-the-way location. It is relatively close to two Metrorail stops, and a quick taxi ride from the city's museums and prime shopping and business district. However, it is advisable to travel by taxi at night and not to walk an appreciable distance in this area. There's a cozy bar and adequate dining room. Children stay free. Guest parking is $12 a night. The hotel has in-house movies. Metro Center or Gallery Place Metrorail stations are three blocks away.
Singles: $125-$185; doubles: $145-$205; suites: $275-$850; weekends: $74-$150 (including parking).

The Hotel Washington

15th St. & Pennsylvania Ave. NW,
Wash., D.C. 20004
• 638-5900,
(800) 424-9540
Fax 638-4275

There was a time, it is said, when the Hotel Washington was home to no fewer than 60 members of Congress. From its legendary top-floor Sky Terrace watering hole, they could look out on the White House or peek around the corner up Pennsylvania Avenue at the Capitol's imposing white dome. Now nearing its 60th birthday, it is the oldest continuously operating hotel in the Washington area. The notables have departed over the years and the hotel has faded a bit, too. But unlike its magnificently restored neighbor, The Willard, the hotel has not been rejuvenated A renovation restored the unique sgraffito designs carved on the building's facade, but the lobby and rooms are dingy, to say the least. The Hotel Washington's location is ideal, and the Sky Terrace still offers one of the best seats in town. Forget the dining room—eat at the Old Ebbitt Grill or the Occidental, both within a block. Children under 14 stay free. Parking is $13.50 a day. Two blocks from Metro Center Metrorail stop. Amenities include in-house movies, exercise room and accommodations for the handicapped.
Singles: $123-$163; doubles: $137-$177; suites: $336-$400; weekends: 25-percent discount, with two-night minimum.

Omni Georgetown Hotel

2121 P St. NW,
Wash., D.C. 20037
• 293-3100, (800) THE-OMNI
Fax 857-0134

First of all, this hotel is not actually located in Georgetown; it's about five minutes from the outskirts of residential Georgetown and a good twenty minutes from the Wisconsin and M Street hub. The Omni Georgetown Hotel is actually just off Dupont Circle, in an area noted for its profusion of art galleries, interesting shops and restaurants. The lobby and rooms are rather sterile, and the restaurant, the Rock Creek Café (named for the park nearby), is adequate, but hardly inspired. Children under 18 stay free.

There is a $14 charge for guest parking. Amenities include a swimming pool, in-house movies, nonsmoking rooms and accommodations for the handicapped.

Singles: $135-$165; doubles: $155-$185; suites: $200-$400; weekends: $89 (including Continental breakfast).

One Washington Circle Hotel

One Washington Circle NW,
Wash., D.C. 20037
• 872-1680
Fax 887-4989

One Washington Circle Hotel is one of several that claim the title of "the city's most popular hotel," and it is located on one of the city's busiest traffic circles, so expect to hear horns blaring at night. It follows an increasingly popular small hotel formula of offering only suites and emphasizing high-quality services. Specific guest services range from grocery shopping to provision of "survival" supplies such as hot hair-rollers and baby-bottle warmers. The hotel is conveniently located in the West End, at a very busy traffic circle, unfortunately. It is a pleasant walk from Georgetown, the Kennedy Center for the Performing Arts or the downtown business area. The small and comfortable lobby, decorated with understated elegance in shades of peach, is inviting, and will be renovated shortly, since the hotel has been sold to a new owner. The rooms tend to be spacious, and all include sofa beds to provide daytime seating and extra sleeping space at night. The West End Café in the basement is very good. Children under 16 stay free. There is a $9-a-day charge for guest parking. Amenities include a swimming pool, nonsmoking rooms and accommodations for the handicapped. Small pets are permitted in rooms.

Suites: $115-$250; weekends: $78-$135 (including parking).

Ramada Renaissance Hotel

1143 New Hampshire Ave. NW,
Wash., D.C. 20037
• 775-0800, (800) 228-9898
Fax 331-9491

Situated at the edge of the West End, the Ramada is worth a look if you're planning to hit the business district by day and Georgetown by night. The hotel is a rung above the garden-variety Ramada, but not in the "luxury" category. It is large, boxlike and modern, without the excitement of the newer hotels. Yet guests say the rooms are big and the service good. The hotel is away from the busiest section of downtown, which makes it feel secluded. A number of Washington's finest downtown restaurants are within walking distance. The nearest Metrorail stop is the Dupont Circle station, four blocks away. Children under 18 stay free. There is a $12 charge for guest parking. Amenities include in-house movies and accommodations for the handicapped. Hotel guests may use a nearby health club.

Singles: $140-$170; doubles: $150-$170; suites: $200-$375; weekends: $93.

The River Inn

924 25th St. NW,
Wash., D.C. 20037
• 337-7600, (800) 424-2741
Fax 337-6520

Every one of the 128 recently redecorated rooms is a suite, and that is why the management offers monthly rates and the staff describes the Inn as a comfortable place for an extended stay. The River Inn is a small hotel, tucked away on a relatively quiet street, in the neighborhood known as Foggy Bottom. It's convenient to many parts of the city and is within walking distance of Georgetown, the State Department and Washington's prime business area. It is also within a few blocks of the Kennedy Center for the Performing Arts, which has made the Inn's Foggy Bottom Café a favorite for after-theater dining. Children under 15 stay free. There is a $9-per-night charge for guest parking. Nonsmoking rooms are available. The room charges may vary, depending on the season.
Suites $110-$160; weekends: $85-$130.

BUDGET

Adams Inn

1744 Lanier Pl. NW,
Wash., D.C. 20009
• 345-3600

The Adams Inn is patterned after the English bed-and-breakfast, and is a real find for the cost-conscious traveler. Some of the rooms have private baths; others have only a wash basin, and you share a bath with fellow guests. A Continental breakfast is included in the daily rate. The Inn is located on a one-way neighborhood street of duplexes near the heart of the multi-cultural Adams Morgan area. You're just a short walk from great ethnic cuisine in a district burgeoning with antique shops and nightspots. You'll recognize the Adams Inn by the Asian chimes hanging on its front porch and the unattractive iron fire escapes along its side. There's a fire station just down the street, so don't be shocked if you're awakened by sirens and flashing red lights. An advance deposit is required for the first night's stay when you make your reservation. Children do not stay free—there's a $5 charge for each additional person in a room. There is also a $5-per-night charge for the parking, which is limited. No smoking is permitted in the rooms. You're close to bus stops, but the nearest Metrorail stop is the Woodley Park–National Zoo station, which is a good fifteen-minute hike.
Singles: $41-$57; doubles: $46-$63.

The Bellevue Hotel

15 E St. NW,
Wash., D.C. 20001
• 638-0900
Fax 638-5132

Don't be alarmed by those two cannons outside the front door. They're just for show, and this is actually a pretty friendly place. It's a bit worn, but in a way that gives the hotel a certain charm. (And they still employ elevator operators here.) The Bellevue is within a few blocks of the U.S. Capitol and the congressional office buildings; the Mall and the Smithsonian museums and galleries are a short walk away, and the newly restored Union Station, with its shops, restaurants and theaters, is several blocks in the other direction. The guest rooms are unexceptional, but tidy and relatively spacious, and many have small refrigerators. For the money, this is a better-than-average hotel, and it is centrally located for tourists. Children under 17 stay free. There is a $9 charge for guest parking. The nearest Metrorail stop is at Union Station, which also serves Amtrak.
Singles: $89.50; doubles: $104.50; weekends: $75.

The Carlyle Suites

1731 New Hampshire
Ave. NW,
Wash., D.C. 20009
• 234-3200
Fax 387-0085

Into art deco? Well, this suites-only hotel is for you—from the black-and-silver art deco awning to the art deco lobby and the art deco units. Here you'll find 176 suites, each with a fully equipped kitchen (but don't expect more than the minimum in plates, flatware and pots). There's even a coin-operated laundry on the premises. This area is still considered "transitional," but lately, a number of big old apartment buildings and giant Victorian houses have been rehabilitated or converted to condos. Walk out the front door, turn left, and you're three blocks from the small avant-garde cafés and art galleries of Dupont Circle. Children under 18 stay free. Free guest parking—a real plus in this traffic-congested area. Amenities include nonsmoking rooms, pet facilities and babysitting.
Singles: $49-$89; doubles: $59-$109; one-bedroom suites $150; weekends: $44.50 (two-night minimum).

Comfort Inn Downtown

500 H St. NW,
Wash., D.C. 20001
• 289-5959, (800) 228-5150
No fax

Surprise! Here's a new budget hotel that doesn't look like every other budget hotel you've ever seen. Architecturally, it blends nicely with the older buildings in this rundown area of the city that is attempting to make a comeback after a long slide. The immediate surroundings still are not terribly inviting, and you should not walk far in any direction. But if you can stand not being in the high-rent district, the location is actually quite convenient. You're right on the edge of Washington's Chinatown and only three blocks from the D.C. Convention Center. But more important, you are just a block away from two Metrorail stops—the Judiciary Square and the Gallery Place stations. The management calls this a "luxury-budget" hotel. "Luxury" may be a bit extreme. But it is a nice, newish hotel—it opened in the fall of 1986—and charges moderate rates. Children under 16 stay free. There is a $10 fee for guest parking. Amenities include a health club, in-house movies, non-smoking rooms, accommodations for the handicapped and Jacuzzis in some rooms.

Singles: $112; doubles: $122; weekends: $59 (including parking).

Connecticut-Woodley Guest House

2647 Woodley Rd. NW,
Wash., D.C. 20008
• 667-0218
No fax

Here's a money-saving tip for the next time you are part of a convention at Washington's gigantic Sheraton Washington Hotel: simply show up for all the daily events, then slip across the street to the Connecticut-Woodley Guest House, where you can spend the night for about $100 less. The guest house, with its blue trim and shutters, seems a bit out of place in the neighborhood. It looks across the street at the Sheraton Washington and the elegant old Wardman Tower, where the likes of former President Richard Nixon once lived. The guest-house location is ideal—just a short walk up Connecticut Avenue to the National Zoo and only 100 feet from the Woodley Park–National Zoo Metrorail station. It also has a coin-operated laundry. Some rooms have private baths, others require sharing with fellow guests. Like most small guest houses, it requires a one-night advance payment. "Crib-size" children can stay for $2 extra, and there is free parking.

Singles: $41-$53; doubles: $48-$60.

Embassy Square Suites Hotel

2000 N St. NW,
Wash., D.C. 20036
• 659-9000, (800) 424-2999
Fax 429-9546

Some regular visitors to Washington maintain that this is one of the best hotel values the city has to offer. The 1960s decor is not the most elegant in the District, but the furniture is comfortable and perfectly adequate. Each of the 250 units is a suite, and some have kitchenettes. Although the mood of the hotel is more utilitarian than romantic, the Black Horse Tavern, located off a walled courtyard and near the outdoor pool, does offer a touch of charm. The Embassy Square Suites Hotel is well-located—close to Dupont Circle, not far from the shops and nightlife of Georgetown and only two blocks from the Dupont Circle Metrorail subway stop. Children under 16 stay free with parents. There is a charge of $7 per day for parking. Amenities include nonsmoking rooms, accommodations for the handicapped, an affiliation with a nearby health center and free Continental breakfast in the restaurant.

Singles: $129-$149; doubles: $149-$169; two-bedroom suites $209-$229.

Hotel Anthony

1823 L St. NW,
Wash., D.C. 20006
• 223-4320, (800) 424-2970
Fax 223-8546

The Anthony is proof that you can stay in the heart of Washington without spending a fortune. Tucked in the middle of the business district, this relatively small hotel offers a good location without big hotel rates. If you're up for a nice stroll, it's only fifteen minutes to Georgetown. The White House is a ten-minute walk away. And you're just a block away from the Farragut West subway stop, from which you can whisk yourself to all the museums and galleries along the Mall or to the Capitol. Most of the Anthony's 99 "junior" suites have full kitchens (some with microwave ovens) or a wet bar, so you can do your own cooking or relax with a drink in your room. On the other hand, you're just minutes from some of downtown Washington's best restaurants, such as The Palm, Le Pavillon, Galileo, and 21 Federal, where you can eat up all your savings. Children under 16 stay free. The Anthony has no parking facilities, but (expensive) lots are nearby. The hotel offers in-house movies and has accommodations for the handicapped. Guests may also use a nearby health facility free of charge.
Rooms: $117-$127; weekend package: $69 (including Continental breakfast).

Hotel Lombardy

2019 I St. NW,
Wash., D.C. 20006
• 828-2600, (800) 424-5486
Fax 872-0503

There's nothing terribly modern about the Lombardy, but that's the point. Walk through the front door into its dark-wood-paneled lobby, and you'll feel as if you've strolled into an old European hotel. The Lombardy's 125 units are a mix of rooms and suites, many with fully equipped kitchens. The location is a big selling point. The hotel looks out onto a small park that separates it from Pennsylvania Avenue. You're just four blocks from the White House, about a twenty-minute walk from the Kennedy Center or Georgetown, and there are two Metrorail stations—Foggy Bottom or Farragut West—within a few blocks in either direction. You'll find lots of young people around the Lombardy because the George Washington University campus is practically across the street. The hotel features a pleasant eatery, the Lombardy Café, and Primi Piatti, a great Italian restaurant, is next door. Children under 16 stay free. There is no parking in the hotel, although there are nearby lots. But expect to pay up to $15 a day for a space in one of them.
Singles: $95-$125; doubles: $105-$140; suites: $125-$155.

Tabard Inn

1739 N St. NW,
Wash., D.C. 20036
• 785-1277
Fax 785-6173

New York has its Algonquin, and Washington has the Tabard Inn, for funky favorites. The Tabard Inn is different, that's the only way to say it. You won't hear any of that synthesized music piped through its cluttered, but comfortable, lobby. No gimmicks such as extra phones next to the toilet or computerized check-out. No, the Tabard Inn is just about the same as it has been for the past 70 years—a perfectly charming, little European-style hotel with only 40 rooms, right next to Washington's business district. It doesn't have that squeaky-clean look. In fact, the place is a tad shabby. The dark-wood-paneled lobby and lounge are filled with antiques, recycled furniture and art of varying quality. In winter, real fires crackle in real fireplaces. The hotel was started during World War I, combining three Victorian townhouses near Dupont Circle, and was named after the hostelry in Chaucer's *Canterbury Tales*. It has survived another world war and an attempted demolition in the early 1970s (protesting neighbors saved it). It has become an institution, a place where native Washingtonians—particularly literary types—congregate to hoist a few in the pub or dine in the excellent restaurant. Some of the less expensive rooms have shared baths. Children under 6 stay free. The hotel has no parking and nearby lots are expensive; however, you're three blocks from the Dupont Circle Metrorail station.
Singles: $95-$125; doubles: $105-$140.

Howard Johnson's Motor Lodge

2601 Virginia Ave. NW,
Wash., D.C. 20037
• 965-2700, (800) 654-2000
Fax 965-2700 ext. 7910

This hotel resembles others across the United States in the Howard Johnson's chain, but it has distinguished itself by gaining a little niche in American political history. It was from a room in this hotel that a surveillance sentry for the Watergate burglars sought—unsuccessfully—to signal the arrival of police to his fellow criminals, who were attempting to bug the offices of the Democratic National Committee in the Watergate office complex across the street. History aside, guests at this "Hojo" can take advantage of Watergate's fashionable shops and restaurants. The hotel is also within two blocks of the hiking-and-biking path that runs along the Potomac River and eventually extends in one direction to Georgetown and in the other past the Kennedy Center, the Lincoln Memorial and other monuments. The decor is simple and slightly shabby, but at least there is a bar and coffee shop. The hotel offers free guest parking (vans not included), and children under 12 stay free. There is an outdoor pool. Nonsmoking rooms and babysitting are available. Small pets are permitted.
Singles: $68; doubles: $76; weekends: $57.

Kalorama Guest Houses

1854 Mintwood Pl. NW,
Wash., D.C. 20009
• 667-6369
No fax

2700 Cathedral Ave. NW
• 328-0860
No fax

For the penny-wise traveler willing to accept the no-frills charm of an Italian pensione, the Kalorama Guest Houses are just the ticket. The best-known is a red-trimmed Victorian house located on Mintwood Place, a residential street near the center of the ethnically diverse Adams Morgan district. The other one is about a fifteen-minute walk away, near the National Zoo. In both places, Continental breakfast is included in the price of the room and both offer some rooms with private baths, while the rest have "community" baths shared with fellow patrons. Regulars at both guest houses describe them as cozy, from their brass beds to their thick comforters. The guest houses require prepayment in full. You get what you pay for, of course, and these aren't on a par with Washington's luxury hotels. But if you want basic comfort at a moderate price, they are a very good value. There is a $5 charge for each additional person. At Mintwood Place, you're close to the bus lines, but about a fifteen-minute walk from the nearest Metrorail stop. At the Cathedral Avenue guest house, you're about two blocks from the same subway stop.

Singles: $40-$80; doubles: $45-$85; suites: $60-$95.

Normandy Inn

118 Wyoming Ave. NW,
Wash., D.C. 20008
• 483-1350, (800) 424-3729
Fax 387-8241

You don't hear much about the Normandy Inn, perhaps because it is a bit off the main drag. The Normandy Inn is a European-style hotel—moderately priced, not flashy, but with all the essentials. It is located just off Connecticut Avenue and on the edge of a very expensive residential area that many wealthy Washingtonians and diplomats call home. It's a short walk down Connecticut to the Dupont Circle area. The interior of the hotel is pretty standard: hotel furniture, hotel carpet, hotel draperies and hotel light fixtures—but its location and good service make it a fine value. Children under 12 stay free. There is a $4 charge for guest parking. The hotel offers accommodations for the handicapped. The nearest Metrorail stop is at the Dupont Circle station, about a ten- to fifteen-minute walk away.

Singles: $76; doubles: $86; suites: $170; weekends: $57

Quality Inn Capitol Hill Hotel

415 New Jersey Ave. NW,
Wash., D.C. 20001
• 638-1616, (800) 228-5151
Fax 638-0707

Great location. Two blocks from the Capitol. A few blocks more to the Mall and its museums. A short stroll to the recently renovated Union Station, which serves Amtrak and Washington's Metrorail. The only problem with this hotel is that it's extraordinarily ordinary and decidedly unexceptional. The lobby has very little character. There's nothing special about the rooms, and everything else about the place is predictably Quality Inn, right down to the children's menu in the Coach and Parlor Restaurant. But if you care

more for a central location than for fancy surroundings, the moderate rates make this hotel good value. Children under 18 stay free. Free indoor guest parking (if there's space available). Amenities include in-house movies, rooftop outdoor swimming pool, nonsmoking rooms, accommodations for the handicapped and babysitting service.
Singles: $99-$125; doubles: $114-$140; suites: $200-$290; weekends: $65-$85.

Windsor Park Hotel

2116 Kalorama Rd. NW,
Wash., D.C. 20008
• 483-7700
Fax 332-4547

This is a simple, moderately priced hotel on the edge of an elegant, very pricey area. The hotel looks out on the rather uninspiring embassy of the People's Republic of China. But walk out the front door and stroll a few blocks to your left, and you'll be in one of Washington's most exclusive neighborhoods, where houses routinely go for $1 million and up. The Windsor Park offers the basics—direct-dial phones, color TVs, private bath, small refrigerator—but there are no amenities such as in-house movies or a swimming pool or a health club. The location puts you only a fifteen-minute walk up Connecticut Avenue from the National Zoo or a half-hour walk in the other direction from the White House. Nearby Rock Creek Park offers scenic paths for runners and walkers. Children under 18 stay free. There is no guest parking, and finding a space on the street is often difficult. The nearest Metrorail stop is Woodley Park-National Zoo, about a ten-minute walk, although buses run frequently, and there is a bus stop just across from the hotel.
Singles: $48-$55; doubles: $56-$64; suites: $68-$78.

ALSO WORTH A LOOK

The Highland Hotel

1914 Connecticut Ave. NW,
Wash., D.C. 20009
• 797-2000, (800) 424-2464
Fax 462-0944

Small, comfortable and close to Dupont Circle. Great for art-gallery buffs.
Singles: $95-145; doubles: $115-165; suites: $135-$204; weekends: $55.

Holiday Inn Capitol

550 C St. SW,
Wash., D.C. 20024
• 479-4000, (800) HOLIDAY
Fax 479-4353

Just like all the other Holiday Inns, but at a great location close to Capitol Hill.
Singles: $125; doubles: $145; suites: $160-$190; weekends: $62.50-$72.50.

Holiday Inn Central

1501 Rhode Island Ave. NW,
Wash., D.C. 20005
• 483-2000, (800) 465-4329
Fax 797-1078

No surprises, but it has reasonable rates for a downtown hotel, although the neighborhood should be avoided on foot.
Singles: $97; doubles: $104; suites: $125; weekends: $70.

Savoy Suites Hotel

2505 Wisconsin Ave. NW,
Wash., D.C. 20007
• 337-9700 Fax 337-3644

Formerly called the Wellington Hotel. Nice area, nice view and a wealth of freebies.
Singles: $65-$95; doubles: $75-$105; weekend package: $49, if available.

The Windsor Inn

1842 16th St. NW,
Wash., D.C. 20009
• 667-0300, (800) 423-9111
Fax 234-3309

Intimate, comfortable hotel on a very busy street.
Singles: $69-$89; doubles: $79-$99; suites: $105-$125; weekend package: $55, when available.

SUBURBAN

MARYLAND

Best Western Ambassador Inn

2715 University Blvd.,
Wheaton, Md. 20902
• (301) 933-1300,
(800) 528-1234
No fax

This hotel is at a busy intersection, where occasionally, engines roar and brakes screech. It sits directly across from a big suburban plaza, with acres of asphalt parking lots. It's not bad, but it's certainly not exceptional, either. Simply put, it is a standard Best Western hotel, stuck out in deep suburbia. Children under 12 stay free. Free guest parking. The hotel has an outdoor swimming pool. If you stay on Friday and Saturday nights, Sunday's rate is half price.
Singles: $50-$55; doubles: $63; suites: $75-$80.

Bethesda Marriott Hotel

5151 Pooks Hill Rd.,
Bethesda, Md. 20814
• (301) 897-9400,
(800) 228-9290
Fax (301) 897-0192

There are often groups of people wandering around the Bethesda Marriott wearing "Hello, My Name Is . . ." tags. That's because, in addition to being an excellent family hotel, it is also a popular conference site. The hotel has a 4,600-square-foot grand ballroom that can accommodate up to 700 people for receptions. Its ample health facilities and exotic Kona Kai restaurant make it a popular spot for business meetings. Located in a semiwooded area that has recently seen tremendous apartment and condo development, it feels somewhat isolated, although it is very close to Wisconsin Avenue, a main artery into the city. When the savvy Marriott marketers decided to offer conference facilities, they surely took note of the hotel's close proximity to the Bethesda Naval Hospital and the huge National Institutes of Health complex, both of which bring in tons of business. Children under 18 stay free, and there is no charge for guest parking. Amenities include an indoor-outdoor swimming pool, tennis courts, health club, in-house movies, pet facilities, nonsmoking rooms and accommodations for the handicapped.

Singles: $99-$160; doubles: $155-$180; suites: $275-$700; weekends: $69-$99 (including Continental breakfast).

Crowne Plaza Hotel

1750 Rockville Pike,
Rockville, Md. 20852
• (301) 468-1100,
(800) 638-5963
Fax (301) 468-1100
ext. 7973

Here is a suburban hotel with personality. The lobby opens onto an eight-story atrium with a huge central gazebo and a twenty-foot waterfall. Towering trees and lush tropical plants throughout enliven what would otherwise be an uninspiring interior. From the outside, there is nothing spectacular about the hotel, which is located on Rockville Pike, a heavily commercial strip that turns into Wisconsin Avenue as you drive into Washington. Rockville Pike is known for its shopping center, with such stores as Ikea and Loehmann's within a few minutes as well. And directly behind the hotel is the Twinbrook Metrorail station, which gives you easy access to the rest of the Washington area. Children stay free, and there is no charge for guest parking. Amenities include swimming pool, health club, limo service, babysitting, in-house movies, pet facilities, nonsmoking rooms and accommodations for the handicapped.

Singles: $123-$138; doubles: $130-$145; suites: $195-$325; weekends: $59-$99.

Econo Lodge Silver Spring

7990 Georgia Ave.,
Silver Spring, Md. 20910
• (301) 565-3444,
(800) 446-6900
No fax

Let's face it, there are few hidden treasures in the hotel game. Most of the time, you get what you pay for. The Econo Lodge Silver Spring is past its prime. It's a big box of a hotel on the edge of downtown Silver Spring, the kind of place that still posts the nightly rates on the side of the building. But then again, its owners don't try to do anything but make it a solid budget hotel. You're right next to a car wash, and the neighborhood is a bit deserted at night. Children under 12 stay free. No charge for guest parking. Pets allowed. Accommodations for the handicapped.

Singles: $51.65; doubles: $54.95.

Holiday Inn of Bethesda

8120 Wisconsin Ave.,
Bethesda, Md. 20814
• (301) 652-2000,
(800) 638-5954
Fax (301) 652-3806

Nothing fancy about this Holiday Inn. Nothing great about the location. Nothing exceptional about its appearance. But for a nondescript hotel stuck on busy Wisconsin Avenue, it does have a pleasant feel. The lobby is warm and comfortable, and many rooms have their own balconies. Walk out the front and you've got a huge choice of eateries—from the highly touted Rio Grande Café, El Caribe and Johnny's, to the cheap Louisiana Express or Il Forno. The hotel is less than half a mile from the massive National Institutes of Health complex and the Bethesda Naval Hospital. Children stay free, and there is no charge for guest parking. Amenities include a swimming pool, in-house movies, nonsmoking rooms and accommodations for the handicapped.
Singles: $80-$92; doubles: $86-$98; suites: $125-$225; weekends: $64.

Holiday Inn Chevy Chase

5520 Wisconsin Ave.,
Chevy Chase, Md. 20815
• (301) 656-1500,
(800) HOLIDAY
Fax (301) 656-5045

This is the perfect place for those who want to get away from the hurly-burly of Georgetown's upscale stores, but who still enjoy a nice, leisurely buyer's paradise where you can shop 'til you drop. Saks Fifth Avenue is across the street. Saks Jandel, Gucci, Brooks Brothers, Yves St. Laurent and others are within a few blocks, and Lord & Taylor is just a short stroll away. Then there's the enclosed shopping mall, Mazza Gallerie (dubbed "Mausoleum Galleria" by locals because of its windowless design), which features scores of stores, including a Neiman-Marcus. The hotel itself has a rather nondescript exterior, but is pleasant enough inside. And it's just a block from the Friendship Heights Metrorail station. You can eat at Tila's, right above the station, for great southwestern food. Children under 19 stay free. No charge for guest parking. Amenities include an outdoor swimming pool, in-house movies, nonsmoking rooms and accommodations for the handicapped.
Singles: $89-$95; doubles: $99-$105; suites: $149-$268; weekends: $62.

Holiday Inn of Silver Spring Plaza

8777 Georgia Ave.,
Silver Spring, Md. 20910
• (301) 589-0800,
(800) HOLIDAY
Fax (301) 587-4791

It's modern. It's fairly new. It's clean, and the concave exterior of the hotel is a little unusual, but almost everything else about it is what you've come to expect from a Holiday Inn. If you've got business in Silver Spring, the location is good. It's close to downtown and a mere five blocks from the Silver Spring Metrorail station. The hotel caters to the business traveler and offers special rates for military personnel and federal government employees, as well as for a number of corporate guests. A small shopping mall is attached to the hotel. Children under 18 stay free, and there is no charge for guest parking. Amenities include an outdoor swimming pool and tennis courts, an exercise room, babysitting service, in-house movies, pet facilities, nonsmoking rooms and a room equipped for the handicapped.

Singles: $76-$85; doubles: $79-$95; suites: $125-$130; weekend packages vary.

Hyatt Regency Bethesda

One Bethesda Metro Center, Bethesda, Md. 20814
• (301) 657-1234, (800) 228-9000
Fax (301) 657-6453

You've surely been here before. This is your carbon-copy Hyatt—the big glass-roofed atrium interior, with the glass-enclosed elevators and the lush ferns clustered in the tile-floored lobby. Architecturally, the outside is extraordinarily ordinary for a Hyatt. What this big, modern hotel has, however, is a superior suburban location. It's in the heart of the booming Bethesda office and retail district and almost sits atop the Bethesda Metrorail station, so you're literally within minutes of the best of Washington. You're also within walking distance of the House of Kao, an excellent Chinese restaurant. Don't forget your ice skates: the hotel features a winter ice rink. Children under 18 stay free. There is a $9 charge for guest parking. In addition to the ice rink, other amenities include a swimming pool, health club, in-house movies, nonsmoking rooms and accommodations for the handicapped. Call about weekend rates.

Singles: $149-$164; doubles: $174-$189; suites: $390-$490.

Quality Hotel

8727 Colesville Rd., Silver Spring, Md. 20910
• (301) 589-5200, (800) 325-3535
Fax (301) 588-1841

Formerly named the Sheraton Inn Washington NW (although a long way from the district), this hotel is located near the heart of Silver Spring, close to the rejuvenated and growing downtown shopping and business area. There's nothing beautiful about the hotel—it fronts right on the street—but once inside, it is comfortable, and regular patrons say the staff is attentive and polite. It is scheduled for a renovation to match its change of name. It's also close (less than three blocks) to the Silver Spring Metrorail station. The clients are chiefly business folk. Children under 18 stay free. Guest parking is free. Amenities include a swimming pool, health facilities, in-house movies and nonsmoking rooms.

Singles: $68; doubles: $78; suites: $100.

VIRGINIA

Best Western Old Colony Inn

625 1st St.,
Alexandria, Va. 22314
• (703) 548-6300,
(800) 528-1234
Fax (703) 548-8032

You'll have to walk about six blocks to reach the quaint row houses and clusters of shops of historic Old Town. But no matter. This is a well-situated hotel with a solid reputation, and it's expanding. In the summer of 1987, it added 110 rooms to its original 216 and began operating a new health club. But for those who want a different variety of exercise, they can get in a few laps at the domed Alexandria Roller Rink, just two blocks away. Children under 18 stay free in their parents' room. No charge for guest parking. Two miles from the National Airport Metrorail station, and National Airport. Amenities include indoor swimming pool, in-house movies, pet facilities, nonsmoking rooms, accommodations for the handicapped and limo service. *Singles: $78-$98; doubles: $88-$108; suites: $135-$165; weekend package: $152 for two nights (including a bottle of champagne and breakfast buffet).*

Crystal City Marriott

1999 Jefferson Davis Hwy.
Arlington, Va. 22202
• (703) 521-5500,
(800) 228-9200
Fax (703) 685-0191

This is a big city hotel in a semi-suburban setting. Its large meeting rooms and proximity to the Pentagon clue you in to its clientele. The lobby, full of greenery and thick carpets, is pleasant, and opens into an atrium restaurant. Outside, the setting is hardly bucolic—you're stuck between hotels and apartment buildings and busy roadways. But the location is good, a three-minute taxi ride from National Airport and just a short walk to the Crystal City Metrorail station. Children under 18 stay free. Amenities include a swimming pool, in-house movies, limo service, babysitting, nonsmoking rooms and accommodations for the handicapped. *Singles: $65-$164; doubles: $65-$184; suites: $250; weekends: from $65.*

Days Inn

2201 Arlington Blvd.,
Arlington, Va. 22201
• (703) 525-0300,
(800) 368-4400
Fax (703) 525-5671

It's déjà vu back to the era of blinking motel signs, if slightly more modern than the cottages occupied by Bonnie and Clyde. The Days Inn, formerly the Imperial Inn, is not much to look at. It is a rambling, two-story structure with a dinky outdoor pool on Route 50. Low rates are the attraction here, since it looks like a late 1950s hotel that was once the rage but has long since lost out. Children under 18 stay free. No charge for guest parking. In addition to the small swimming pool, amenities include in-house movies and a free van service to and from National Airport and the Rosslyn Metrorail station, the nearest subway stop, which is slightly more than a mile away. *Singles: $52-54; doubles: $59.*

Econo Travel Motor Hotel

3335 Lee Hwy.,
Arlington, Va. 22207
• (703) 524-9800,
(800) 446-6900
No fax

You have to climb a steep hill to get to the Econo Travel Motor Hotel, but there's nothing steep about the prices. This is pretty much a budget place, which explains the lack of amenities. As the crow flies, it's not far from downtown Washington, and it's very close to a main artery (I-66) which takes you into the city. But it is remote in the sense that there's very little of interest immediately around the hotel, save some gas stations and a few used-car lots. Children under 12 stay free, and there is no charge for guest parking. Pets are permitted (call ahead to make arrangements), and there are accommodations for the handicapped.
Singles: $46.95; doubles: $49.95.

Embassy Suites Hotel at Tysons Corner

8517 Leesburg Pike,
Vienna, Va. 22182
• (703) 883-0707,
(800) 362-2779
Fax (703) 883-0694

Located out on the heavily commercial "strip" in the Tysons Corner area, the Embassy Suites Hotel is big (232 suites) and modern. Inside, the small lobby leads into a large triangular atrium that has eight floors, each with its own wraparound balcony. The hotel has a restaurant and lounge. Public transportation is a bit of a problem. The closest Metrorail station is miles away, and although buses run by, it's a long ride into the city (about fifteen miles) and sometimes requires changing to Metrorail. It's best to rely on your own car, and the only reason for staying this far out would be business in the vicinity. Children under 16 stay free, and there is no charge for guest parking. Amenities include an indoor swimming pool, in-house movies, a sauna, Jacuzzi, nonsmoking rooms and accommodations for the handicapped. Complimentary breakfast.
Rooms: $124-$154; weekends: $79-$89.

Howard Johnson's Crystal City

2650 Jefferson Davis Hwy.,
Arlington, Va. 22202
• (703) 684-7200,
(800) 654-2000
Fax (703) 684-3217

You don't even have to enter the hotel to smell the frying burgers at Bob's Big Boy restaurant, connected to the lobby.This is, well, a Howard Johnson's—clean, predictable and in this case, unexciting. You're close to the airport, but you could do a lot better in Crystal City than this. It's at the end of a canyon of hotels, office buildings and apartment complexes, and the setting isn't great, unless you love concrete. But the rates are moderate, and those Big Boy burgers are just an elevator ride away. Children under 18 stay free when in the same room with two adults. Guest parking is free. Amenities include an outdoor swimming pool, in-house movies, nonsmoking rooms, accommodations for the handicapped and a health club.
Singles: $64-$102; doubles: $72-$110; weekends: $55-$65.

Hyatt Arlington

1325 Wilson Blvd.,
Arlington, Va. 22209
• (703) 525-1234,
(800) 228-9000
Fax (703) 875-3393

This is not a big, glitzy Hyatt, with the great atrium and the glass-enclosed elevators. The lobby is small and unexceptional. The setting is cold—you are tucked in among the concrete high-rises of Rosslyn. But you're close to Washington. Close enough, in fact, that you can walk across the Key Bridge to Georgetown, or take the metro (the Rosslyn Metrorail stop is just outside the hotel) to any of the city's sights. You can also stroll to the Iwo Jima Monument or through Arlington National Cemetery, both a short distance from the hotel. Children under 18 stay free, and there is no charge for guest parking. Amenities include in-house movies, nonsmoking rooms and accommodations for the handicapped.

Singles: $127-$149; doubles: $149-$159; suites: $185-$400; weekends: $79.

Key Bridge Marriott

1401 Lee Hwy.,
Arlington, Va. 22209
• (703) 524-6400,
(800) 228-9290
Fax (703) 524-8964

If you want easy access to the Virginia suburbs, but still want to feel as if you're visiting Washington, this hotel is the best compromise. A quick walk across the Key Bridge, and you're in Georgetown. The higher floors and "The View" rooftop restaurant looking out the front offer a spectacular view of Washington all the way up the Mall to the Capitol. If you're coming by car, this is just off I-66, a main artery into Washington. The hotel has a pleasant interior and is set off from the rather imposing and impersonal high-rise office buildings of the urban sprawl area of Rosslyn. Children under 18 stay free. No charge for guest parking. Amenities include a swimming pool, health club, babysitting, in-house movies, nonsmoking rooms and accommodations for the handicapped. Small pets are permitted in rooms.

Singles: $149; doubles: $169; suites: $195-$225; weekends: $79-$99.

Morrison House

116 S. Alfred St.,
Alexandria, Va. 22314
• (703) 838-8000,
(800) 367-0800 (out of Va.),
(800) 533-1808 (in Va.)
Fax (703) 684-6283

This is a jewel of a hotel, nestled among a mix of some very old historic row houses and a few modern, unattractive low- and midrise office and commercial buildings. It's slightly off the heavily traveled tourist routes of Old Town Alexandria, but it's just a short walk across Washington Street to the heart of the Old Town shopping district. The Morrison House itself is not especially old, but its colonial architecture and charming early American interior make you feel as if you're in a place that has been around forever. Tea is served daily in the parlor. The 47 rooms and suites have four-poster mahogany beds, brass chandeliers and sconces. Children under 12 stay free, with a $20 charge for rollaways. The guest parking costs $7.50. Nine blocks from the King Street Metrorail station. Amenities include in-house movies, babysitting and accommodations for the handicapped.

Singles & doubles: $135-$155; suites: $230-$385; weekends: $99-$139 (double), $179-$200 (suite), including parking.

Old Town Holiday Inn

480 King St.,
Alexandria, Va. 22314
• (703) 549-6080,
(800) 368-5047
Fax (703) 549-7070
ext. 7777

This isn't a typical, cookie-cutter Holiday Inn. Step inside the wood-paneled colonial lobby, settle down in a wing chair below expensive brass chandeliers, listen to the tick-tock of the antique grandfather clock, and you can catch the hint of an eighteenth-century inn. Despite its Early American decor, this particular Holiday Inn has all the modern hotel attractions, including an all-weather swimming pool. You're paying for location here. The hotel is on the main shopping drag in historic Old Town Alexandria, and it's just a short stroll down to the Potomac waterfront. Right next door is Santa Fe East, an excellent southwestern restaurant. Children under 18 stay free. There's no charge for guest parking. The nearest subway stop is a good hike—about twelve blocks to the King Street Metrorail station. But there is complimentary shuttle bus service to National Airport, located about three miles away, where you can catch the subway. Amenities include in-house movies, babysitting service, nonsmoking rooms and accommodations for the handicapped.

Singles: $99-$125; doubles: $114-$140; suites: $165-$225.

Quality Inn

6461 Edsall Rd.,
Alexandria, Va. 22312
• (703) 354-4400,
(800) 228-5151
Fax (703) 354-8359

You'll recognize the Quality Inn, formerly the Imperial 400, by the unsightly satellite dish stuck in the lawn outside its Greenhouse Restaurant. Not that you'll have any trouble finding the place: The Quality Inn is about the only hostelry in the immediate area. You get what you pay for, of course, and for the money, this is good value. The motel has recently been renovated. It caters to student and tour groups. It's a bit far from Metrorail—about five miles—but a straight shot by car up I-395 to downtown Washington. Children under 16 stay free. No charge for guest parking. Amenities include an outdoor swimming pool, free in-house movies and an indoor exercise facility. Small pets are permitted in the rooms.

Singles & doubles: $45-$78.

Radisson Mark Plaza Hotel
5000 Seminary Rd.,
Alexandria, Va. 22312
• (703) 845-1010,
(800) 228-9822
Fax (703) 820-6425

A big (500 rooms) high-rise hotel, this one has it all—health club, swimming pool, tennis courts, four racquetball courts. Even an artificial lake. Its marble lobby is airy and inviting, and the hotel, taken as a whole, is almost a self-contained, modern resort. The location is nearly four miles from the nearest Metrorail station, but limo service is available, and the hotel is large enough that taxis are usually waiting outside. Children under 18 stay free. There is a charge for guest parking. Other amenities include a babysitting service, in-house movies, nonsmoking rooms and accommodations for the handicapped. Small pets are permitted.

Singles: $119-$149; doubles: $139-$169; suites: $269-$488; weekends: $72.

Rosslyn Westpark Hotel
1900 N. Fort Myer Dr.,
Arlington, Va. 22209
• (703) 527-4814,
(800) 368-3408
Fax (703) 522-3653

The Westpark is short on personality. But then, it's located across the Potomac River from D.C. in Rosslyn, a steel-and-glass office-building jungle that has no personality, either. The Westpark's lobby is small and uninviting. But the hotel's location is great. It is just one block from the Rosslyn Metrorail station (the escalator to the subway is one of the longest in the world), and you can also walk across Key Bridge into Georgetown. Many of the rooms look out on the Potomac and over to Northwest Washington. The hotel also has a rooftop restaurant with a nice view. Children under 18 stay free. No charge for guest parking. Amenities include a swimming pool, health club, in-house movies, pet facilities and accommodations for the handicapped.

Singles & doubles: $95-$97; suites: $107-$150; weekends: $65.

Sheraton Crystal City Hotel
1800 Jefferson Davis Hwy.,
Arlington, Va. 22202
• (703) 486-1111,
(800) 325-3535
Fax (703) 979-3556

A rather unexciting hotel, but a good value for the money. It's midway between National Airport and the Pentagon, which are both just short taxi rides away. The hotel caters to meetings and conferences—it offers nine meeting rooms and a grand ballroom that accommodates nearly 900 people. A pleasant atrium lounge overlooks a rather uninspiring roadway. Children stay free, and there is a $3-per-night charge for guest parking. Amenities include a swimming pool, health club, in-house movies, accommodations for the handicapped and limo service.

Singles: $95-$150; doubles: $113-165; suites: $250-$650; weekends: $79 (including breakfast buffet).

Sheraton Tysons Corner Hotel

8661 Leesburg Pike,
Vienna, Va. 22182
• (703) 448-1234,
(800) 325-3535
Fax (703) 893-8193

This hotel is located in the booming Tysons Corner area, which is one of several "satellite" cities that are springing up in Greater Washington. It is one of the best hotels in northern Virginia, and, with 455 rooms, it may also be the largest. The hotel caters to almost every type of clientele. It has 25 meeting rooms for business conferences, a trendy nightclub and health and recreational facilities that include indoor and outdoor lap pools, a jogging trail, three racquet-ball courts and a sauna. The closest Metrorail stop is four miles away at the Dunn Loring station, so you'll have to rely on ground transport. There is a complimentary shuttle bus to and from Dulles Airport, which is fifteen minutes away. Children under 17 stay free, and there is no charge for guest parking. Other amenities include nonsmoking rooms, cable and pay television, and accommodations for the handicapped.

Singles: $98-$150; doubles: $113-$165; suites: $250-$650; weekends: $79 (including breakfast buffet).

Stouffer Concourse Hotel at Washington National Airport

2399 Jefferson Davis Hwy.,
Arlington, Va. 22202
• (703) 979-6800,
(800) HOTELS-1
Fax (703) 486-2014

The hotel is adjacent to National Airport, and if you're traveling light, you can literally pick up your bags and walk to your flight. There's not much charm to the exterior of the hotel. It's set in a canyon of concrete office and residential structures and overlooks busy Jefferson Davis Highway. But it is a comfortable place. The wood-paneled lobby is inviting. Across the road is the Crystal City Comedy Club, in case you need a shot of humor, and there are movie theaters within easy walking distance. The Crystal City Metrorail station is three blocks away, as is the Crystal City Underground Shopping Mall. Children under 18 stay free. No charge for guest parking. Amenities include a swimming pool, health club, babysitting, in-house movies, nonsmoking rooms, accommodations for the handicapped and limo service.

Singles: $154-$204; doubles: $174-$224; suites: $350; weekends: $85-$105.

NIGHTLIFE

INTRODUCTION

AFTER DARK: WASHINGTON'S NIGHTLIFE

For skeptics, the phrase "Washington nightlife" is an oxymoron, along the lines of "business ethics" or "military intelligence." There is plenty of evidence to support the conclusion that the nation's capital will never be more than a weekend town, that the city is full of workaholics who spend their weeknights resting up for another twelve-hour day at the office and their weekends in the sunshine to reduce the pallor known locally as a "Capitol Hill tan." But optimistic observers believe—with some basis—that Washington finally is on its way to becoming a sophisticated world capital, a place of excitement, variety and dance floors that never empty. The truth, as usual, lies somewhere in between. During the week, many bars and theaters do lack for customers, thanks partly to a regional work ethic that places a premium on getting in early and getting out late, and partly because Washington likes to entertain at home. Yet today's Washington is definitely a much livelier place than the city of a decade ago. An assortment of comedy clubs, offbeat theaters, dance spots, jazz havens and sleek saloons has sprung up, creating the big-city excitement that the District needed. Washington now has a pair of nightlife hubs.

Georgetown, with its ever-changing collection of bars and restaurants, has long been a favored party zone, and once had no equal. Particularly on weekends, its sidewalks are jammed with young sophisticates and college kids doing the M Street rounds. But now there's a serious challenge to Georgetown's status as *the* nighttime locale, thanks to the revivification of Adams Morgan, an old-time neighborhood in the vicinity of 18th Street and Columbia Road NW. Easily Washington's most diverse section, Adams Morgan has a lively street scene and a multinational flavor, buttressed by Latino restaurants, Ethiopian eateries and Euro-disco dance clubs, along with all the interesting shops and bars that have taken root in a neighborhood whose history extends back more than 90 years.

Another favorite with people of the night is Dupont Circle, from the crowded gay bars of P Street to the strategically placed sidewalk cafés of Connecticut Avenue. Capitol Hill has two nightlife enclaves: the neighborhood bars along Pennsylvania Avenue and the tonier, but still casual, restaurants on Massachusetts Avenue, not far from Union Station. And at midtown, where the area north of Pennsylvania Avenue between 5th and 13th streets has been marked for wholesale demolition and recon-struction, instant nighteries are popping up in curious settings, such as retired bank vaults and aged office buildings, with life expectancies no longer than the month-to-month leases that their owners hold. Until the hammer comes down, however, the

Give an extra special scotch to someone who deserves it.
You.

EXTRA **12** SPECIAL

Johnnie Walker
BLACK LABEL

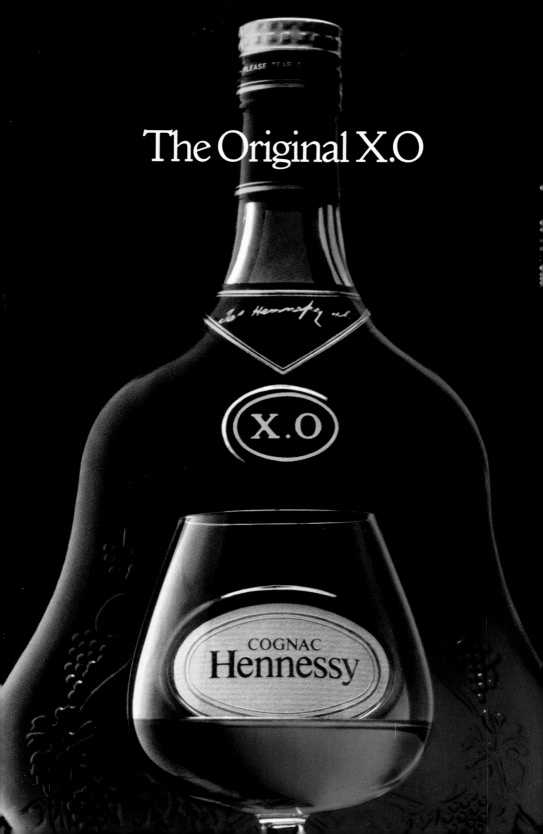

different scenes thereabouts are among the most invigorating that Washington has to offer. Keep in mind that a nightspot is not a museum; by the time you read these pages, some of their contents may be yesterday's news. To be safe, call ahead.

BARS

The Brickskeller
1523 22nd St. NW
• 293-1885

This is a beer-drinker's paradise, stocking more than 500 brands of American and imported brews. If they don't have your hometown beer, you don't have a hometown. The subterranean pub is conducive to long drinking fests; should the elbow-bending make you hungry, order a bison burger or the spicy chicken wings, two of the house specialties. Other popular pastimes here are darts (a game that, after a few beers, anyone thinks can be mastered) and studying, with proper reverence, the huge antique beer can collection.
Open Mon.-Fri. 11:30 a.m.-2 a.m., Sat. 6 p.m.-3 a.m., Sun. 6 p.m.-2 a.m. All major cards.

Bullfeathers
410 1st St. SE
• 543-5005

A posh public house in the shadow of the Capitol, Bullfeathers is the place where lobbyists run up tabs fine-tuning the art of liquid persuasion. This is where many congressional staffers—the Hill's true muscle—stop to gossip, drop names or follow up on meaningful eye contact made in the halls of Congress. When Congress is in session, the long bar usually is packed, as is the adjoining restaurant, which serves above-average bar food. Don't expect normal bar conversation—one of the Hill's folkways demands that staffers refer to their bosses as "members," which means that a conversation can include sentences along the lines of, "My member's real tired this week," uttered with a perfectly straight face. Recent scandals involving current and former members and their amorous and imbibing habits don't seem to have hurt business much.
Open Mon.-Fri. 11:30 a.m.-2 a.m., Sat. 11:30 a.m.-3 a.m., Sun. 10:30 a.m.-midnight. All major cards.

Champions
1206 Wisconsin Ave. NW
• 965-4005

An honest-to-God shrine to athletic competition, Champions boasts soiled shirts and signed photos of sports stars on its walls; $15,000 worth of football and baseball cards embedded in the surface of the downstairs bar; and the city's top baseball trivia wizard, the portly Baseball Bill, who

holds forth from behind the upstairs bar. You can, on occasion, see real jocks hanging out here, but, mainly, this is a place to congregate with like-minded fans and scream at the big screens on both floors. When there's no major sporting event, Champions becomes a Georgetown singles bar, where as many women as men circulate among the boxing gloves and hockey pucks. One sign of this bar's success: plans are underway to replicate it in other cities, under the auspices of a major hotel chain.
Open Mon.-Thurs. 5 p.m.-2 a.m., Fri. 5 p.m.-3 a.m., Sat.-Sun. noon-3 a.m. All major cards.

Childe Harold
1610 20th St. NW
• 483-6700

A Dupont Circle institution that hasn't fallen prey to the notion that what a good bar needs these days is a lot of sunshine, Childe Harold is dark and down-to-earth, which is why it remains a favorite hangout in a neighborhood heavy with designer cookie shops and ice-cream boutiques. The upstairs restaurant is, for the most part, uninspired. But the downstairs saloon is the real thing, from dark wood tables tucked into various nooks to an eclectic jukebox. There are few other venues where a listener can choose between tunes by Jimi Hendrix and Patsy Cline.
Open Mon.-Sat. 11:30 a.m.-2 a.m., Sun. 10:30 a.m.-1 a.m. All major cards.

Clyde's Georgetown
3236 M St. NW
• 333-0294

Once the ultimate Georgetown singles bar, Clyde's spawned the ferns-and-fans look. But in some ways, Clyde's is a victim of its own success. Critics say it attracts too many tourists and that too many of its diners and drinkers probably had lunch at the Air and Space Museum cafeteria. Some of its luster may have faded, but Clyde's remains a classic upscale watering hole, with a first-rate bar menu and an atrium dining room with abundant plant life. Another feature is the Omelet Room, where locals invariably take out-of-town guests for Sunday brunch.
Open Mon.-Thurs. 7:30 a.m.-2 a.m., Fri. 7:30 a.m.-3 a.m., Sat. 10 a.m.-3 a.m., Sun. 9 a.m.-2 a.m. All major cards.

Hawk and Dove
329 Pennsylvania Ave. SE
• 543-3300

A sometimes rowdy, but always comfortable, saloon whose habitués tend to be less uptight than at most Capitol Hill bars. Maybe it's the lively jukebox, maybe it's the coterie of diehard sports fans. Whatever the reason, the Hawk, with its three bars, remains a place where usually cautious Hill denizens can drop their guards.
Open Sun.-Thurs. 10 a.m.-2 a.m., Fri.-Sat. 10 a.m.-3 a.m All major cards..

J. R.'s Bar & Grill
1519 17th St. NW
• 328-0091

A Dupont Circle–area bar with a Texas-style menu, J. R.'s has a largely gay clientele. The big draw is the giant video screen, on which you can watch Liza Minelli one night and television clips another. Dance music, of course, is played during the commercials.
Open Sun.-Thurs. 11 a.m.-2 a.m., Fri.-Sat. 11 a.m.-3 a.m. Cards: AE, MC, V.

J. Paul's
3218 M St. NW
• 333-3450

A high-ceilinged, handsome Georgetown pub, J. Paul's is ideal for gazing and grazing. Behind the raw-seafood (shrimp-and-oyster) bar is an open room, with an earnest young crowd that's particularly dense on weekends. If you prefer to watch the action out front, the best vantage point is the casually chic dining room elevated above the fray. The fare, which is of the burger, steak and seafood persuasion, is above average, and on weekends it's served until 2 a.m. In short, J. Paul's is a big American bar for people with small foreign cars.
Open Mon.-Thurs. 11:30 a.m.-1:30 a.m., Fri.-Sat. 11:30 a.m.-3 a.m., Sun. 10:30 a.m.-1:30 a.m. All major cards.

Kramerbooks & Afterwords
1517 Connecticut Ave. NW
• 387-1462

Every *real* city has a late-night bookstore and browsing spot, and this is Washington's. Located a cobblestone's throw north of Dupont Circle, it has become a gathering spot for bibliophiles, artists and gays, who come not only to peruse the latest titles, but also to hang out at Afterwords Café. There, they sip wine or coffee or sample salads and desserts as they swap opinions on literature, the arts and neighborhood gossip. On weekends, folk musicians usually provide accompaniment.
Open Mon.-Thurs. 7:30 a.m.-1 a.m., Fri. 8 a.m.-midnight, Sat. noon-midnight, Sun. noon-1 a.m. Cards: AE, MC, V.

Millie & Al's
2440 18th St. NW
• 387-8131

This neighborhood Adams Morgan dive hasn't given up its soul in the face of success. Large groups of young, upwardly mobile types gather here to spill beer, wolf pizzas and generally act as if they're celebrating the end of finals week. The place has a lived-in look, with tattered booths, battered tables and bar decorations dating to the days when you could drink on a handful of change. Don't let the fact that one or both of the TVs is on discourage you from using the wide-ranging jukebox. Millie & Al's is a mixed-media kind of place.
Open Mon.-Thurs. 4 p.m.-2 a.m., Fri.-Sat. noon-3 a.m., Sun. 1 p.m.-2 a.m. No cards.

Nathan's

3150 M St. NW
• 338-2000

It has a great location at Georgetown's main intersection and a respected Italian kitchen, but it's the understated atmosphere of the front bar that has made Nathan's a favorite of Georgetown pub crawlers. With an impressive selection of champagnes, it draws a slightly older, more sophisticated crowd than most M Street bars. The background music, much of it Motown, isn't loud enough to interfere with conversation. And while some people are clearly there to be seen, Nathan's also has quiet niches for those moments that call for discretion, if not solitude.
Open Mon.-Thurs. 11 a.m.-2 a.m., Fri. 11 a.m.-3 p.m., Sat. 9 a.m.-3 a.m., Sun. 9 a.m.-2 a.m. All major cards.

Old Ebbitt Grill

675 15th St. NW
• 347-4800

A few years ago, the same trendsetters who opened Clyde's spent $5 million to open a high-style, downtown saloon for fern-bar refugees. The result is the Old Ebbitt, a striking place with a massive mahogany bar; enough tastefully appointed tables to seat the residents of an entire zip code; suitably chic gas sconces; wine by the glass; fresh salmon daily; and a raw-seafood bar. The menu runs the gamut of pasta dishes and nouvelle grills, but many regulars swear by the burgers. A short walk from both the White House and the National Theater, it draws many patrons with an interest in actors.
Open Sun.-Thurs. 7:30 a.m.-2 a.m., Fri.-Sat. 11 a.m.-3 a.m. All major cards.

Paper Moon

1073 31st St. NW
• 965-6666

Ostensibly a Georgetown pizza-and-pasta restaurant, Paper Moon is, in fact, more like a fashion show with food. The neon and pastel decor, high-energy soundtrack and strategically placed spotlights—each table has its own—create a rare Washington blend of high style and informality. The clients are some of the city's hippest dressers, who either parade around the front bar or lounge through long meals at the marble tables. Don't worry about missing the passing parade or being missed—the terrace layout means that no matter where you sit, you can see everyone and everyone can see you.
Open Sun.-Thurs. 5:30 p.m.-midnight, Fri.-Sat. 5:30 p.m.-3:00 a.m. Cards: AE, MC, V.

Au Pied de Cochon

1335 Wisconsin Ave. NW
• 333-5440

More a French bistro than a bar, this restaurant's reputation is based on two essential facts: being one of the few places in town open all night (the only break is the wee hours on Monday), and being the spot where, a few years ago, a Russian defector walked away from his FBI protector and strolled up the hill to the Soviet Embassy, where he begged

forgiveness. This incident inspired the barman to invent the "Yurchenko Shooter," celebrated on a sign over the door. But don't go looking for international intrigue. More than anything, the Pied is a casual escape from the Georgetown street scene and a swell site to sit over an after-hours omelet; a bowl of bean soup; a mug of coffee; or a delectable order of pigs' feet.
Open daily 24 hours. All major cards.

Quigley's Jenkins Hill
223 Pennsylvania Ave. SE
• 544-6600

It has all the elements of the archetypal Baby Boomer saloon: hardwood floors, ceiling fans, Tiffany shades. But despite the trendy trappings, this boîte feels like a corner bar. The lunch crowd tends toward government types talking shop, but at night the bar is a gathering place for those who make this fashionable neighborhood their home. As always, the mating game is played here, but without the mad abandon characteristic of some hard-core singles bars. The pace picks up considerably on Saturday nights, when Motown devotees gather to dance to the songs that moved the *Big Chill* generation.
Open Sun.-Thurs. 9:30 a.m.-2 a.m., Fri.-Sat. 10:30 a.m.-3 a.m. All major cards.

Rumors
1900 M St. NW
• 466-7378

A perennial front-runner in the singles-bar derby, Rumors is a tribute to the popular theory that given a sufficient supply of alcohol, a dance floor and good sightlines, anything is possible among consenting adults. It's a favorite downtown oasis for the young and the restless. On weekends, except in the dead of winter, there's a line outside. Once inside, clients go looking for love in all the right places—the tables in the open front room, the two bars and, of course, the small dance floor.
Open Sun.-Thurs. 11 a.m.-2 a.m., Fri.-Sat. 11:30 a.m.-3 a.m. All major cards.

Sign of the Whale
1825 M St. NW
• 223-0608

By day a saloon known for its seafood and burgers, the Sign of the Whale by night is a bar known for its mating rituals. The long bar can get pretty crowded, but the patrons, most of them thirtysomething professionals, don't seem to mind at all. Prerecorded tapes provide background music that's loud enough to allow you to avoid the come-ons of a troglodyte, but soft enough to engage in verbal foreplay with someone who fills the night with possibilities.
Open Mon.-Thurs. 11:30 a.m.-1:30 a.m., Fri.-Sat.11 a.m.-2:30 p.m., Sun. 11 a.m.-2:30 a.m. All major cards.

145

The Sky Terrace

Hotel Washington,
15th St. & Pennsylvania
Ave. NW
• 347-4499

Building restrictions render rooms with views scarce in the heart of Washington. That explains the appeal of the Sky Terrace atop the Hotel Washington, a favorite place to savor the charm of Washington in late spring, early fall and even during the dog days of summer. From a seat on the covered balcony, you can watch jets approaching or leaving National Airport and, if the timing's right, presidential helicopters setting down or lifting off at the White House. It's no World Trade Center, but it's one of the few places in town where you can get both a cold drink and the Big Picture.
Open daily (May-Oct. only) 11 a.m.-1 a.m. All major cards.

Stetson's

1610 U St. NW
• 667-6295

A casual, friendly, fernless place that has character and characters in plentiful supply, Stetson's also has Mexican food and Texan hospitality. One key to Stetson's engaging personality is its jukebox, whose offerings range from Lou Reed's "Walk On The Wild Side" to Kate Smith's "God Bless America."
Open Mon.-Tues. 11 a.m.-2 a.m., Fri. 11 a.m.-3 a.m., Sat. 4 p.m.-3 a.m., Sun. 4 p.m.-2 a.m. Cards: AE, MC, V.

Third Edition

1218 Wisconsin Ave. NW
• 333-3700

This Georgetown establishment has survived for years with a semi-split personality. The downstairs bar, with its dark wood and leather, draws an older, more subdued crowd whose conversation is as likely as not to revolve around stock options. Upstairs is the domain of the college crowd, whose members are more likely to be talking dating options. On weekends, a deejay plays records and Third Edition is transformed into one big fraternity party.
Open Sun.-Thurs. 11:30 a.m.-2 a.m., Fri.-Sat. 11:30 a.m.-3 a.m. All major cards.

The Tune Inn

331 1/2 Pennsylvania Ave.
SE
• 543-2725

The Tune Inn was once a hard-edged Capitol Hill saloon where the fights were frequent, the beer s cheap and stock car races the favorite TV fare. Then it was discovered by Hillsters, drawn by low prices and the chance to loosen their ties. Today the Tune Inn is an after-work tonic for the troops who patrol the halls of Congress. You're more likely to hear talk of Euro-dollars than cam shafts, but the waitresses are as surly as ever, and Hank Williams is still on the jukebox. A great place for a greasy weekend breakfast.
Open Sun.-Thurs. 8 a.m.-2 a.m., Fri.-Sat. 8 a.m.-3 a.m. No cards.

COMEDY CLUBS

Comedy Café
1520 K St. NW
• 638-5653

More than one comic has died in front of the brick wall here, but often they're the life of the party. The café brings in promising standups from New York and Los Angeles, mixes them with local comedians, and the result is a barrage of one-liners aimed at anything and everything. If you're feeling especially masochistic, go early and take a table beside the stage; with luck, the comics may leave you a shred of dignity. Reservations are a must, except on Thursdays, when anyone with a sense of humor and advanced neurosis can go onstage and try to squeeze laughs out of strangers. *Open Thurs. 8 p.m.-11 p.m., Fri. 8 p.m.-12:30 p.m., Sat. 7 p.m.-1:30 p.m. Shows Fri. 8:30 p.m. & 10:30 p.m., Sat. 7:30 p.m., 9:30 p.m. & 11:30 p.m. Cover $3.49-8.49. All major cards.*

Garvin's Comedy Club
1335 L St. NW
• 726-1334

During the evening, it's an expense-account restaurant; at night, it's a singles bar with substantial drinks. But on weekends, the tables are turned, and a cavalcade of New York and local comics climbs up on the tiny stage and opens fire, usually with deadly and humorous accuracy. *Open Tues..-Fri. 5 p.m.-2 a.m., Sat. 6 p.m.-2 a.m. Shows Fri. 8:30 p.m. & 10:30 p.m., Sat. 7:30 p.m., 9:30 p.m. & 11:30 p.m. Cover $10. Cards: AE, MC, V.*

DANCING/NIGHTCLUBS

Badlands
1415 22nd St. NW
• 296-0505

Badlands is a gay dance club with staying power, partly because it's strategically located in the gay stronghold of the Dupont Circle area, and partly because it has never failed to appreciate the power of a relentless beat. A deejay spins tunes from 9 on, but the fun starts around midnight. *Open Tues. &Thurs.-Sun. 9 p.m.-2 a.m., Fri.-Sat. 9 p.m.-3 a.m., Sun. 9 p.m.-2 a.m. Cover $5 weekends, $2 weeknights. No cards.*

Cagney's

1 Dupont Circle NW
• 659-8820

A British-flavored club just off Dupont Circle, Cagney's boasts the steady pulse of new music, which draws a good share of punkers, although most are weekend warriors rather than hard-core skinheads. Basic black is the color of choice.
Open daily 4:30 p.m.-2 a.m. Cover $3 weeknights, $8 after 10 p.m. on weekends. Cards: AE, MC, V.

Chelsea's

1055 Thomas Jefferson St. NW
• 298-8222

If Latin rhythms drive you insane, take a straitjacket with you to this Georgetown club, which doubles as an Italian restaurant during the day. Deejays provide the beat on Tuesdays and Wednesdays, but the rest of the week local Latin bands take over, and on weekends the dance floor is a shrine to salsa.
Open Tues.-Thurs. & Sun. 10 p.m.-2 a.m., Fri.-Sat. 10 p.m.-4:30 a.m. Cover $5 Thurs., $10 Fri., $12 Sat.

Christini's

1140 Connecticut Ave. NW
• 296-9500

Like Chelsea's, this is a part-time party place for salseros, located in a downtown district that's usually deserted after dark. However, the subterranean location—beneath the sidewalks of Connecticut Avenue—belies a softly lit, elegant room that soothes spirits charged up by the insistent beat, and lets the dancer return to the floor with renewed enthusiasm. If you want to fuel up beforehand, Christini's offers a northern Italian menu until 9:30 p.m.
Open Tues.-Sat. 5 p.m.-3 a.m. Cover $10 Fri.-Sat. All major cards.

Cities

2424 18th St. NW
• 328-7194

Cities is a multilevel exercise in postindustrial chic set in the poured-concrete confines of a former Chevrolet dealership. The street-level bar features glass-front garage doors raised in all but the least clement weather, guaranteeing a steady stream of gawkers and gazers along Adams Morgan's main drag. The restaurant at the back of the first floor changes its menu in line with whichever city is being featured, and the fixed-price special generally is a fine buy. Upstairs, the dance floor attracts punkers, posers and various fashion victims (like an inventive young woman who appeared one night in a T-shirt dress that seemed excessively demure—until she turned around to reveal that the back had been scissored from the nape of her blonde neckline to her ischial dimples). On Wednesdays and Thursdays, Cities hosts live bands playing world-beat riffs, but every night is a show.
Open Thurs.-Sat. 9:30 p.m.-2 a.m. Cover $5 Thurs., $8 Fri.-Sat. All major cards.

Club Soda
3433 Connecticut Ave. NW
• 244-3189 (message)
244-4084

A nostalgia bar based on the premise that life was better when Motown ruled the world and the Beatles were lovable waifs who made Ed Sullivan nervous, Club Soda has two rooms. One features mainly '50s and '60s hits, but this venerable space also sometimes hosts local fretburner Danny Gatton, whose "redneck jazz" guitar stylings have earned him a national reputation. Deejays rule one room seven nights a week; the other is the turf of local bands Wednesday through Saturday. This is a place where you can twist with impunity and act the way you did in premortgage days.
Open Sun.-Thurs. 4:30 p.m.-2 a.m., Fri.-Sat. 4:30 p.m.-3 a.m. Cover $3 weekends, $10 for specials. Cards: MC, V.

Dakota
1777 Columbia Road NW
• 265-6600

This is the reigning palace of pulse in Adams Morgan, where disco never quite died. Designed within an inch of its life, Dakota is like certain mixed drinks: best experienced late and in the company of serious revelers. The crowd tends toward weekend hipsters and the rather young, but the food in the restaurant is fresh, well-presented and fairly priced, and the music never stops.
Open Tues.-Thurs. & Sun. 6:30 p.m.-2 a.m., Fri.-Sat. 6:30 p.m.-3 a.m. Cover $7 Fri.-Sat. after 9 p.m.

Déjà Vu
2119 M St. NW
• 452-1966

A huge, consciously unfashionable dance club between Georgetown and downtown, Déjà Vu makes up in enthusiasm what it lacks in hipness. You can frug here. You can shag here. You can even jitterbug on Thursday nights—and at midnight, they slow things down with a wet T-shirt contest. The music is pop hits, with an emphasis on oldies, and if you feel you haven't enough room to let your backbone slip, move to one of the many dance floors spread throughout the place. In some ways, it's like a teen club dance with booze; the dress code bans tennis shoes or collarless shirts, no matter how old their wearers might be.
Open Sun.-Thurs. 8 p.m.-1:30 a.m., Fri. 8 p.m.-2:30 a.m., Sat. 8 p.m.-3 a.m. No cover. All major cards.

East Side
1824 Half St. SW
• 488-1205 (message)
488-1206

A warehouse-district gay disco, East Side has had a facelift and personality transplant and is trying to make it as a slick rock-and-new-wave dance club. That's the East Side story. Judging from the crowds that gather on the video dance floor downstairs or the rock lounge upstairs—which features up-and-coming rock bands—it's headed for a happy ending.
Open Thurs.-Sat. 10 p.m.-5 a.m. Cover $7. No cards.

Fifth Column

915 F St. NW
• 393-3632

A meld of art bar and danceteria that's set in the sobering reality of a former bank, the Fifth Column used to be called "The Bank." But that was then; this is now, and what's happening now is art, which is only business conducted by other means. You can still smell the money, and the artwork's not half bad, but the real reason to pass through is to hear the volume pumped up amid granite and marble. Weekends, get in before 11 p.m. or risk wasting prime dance time standing in line.

Open Tues.-Wed. & Sun. 10 p.m.-2 a.m., Thurs. 9 p.m.-2 a.m., Fri-Sat. 9 p.m.-3 a.m. Cover $3 Tues., $5 Wed.-Thurs. & Sun., $7 Fri.-Sat.

Ibex

5832 Georgia Ave. NW
• 726-1800

Ibex is a big uptown club, crowned by a third-floor disco that features the latest inner-city dance hits. If you need a break from the fast action, you can chill in the first floor lounge, where national and local jazz acts express themselves, or in the Marvin Gaye Room, where rising black comedians hold forth on life in the big city.

Open Thurs. 9 p.m.-2 a.m., Fri.-Sat. 9 p.m.-3 a.m. Cover $6 Thurs., $7 Fri., $8 Sat.

Kilimanjaro

1724 California Ave. NW
• 328-3838 (message),
328-3839

Washington considers itself an international city, but this sprawling club in the melting pot of Adams Morgan is the only place where you can regularly hear first-rate African and Caribbean music, from reggae to soukous. During the week, there's dancing to recorded Third World hits; on weekends, bands take over, including top acts from Africa.

Open Mon.-Thurs. 5 p.m.-2 a.m., Fri. 5 p.m.-4 a.m., Sat. 6 p.m.-4 a.m., Sun. 6 p.m.-2 a.m. Cover $3-$8. Cards: MC, V.

The River Club

3223 K St. NW
• 333-8118

The River Club is a sleek joint where the buttoned-up come to get down, at least as far as they're capable. The best way to experience The River Club is late on a Saturday night, men in black tie (or, at the minimum, the required collared shirt and sports jacket), women in strapless taffeta. Muster the attitude necessary to sweep past the pathetic creatures huddled at the door; nod at the doorman; and step inside to survey a roomful of gray suits and power dresses, serene in the knowledge that you could leave it all behind in a moment if you wanted to. But you don't want to.

Open Mon.-Thurs. 6 p.m.-2 a.m., Fri.-Sat. 6 p.m.-2:30 a.m. No cover. All major cards.

Tracks

1111 1st St. SE
• 488-3320

A warehouse-district gay club that also draws a large straight crowd, with its large, lively dance floor and separate video dance room, Tracks 's clientele is the antithesis of the straitlaced Washington stereotype. The music is usually high-energy disco, but on Wednesdays, it slows down to rhythm and blues. Something different always seems to be going on here, whether it's the flashy fashion shows or the all-night volleyball games on the outdoor court during the summer.

Open Mon.-Fri. 8 p.m.-4 a.m., Sat. 9 p.m.-6 a.m., Sun. 2 p.m.-2 a.m. Cover $5 Fri.-Sat. No cards.

Winston's

3295 M St. NW
• 333-3150 (message)
333-3151

A long-time fixture on the M Street strip, Winston's nonetheless displays modernist tendencies. Most evenings, the fare is beer and boogie, but on Wednesdays, the floating "Club Random" beams down to transform the room into a progressive dance-pop scene.

Open Sun.-Thurs. 8 p.m.-2 a.m., Fri.-Sat. 8 p.m.-3 a.m. Cover varies. All major cards.

JAZZ

Anton's 1201

1201 Pennsylvania Ave. NW
• 783-1201

A 250-seat attempt at supper-club suavity, Anton's succeeds in spite of its proximity to the seat of power, or possibly because of it. Acts such as Bobby Short show up at the top end of the scale, but even at the bottom end, we're talking class, and plenty of it. Elegance you can afford, provided you don't try to afford it too often.

Open Tues.-Sun. 6 p.m.-closing varies. Shows Tues.-Thurs. & Sun. 8:30 p.m., Fri.-Sat. 8:30 p.m. & 10:45 p.m. Cover $19.50-$26.50 All major cards.

Blues Alley

1069 Wisconsin Ave. NW
(rear)
• 337-4141

So much a local institution, Blues Alley has a real alley named after it, and Japanese investors are planning to clone it all over Dai Nippon. And why not? The club's attributes are many: a steady parade of big-name jazz acts—Wynton Marsalis, Dizzy Gillespie, Mel Torme, Stan Getz, McCoy Tyner, Ramsey Lewis, to name but a few: first-rate acoustics, and no truly bad seats. In fact, some seats are so good, the management may get carried away and try to pack several people into them. If you want a good table, make a dinner reservation; the food, with the exception of some of the Creole specialties, isn't memorable, but it's better than usual jazz-club fare. Drawback: on crowded nights, the management clears the room after every show, so if you want to hear it one more time, you'll have to pay again. *Open nightly 6 p.m.-closing varies. Shows nightly 8 p.m. & 10 p.m., (occasional midnight shows Fri.-Sat.) Cover $7-$40 (plus $5 minimum). All major cards.*

Colonel Brooks' Tavern
901 Monroe St. NE
• 529-4002

A friendly saloon near Catholic University, where restaurants are hard to find, on Tuesdays the Tavern turns into a Dixieland bandstand. The Federal Jazz Commission and the Pontchartrain Causeway Jazz Band alternate. *Open Mon.-Thurs. 11:30 a.m.-2 a.m., Fri.-Sat. 11:30 a.m.-3 a.m., Sun. 11 a.m.-2 a.m. No cover. Cards: MC, V.*

Hazel's
1834 Columbia Rd. NW
• 462-0415

Hazel's is an Adams Morgan restaurant best known for the southern recipes of owner Hazel Williams; but on weekends the tiny upstairs lounge is a good place to slide into one of the sultry moods summoned only by jazz at midnight. If you're eating light, the homemade chicken-noodle soup is a sure hit. So are the Buffalo chicken wings. *Open Tues.-Sun. 4 p.m.-2 a.m. Two-drink minimum Tues.-Thurs. & Sun. Cover $4 (plus two-drink minimum) Fri.-Sat. All major cards.*

One Step Down
2517 Pennsylvania Ave. NW
• 331-8863

It's cramped and it's smoky; the menu is basic; and you can hear Charlie Parker on the juke box. What more do you need to know? There's nothing slick about this bar at the edge of Georgetown; it's a tiny, unassuming club, straight out of a time capsule. Weekends usually feature New York trios and quartets; weeknights, it's top local musicians, including bassist Steve Novosel, pianist Reuben Brown and vibraphonist Lennie Cuje. Go early; they don't take reservations. *Open Mon.-Thurs. 10 a.m.-2 a.m., Fri.-Sun. noon-3 a.m. Cover $5 -$12.50 (plus two-drink minimum). All major cards.*

Philly's Finest
1601 Rhode Island Ave. NE
• 635-7790

Once known as Mr. Y's, this tavern keeps alive some of its predecessor's traditions, such as the late-Saturday-to-early-Sunday breakfast jam. No limp fusion music here; the jazz is straight-ahead, the way the crowd likes it. The roster mixes national acts, such as Houston Person and Etta Jones, and local notables such as longtime Washington singer Mary Jefferson. *Open Tues.-Thurs. 11:30 a.m.-midnight, Fri. 11:30 a.m.-2 a.m., Sat. 1:30 p.m.-2 a.m. Cover varies. No cards.*

219 Basin Street Lounge

219 King St.,
Alexandria, Va.
• (703) 549-1141

The Lounge is a real bargain for lovers of traditional jazz, in light of the downstairs restaurant's upscale prices. It's only fitting that the musicians seem to have so much fun; the room, with its heavy drapes, dark floral wallpaper and long bar, feels like one big, happy bordello.
Open Mon.-Thurs. 11:30 a.m.-1:30 a.m., Fri.-Sat. 11:30 a.m.-3 a.m. Sun. 10 a.m.-midnight. Music nightly. Cover $3 weeknights, $5 weekends. All major cards.

MUSIC

BBQ Iguana

1413 P St. NW
• 310-1409

A northern outpost of the midtown boho empire, the "Ig" serves, besides massive amounts of beer and attitude, local bands performing original material, touring up-and-comers from the provinces, and cusp-of-a-contract outfits from more established scenes such as Athens, Georgia and points south.
Open Thurs.-Sun. 9 p.m.-2 a.m. Showtimes vary. Cover $5 weeknights, $6 weekends.

The Bayou

3135 K St. NW
• 333-2897

A Washington institution, The Bayou is, like many of its ilk, overrated. It started out as a Dixieland jazz club 50 years ago and was even a gangster hangout for a time before embracing rock and roll in the '60s. It became the place to see acts on the way up. Hall and Oates, Billy Joel, Foreigner and Dire Straits are among the aces who played the room in their salad days. Today, you can hear straightforward rock and roll or new wave or blues from touring bands. But stay on the good side of the roving gangs of bouncers, who have a reputation for acting first and asking questions later. More a concert hall than a bar, the place can fit about 450 people. The high ceiling and sloping stage create first-rate acoustics. Most live acts appear during the week; on weekends, The Bayou becomes a rock-and-roll dance club. If you work up an appetite, basic bar food is available.
Open Sun.-Thurs. 8 p.m.-2 a.m., Fri.-Sat. 8 p.m.-3 a.m. Showtimes vary. Cover $2-$18.

The Birchmere

3901 Mt. Vernon Ave.,
Alexandria, Va.
• (703) 549-5919

A home for hearts that ache in the presence of bluegrass, the Birchmere is one of the best acoustic music clubs in the country. Steeped in bluegrass and "newgrass," it's also a place to see folksingers on the comeback trail—people like Tom Paxton, Tom Rush, Jesse Winchester and Arlo

Guthrie. This casual, unassuming club has a welcome no-talking policy during sets. Shows start at 9 p.m., but get there early; the club takes no reservations. The food is basic and mediocre at best.

Open Tues.-Sat. 7 p.m.-1 a.m. Shows Tues.-Sat. 9 p.m. Cover $10-$20. Cards: MC, V.

Café Lautrec
2431 18th St. NW
• 265-6436

The first distinguishing characteristic of this place is the giant Toulouse-Lautrec likeness on the facade. The second is this café's dedication to the lost art of bar tap dancing. When in town, tapdancer John Forges struts his stuff on the hardwood surface that only a few seconds earlier was a swizzle stick graveyard. This is a neighborhood saloon with a bohemian style that fits well with Adams Morgan's urban flavor. The food is French, but simple. If you arrive early enough, you can grab a table next to the piano or one of the two on the tiny balcony.

Open Sun.-Thurs. 5 p.m.-1:30 a.m., Fri.-Sat. 5 p.m.-2:30 a.m. Music nightly until 1 a.m. $6 minimum after 9:45 p.m. All major cards.

Dar es Salam/ Sheherezade
3056 M St NW
• 342-1925

This is Washington's only venue for live Arabic music, played by a polyglot band of stellar instrumentalists. The trick is to have an expansive Morrocan dinner upstairs at restaurant Dar es Salam, then arrive downstairs at nightclub Sheherezade in time to listen to the musicians warm up the crowd for the belly dancer. Their repertoire ranges across the map of the Mideast, but once the dancers hit the floor, the music definitely takes second place to the hips, the hands, the lips and all the rest. (See also Dar es Salam in the Restaurants chapter, page 54.)

Dar es Salam: open nightly 5 p.m.-11 p.m. Sheherezade: open Wed.-Sat. 10 p.m.-3 a.m. $7 minimum Wed.-Thurs., cover $12 Fri., $15 Sun.

D.C. Space
433 7th St. NW
• 347-1445

For a taste of the city's avant-garde culture, spend some time in this artsy, slightly ragged restaurant. One night you might hear poetry, another progressive jazz, another folk-punk. It seems as if everyone in the crowd knows everyone else, but everybody's welcome. The menu is limited, but the food is better than most bar fare. On Friday and Saturday nights, the satiric troupe Fresh Victims takes the stage and skewers pretensions in a lively revue that starts at 7:30 p.m.

Open Mon.-Fri. 11 a.m.-2 a.m., Sat. 4 p.m.-3 a.m. Cover $3-$7.50.

The Dubliner
520 N. Capitol St. NW
• 737-3773

This is an Irish pub as only Yanks can manufacture them, but it is still a big, warmhearted bruiser of a bar, where drink and merriment are taken seriously. One room is dominated by a long bar serving Guinness on tap, not to mention other favorites such as Harp and Bass ales, and all manner of Irish whiskey, from Jameson to potcheen. The other is filled with tables around a small stage where folksingers do their part to keep the culture alive. Should you develop an appetite, order fish and chips—naturally, a house specialty. Overall, a convivial place where you can't help but have fun.
Open Mon.-Thurs. 11 a.m.-1:30 a.m., Fri.-Sat. 11 a.m.-2:30 a.m., Sun. 11:30 a.m.-1:30 a.m. Shows nightly 9 p.m. (Sun. 7 p.m.) No cover. All major cards.

Dylan's
3251 Prospect St. NW
• 337-0593

Dylan's is an oddly shaped but endearing second-floor room where local and national folkies hold forth. You'll find good sound, an amiable atmosphere and a chance to hear someone like Gene Clark sing something like "Eight Miles High" in the original modal tuning.
Open Tues.-Thurs. 5 p.m.-1 a.m. Cover $3 Thurs.-Sun. Showtimes vary. All major cards.

Gallagher's
3319 Connecticut Ave. NW
• 686-9189

A relaxing neighborhood pub with low lights and Irish inclinations, Gallagher's has become a favorite after-movie wateringhole for patrons of the big-screen Uptown Theater across the avenue. The well-worn wooden tables mark it as a place of rambling conversations and prolonged elbow-bending, but the local folk artists are another draw. To get in the spirit of things, order Irish stew, the house specialty.
Open Mon.-Thurs. 5 p.m.-2 a.m., Fri. 5 p.m.-3 a.m., Sat.-Sun. noon-2 a.m. Music Thurs.-Sun. (showtimes vary). No cover. All major cards.

Grog & Tankard
2408 Wisconsin Ave. NW
• 333-3114

A neighborhood fixture in Glover Park, the next section up Wisconsin Avenue from Georgetown, the Grog has evolved into an active outlet for talented local and regional musicians performing original material in a cozy—some might say elbow-to-elbow—setting. On some nights the show reverts to Grateful Dead covers, on some the sound is acoustic Piedmont blues; either way, the joint always jumps.
Open Sun.-Thurs. 4 p.m.-2 a.m., Fri.-Sat. 4 p.m.-3 a.m. Showtimes vary. Cover $4-$7. Cards: AE, MC, V.

Mr. Henry's Adams Morgan
1836 Columbia Rd. NW
• 797-8882

Forget that it feels like a motel lounge. Pay no attention to the red leather booths. The appeal of this otherwise non-descript restaurant comes from Julia and Company, the R&B group led by singer Julia Nixon. Nixon has a powerful voice that won her a lead role in *Dreamgirls* on Broadway, and when she sings gospel—well, if that doesn't lift your spirits, you need professional help.
Open Mon.-Fri. 4 p.m.-2:30 a.m., Fri.-Sat. 8 a.m.-2 a.m. Music Thurs.-Sun. (showtimes vary). Cover $2-$7.50. All major cards.

Ireland's Four Provinces
3412 Connecticut Ave. NW
• 244-0860

A cavernous drinking hall with a long bar suitable for standing, Ireland's Four Provinces has a reputation for revelry. The music is all Irish and the sing-along potential is high; it's not unusual to see a roomful of people of every conceivable ancestry singing longingly of Galway Bay. Irish bars will do that to you. For authenticity's sake, there are fish and chips and lamb chops on the menu and Guinness and Harp on tap.
Open nightly 5 p.m.-2 a.m. Shows Tues.-Thurs. & Sun. 9 p.m., Fri.-Sat. 9:15 p.m. Cover $2 Fri.-Sat. Cards: AE, MC, V.

The Irish Times
14 F St. NW
• 543-5433

An very Irish pub, which is to say a bit shopworn; a touch eccentric (How many Irish pubs sport rotogravure portraits of Frederick Douglass?); and thoroughly without pretense, literary or otherwise. Downstairs on weekends, The Chamber floating club hosts live rock.
Open Sun.-Thurs. 10 a.m.-2 a.m., Fri.-Sat. 10 a.m.-3 a.m. Shows Wed.-Sat. 9 p.m. No cover. All major cards.

Nightclub 9:30
930 F St. NW
• 393-0930 (message)
638-2008

It's enormously loud and enormously grungy, which helps to explain why the 9:30 is Washington's reigning edgecutter club. For hard-core breeds of night crawlers—moshers, stagedivers, headbangers and thrashers of all varieties—this is home base. Reggae and go-go bands often are rotated into the mix, creating one of the city's more eclectic dance floors. You can jam to the sounds of The Feelies, The Fangs and Severed Heads as well as better-known acts such as Pyschedelic Furs and Marianne Faithfull. The only place in Washington to see both Peter Case and George Clinton in the same summer.
Open Tues.-Sun. 9 p.m.-closing varies. Showtimes vary. Cover $2-$20. No cards.

The Roxy
1214 18th St. NW
• 296-9292 (message)
296-9293

A once-seedy rock club near Dupont Circle, The Roxy has cleaned up its act and now serves decent meals with its music. It's become a good spot to listen to blues, rock or reggae, played by a mix of local and touring acts. There's room for dancing, especially on Saturdays—usually set aside for high-energy reggae bands.
Open Mon.-Tues. 8:30 p.m.-midnight, Wed.-Thurs. 8:30 p.m.-1 a.m., Fri.-Sun. 8 p.m.-2 a.m. Music Thurs.-Sat. 8 p.m.-2 a.m. Cover $4-$10.

Twist & Shout
Bethesda American Legion,
4800 Auburn Ave.,
Bethesda, Md.
• (301) 681-8536

This is a thoroughly satisfying try at recreating a Louisiana social club in the shadows of an expanding suburban center. Twist & Shout has a beer-on-the-floor, blues-in-the-air atmosphere that brings out the raucous in almost everyone. Besides local rockers, the room takes care to book rarely heard national talent, such as heavylidded country-blues veteran Sleepy LaBeef.
Open Thurs.-Sat. 9 p.m.-2 a.m. Cover varies.

The Vault
911 F St. NW
• 347-8079

Another doomed bank revived by music lovers, The Vault is dedicated to the proposition that a short lease and a loud bass line can make for an interesting half-life. Big hair, big clothes, big attitude—and big fun, if your heart can take it.
Open Wed.-Thurs. 9 p.m.-2 a.m., Fri.-Sat. 9 p.m.-3 a.m. Cover (after 10 p.m.) $4 Wed., $3 Thurs., $5 Fri., $7 Sat. Cards: AE, MC, V.

PIANO BARS & CABARETS

Anton's Loyal Opposition
400 1st St. SE
• 546-4545

This Capitol Hill restaurant is popular during the day as a lunch spot and a venue for congressional gossip. But at night, folks savaged by a day of politicking come to be soothed by the music of Elizabeth Flood and other talented ivory ticklers.
Open Mon.-Sat. 7 a.m.-2 a.m., Sun. 7 a.m.-11 p.m. Music Tues.-Sat. 7:30 p.m.-12:30 p.m. All major cards.

21 Federal
1736 L St. NW
• 331-9771

One of Downtown's snazzier eating rooms sprouts musical notes at sundown, as pianist Kendra Holt holds forth.
Open Mon.-Fri., music 6 p.m.-10 p.m.

**Westin Hotel's
Lobby Lounge**
2401 M St. NW
• 429-2400

Offering an elegant middle ground between piano bar and lobby music, the Westin Hotel's Lobby Lounge is set in one of the glitzier foyers in the West End; for plush dining, the Grand Bistro restaurant and bar is just across the foyer. *Open daily 4 p.m.-midnight. Music nightly 5 p.m.-11:45 p.m. All major cards.*

THEATER

Washington is a place geared more to the glitzy Broadway spectacle than to the brooding, powerful, avant-garde gem. Few theater devotees were surprised when director Peter Sellars's American National Theater—his much-heralded attempt to bring experimental productions to the Kennedy Center—fizzled after one season. The District may not be a great theater town, agreed, but things are looking up. For many Washingtonians, a night at the theater still means a visit to the Kennedy Center, the National Theater or Ford's Theater. But Arena Stage, one of the country's leading regional theaters, remains consistently innovative. Morever, small operations, such as Studio Theater, Woolly Mammoth, Horizons Theater and Source Theater Company, are building loyal audiences for their off-Broadway fare. It's no longer *A Chorus Line* or nothing. For those whose love of theater exceeds their budget, the best bet is TICKETplace (F Street Plaza, between 12th and 13th streets NW; 842-5387). Not far from the Gallery Place Metro stop, it offers same-day tickets to most of the city's major theaters at 40 percent off. Payment, however, is by cash only. Hours are Tuesday through Friday 1 a.m. to 4 p.m.; Saturday 11 a.m. to 5 p.m. Tickets for Sunday performances are sold on Saturday. Also available: full-price tickets for a variety of concert and theater venues. To find out what's available, call TIC-KETS. If you're willing to pay more than top dollar for the best seats in the house, consider Premiere Theater Seats (533-1600), Top Centre Tickets (452-9040) or the Ticket Connection (587-6850). These outfits buy concert and theater tickets through classified ads and resell them at prices $15 to $25 higher than what you'd pay in the theater. Obviously no bargain, but it's one way to get into a must-see show on short notice or when tickets are rarer than congressmen on the weekends. You can order tickets for most theater events through Ticketron (1101 17th Street NW, 659-2601). They can be purchased at the main office or at twelve Woodward and Lothrop stores and five area Sears stores. The fee is $1.25. Instant Charge (467-4600) sells tickets to Kennedy Center events. There is no charge.

JOHN F. KENNEDY CENTER FOR THE PERFORMING ARTS

For years ridiculed as a cultural backwater, Washington joined the big leagues of performing arts when this imposing center opened in September 1971 with the world premiere of Leonard Bernstein's *Mass*. Now about 8,000 people visit the Center daily, some simply to stroll through its grand, red-carpeted hallways, others to take in the striking views from its rooftop terrace of the Potomac River and the infamous Watergate complex next door. But most of the visitors are there for the shows—ranging from blockbuster theater productions like *Les Miserables* and operas starring Placido Domingo to performances of American Ballet Theater or concerts by the resident National Symphony Orchestra under the direction of Mstislav Rostropovich. Ticket prices can also hit the blockbuster range—$45 for top shows—but really to appreciate Washington's blossoming cultural life, you should spend an evening in one of the center's concert halls. Critics call it a high-priced haven for highbrows, but the Center does offer half-price tickets to fulltime students and people 65 and older. They're available at the Friends of the Kennedy Center booth (416-8340; open daily 10 a.m. to 9 p.m.) in the Center's Hall of States. Another bit of advice: the theaters hold onto a few prime "house seats" for drop-in VIPs, but if no one drops in, these excellent seats go at face value a few minutes before curtain to the patient stalkers who wait until the lights are going down to ante up. Kennedy Center is located at New Hampshire Avenue NW and Rock Creek Parkway; for information, call 467-4600. Its halls include the following listings:

American Film Institute Theater
• 785-4600

Next to its more formal counterparts, the AFI Theater seems tiny and rather ordinary, but its screen and sound system are grand compared to those of most modern matchbox moviehouses. Located in the Hall of States, it seats 225 and presents two films a night at 6:30 p.m. and 8:45 p.m. Usually, one is a fairly recent release, the other a film classic; there's always an eclectic but interesting lineup.
Box office open daily 5 p.m.-9 p.m. All major cards.

The Concert Hall
• 467-4600

From the gold-and-white walls to the grand Norwegian chandeliers, this 2,750-seat concert hall is a study in elegance. It's home base for the National Symphony Orchestra, and the place to see performances by the world's leading orchestras and choral groups. Acoustics throughout are excellent, although insiders say they are particularly wonderful in Row W.
Box office open Mon.-Sat. 10 a.m.-9 p.m., Sun. noon-9 p.m. All major cards.

The Eisenhower Theater
• 467-4600

This 1,200-seat theater hosts major touring productions, often before they open on Broadway, such as *Death of a Salesman*, starring Dustin Hoffman, or *The Iceman Cometh*, with Jason Robards. This theater is best known in recent years as the stage where wunderkind director Peter Sellars tried to create an avant-garde national theater, but succeeded only in annoying critics and confusing audiences. *Box office open Mon.-Sat. 10 a.m.-9 p.m., Sun. noon-9 p.m. All major cards.*

The Opera House
• 467-4600

A three-tiered, 2,300-seat formal theater, the Opera House from November through February features the acclaimed Washington Opera (416-7800), which has become one of the hottest destinations in town. The rest of the year, groups as diverse as the Dance Theater of Harlem and the Stuttgart Ballet take the stage. The best seats, as you might expect, are Rows A-J in the center section. *Box office open Mon.-Sat. 10 a.m.-9 p.m., Sun. noon-9 p.m. All major cards.*

The Terrace Theater
• 467-4600

The smallest and most intimate of the Kennedy Center halls, the Terrace has only 500 seats, but has a repertoire of consistently good chamber and choral music. It also hosts the American College Theater Festival every April. *Box office open Mon.-Sat. 10 a.m.-9 p.m., Sun. noon-9 p.m. All major cards.*

OTHER THEATERS

Arena Stage
6th & M Sts. SW
• 488-3300

Many Washington theaters have come and gone, but Arena has endured for nearly 40 years and in the process become one of the nation's leading regional theaters. It has premiered plays such as *The Great White Hope* and *K2*, and brings high-quality, imaginatively staged productions to its devoted patrons. A cultural oasis in Washington's restaurant-heavy waterfront district, the theater actually has three components: the namesake Arena, a spare, 800-seat theater with the stage in the middle; the Kreeger Theater, a more recent and somewhat smaller (500 seats) venue; and the Old Vat Room, a cozy club that for seven years has featured Washington's longest-running act, Stephen Wade, who clog-dances, flails at his banjo, and tells tall tale upon tall tale in his one-man show, *On the Way Home*. The Arena is heavily subscribed; tickets may be hard to find on weekends. *Box office open Sun.-Mon. noon-6 p.m., Tues.-Sat. 10 a.m.-6 p.m. Cards: MC, V.*

Ford's Theater
511 10th St. NW
• 347-4833 (information),
432-0200 (tickets)

This is the city's oldest theater—known mainly and unfortunately as the place where Abraham Lincoln was shot. Don't hold that against it, however; Ford's has been beautifully and meticulously restored, and has rebuilt its reputation by booking a mix of small-stage touring productions, from musicals such as *Godspell* to serious drama like Arthur Miller's *All My Sons*. Tickets are in the $20 range. As you might expect, the theater's basement houses a small museum where you can view the clothes Lincoln was wearing on the night he was shot and the derringer John Wilkes Booth used. The museum is free, but will be closed for renovations until the summer of 1990.
Box office open Mon.-Fri. 10 a.m.-6 p.m., Sat. noon-4 p.m., Sun. noon-6 p.m. All major cards.

National Theater
1321 E St. NW
• 628-6161 (information),
(800) 233-3123 (tickets)

Rich in history—the Booths, Barrymores and Bernhardt appeared on its stage—and recently refurbished, the National is a showcase for big, brassy Broadway shows. Fittingly, it reopened a few years ago with *42nd Street* and hasn't lost much steam, booking the likes of *Cats* and all of Neil Simon's recent autobiographical trilogy. What you see here is not the most imaginative theater, but the National's owners, the Shubert Organization, consider it a far better thing to entertain an audience than to challenge it. For the privilege, customers pay up to $35 a seat.
Box office open Mon. 10 a.m.-6 p.m., Tues.-Sat. 10 a.m.-9 p.m., Sun. noon-9 p.m. All major cards.

Olney Theater
2001 Rte. 108,
Olney, Md.
• (301) 924-4485,
(301) 924-3400

A summer stock house, the Olney began edging toward year-round status in 1989, with the addition of insulation and a heating system. Offerings range from *The Nerd* to *A Shayna Maidel*, with frequent forays into door-slamming bedroom farces such as *Noises Off*.
During season (May-Oct.): box office open Mon. 10 a.m.-6 p.m., Tues.-Sat. 10 a.m.-9 p.m., Sun. noon-9 p.m. Off-season (Nov.-Apr.): open Mon.-Fri. 10 a.m.-6 p.m., Sat. 10 a.m.-1 p.m. Cards: MC, V.

Shakespeare Theater at the Folger
201 E. Capitol St. SE
• 546-4000

Shakespeare had a few nasty things to say about politicians, so it is only appropriate that he be celebrated regularly in this authentic re-creation of a sixteenth-century theater not far from the Capitol. Located in the Elizabethan Folger Shakespeare Library, the theater stages the "Best of the Bard," usually inventively. (It once set *Romeo and Juliet* in a circus.) In recent years, the Folger has attracted some stellar talent; Kelly McGillis has starred as Portia in *The Merchant of Venice*, and as Viola in *Twelfth Night*. The

Folger also presents other classic theater by such play-wrights as Molière and Chekhov, mixed in with more contemporary works. There are regular Saturday and Sunday matinees.

Box office open Mon. 10 a.m.-6 p.m., Tues.-Sat. noon-8 p.m., Sun. noon-7:30 p.m. All major cards.

Source Theater
1835 14th St. NW
• 462-1073

This is but one of the small but energetic companies scratching out a niche for itself along a street evolving from auto repair outlets to box offices. Imaginatively staged and often excitingly acted, the Source's offerings include a wide range of new works and revivals.

Box office open Tues.-Sat. noon-6 p.m., Sat. & Sun. noon-8 p.m. All major cards.

Studio Theater
1333 P St. NW
• 265-7412

Sure, it's tiny. Sure, it's not in the best part of town (hookers cruise the sidewalks outside). But some people swear by the Studio, and with good reason. It consistently presents intelligent, imaginative dramas and isn't afraid to take chances. Also, the Studio has a knack for discovering some of the city's most promising actors. Productions here are never glitzy but are usually polished.

Box office open Mon.-Tues. 10 a.m.-6 p.m., Wed.-Fri. 10 a.m.-8 p.m., Sat.-Sun. noon-8 p.m.; when dark, Mon.-Fri. 10 a.m.-6 p.m. All major cards.

Woolly Mammoth Theatre Co.
1401 Church St. NW
• 393-3939

An intimate, avante-garde theater now in its second decade, the Woolly Mammoth offers unusual productions of new and rarely produced works by playwrights such as Wallace Shawn, Harry Kondoleon, John Patrick Shanley and others.

Box office open daily noon-6 p.m. All major cards.

Seven ways to say three words.
Diamond, emerald, ruby
and sapphire rings from Tiffany.
Available at Tiffany & Co.,
Fairfax Square at Tyson's Corner,
703-893-7700.

TIFFANY & CO.

CHANEL

SHOPS

CONSPICUOUS CONSUMPTION IN THE CAPITAL CITY

O h sure, you could spend your day drowning yourself in culture at the museums, catching a star-studded matinee at the Kennedy Center, wallowing in a local pub or jogging, but if your favorite pastime is reaching into your wallet or even just dreaming about it, you're in for a treat. Washington is a city with many options for a grand prize in shopping. If you take the time to search for it, you can find just about anything you desire—and, after all, looking is nearly as much fun as buying. You can find old and new, designers and discounts. Unlike New York's Fifth Avenue or Chicago's "Magnificent Mile," there is no one center of Washington shopping. Some of the best antiques are to be found in the suburbs of Kensington, while for funky clothes and jewelry, you'll do as well in Old Town as Georgetown.

ANTIQUES

THE DELIGHTS OF OLD

G iven Washington's history, it should come as no surprise that the city and its environs offer an outstanding variety of antique shops, enough to satisfy the tastes of virtually every connoisseur. The best sources on where to go are the antique publications readily available in most area antique shops, as well as the dealers themselves. Also look in the papers for announcements of auctions; Wexler's and Sloan's are the two big auction houses. But for those on a tight timetable, a delightful day of roaming, browsing and buying can be had in the metropolitan area. For our reviews, we have concentrated on two antiques enclaves within a few miles of downtown: Old Town Alexandria, Virginia, and Kensington, Maryland.

Old Town Alexandria, a historic delight of a community, offers far more than its antique stores, and should be visited even if you aren't shopping. Maps and guides for Old Town antique exploring are available in every local shop. We suggest you leave your car and walk the route through the heart of town, driving only to the most far-flung stores.

The second "must" for antique addicts is Kensington, only four miles due north of the Washington city limits, and about 30 minutes from downtown. There you'll find an incredible variety of antique stores that specialize in collectibles of every stripe, color and style. We suggest that if you are looking for a specific item, you try the Howard Street warehouses, which have huge selections of European and American antiques. You might also chat with the friendly Kensington dealers who know the area and their colleagues' offerings well. One caution: many of the Kensington stores fudge a bit on their listed hours during the week. It might be wise to call ahead before making a weekday trip, if you're interested in a particular shop.

While Georgetown has another cache of shops, it takes a lot more cash to shop there. The high rents of Georgetown have taken their toll on the prices of the antiques. Because of these prices, we have not reviewed the Georgetown shops, but suggest that, since every stay in Washington should include a visit to Georgetown, the antiques adventurer should just poke around a bit and see what's available. Most of the antique shops are located "up the hill" on Wisconsin Avenue, starting at about N Street. At the very least, you'll enjoy the quaint streets, stores and historic buildings.

Lastly, the caveat, "Buyer beware," applies to Washington antique shops, as well as to any store, anywhere. If it looks too new to be old, it is probably a reproduction or a copy. A reputable shop will have back-up material on their gems and won't find it the least bit unreasonable if you insist on an independent appraisal before concluding a major deal.

OLD TOWN ALEXANDRIA

Burke's Peerage, Ltd.
128 S. Royal St.,
Alexandria, Va.
• (703) 549-5155

The prices for the primarily English antiques in this shop on a quiet side street in Old Town are very high, but the pieces are also very well chosen, with an eye to the particularly distinctive. The owner once lived in London and has lots of English contacts who help him locate fine pieces, especially from the Regency period. Besides furniture, prints and lamps, the shop also specializes in costly antique garden ornaments.
Open Tues.-Sat. 10:30 a.m.-5:30 p.m.

C & M Antiques/ Eagle Antiques
311 Cameron St.,
Alexandria, Va.
• (703) 549-7611

These two stores share several spacious rooms on the second floor of the historic Norford Inn, and offer a wide variety of silver, linens, glass, porcelain, china, quilts and paintings. If you want a chocolate mold, a cast-iron cornbread pan or any sort of antique kitchen equipment, this is the place to look and stay within budget. Although some of the items are a bit tacky, the historical paintings and old American clocks (they work, too) are outstanding. Moreover, it's a fun place to browse, if only for the building itself.
Open Mon.-Sat. 11 a.m.-5 p.m., Sun. noon-5 p.m.

Donna Lee's Collectibles

206 Queen St.,
Alexandria, Va.
• (703) 548-5830

At first glance, you might find the Americana in this shop of questionable taste. But once you're over the shock of seeing display cases full of pickaninny dolls and Aunt Jemima figurines, you will discover that this is the only shop in the Washington area specializing in black memorabilia. Owner Donna Lee Wilson has been collecting rag dolls, china figures, pictures, old books, music and wall hangings representing the black experience in America for four years. Her offerings date from the 1880s to the 1950s and range in price from $10 to $20 for some of the newest items, to $200 or $250 for the oldest and rarest. Donna Lee prides herself on keeping prices down so that more people can enjoy collecting without making a major investment. A separate book store upstairs specializes in rare books, mostly on American and military history.
Open daily 11 a.m.-4 p.m.

Ethridge, Ltd.

220 S. Washington St.,
Alexandria, Va.
• (703) 548-7722

A first-class shop, this place specializes in seventeenth-, eighteenth- and nineteenth-century English and American furniture, nineteenth-century paintings, Oriental rugs and eighteenth-century decorative accessories. Secretaries, desks, cupboards, small tables, mirrors, clocks, chairs—everything except beds—of fine quality and in excellent condition, are featured here. The furniture is selected piece by piece in both the United States and Britain. Don't let the thought of shipping furniture stop you from falling in love with something precious here. The shop owners are glad to arrange transport and delivery. It's expensive, but worth the price.
Open Wed.-Sat. 11:30 a.m.-5 p.m. and by appt.

Lenore and Daughters

130 S. Royal St.,
Alexandria, Va.
• (703) 836-3356

An informal, neighborly air pervades this shop, thanks to the chatty, friendly owner, Lenore Binzer. She doesn't stock much furniture, because she has trouble lugging it around. What she does offer is a good collection of antique porcelain, glassware and faience, as well as silver flatware and other small silver items. This shop is a particularly good place to find a wide selection of early twentieth-century fashion prints and hand-colored nineteenth- and twentieth-century floral engravings. The prices generally seem quite reasonable, a point on which Binzer says she prides herself.
Open Mon.-Sat. 10 a.m.-5 p.m., Sun. 1 p.m.-5 p.m.

Lloyd's Row

119 S. Henry St.,
Alexandria, Va.
• (703) 549-7517

Some Old Town shops match Georgetown prices. Lloyd's Row occupies an entire eighteenth-century townhouse. When you walk in, you might think you are disturbing owner R. J. Mraz in his living room. In fact, Mraz does live here, and part of the elegance of this shop lies in how the fine eighteenth-century American furniture and accessories are tastefully displayed in a period setting. A former teacher who got into the antique business fourteen years ago, Mraz will discuss the individual pieces and prices, but brace yourself for a shock before asking about prices. A pair of chairs recently sold for $35,000.
Open Wed.-Sat. 11 a.m.-5 p.m., Sun. noon-5 p.m.

Micheline's Antiques

1600 King St.,
Alexandria, Va.
• (703) 836-1893,
(703) 256-0950

Micheline's has been around far longer than the current French- country craze. Even people who don't usually care for this style will be in awe of the variety and selection at Micheline's. In business for ten years, the owners are a mother-and-son team who do all their buying in France, particularly in Normandy. Their specialty is armoires, and they have the most extensive selection of art deco clocks in the area. In addition to the furnishings, which are not priced for the fainthearted, Micheline's offers a wonderful selection of traditional country fabrics by Les Olivades, produced near Avignon. Exquisite, attractively priced silk tassles and braidings are available, as well as a selection of faiences and other French pottery. Strictly for the discriminating buyer, Micheline's draws many regular customers from up and down the East Coast. The store will accept out-of-town checks.
Open Tues.-Fri. 11 a.m.-4 p.m., Sat. 11 a.m.-5 p.m., and by appt.

Old Colony Shop

222 S. Washington St.,
Alexandria, Va.
• (703) 548-8008

The Old Colony Shop, situated in the basement of a historic Old-Town residence, features an impressive collection of sixteenth- through nineteenth-century prints, maps and documents. The shop also specializes in museum framing and art conservation. Sales personnel will gladly discuss any special art projects you may have in mind.
Open Tues.-Fri. 10 a.m.-6 p.m., Sat. 10 a.m.-5 p.m.

Silverman Galleries, Inc.

110 N. Saint Asaph St.,
Alexandria, Va.
• (703) 836-5363

For almost 30 years, Silverman's has specialized in eighteenth- and early nineteenth-century decorative arts, including a fine collection of estate jewelry, silver, clocks, porcelain and ceramics as well as furniture. With a jeweler on the premises, it's no surprise that all of Silverman's

antique clocks work. These folks are willing to try to repair your clocks and watches, however impossible the task may seem. Silverman's jeweler also does custom design work and appraisals by appointment. A two-room gallery featuring nineteenth-century American paintings opened upstairs in September 1986.
Open Tues.-Sat. 11 a.m.-5 p.m.

Studio Antiques and Fine Art
628 N. Washington St., Alexandria, Va.
• (703) 548-5188

The fine eighteenth- and nineteenth-century furnishings in Studio Antiques are among the best documented we found, with full history, dates and descriptions offered on every piece. Prices here are fair, and reflect the high quality of the merchandise. This shop specializes in nineteenth-century American, English and Continental paintings, with a selection so distinctive that 40 percent to 50 percent of the shop's business is with local art galleries. You can also find some interesting decorative porcelain, Asian ceramics, eighteenth- and nineteenth-century tobacco boxes, thimbles and accessory items. Studio prides itself on offering furniture and paintings that are perfectly restored.
Open Mon.-Sat. 10 a.m.-5 p.m., Sun. noon-5 p.m.

Trojan Antiques and Teacher's Pet
210 N. Lee St., Alexandria, Va.
• (703) 549-9766

These two stores share a large open area and offer an unlikely combination of costume jewelry, accessories and small craft items. Anybody heading off to a costume party should stop here first and check out the six cases of costume jewelry, mostly from the twenties and thirties. Also, an eccentric array of country and formal furniture, paintings, art deco accessories, old holiday collectibles, postcards, glass and wooden items is crammed into 1,400 square feet.
Open Mon.-Sat. 11 a.m.-6 p.m., Sun. noon-5 p.m.

Warehouse Antiques
218 N. Lee St., Alexandria, Va.
• (703) 548-2150

A small, cheery shop featuring English country and turn-of-the-century American furniture and accessories. You'll find trunks, iron and brass beds, armoires, tables and a wide selection of stained glass here. Everything is carefully arranged and is in good condition. If you don't see exactly what you want, don't hesitate to ask for it. There's a three-story warehouse for overflow stock, as well as a second shop in Frederick, Maryland.
Open Mon.-Sat. 10 a.m.-5 p.m., Sun. 1 p.m.-5 p.m.

KENSINGTON

Brenda's Antiques & Collectibles

3762A Howard Ave.,
Kensington, Md.
• (301) 942-2611

A funky shop for the eclectic collector, Brenda's features small, reasonably priced specialty items, from glassware to jewelry, china to linens and vintage clothing. Brenda's has one of the most interesting collections of old sheet music you'll find in the area, as well as postcards and other paper items. On occasion, she carries some lovely furniture pieces, sometimes art deco. Variety is Brenda's trademark; if you don't see what you want, ask: the treasure you seek may be in stock, but not on display.
Open Mon.-Sat. 10 a.m.-5:30 p.m., Sun. noon-5:30 p.m.

Bobbie's Antiques and Interiors

3760 Howard Ave.,
Kensington, Md.
• (301) 949-5552

Don't miss this large, charming store. Thomas Kruez has collected a wide variety of unusual American furnishings from the eighteenth and nineteenth centuries. His impressive display of restored and polished gas and electric lighting fixtures are alone worth a visit. Cards on the furniture describe and price each item, and the more expensive pieces boast their own appraisal documents. Gourmet alert: this was the first shop in the Kensington area where we spotted a pie safe and a pie cupboard, circa 1830 and 1875, respectively. A Georgia pine cigar-rolling table from the 1840s is an ideal gift for the do-it-your-selfer who can't obtain (still illegal to import) Cuban cigars. Check it out.
Open Mon.-Wed. 10 a.m.-5:30 p.m., Thurs. 10 a.m.-8 p.m., Fri.-Sat. 10 a.m.-5:30 p.m., Sun. noon-5:30 p.m., evenings by appt.

Bruton Antiques

4125 Howard Ave.,
Kensington, Md.
• (301) 564-1226

The emphasis of this warehouse operation is chiefly on nineteenth-century antiques from England, Wales, Ireland and Scotland, and you'll frequently find pieces that are less expensive than the cost of obtaining them abroad and shipping them home. The owner of the store lives in Wales, does the buying himself, and sends over containers full of wonderful items several times a year. In addition to a wide and varied selection of furniture, you'll find numerous decorative accessories.
Open Mon.-Sat. 10 a.m.-5:30 p.m., Sun. noon-5 p.m.

The Crowded Attic

3730 Howard Ave.,
Kensington, Md.
• No phone

Five separate antique dealers are jammed into this crowded space. Much of the merchandise lacks allure, but Kensington Station Antiques has a well-chosen selection of country oak furniture—tables, cabinets, dressers and bookcases—that the owners seek out in Pennsylvania and Ohio. The pieces date mainly from 1900 to 1920. Since many were once painted, they are refinished by Pennsylvania craftsmen before they are put on sale. Another interesting shop is The Highwayman, specializing in early American antique country furniture and accessories. Especially interesting is the collection of kitchen utensils and containers, including trays, rolling pins and painted metal canisters. It is also one of the three shops in the enclave that sell old quilts. Most items date from the mid-1800s, with few earlier than 1820. You can find wooden chests and painted wooden furniture, as well as game boards, washboards and a variety of other objects whose functions often aren't immediately apparent. *Open Mon.-Sat. 11 a.m.-5 p.m., Sun. noon-5 p.m.*

Dark Horse Antiques
3784 Howard Ave.,
Kensington, Md.
• (301) 942-0016

If wonderful oak furniture is your thing, then Dark Horse is your place. The lovely casual oak furniture and accessory pieces in this shop are a welcome break from the formal offerings in most other Kensington stores. All of the furniture here, both old and new, is in exceptional condition and fairly priced. This shop carries an impressive stock of dining tables and chairs, as well as some handsome marble-top chests, sideboards and an oak mantle just waiting for the perfect fireplace. And for a special gift, the shop features some stunning reproductions of merry-go-round horses and circus animals.
Open Sat. 11 a.m.-5:30 p.m., Sun. noon-5 p.m.

Diane, Diane Too! & The Three of Us
3758 Howard Ave.,
Kensington, Md.
• (301) 946-4242

Three tiny arcade shops, side by side and all under the same ownership, are full of whimsical and amusing objects. You'll find everything from antiques to art deco and art nouveau furniture, accessory items and some unusual decorative pieces. Be sure to take a look at the stuffed animals and animal heads peeking out from "The Three of Us." You could find the perfect surprise for a child you know.
Open Mon.-Wed. & Fri.-Sat. 10 a.m.-5:30 p.m., Thurs. 10 a.m.-8:30 p.m., Sun. noon-5:30 p.m.

Georgian Shell Interiors/Antiques, Inc.
10419 Fawcett St.,
Kensington, Md.
• (301) 631-1022

In addition to offering some lovely reproductions of formal eighteenth-century furniture, Georgian Shell does furniture refinishing, repairs and custom carpentry work. This large shop carries elegant bedroom suites, dining room tables for ten, settees, loveseats and accent pieces, most in mahogany, walnut or cherry. Shop owners Bob Farrow and Bill Autry will duplicate furniture or seek out truly unusual pieces and decorative items if you have your heart set on a certain something. They specialize in vintage furniture—

mostly from the 1920s and 1930s—and look for age, style and condition in what they sell. They also stock some special stained glass pieces, Tiffany-style lights, chandeliers and hard-to-find crown and chair moldings.
Open Wed.-Sun. 10 a.m.-5 p.m., Tues. by appt.

Gonzales Antiques
4233 Howard Ave.,
Kensington, Md.
• (301) 564-5940

This store specializes in chandeliers and wall sconces, and will do restoration and cleaning as well. Otherwise, its stock tends to unusual, often quite ornate furniture from England, France and Italy, as well as interesting china and other ornaments. It's been known to stock some smashing andirons and fireplace screens.
Open Mon.-Sat. 10 a.m.-5 p.m.

Jill and Co. Antiques
3744 Howard Ave.,
Kensington, Md.
• (301) 946-7464

While many of the items carried are antique, some are contemporary crafts from the hills of West Virginia and Kentucky. They carry primarily American primitive furniture and contemporary folk accessories such as quilts, rag rugs, dried flowers, wreaths and baskets. The shop does a lot of dealer and decorator trade, and is the new darling of certain English decorators.
Open daily 11 a.m.-5 p.m.

JoAnne's Antique Alley
3746 Howard Ave.,
Kensington, Md.
• (301) 933-6939

Owner JoAnne Alley began her antique business dealing only in glassware, but gradually expanded into fine mahogany and walnut furniture—no oak. She buys most of her pieces from local estate sales, and estimates that her stock turns over every four to six weeks. This is a good place to look if you're in search of a special mirror. Since her first love was glassware, JoAnne also offers an interesting selection of fine china, glassware and curiosity items.
Open Mon.-Wed. & Fri.-Sat. 11 a.m.-5:30 p.m., Thurs. 11 a.,-8:30 p.m., Sun. noon-5:30 p.m.

Just for You Antiques
3730 Howard Ave.,
Kensington, Md.
• (301) 933-5067

With owner Janet Gilden sitting in this tiny store, there's barely room for more than one customer at a time. But do stop in for a look at her collection of china and glass, which includes some nice pieces of good, oldfashioned cut glass from somebody's grandmother's house. She might have just the thing you need.
Open Wed.-Sun. noon-5 p.m.

Lost and Found

3734 Howard Ave.,
Kensington, Md.
• (301) 946-8666

Specializing in assorted everythings, Lost and Found is a delightful shop to browse around in and recapture a bit of the past. Owner Julia Moed carries primarily pre-1930 kitchen items and country accessories, toys and children's items. She also stocks paper goods, from postcards to trading cards, and every few months, the shop mounts a different exhibit, often featuring objects from her customers' collections.
Open Mon.-Sat. 11 a.m.-5 p.m., Sun. noon-5 p.m.

Maria's Place

3758 Howard Ave.,
Kensington, Md.
• (301) 949-2378

Maria's place is crammed with a mix of furniture, from casual oak to more formal pieces, and accessory items. Ask about the Christmas plates from Denmark, and you'll discover that there are plenty of secret hiding places in this shop for special objects too numerous to display.
Open Mon.-Sat. 10 a.m.-5:30 p.m., Sun. noon-5:30 p.m., Thurs. 10 a.m.-7 p.m.

Miniatures by B.R.

3768 Howard Ave.,
Kensington, Md.
• (301) 942-0709

For the little girl you know or the little girl you remain, here's a store that features a complete selection of doll houses and accessory items. Your choice of new, hand-crafted or antique doll houses and furnishings for hours of pleasure.
Open Mon.-Sat. 10 a.m.-5:30 p.m., Sun. noon-5:30 p.m.

Nautical and Scientific Shop

3762 Howard Ave.
(upstairs), Kensington, Md.
• (301) 942-0636,
(301) 384-1394

This place is a true delight. Here, you'll find antique scientific instruments: laboratory, meteorological, nautical, optical, photographic, telegraphic, geological, carto-graphic, navigational. Half of the customers are women seeking presents for men, so if Father's Day or a special someone's birthday is posing some gift-buying problems, this is a good place to investigate.
Open Sat.-Sun. noon- 5 p.m. or by appt.

Onslow Square

4131 Howard Ave.,
Kensington, Md.
• (301) 530-9393

Onslow Square has an extensive selection of eighteenth- and nineteenth-century English antiques, including ar-moires which can be converted into television or stereo cabinets. You'll also find an unusual collection of accessory items, especially silver. Fully 5,000 square feet of warehouse space are filled with wonderful furnishings, and the stock is frequently updated with spoils obtained on buying trips abroad.
Open Mon.-Sat. 10 a.m.-5:30 p.m., Sun. noon-5 p.m.

Prevention of Blindness Antique Shop

3716 Howard Ave.,
Kensington, Md.
• (301) 942-4707

How delightful to shop in the knowledge that whatever you spend is going to a good cause! The antiques and collectibles here are all donated items, so the variety is exceptional and quite unpredictable. This is a great secondhand shop for someone furnishing a home with functional, reasonably priced furniture. In addition, there's a good selection of glassware, china and paintings, rustic collectibles and even some old books and jewelry. There's truly a little bit of everything in this pleasant, well-organized store.
Open Tues.-Sun. 10:30 a.m.-5 p.m.

Pritchard's

3748 Howard Ave.,
Kensington, Md.
• (301) 942-1661

Pritchard's offers a little bit of everything—and a cheerful atmosphere to boot. Here a young couple just starting out could find an attractive, inexpensive antique, as could anyone looking for something nice, but not too costly. There are some lovely stained-glass items, old leaded-glass windows, beautiful perfume bottles, lamps, nineteenth- and twentieth-century American furniture and jewelry. Owner Kurt Pritchard also runs a custom stained- and etched-glass business nearby.
Open Mon.-Sat. 10 a.m.-5:30 p.m., Sun. noon-5:30 p.m.

Sparrows

4115 Howard Ave.,
Kensington, Md.
• (301) 530-0175

Sparrows specializes in an interesting selection of formal French furniture, from Henri II, Louis XV and Louis XVI to art nouveau and art deco. You'll also find a good selection of accessories, including lamps.
Open Mon.-Sat. 10 a.m.-5 p.m., Sun. noon 5 p.m.

Phyllis Van Auken Antiques

10425 Fawcett St.,
Kensington, Md.
• (301) 933-3772

One of the highlights, although it could be an expensive one, of a day of antiquing in Kensington, is a stop at this gleaming little shop. Owner Van Auken has assembled one of the area's finest selections of antique candlesticks, chandeliers and fireplace implements. Her specialties include turn-of-the-century American lighting fixtures and an extensive array of brass candlesticks. Most of the latter are from the eighteenth and nineteenth centuries, but she sometimes has a few dating from the seventeenth century. A limited selection of antique furniture is also on display, mainly small tables in various late eighteenth- or early nineteenth-century styles. This shop is a good place to search for striking picture and photograph frames, most of them products of nineteenth- and twentieth-century America.
Open Mon.-Fri. 10:30 a.m.-4:30 p.m., Sat. 10 a.m.-5 p.m., Sun. noon-5 p.m.

WASHINGTON & ENVIRONS

Cherishables
1608 20th St. NW
• 785-4087

This pleasant store is one of just a few in the area specializing in eighteenth- and nineteenth-century country antiques, folk art and quilts. Much of the furniture consists of American copies of well-known English designs. Etchings of various types are available, including excellent botanical drawings, and there is a small interior-design section with fabrics in traditional patterns. The wares are chosen with a very discriminating eye, yet many of the prices seem outlandish, even in the expensive Washington antique market. *Open Mon.-Sat. 11 a.m.-6 p.m.*

Heller Antiques, Ltd.
5454 Wisconsin Ave. NW, Chevy Chase, Md.
• (301) 654-0218

The display cases of this elegant shop gleam with one of the finest selections of antique silver to be found in the Washington area. Dazzling displays of important jewelry, both antique and contemporary, are also featured. There is an impressive collection of antique tea and coffee services, along with platters, candlesticks and flatware, some of it handmade. Much of the silver is English, especially from the late Victorian era, which the shop's owners purchase in Britain. There is a handsome array of small silver items, including boxes, napkin rings, salt cellars, picture frames and goblets. There is also a well-chosen selection of antique jewelry, often including unusual heavy gold chains and elaborate earrings. The rings are outstanding. Jewelry design services are available, as are restorations and appraisals. The sales personnel is expert and generally friendly, but don't expect to find bargains here; the prices fit the quality of the merchandise. *Open Mon.-Sat. 10 a.m.-5:30 p.m.*

Marston Luce
1314 21st St. NW
• 775-9460

If you're interested in painted nineteenth-century country furniture, this shop is worth a visit. Some of the tables and chests are quite attractive, but many of the painted cupboards and other such items obviously have suffered much wear and tear through the years. There are also some moldings and other architectural fragments in stock, as well as mirrors, china and a large selection of quilts. *Open Mon.-Sat. 11 a.m.-6 p.m.*

Seidner Galleries
1333 New Hampshire Ave. NW
• 775-8212

An exciting recent addition to the Washington antique world, this gallery offers an admirable array of European antique furniture dating from the sixteenth century. As you wander among the choice objects, you feel as if you've stepped into a particularly selective small museum. The

desks, chests and tables from Spain, England, France and Italy are truly outstanding. Many feature lovely inlaid ivory or a variety of wood inlays. There is also an extensive collection of small terra-cotta, wooden and stone sculptures and a selection of nineteenth-century German kitchen items, as well as metal objects from more exotic places. The eclecticism of the offerings stems from the fact that the owners, a former foreign service officer and his wife, formed the collection during the six years they lived in Heidelberg and Paris. The merchandise bears no price tags, though price lists are willingly provided. The tariffs are steep, indeed, but perhaps understandably so in a town where antique furniture is almost automatically English or American, rather than Continental.
Open Mon.-Sat. 11 a.m.-6 p.m.

Trocadero Asian Art
1501 Connecticut Ave. NW
• 234-5656

One of the nicest selections of Asian antiques is to be found, not in the city's Chinatown area, but in this wedge-shaped shop on Dupont Circle. Ceramics, prints and furniture from China, Japan and India are featured, with especially handsome carved chairs, tables and chests. There is a large selection of small figurines and vases, as well as Indian stone carvings.
Open Tues.-Thurs. 10:30 a.m.-6 p.m. by appt., Fri.-Sat.10:30 a.m.-6 p.m.

AUCTION HOUSES

Charles H. Olin
9447 Rabbit Hill Rd.,
Great Falls, Va.
• (703) 759-3581

Olin works with paintings of all types, but his specialty is correcting and salvaging others' botched efforts at restoration. He has worked at the Metropolitan Museum of Art in New York, was chief conservator of the National Portrait Gallery and has sent students to the major museums of the nation.
Open by appt. only.

New England Antique Furniture Repair Shop
1118 N. Jackson St.,
Arlington, Va.
• (703) 528-1800

The Ohmke brothers—Horst and Jürgen—are perhaps the best German imports since the Volkswagen. For nearly 40 years, they have been practicing their almost-magic craft on damaged furnishings from the White House and other upscale clients as well as on the sagging cane seat from Granny's rocker. They pick up and deliver, and are outrageously reasonable for the quality of their work.
Open Mon.-Fri. 7 a.m.-4 p.m., Sat. 10 a.m.-noon.

C. G. Sloan & Co., Inc.
4920 Wyaconda Rd., Rockville, Md.
• (301) 468-4911

Sloan's is Washington's own home-grown Sotheby's, but Sloan's has abandoned its convenient downtown location to follow the folks with the money to buy at auction. Thus, a move to the Maryland suburbs. A fine-arts and antiques auction house founded in 1853, Sloan's holds eight to ten nationally advertised catalog auctions a year. Exhibitions are open to the public, for an admission charge of $1, which benefits local art institutions. Admission to the auctions themselves is by catalog, which costs $15 for two at the door. The merchandise comes primarily from estates, although the firm also sells items for individuals and museums on consignment. Sloan's boasts a full staff, capable of doing appraisals of all types. Phone for information on the dates of the exhibitions and sales; there's no set schedule.
Open: hours vary with auctions and exhibitions.

Catherine Valentour
3442 Oak Wood Terrace NW
• 265-2162

Ms. Valentour is a private specialist in ethnographic objects—basketry and artifacts from far-flung civilizations and peoples, including Native Americans and peoples of the Pacific Rim.
Open by appt. only.

Adam A. Weschler & Son
905 E St. NW
• 628-1281

Virtually every Tuesday, Weschler, one of Washington's premier auction houses since 1890, puts an extensive array of household merchandise on the block: used furniture and the like for either consignment sales or local estate settlements. It's a walk-in auction, and some real treasures can be found, as witnessed by the number of antique dealers who routinely show up for these sales. Exhibitions for the weekly auctions are on Mondays, usually from 9 a.m. to 5 p.m., while the auction itself runs all day Tuesday, from around 9:30 a.m. to 3:30 or 4 p.m. In addition to the regular weekly auctions, Weschler's conducts fine-arts and antiques auctions about eight times a year, for which catalogs are available. The fine-arts and antique auctions are spectacular. Each year brings four three-day estate auctions, and five gallery sales, held on Saturdays. A phone call will alert you to what is coming up, and a visit is definitely worthwhile. Weschler also does appraisals of fine arts and antiques.
Open: hours vary with auctions and exhibitions.

BEAUTY

IN SEARCH OF PERFECTION

In Washington, beauty salons go in and out of fashion as quickly as restaurants. It's for the same reason: it's who goes there that counts. During the Reagan years, Robin Weir trimmed the First Tresses, so his Dupont Circle salon was the place to be coiffed. Mrs. Bush hasn't annointed a hairdresser, so many are now on the accepted list, depending on who goes there, of course. Salon services and atmospheres are so distinctive that Washington stylists usually establish regular and loyal clienteles known to everyone in the shop. A day of beauty care then becomes a social, as well as an aesthetic, ritual. But if you're a first-time customer, never fear. Competition is so intense that successful salons go out of their way to pamper their customers. If your first choice doesn't satisfy you, another salon surely will. Most top establishments offer full skincare and makeup services. Major department stores also provide a variety of excellent cosmetic advisers and makeup specialists and some, such as Garfinckel's, even offer a decent, well-priced haircut.

HAIR SALONS

MEN & WOMEN

Bogart, Inc.
1063 Wisconsin Ave. NW
• 333-6550

Bogart, an award-winning styling salon, prides itself on its great team of hair designers, who keep abreast of new developments in hair care and stylings. Some staff members have trained in London and Japan. A shampoo, haircut and blow dry will cost $35. Susan Ireddell operates a separate business at the back, offering massages, facials, makeup application, makeup lessons and facial waxing. Co-owner Fernando is so popular that appointments should be made four to eight weeks ahead, but you can book an appointment with another stylist on short notice—usually on the same or the following day.
Open Tues.-Wed. & Fri. 10 a.m.-6 p.m., Thurs. 10 a.m.-7 p.m., Sat. 9 a.m.-4 p.m.

Hair Cuttery
1645 Connecticut Ave. NW
• 232-9685

Just walk right in, and someone will be with you shortly. No appointments taken, let alone necessary. A steady snip-snip-snip is the sound that greets clients when they enter the Hair Cuttery. This Dupont Circle salon is part of a

popular Washington chain, with over 75 branches (many of which are open on Sundays). Prices are rock-bottom, but don't ask for a complicated cut, unless you know the stylist. Nor should you get too attached to the personnel in this here-today-gone-tomorrow world of fast turnover. Check phone book for numbers of other branches.
Open Mon.-Fri. 8 a.m.-9 p.m., Sat. 8:30 a.m.-7 p.m., Sun. 11 a.m.-5 p.m.

Ilo
1637 Wisconsin Ave. NW
• 342-0350

Ilo is a full-service salon, with a complete skincare clinic that provides facials, electrolysis, waxing, massage—even aromatherapy, which involves the use of different oils on different parts of the body to relieve tension. Ilo's fifteen stylists pamper a wide range of clients: college students, professional people, government officials and television personalities. The house color specialist was a top colorist in Paris before joining Ilo's staff. Shampoo, cut, blow dry and styling will run $45 for women, $30 for men.
Open Mon.-Wed. &Fri. 10 a.m.-6 p.m., Thurs. 10 a.m.-7 p.m., Sat. 9 a.m.-5 p.m.

Noelle, The Day Spa & Hair Design
7200 Wisconsin Ave.,
Bethesda, Md.
• (301) 986-9293

Either men or women can escape from the office for a few hours and have a relaxing massage and a haircut here, or an entire morning (or day) of luxury. Noelle, located at the far reaches of Bethesda, unfortunately for downtown executives of both sexes, offers the most comprehensive pampering and pounding of any salon in the area. There are herbal wraps, paraffin treatments, massages, facials, waxing, cellulite toning and mud rubs. Then, there are the usual manicures, pedicures and everything you ever wanted done to your hair or scalp. The shop looks rather Swedish and modern, so even the most macho man would feel comfortable walking in the front door.
Open Mon.-Tues. & Fri.-Sat. 9 a.m.-6 p.m., Wed.-Thurs. 9 a.m.-8 p.m.

Okyo
1519 Wisconsin Ave. NW
• 342-2675

Bernard Portelli, the French-born stylist and owner of Okyo, is particularly enamored of long hair. He prides himself on offering modern European styling, classic rather than trendy. "There's no blue and green hair here," he notes. Bernard's beautifully designed shop is equipped with a video system that allows customers to watch a movie while waiting for their perms or color to take. The colorist at Okyo is one of the best in the business, with clients who come from as far as California and New York. The full-service salon offers body massages, make-up services, skin care,

waxing, full nail care and a solarium. First-time customers are limited to a haircut and blow dry, priced at $45 for women, $30 for men, "a little less than other big names in Washington," Bernard explains. Once the cut is right, Bernard and his stylists steer the client to other services as needed. Portelli's strategy is supremely successful, as witnessed by his clientele of political figures, congressional wives and television stars.
Open Mon.-Wed. & Fri. 10 a.m.-6 p.m., Thurs. 10 a.m.-7 p.m., Sat. 9 a.m.-5 p.m.

Roche
2445 M St. NW
• 775-0775

Relatively new on the scene, Roche offers hair and beauty treatments, makeup artistry, body massage, waxing, skin care and a nail artist who does manicures, pedicures, sculptures, tips and acrylics. For women, a shampoo, cut, blow dry and styling will cost $45. The same services for men are $30. West End Haircutters, Inc. is also owned by Dennis Roche and his wife, Sang Benkirade. Located at 2130 Pennsylvania Avenue NW (466-4403), it offers standard salon services. But for that special something extra, give Roche a try.
Open Mon.-Sat. 10 a.m.-6 p.m.

Salon Roi
2602 Connecticut Ave. NW
• 234-2668

If you've suffered enough stuffiness in the course of the day, unwind while being coiffed at Salon Roi. What's memorable about this full-service shop is the staff's special warmth and enthusiasm. Whether you're interested in the latest style or cut, a classic "do" or funky punk, you can get precisely what your heart desires at Salon Roi. Excellent stylists offer considerable expertise, but there's a lot of laughter and lighthearted conversation to be had here, as well. From heavenly shampoos and massage to pedicures and manicures, from luxurious facials and bikini waxing to skin care and makeup services, Salon Roi has it all. Coloring, highlighting and perms are excellent. The location is superb: just a stone's throw from the Zoo exit on Metro's Red Line. Salon Roi takes extra care with children, especially those coming for their first haircuts. A shampoo, cut and blow dry by the owners runs $52; $20 for children.
Open Tues.-Fri. 9 a.m.-7 p.m., Sat. 9 a.m.-4 p.m.

Watergate Salon
2532 Virginia Ave. NW
• 333-3488

You won't find a sun room or a sauna here, but virtually every other service—including body massage for women only—is available at the Watergate Salon. Nine stylists do both traditional and modern styles, and customers are pampered in what can only be described as the slightly

affected Watergate style. A shampoo, cut and blow dry will run $40 to $50 for women, depending on hair length, condition and setting lotion required. For men, haircuts are $20. Skin care, manicures and pedicures are available for both men and women.
Open Mon.-Sat. 9 a.m.-5 p.m.

Robin Weir and Co.
2134 P St. NW
• 861-0444

While former First Lady Nancy Reagan may be taking her tresses to a Hollywood hairdresser now, Robin Weir remains the glitziest "in" hairdresser, tending the heads of television journalist Lesley Stahl to sex therapist Dr. Ruth. If you would like to join this august company, an appointment with Weir should be made two weeks in advance. The first visit commands a flat $150 fee, which covers a consultation, haircut and perm or color if needed. After that initial premium, Weir's rates drop to those charged by his other stylists—a cut and styling will run $45. The salon offers a full range of services for hair, skin and nails. This is a big salon, with sixteen stylists, and thus lacks the warmth of some of its top-of-the-line counterparts. But warmth is secondary in a shop like this, where people come to see and be seen.
Open Mon.-Fri. 8 a.m.-6 p.m., Sat. 8 a.m.-4 p.m.

MEN ONLY

Pietro Hair Salon
1001 16th St. NW
(Capitol Hilton Hotel)
• 393-1000, 628-3706

Some women, primarily hotel guests, are relegated to the rear of this modern shop at the back of the Hilton lobby, but the specialty here is prize-winning hair cutting and wig making for men by Pietro Santori and his family. Washington isn't a very sybaritic city, but a facial by Attilio Santoro and a manicure by Arlette Weiner can be as relaxing as eighteen holes at the Burning Tree Golf Club.
Open Mon.-Fri. 8:30 a.m.-5:30 p.m., Sat. 9 a.m.-2 p.m.

Milton Pitts
16th & K Sts. NW
(Sheraton Carlton Hotel)
• 628-9425

If a visitor to Washington wants to feel like part of the power elite, this is the place to go. Barbering impresario Milton Pitts has been cutting presidential hair since the 1960s, but he and his associates also tend to less exalted heads for $25 per shampoo, cut and style. Pitts has a shop in the White House, where he spends approximately one day a week (shearing George Bush about once a fortnight). Since LBJ, only Jimmy Carter has eschewed Pitts' services.
Open Mon.-Fri. 9 a.m.-6 p.m., Sat. 9 a.m.-2 p.m.

House Barber Shops

B-323 Rayburn House Office Building, U.S. Capitol
• 225-7024

Senate Barber Shop

B-68 Russell Senate Office Building, U.S. Capitol
• 224-4560

You never know who'll be sitting in the next chair, so lobbyists consider this the place to be sheared. Although intended for male members of Congress and their staffs, the House and Senate barbers will accept other worthies if the appointment is made by a member's office—but you'll have to wait if a member walks in. Once the equivalent of the Main Street barber in Anytown, U.S.A., the Capitol shops have recently been tricked up so that they now provide all sorts of services desired by the modern politician, including coloring and a hair-spray job that would make Ann Miller green with envy. Prices are reasonable, and the barbers love to work here because they share in the great congressional "perks" program.
Open by appt. only (both locations).

BOOKS & PERIODICALS

GENERAL INTEREST BOOKSTORES

Ampersand Books

118 King St., Alexandria, Va.
• (703) 549-0840

Small, modest, this is the kind of place where you'd expect to find the latest political memoir or another reassessment of the Vietnam adventure. Given the plethora of Capitol Hill and lobbyist types living in the Old Town Alexandria neighborhood, this is why, no doubt, it attracts so much of the local clientele. Don't expect much more than recent releases, but there's a decent selection of those.
Open Mon.-Thurs. 10 a.m.-10 p.m., Fri.-Sat. 10 a.m.-11 p.m., Sun. noon-10 p.m.

B. Dalton Bookseller

The Shops at National Place, 1331 Pennsylvania Ave. NW
• 393-1468

Union Station, 50 Massachusetts Ave, NE
• 289-1724

It's a short sight better than a hotel newsstand. Actually, as chain bookstores go, this one boasts considerably more than current bestsellers. Since the demise of a small version of New York's Barnes & Noble a few years ago, this section of Washington's old downtown has needed a decent bookstore. So here it is, just off the Press Building's glitzy new shopping concourse. It's located in the attached J. W. Marriott Hotel, as a matter of fact, near the newsstand. There's another B. Dalton at the Mazza Gallerie, Union Station; others are sprinkled around area shopping malls.
National Place branch: open Mon.-Fri. 10 a.m.-9 p.m., Sat. 10 a.m.-7 p.m., Sun. noon-5 p.m. Union Station branch: open Mon.-Sat. 10 a.m.-9 p.m., Sun. 10 a.m.-7 p.m.

Bridge Street Books

2814 Pennsylvania Ave. NW
• 965-5200

While most other bookstores are trendy, and finding a book published prior to this year is impossible, Bridge Street is a quiet refuge from Georgetown's bustle—with a thoughtful selection of books. Upstairs, in the fiction section, is quietest. Lean back, relax and scan the shelves for that Thomas Hardy you've been wanting to reread. The shop deals in "quality books." That generally means serious stuff—philosophy, history, a rack devoted to Judaica—but there's a fine humor collection, too. Some good bargains can be found, usually, in a stall out front.
Open Mon.-Thurs. 10 a.m.-7 p.m., Fri.-Sat. 10 a.m.-11 p.m., Sun. 1 p.m.-6 p.m.

Calliope Bookstore

3424 Connecticut Ave. NW
• 364-0111

This is another "quality" shop, with a good poetry section and lots of university press offerings. There isn't much Stephen King here. Instead, there's lots of serious fiction, mostly current, and a broad selection from the social sciences.
Open Mon.-Fri. 11 a.m.-11 p.m., Sat. 10 a.m.-midnight, Sun. noon-9 p.m.

Chapters Literary Bookstore

1500 K St. NW
• 861-1333

Well, okay, a "literary" bookstore does sound a bit redundant, if not pretentious. But this little place's intended clientele, Washington's rather sparse and loosely knit American Literature—loving community, might have overlooked it under a less obvious name. As it happens, the store has expanded from a Saturdays-only schedule. Look for shelfloads of literary criticism, small-press offerings and, of course, all kinds of writers' self-help books.
Open Mon.-Fri. 10 a.m.-6:30 p.m., Sat. 11 a.m.-5 p.m.

Crown Books

2020 K St. NW
• 659-2030

This is the Washington area's own discount book chain, now reaching into every possible mall vacancy in the land, or so it seems. Founded by the very smart and aggressive son of a pharmacy-chain owner (himself very smart and aggressive), Crown offers big savings on *New York Times* bestsellers to lure customers. There's usually an aisle or two of remaindered bargains, which, if you really were looking for the 946-page *A New Encyclopedia of Freemasonry,* can help fill your home library for a pittance. Service is a problem at Crown: part of the reason the prices are lower is that the staff is not trained to help. If you see what you're looking for, great. If you don't, chances are the staff won't help. Crown, always quick to smell out new reading trends, was one of the first chains to jam its shelves with computer books and supplies. Branch locations almost everywhere.
Open Mon.-Fri. 9 a.m.-8 p.m., Sat.-Sun. 10 a.m.-6 p.m.

Gilpin House Book Shop
208 King St.,
Alexandria, Va.
• (703) 549-1880

Note the slightly earlier opening on Sunday. That's when the Sunday *New York Times* gets dumped in massive bundles outside Gilpin's door. It's become something of an Old Town Alexandria tradition, the convenience of home delivery notwithstanding, to saunter out for Sunday brunch, stopping at Gilpin's for the *Times* along the way. But this store is a good deal more than a newsstand. Current nonfiction books line one wall, and there's a wide selection of local literature and history.
Open Mon.-Thurs. 10 a.m.-10 p.m., Fri.-Sat. 10 a.m.-11 p.m.

Francis Scott Key Book Shop
28th & O Sts. NW
• 337-4144

This shop is considered a hidden treasure by locals. As its name implies, this store's strongest suit is local lore, both historical and current, which means anything from Civil War biographies to the latest bombshell by Seymour Hersh. There is also a good selection of travel, cooking and art books. Tucked away on one of Georgetown's quieter side streets, the shop celebrated half a century of business in 1988.
Open Mon.-Sat. 9:30 a.m.-6 p.m.

Sidney Kramer Books
1825 I St. NW
• 293-2685

This companion store of Kramerbooks recently moved to the heart of the city's business and financial district. The place still specializes in books for professionals in the social sciences, especially economics, political science and computers. But, hold on, there's more: look for a wider range of travel books as well.
Open Mon.-Thurs. 7:30 a.m.-1 a.m., Fri. 7:30 a.m.-midnight, Sat. 24 hours, Sun. midnight-1 a.m.

Kramerbooks
1517 Connecticut Ave. NW
• 387-1400

New York has Shakespeare & Co., and Washington has Kramerbooks, as popular as the "Social Safeway" or a singles bar for meeting people, plus a comprehensive bookstore-cum-café, too. This popular spot, with its Afterwords café at the back, can sometimes be a jumble of browsers, employees and queueing diners, especially when nearby think-tank and other office buildings empty for lunch or the end of the day. But the sophisticated selection of current works is a major compensation. Staffers' current literary "picks," posted near the cash register, are usually offbeat and intriguing, often beating local book reviewers to the draw.
Open Mon.-Thurs. 7:30 a.m.-1 a.m., Fri.-Sat. 24 hours, Sun. midnight-1 a.m.

Olsson's Books & Records

1239 Wisconsin Ave. NW
• 338-9544

Like everything else about Georgetown, there's a serious side behind the funky exterior. Don't let the green and purple hair—on patrons and employees alike—throw you. Beyond the record bins, there exists one of Washington's more serious bookstores, complete with earnest young clerks happy to help you pore over the catalogs in search of hard-to-find titles. Actually, there's a sizable assortment of the obscure and arcane already in stock. A very respectable array of current offerings is displayed near the front of the store—near the records and the green and purple hair. There's a quieter branch operation, for the determinedly unpunk, in Alexandria, Virginia, at 106 South Union Street. Added attraction there: a tea room overlooking the Potomac River.
Open Mon.-Thurs. 10 a.m.-10:45 p.m., Fri.-Sat. 10 a.m.-midnight, Sun. noon-7 p.m.

Politics & Prose

5015 Connecticut Ave. NW
• 364-1919

This delightful store, which recently moved almost doubling its original size, has become one of literary Washington's few landmarks, but the array of books and almost librarylike atmosphere explain why some passersby occasionally do confuse Politics & Prose with a branch of the public library. Browsing is not just welcome, it's actively encouraged. You may even see the odd well-known author there, not to sign books, but to shop for them. A particular favorite of Washington journalists, many of whom throw their book parties here.
Open Mon.-Sat. 10 a.m.-10 p.m., Sun. 11 a.m.-6 p.m.

Waldenbooks

1700 Pennsylvania Ave. NW
• 393-1490

This is a fairly predictable, although well-stocked, variation on the chain's nationwide formula. Waldenbooks has more than a dozen other locations in the Washington area.
Open Mon.-Fri. 9:30 a.m.-6 p.m., Sat. 10 a.m.-6 p.m.

SPECIAL-INTEREST BOOKSTORES

Audubon Naturalist Book Shop

8940 Jones Mill Rd.
Chevy Chase, Md.
• (301) 652-3606

Washington is chock-full of specialized bookstores, many of them, like this one, operated in conjunction with national organizations headquartered here. This store, operated by the Audubon Naturalist Society, happens to be one of the best. Not just for bird-fanciers, but for nature lovers of all kinds, it stocks some of the best photographic books going.
Open Mon.-Wed. & Fri.-Sat. 10 a.m.-5 p.m., Thurs. 10 a.m.-7 p.m.

Franz Bader Bookstore

1911 I St. NW
• 337-5440

Washington does not have a bookstore like New York's Rizzoli, a Tiffany of coffee-table books. However, one of Washington's better private galleries also boasts a quite respectable selection of art books. Sure, you might do as well at the National Gallery gift shop, but half the value of buying a pricey art book is knowing another copy won't be sitting on your neighbor's coffee table. Besides, private shops tend to reflect the private biases of their owners, which can yield surprises. This one has a German-language section, for instance.
Open Mon.-Sat. 10 a.m.-6 p.m.

Common Concerns

1347 Connecticut Ave. NW
• 463-6500

Where do all the Kennedy liberals find fodder for their causes? Right here. Whether it's famine in Africa, land reform in Central America or the exploitation of immigrant labor in the U.S., this Dupont Circle book shop contains something to make your blood boil. Then you can buy a T-shirt to announce your position to the world at large, and a greeting card with which to proselytize a friend. But there's more here than literature on the latest "flavor-of-the-week" cause. Development issues, East-West relations, black studies and labor movement literature are all represented. Common Concerns's co-owner, David Marcuse, is also the latter half of Chuck & Dave's in Takoma Park, Maryland (7001 Carroll Avenue; 301-891-2665). It's a general-interest bookshop specializing in children's and New-Age literature.
Open Mon.-Fri. 10 a.m.-8 p.m., Sat. 10 a.m.- 6 p.m., Sun. noon-5 p.m.

Dream Wizards

104 -G Halpine Rd.,
Rockville, Md.
• (301) 881-3530

For fans of Dungeons & Dragons and other fantasy games, and for a dizzying array of sci-fi literature, this shop is worth a visit. It also dabbles in magic and other black arts. It's a bit hard to find, so call for directions.
Open Mon.-Tues. 11 a.m.-6 p.m., Wed.-Fri. 11 a.m.-8 p.m., Sat. 10 a.m.-6 p.m., Sun. noon-5 p.m.

Lambda Rising

1625 Connecticut Ave. NW
• 462-6969

Washington's gay and lesbian community, which counts the Dupont Circle area as its hub, considers this store, a block from the Circle, its most important intellectual resource. Indeed, Lambda Rising is a fine general bookstore, too, well laid out and intelligently stocked. There are many volumes on sexual politics and human relationships, of course. But the selection ranges well beyond those areas, keeping up with the eclectic tastes of its core clientele.
Open daily 10 a.m.-midnight.

Georgetown University Leavey Center Bookshop
3800 Reservoir Rd. NW
• 687-7525

This snappy store, which is triple the size of the old one, has an extensive selection of international papers and magazines. As you would expect, there's also a good number of fields represented, including theology, history, reference works, travel, cooking and test preparation. If you've always wanted a university T-shirt, this is the right place to make the purchase.
Open Mon.-Fri. 8:30 a.m.-8 p.m., Sat. 9 a.m.-5 p.m., Sun. 11 a.m.-4 p.m.

The Map Store
1636 I St. NW
• 628-2608

Maps aside, this is the best travel book store in town. Of course, you can get a perfectly adequate highway guide from the auto club, but can you get one with a leather binding? This busy, little shop doesn't just serve travelers, it seeks to inspire them. In the middle of all the globes and antique map reproductions and travel aids, you'll find a broad array of travel books.
Open Mon.-Fri. 9 a.m.-5:30 p.m., Sat. 10 a.m.-4 p.m.

Modern Language Bookstore
3160 O St. NW
• 338-8963

Let's pretent that you awake one night and can't possibly go back to sleep without reading *Death in Venice* as Thomas Mann wrote it—in German. A translation just won't do. Although you'll have to wait until morning, check out Modern Language for volumes in many foreign languages, as well as cards and videos.
Open Mon.-Sat. 10 a.m.-7 p.m., Sun. noon-6 p.m.

Pyramid Bookstore
2849 Georgia Ave. NW
• 328-0190

1421 Good Hope Rd. SE
• 889-0002

3500 East-West Hwy.
Hyattsville, Md.
• (301) 559-5200

For a city whose population is at least two-thirds black, Washington has astonishingly few stores specializing in black literature. This one, located near Howard University, offers "books by and about people of African descent." The range is modest, but it includes titles on Islam, black politics and the arts. There's even an assortment of children's books for those to whom the Hardy Boys seem like odd role models.
Open daily 11 a.m.-7 p.m.

Reiter's Scientific & Professional Books
2021 K St. NW
• 223-3327

Were it not for all those earnest browsers in dark suits, this might almost seem like computer hacker heaven. The computing department has about the best collection of titles this side of Stephen Jobs's study. But don't bother if all you want to do is write a program to balance your checkbook. This is a store for professionals, and not just in the computer industry. All the sciences are well covered.
Open Mon.-Fri. 9 a.m.-7:30 p.m., Sat. 9:30 a.m.-6 p.m., Sun. noon-5 p.m.

Revolution Books

2438 18th St. NW
• 265-1969

For activists, and students of activists, this is virtually a mandatory stop. In the heart of Washington's ethnically diverse Adams Morgan section, the store offers the usual assortment of "movement" material—buttons, posters, tracts and other paraphernalia—plus an assortment of Third World periodicals and literature.
Open Mon. &Wed.Fri. noon-7 p.m., Sat. 11 a.m.-7 p.m., Sun. noon-5 p.m.

Sports Books, Etc.

Ravensworth
Shopping Center,
5224 Port Royal Rd.,
Springfield, Md.
• (301) 321-8660

Sports literature has blossomed in recent years to the point where a few stores specializing in it have begun to spring up as well. This one, in a suburban Springfield, Virginia shopping mall, recently merged with a memorabilia-and-baseball-cards shop. It offers souvenirs and other sporting odds and ends to supplement its inventory, but its first allegiance is obvious: it stocks biographies and how-to books for every popular sport, and a few more exotic ones as well.
Open Mon.-Fri. 10 a.m.-8 p.m., Sat. 10 a.m.-6 p.m., Sun. noon-5 p.m.

Travel Books Unlimited & Language Center

4031 Cordell Ave.,
Bethesda, Md.
• (301) 951-8533

Without doubt, this store has the largest and most complete selection on travel books in the area. There are guidebooks, travel narratives and maps galore from which to choose. Don't forget the foreign-language cassettes, money belts and currency changers, either.
Open Tues.-Sat. 10 a.m-9 p.m., Sun. noon-5 p.m.

Yes! Bookshop

1035 31st St. NW
• 338-7874

With the soothing strains of a meditation cassette playing gently over the speaker system, browsers at Yes! can sometimes be found staring off into the middle distance, all but unconscious of the book they've just picked up or the lunch date they'll be late for. It's that kind of place. Huge self-improvement and preventive medicine selections and lots on philosophy, psychology and religious themes stare you in the face. Even the fiction gets slotted into social science categories. You'll find Robertson Davies, for instance, in the Jungian psychology department. And—yes!—you can buy the tapes.
Open Mon.-Sat. 10 a.m.-10 p.m., Sun. noon-6 p.m.

USED & RARE BOOKS

The Book Cellar
8227 Woodmont Ave.,
Bethesda, Md.
• (301) 654-1898

This store, just off the Maryland end of Wisconsin Avenue, boasts a "half mile of fine browsing." We haven't checked the claim with a pedometer, but the place is well worth the extra several miles it takes to get there. It is truly a massive collection, in all major categories. And if the book you want is out of print or not in stock, the store's respected search service can often track it down, given a few weeks.
Open Mon.-Fri. 11 a.m.-6 p.m., Sat. 10 a.m.-5 p.m., Sun. 11 a.m.-5 p.m.

Booked Up
1209 31st St. NW
• 965-3244

This could be considered the dowager empress of local bookstores. Here is where Georgetown's gentry comes to find the nice, little leather-bound first edition for the library. Well-stocked with travel memoirs and other international memorabilia—as befits a neighborhood heavy with current and former diplomats and statesmen. It's a labyrinth of little rooms; finding your way around is an adventure in itself.
Open Mon.-Fri. 11 a.m.-3 p.m., Sat. 10 a.m.-12:30 p.m.

Bryn Mawr Lantern Bookshop
3222 O St. NW
• 333-3222

There must be an impressive number of Bryn Mawr alumna scattered up and down Georgetown's narrow streets, because this crowded shop in a townhouse is jammed with second-hand bargains, many of them the sort of erudite works one would expect Bryn Mawr women to have read. Whether it's the *Ann Landers Encyclopedia* or the 1911 Oxford University Press edition of *The Complete Works of Shakespeare*, the prices are usually exceptionally low.
Open Mon.-Fri. 11 a.m.-4 p.m., Sat. 11 a.m.-5 p.m., Sun. noon-4 p.m.

Idle Time Books
2410 18th St. NW
• 232-4774

This Adams Morgan shop offers a good, cheap read in an eclectic assortment of categories, reflecting the source of most of its volumes, the highly heterogeneous inhabitants of its neighborhood. You probably will not stumble across much that's rare, but the informal, almost studious atmosphere is nice, anyway. Each room offers couches and chairs, so you can sit and relax and sample, sample, sample.
Open daily 11 a.m.-10 p.m.

Second Story Books
2000 P St. NW
• 659-8884

You'll be able to spot this popular shop by the crowd browsing at book bins placed on the corner. A Dupont Circle mainstay, Second Story is a favorite haunt for the mildly bohemian folk who live in the neighborhood, and, during the day, for the young professionals who work nearby. Poetry, history and the humanities are particular strengths. A selection of first editions, not vast, is kept behind glass, and a few autographed and other rare volumes can always be found. Other locations in Bethesda (4836 Bethesda Ave. 20814, 656-0170) and Baltimore, Maryland.

Open daily 10 a.m.-10 p.m.

NEWSSTANDS

B & B News Stand
2621 Connecticut Ave. NW
• 234-0494, 234-0497

Billed as "one of the world's largest newsstands," B & B also stocks one of the world's largest collections of things newsstand habitués wouldn't want to buy. Pinball machines, for instance. Nonetheless, it has an enormous selection of out-of-town newspapers and periodicals, all kept in reasonable order—rare enough in this business. Despite the array of "adult publications," there is plenty of more serious material to be found.

Open Mon.-Fri. 9 a.m.-11 p.m., Sat.-Sun. 7 a.m.-11 p.m.

Hudson News
The Shops at National Place,
529 14th St. NW
• 783-1720

The old National Press Building, before it was gutted and renovated, boasted a decidedly dowdy-looking newsstand, which, despite its appearance, managed to keep the *Investor's Daily* from overflowing onto the *Wall Street Journal*, and got out-of-town papers on the racks before they had yellowed into history. The old stand's successor, although more pleasant to look at, has been somewhat less successful at the basics thus far. The growing array of souvenir T-shirts, sunglasses and chewing gum tell part of the story. A stray comment from a clerk tells another part: "We're not just a newsstand, you know," she explained when a customer complained about the non-news clutter.

Open Mon.-Thurs.. 8 a.m.-9 p.m., Fri. 8 p.m.-7 p.m., Sat. 10 a.m.-7 p.m., Sun. noon-5 p.m.

Key Bridge News Stand
3326 M St. NW
• 338-2626

It may look like a small convenience store, but this slightly out-of-the-way Georgetown shop does its main job—selling newspapers and magazines—quite adequately, thank you. *The Times* of London stays in its allotted space and the *Far Eastern Economic Review* will be right where it's supposed to be.

Open daily 8 a.m.-8 p.m.

News Room

1753 Connecticut Ave. NW
• 332-1489

Just what a good newsstand ought to aspire to be, the News Room enjoys a vast following among Washington's news junkies. You can buy collector's edition papers of the past —reporting on the first moon walk or the King assassination—or a wide assortment of foreign journals more or less of the present. Literary and academic journals are kept on one set of stands and computer publications on another. It's by no means an uncluttered place, but there is a sense that order is being maintained, however tenuously.
Open Mon.-Fri. 7 a.m.-10 p.m., Sat. 7 a.m.-midnight, Sun. 7 a.m.-9 p.m.

Periodicals

International Square,
1825 I St. NW
• 223-2526

Washington may be a competitive news town, but it's an even more competitive newsstand town, judging from the repeated openings and closings of this store's Georgetown outlet (3109 M Street NW). Fortunately, the International Square branch is still going strong, thriving apparently on the global news interests of nearby K Street law offices and news bureaus. It's well organized and well stocked. Even more, it's bright and clean, a rarity, indeed, in this retail sector.
Open Mon.-Fri. 7 a.m.-7 p.m., Sat. 10 a.m.-5 p.m.

CHILDREN

BOOKS

The Cheshire Cat Children's Book Store

5512 Connecticut Ave. NW
• 244-3956

The brainchild of four former schoolteachers, this shop near Chevy Chase Circle is a delight. The owners are knowledgeable, and eager to help you select books that will intrigue even "reluctant readers." There's a play area for little kids, to give parents more time to peruse the wide selection of books, records, maps and atlases, and coloring books about historic figures. The stock includes such unusual items as a huge chart depicting the monarchs of England, for pint-size history buffs. Authors of children's books often give readings here on weekends. Ask to receive the newsletter that lists the schedule and which also includes brief notes on new books for kids of all ages.
Open Mon.-Wed. & Fri.-Sat. 9:30 a.m.-5:30 p.m., Thurs. 9:30 a.m.-8 p.m.

A Happy Thought
4836 MacArthur Blvd., NW
• 337-8300

A big wooden goose tied with a red ribbon is the sign that you're at the right row house in what is a small commercial strip in a residential neighborhood. There is a play area where children can amuse themselves while parents peruse the shelves, and for those looking for gift books, the staff is happy to discuss what books are appropriate for which ages.
Open Mon.-Sat. 10 a.m.-5:30 p.m.

CLOTHES

Blue Moon Kids
Wildwood Center,
10231 Old Georgetown Rd.,
Bethesda, Md.
• (301) 530-4977

If your children are more at home in mud baths than at tea parties, Blue Moon may be the best place to shop. The clothes are hardly inexpensive, but they are extremely durable—100-percent cotton, from which the grime easily washes out. The fabrics come in prints as well as solids, and the styles are as classic as the problems of children getting dirty.
Open Mon.-Wed. & Fri.-Sat. 10 a.m.-6 p.m., Thurs. 10 a.m.-9 p.m.

Full of Beans
Tavern Square Mall,
109 N. Pitt St.
Alexandria, Va.
• (703) 632-8566

This pleasant shop is a little hard to find: it's tucked inside a tiny shopping mall, which, for purposes of architectural harmony, the city fathers forbid to be decked with commercial signs. It is worth seeking out if you want to find attractive, unusual clothes for boys and girls up to size six large. Much of the merchandise, including christening dresses, underwear, playclothes and pajamas, is 100-percent cotton. There are dainty, hand-smocked and hand-embroidered dresses for girls and nifty play clothes for both sexes. You'll also find a few toys and some colorful, kid-sized sleeping bags. Prices are moderate to expensive.
Open Mon.-Sat. 10 a.m.-5 p.m., Sun. 1 p.m.-5 p.m.

Just Boys
Foxhall Square,
3301 New Mexico Ave. NW
• 966-2697

If Dad is a Brooks Brothers man during the day and wears Polo in his off hours, then Just Boys will be just right for the little guy in the family. The shop, with a large model racing car in the center of the room, is decorated to look like a liliputian version of a wood-paneled men's store, and the clothes are for young gentlemen who will someday be wearing club ties, if not regimental ones. Just Boys is where you can find the best selection of short pants and blazers, bow ties and velvet knickers. This shop is for ages four and up, or until they are old enough to go to Dad's favorite salesman at Brooks Brothers.
Open Mon.-Sat. 9:30 a.m.-5:30 p.m.

Just So

Foxhall Square,
3301 New Mexico Ave. NW
• 244-0500

If success in business is location, location and location, this is a sure winner. Along with a shoe store, called Just Shoes, and a toy store, this is the sister shop of Just Boys, and all are located in a building with a lot of pediatrician offices. Just So specializes in clothes for older girls, and also has a good selection of infant and toddler clothes for both sexes, including some costly, but lovely, French cottons.
Open Mon.-Sat. 9:30 a.m.-5:30 p.m.

The Kid's Closet

1226 Connecticut Ave. NW
• 429-9247

1900 K St. NW
• 466-5589

A good selection of clothing for boys and girls up to size fourteen is stocked here, as well as Nike tennis shoes and other accessories. Busy working mothers will appreciate the store's shopping service. Customers fill out a form—available at the store or by mail—with their children's ages, sizes and color preferences, noting whether the kids are in school or day care, and whether the clothing is needed for special occasions. The store assembles a selection of outfits, and parents arrange for a convenient time to make their choice.
Connecticut Ave. branch: open Mon.-Fri. 10 a.m.-6 p.m., Sat. 11 a.m.-5 p.m. K St. branch: open Mon.-Fri. 10 a.m.-6 p.m.

Kids-R-Us

11818 Rockville Pike,
Rockville, Md.
• (301) 770-0660

3540 S. Jefferson St.,
Falls Church, Va.
• (703) 820-0034

These huge stores are an absolute boon for parents who would like to make shopping for their kids' clothes a one-stop outing. There are masses of attractive garments here, in infants' and children's sizes up to fourteen, as well as shoes, boots and sandals. What's more, prices are slightly discounted for merchandise that appears to be of good quality. You can find fashionable sportswear that elementary school girls will love because it is just like what their teen-age sisters are wearing, and pretty accessories such as headbands, bows and purses. The boys' departments stock an exceptionally large range of cute, unusual things for little boys. The Rockville store is about two blocks north of the White Flint metro stop.
Open Mon.-Sat. 10 a.m.-9 p.m., Sun. 11 a.m.-5 p.m.

Little Sprout, Inc.

Georgetown Park Mall,
3222 M St. NW
• 342-2273

This store bills itself as a gift store for children, but doting parents who also want to find special (read: expensive) clothes for infants and young school kids will find it worth a stop. The stock includes hand-painted underwear, T-shirts and socks, as well as very attractive handmade sweaters. There are some amusing T-shirts with prehistoric animals on them and satin baseball-style jackets with car appliques. Items like pajamas, overalls, patchwork banners, wooden coat racks and piggy banks can be monogrammed.
Open Mon.-Sat. 10 a.m.-9 p.m., Sun. noon-6 p.m.

Monday's Child

218 N. Lee St.,
Alexandria, Va.
• (703) 548-3505

Parents and grandparents who plan to make their favorite infant's baptism a major event will find an exquisite collection of cotton christening dresses in this tiny shop. Some of the lovely, delicate garments are made in the Philippines, then hand-smocked by three local women. There's a small, well-chosen selection of clothing for older children, but the nicest choices are for infants, including charming sweaters knitted in France and pretty blankets from Churchill Weavers in Berea, Kentucky. The shop sells one of the most imaginative baby shower gifts going. Set on a frilly doily is an array of infant necessities—diapers, a bottle and such—formed into the shape of a birthday cake!
Open Mon.-Sat. 10 a.m.-5 p.m.

Marelle

5301 Wisconsin Ave. NW
• 686-2040

If you've always wondered why your children do not look as cute as those wandering the streets of Paris, buy their clothing here, and they will. While this line of classic French children's clothing is very well known on the other side of the Atlantic, there are only a few shops in the U.S. This one opened late in 1989, and was an instant success. The smocked dresses, sailor suits, jumpers and woolen tights are adorable, simple and expensive. But it's still cheaper than a trip to France to buy the togs.
Open Mon.-Sat. 10 a.m.-5 p.m.

Twinkles

5232 44th St. NW
• 363-6211

Galleria at Tyson's II,
2255 International Dr.,
McLean, Va.
• (703) 734-8704

Twinkles is for kids who want to be stars. Or for kids whose parents are already stars, so they can afford the clothes. There is nothing classic about this selection. Rather than coats with velvet collars, Twinkles sells $300 studded leather jackets. Everything is top quality, with top price tags. This is the store where trendy parents dress their trendy kids. It's hip, cool, and who cares if the styles go out of fashion within a year? The kids will have outgrown their $500 outfits long before then. But if you want your child to make a fashion statement, this store is the Dianne B. of the toddler set.
Washington branch: open Mon.-Sat. 10 a.m.-5 p.m. McLean branch: open 10 a.m.-9:30 p.m. & 11 a.m.-6 p.m.

Why Not

200 King St.,
Alexandria, Va.
• (703) 548-4420

It's a toss-up whether this is a clothing store with a sideline of toys, or a toy store with a sideline of clothes. It's the clothing here that caught our attention, up to size seven for boys and size fourteen for girls. A big playpen equipped with lots of toys occupies toddlers while parents shop. The large selection of infants' wear features adorable baby bonnets and bibs, perfect for gift giving. Clothing can be personalized, with a child's name hand-painted on overalls

and shirts. For older children, consider the lovely hand-smocked dresses signed by South Carolina craftswomen, as well as amusing T-shirts and nifty play and school clothes for both boys and girls. Aspiring ballerinas will sigh for the pink and blue net tutus sparkling with silver trim, the matching headbands and ballet slippers.
Open Mon.-Wed. 10 a.m.-5:30 p.m., Thurs.-Fri. 10 a.m.-9 p.m., Sat. 10 a.m.-5 p.m., Sun. 1 p.m.-6 p.m.

FURNITURE

Lewis of London
12248 Rockville Pike, Rockville, Md.
• (301) 468-2070

Loehmann's Plaza, 7249 Arlington Blvd., Falls Church, Va.
• (703) 876-9330

This is just the place for wealthy grandparents or expectant couples with money to burn. Featured here is a large array of high-priced, high-quality nursery and juvenile furniture: dressers and beds, as well as rocking chairs and toy chests that can be personalized with a child's name. A handsome collection of bed linens includes charming, cozy comforters. Many of the bright, cheery wall hangings also can be personalized. Expensive designer clothes for infants and toddlers, like the Baby Dior line, are available to tempt shoppers to further extravagance. Steer clear of the toys. You can find the same things elsewhere for less.
Rockville branch: open Mon.-Wed. & Fri.-Sat. 10 a.m.-6 p.m., Thurs. 10 a.m.-9 p.m., Sun. noon-5 p.m. Falls Church branch: open Mon.-Wed. & Fri.-Sat. 10 a.m.-6 p.m., Thurs. 10 a.m.-8:30 p.m., Sun. noon-5 p.m.

TOYS

Child's Play
The Shops at National Place, 1331 Pennsylvania Ave. NW
• 393-2382

This charming two-room store, crammed with toys and stuffed animals, aims to delight the younger child with a nice selection of simple toys and games. The stuffed animal menagerie will entice shoppers of all ages. But the real attractions here are the tiny, funny novelty items, such as wind-up somersaulting mice and kangaroos or the battery-powered gorilla that shoots sparks from its mouth when it walks. The staff includes a couple of chatty, zany salespeople who know the stock well and can't contain their eagerness to show off a few of their favorite toys.
Open Mon.-Wed. & Fri. 10 a.m.-7 p.m., Thurs. 10 a.m.-8 p.m., Sat. 10 a.m.-7 p.m., Sun. noon-5 p.m.

FAO Schwarz

Georgetown Park Mall,
3222 M St. NW
• 342-2285

Mazza Gallerie
5300 Wisconsin Ave. NW
• 363-8455

Neither of these outlets of the famed New York store can begin to rival their namesake. Nor are they a match for Toys-R-Us or the other large toy stores in the area, but they do carry a respectable array of stuffed animals, dolls, battery-operated and remote- or radio-controlled cars and other vehicles. Infant toys are not neglected, but while there is a good selection of games for young children, the store maintains only a small section of games for older youths and adults.
Open Mon.-Fri. 10 a.m.-9 p.m., Sat. 10 a.m.-7 p.m., Sun. noon-6 p.m.

Flights of Fancy

The Shops at National Place,
1331 Pennsylvania Ave. NW
• 783-2800

This whimsical store is home to a few traditional, cuddly, stuffed bears and dogs, but the real focus is on stuffed cloth creations. On hand are exotic animals such as flamingos and toucans, and some wildly imaginative one-of-a-kind creatures. You'll also find cloth-art dolls with loads of personality. Beware, none of these beasts comes cheap, and some of the larger dolls and animals sell for well over $100.
Open Mon.-Wed. & Fri. 10 a.m.- 7 p.m., Thurs. 10 a.m.-8 p.m., Sat. 10 a.m.-7 p.m., Sun. noon-5 p.m.

Georgetowne Zoo

3222 M St. NW
• 338-4182

Adults have been known just to gaze in wonderment at the window of this shop in the Georgetown Park shopping mall. There are not only bears, bears and more bears, but there are also stuffed anteaters, snakes, dolphins and alligators. Stuffed animals are the only inhabitants of this shop, and they range in price from imported and outrageously expensive, to reasonably priced and just as cute. Even if you have no intentions of buying, look in the window and smile.
Open Mon.-Sat. 10 a.m.-9 p.m., Sun. noon-6 p.m.

Lowen's

7201 Wisconsin Ave.,
Bethesda, Md.
• (301) 652-1289

Lowen's is popular among local parents for its selection of unusual, innovative toys, ranging from the likes of a six-foot-long lion to plastic dollhouse furniture and wooden infants' toys from Sweden. There are Lego sets galore, some with power packs that allow construction of elaborate machinery with moving parts. Dozens of new and traditional board games are always in stock, as well as art supplies, scale-model kits and children's books. There's even a shoe section for tiny feet and an ice-cream parlor to provide a little quick energy for tired shoppers. An extra bonus: the store is near the Bethesda metro stop.
Open Mon.-Wed. & Fri.-Sat. 9:30 a.m.-6 p.m., Thurs. 9:30 a.m.-9 p.m., Sun. noon-5 p.m.

Red Balloon

1073 Wisconsin Ave. NW
• 965-1200

Both parents and kids will have fun browsing among the displays of whimsical, unusual toys at Red Balloon. Weekends can be a bit hectic in this narrow store, just a block off Georgetown's main drag, with customers examining the interesting imported toys for infants, the scientific toys and some off-beat board and card games. The front of the shop features lots of clever little items perfect for party favors and Christmas stocking-stuffers, for which kids willingly shell out a couple of dollars of their allowance. The toys are supplemented by a small selection of children's clothes, including togs for infants and toddlers that feature funny animal appliqués.

Open Mon.-Thurs. 10 a.m.-10 p.m., Fri.-Sat. 10 a.m.-11 p.m., Sun. noon-6 p.m.

Tiny Dwelling

1510 King St.,
Alexandria, Va.
• (703) 548-1223

The plans for Dolly's dreamhouse can be purchased here, along with all the necessary building materials: molding, shingles, bricks, wallpaper, special kits for bay windows, hot tubs and gazebos and other "essentials" for a lavish mini-mansion. Tiny Dwelling boasts one of the widest ranges of dollhouse furniture in the area, from inexpensive wooden pieces for real kids to elaborately carved reproductions of Tudor four-poster beds and other miniatures for affluent adult dollhouse addicts. Those fond of miniatures will melt before the array of tiny accent pieces, from picture frames to birthday cakes to brooms and dustpans. The staff is friendly and helpful, and in case you don't have the time or skill to do it yourself, they can arrange for your dollhouse to be built from the kit you select. The store is near the King Street metro stop.

Open Tues.-Sat. 10 a.m.-5:30 p.m., Sun. noon-5 p.m.

Toys-R-Us

11800 Rockville Pike,
Rockville, Md.
• (301) 770-3376

Somehow, any Saturday afternoon at this toy department store manages to look like the Christmas rush, with parents pushing loaded shopping baskets through the aisles while they try to ride herd on gaggles of giggling tykes. The sheer volume of merchandise is daunting; you'll find party favors, dolls, balls, wagons, bikes, elaborate electronic games and more. The directories hung near the entrances are a true blessing, as are the signs posted over each aisle. To avoid frazzled nerves, try to shop early or late in the day. The childless shopper should be prepared for a potentially terrifying experience, especially near the holidays. The Rockville location of Toys-R-Us is near the White Flint metro stop, and there are several other locations in suburban Maryland and Virginia accessible by car.

Open Mon.-Sat. 9:30 a.m.-9:30 p.m., Sun. 11 a.m.-6 p.m.

Tree Top Toys

**Foxhall Square Mall,
3301 New Mexico Ave. NW
• 244-3500**

This toy store is where you can park one child while taking the others to the pediatrician upstairs. It is a small toy store, but each of the shelves and aisles is crammed full of toys that will appeal to all ages, from infants' items all the way up to complicated models for older boys and girls. There is a small section of books and videotapes. A great feature of Tree Top Toys is that they have a counter devoted to seasonal holidays, such as Halloween or Christmas.
Open Mon.-Sat. 9:30 a.m.-5:30 p.m.

Washington Doll's House & Toy Museum

**5236 44th St. NW
• 363-6400**

Begin your visit to this combination museum and miniatures store with a stroll through the fascinating collection of antique toys and dollhouses. Serious miniaturists consider this store the best place in the area to find the expensive and elegant furniture, lighting fixtures, wine glasses and other accessories that can turn their dollhouses into convincing replicas of real dwellings. Tiny reproductions of nineteenth-century silver tea-and-coffee services and tin-lined copper cooking pots are produced for the store by artisans who originally produced such items in full scale, but got hooked on the fun of creating them in miniature. Some building supplies are also stocked, but you won't find much of the cruder wooden or plastic furniture that is more appropriate for youngsters working on their first dollhouse. The Friendship Heights metro stop is close by.
Open Tues.-Sat. 10 a.m.-5 p.m., Sun. noon-5 p.m.

CLOTHES (See Children's shops, page 191; Department Stores & Shopping Centers, page 198; Menswear, page 254; Womenswear, page 271)

COMPUTERS

Advanced Computer Concepts

**1555 Wilson Blvd.,
Rosslyn, Va.
• (703) 276-7800**

You can find all the top brands of personal computers here—Leading Edge, IBM, Kaypro, Epson, Toshiba, Sharp, to name a few—in this cluttered, busy suburban shop. But don't be put off by the zillions of boxes jamming the sales area or the frantic pace around you, because the prices are all discount—and the savings make the lack of ambience worth it. In addition to computers, you will find a full range of accessory items here, also at better prices than most outlets in the area. Discounts range as high as 20 to 25 percent, with the savings—as always—improving with the size of the purchase. This store, which also has a small

branch location at Tyson's Corner, is an authorized dealer for most of its products, and the salespeople are technically trained to service what they sell.
Open Mon.-Fri. 9 a.m.-7 p.m., Sat. 10 a.m.-5 p.m.

Rent-a-Computer, Inc.
4853 Cordell Ave.,
Bethesda, Md.
• (301) 951-0811

This rental store claims four-hour service in getting a computer to you, including delivery. They offer both short- and long-term rentals and specialize in IBM equipment. A sample price: a basic IBM PC rents for $120 a month.
Open Mon.-Fri. 8:30 a.m.-5:30 p.m.

DEPARTMENT STORES & SHOPPING CENTERS

ONE-STOP SHOPPING

There are few months in which wandering the streets of Georgetown or downtown to find specialty shops is a pleasant stroll—namely, during spring and fall. Washington abounds in fascinating specialty stores, but the seasoned shopper will realize that a tour of the capital's department stores is an efficient and entertaining way to organize a shopping spree. About the only thing you can't find in Washington department stores is, curiously, a decent selection of toys. Virtually anything else can be nosed out on some floor, in some department, from everyday necessities to objects rare and bizarre. For example, the furniture sections in the better department stores often outshine the specialty furniture stores in town, and the same goes for menswear and shoe departments. Department stores offer hard-to-beat selections of stationery, cosmetics, fragrances and costume jewelry.

Most of the major shopping malls are well outside the city, in Virginia and Maryland. Several have branches of the three major downtown department stores—Garfinckels, Hecht's and Woodward & Lothrop—but none of the branches can compare with the downtown flagship stores. For visitors from New York, the Washington suburbs do offer outposts of Saks Fifth Avenue, Lord & Taylor and Bloomingdale's, so the credit cards can be put to good use.

DEPARTMENT STORES

Bloomingdale's

Tyson's Corner Shopping
Center,
1961 Chain Bridge Rd.,
McLean, Va.
• (703) 556-4600

White Flint,
11301 Rockville Pike,
North Bethesda, Md.
• (301) 984-4600

It's not New York, but it's Bloomies. This is the wonderful store where you can find a pair of red Dr. Denton's with "Bloomies" stamped on the drop seat, men's bikini underwear featuring a giant ice cream cone where it counts, or the perfect gift for your sedate, elderly grandmother. Here the bizarre blends with the standard, accented by the elegant and the unusual, in a marvelous, exciting atmosphere that makes browsing a pleasure and buying a delight. Great furniture, housewares, linens, lighting, china, glassware, crystal, silver and exceptional gift items make this store's reputation, sold at what are often surprisingly reasonable prices. The menswear department and the women's clothing sections, including lingerie and a special section for larger women, are first-rate. You can find it all at Bloomingdale's, and have loads of fun in the process.
Open Mon.-Sat. 10 a.m.-9:30 p.m., Sun. 11 a.m.-6 p.m.

Garfinckel's

1401 F St. NW
• 628-7730

Georgetown Park Mall,
3222 M St. NW
• 628-8107

4820 Massachusetts Ave. NW
• 363-7700

Garfinckel's is Washington style. Which means you'll see a lot of conservative clothes, with a smattering of international style. It's the bastion of old-line Washington good taste and style, and insecure newcomers know that if it comes from Garfinckel's, it fits in Washington society. Of the major downtown department stores, Garfinckel's is unbeatable for its variety of merchandise and prices. The menswear department is outstanding, especially for shirts, ties, sweaters and accessories. You'll find a wide selection of sportswear for both men and women (albeit a tad on the stuffy side), as well as everything from casual wear to business suits, and from designer sportswear to furs and evening wear for women. Recently, the store added a good section of clothing for larger women. Garfinckel's bridal salon is a particular favorite of Washington brides-to-be. For those who are guests, and not the main attraction at the wedding, this is a superb source of gifts for the occasion, with china, crystal and silver offerings among the best in the city. The Garfinckel's box alone makes a statement. You'll find a solid stationery department, an excellent jewelry section both for costume and top-of-the-line pieces, good shoes and hosiery, and an impressive cosmetics and fragrance department. There's also a nice little restaurant, popular with impeccable, blue-haired older ladies, that offers a good, quiet place to lunch for a reasonable price—a rarity in downtown Washington.
F St. branch: open Mon.-Wed. & Fri.-Sat. 10 a.m.-6 p.m.,

Thurs. 10 a.m.-7 p.m. Georgetown Park Mall branch: open Mon.-Fri. 10 a.m.-8 p.m., Sat. 10 a.m.-7 p.m., Sun. noon-5p.m. Massachusetts Ave. branch: open Mon.-Wed. & Fri.-Sat. 10 a.m.-6 p.m., Thurs. 10 a.m.-7 p.m.

Hecht's
1201 G St. NW
• 628-6661

Of the major downtown department stores, Hecht's is the solid option for Washington shoppers on a less-than-unlimited budget. The merchandise at Hecht's holds up well by virtually every standard, but the sales clerks are disappointingly inattentive (but then sales staff is not the strong suit of any of the downtown stores). Recently, Hecht's moved into a new location in the heart of downtown at Metro Center, acquiring a new elegance in the process. Particularly noteworthy here are the good, reasonably priced small appliances, electronics, housewares, linens and home furnishings. Women's and men's clothing and jewelry also merit your attention. Hecht's operates a furniture warehouse in suburban Virginia that boasts some of the best values around.
Open Mon.-Sat. 10 a.m.-8 p.m., Sun. 11:30 a.m.-6:30 p.m.

Lord & Taylor
5255 Western Ave. NW
• 362-9600

Nestled in the shadow of glitzier Mazza Gallerie, Lord & Taylor is primarily for women who wear sensible shoes. It is the best place for "safe" shopping for women who wish to be very proper, very conservative and want nothing to do with trends. It is particularly good for shoes, handbags, belts, jewelry and other accessory items. You'll find all the classics here in the designer departments, but not a great deal of spark or drama. Yet, every once in a while, you'll find an in-house design that is exceptionally stylish. The menswear is utterly predictable. The furniture at Lord and Taylor gets good marks, and the excellent sales seem to be never-ending. The store is certainly worth a visit.
Open Mon.-Fri. 10 a.m.-9:30 p.m., Sat. 10 a.m.-7 p.m., Sun. 11 a.m.-6 p.m.

Macy's
The Galleria at Tysons II,
2255 International Dr.,
McLean, Va.
• (703) 556-0000

Pentagon City,
Fashion Center
1000 S. Hayes St.,
Arlington, Va.
• (703) 418-4488

It all started when Saks Fifth Avenue established a beachhead in Washington more than twenty years ago, and the out-of-town stores have just kept coming, especially from New York. It was inevitable that the region was due for a Macy's, "the biggest store in the world at Herald Square," and now a big force in the Washington economy. Unlike Bloomingdale's, whose boutiques force you to have to look for blouses in ten places, it is easy to find your way around Macy's. Macy's will have what it is you are looking for. It can be feather boas, rugs, housewares, pâté, washing machines or buttons. Macy's has a department for everything. Shop here: that is, if you don't mind a frantic pace and a rude sales staff. You can usually save money at the sale times, and this is a truly full-service department store, with the emphasis on middle-range merchandise.

McLean branch: open Mon.-Sat. 10 a.m.-9:30 p.m., Sun. 10 a.m.-6 p.m. Arlington branch: open Mon.-Sat. 10 a.m.-9:30 p.m., Sun. 10 a.m.-6 p.m.

Neiman-Marcus

Mazza Gallerie,
5300 Wisconsin Ave. NW
• 966-9700

The Galleria at Tysons II,
2255 International Dr.,
McLean, Va.
• (703) 761-1600

Known to many who still flock there as "Needless Markup," Neiman-Marcus rode into Washington from Texas and took the town by storm. From its cosmetic department, where you can be almost assaulted by salespeople or frozen out, depending on how you are dressed, to the pricey costume-jewelry section, or the designer salon with every name you've read on the pages of *Vogue*, or the epicure department, with private-label liqueur cakes, to the best fur department in the region, or the handbag boutique with its designer purses, N-M carries the top of the line, and not much else. Neiman's rewards its frequent shoppers by giving them membership in the In Circle. This means free gift-wrapping, magazine subscriptions, and, according to how many points you earn, perhaps even a trip to London or Paris. The staff can be charming and helpful, or haughty and acting as though they are doing you a favor by taking your money—the attitude is a crap shoot. Do watch for the sales, however, since not everyone can afford designer everything, so a lot of it ends up on sale.

Open Mon.-Fri. 10 a.m.-9 p.m., Sat. 10 a.m.-6 p.m., Sun. noon-5 p.m.

Nordstrom

The Galleria at Tysons II,
2255 International Dr.,
McLean, Va.
• (703) 761-1121

Pentagon City,
1100 S. Hayes St.,
Arlington, Va.
• (703) 415-1121

The story made the front page of the business section of *The Washington Post*: Nordstrom had arrived, with its legendary customer service, its fabulous merchandise and more legendary service. And it's true. It's not that you'll find that much more at Nordstrom than in any other store, but the Seattle-based retail chain does give service with a smile. They take back merchandise if you don't have the sales receipts; they take you from department to department to accessorize an outfit. In the shoe department, which is one of the stores' highlights, a salesperson wanders around with a small walkie-talkie to alert staff members if a person is sitting and looking forlorn. You won't find dishwashers or sewing notions, but you will find complimentary personal shopping service—with a capital S.

Open Mon.-Sat. 10 a.m.-9:30 p.m., Sun. 11 a.m.-6 p.m.

Saks Fifth Avenue

5555 Wisconsin Ave.,
Chevy Chase, Md.
• (301) 657-9000

It was considered a sign of civilization reaching the banks of the Potomac when Saks opened in 1964. Saks is probably the best across-the-board department store (no furniture) in the Washington area, for price, variety and quality. Just across the District line on Wisconsin Avenue, Saks offers men's and women's clothing from the casual to the formal, a wonderful women's shoe deparment, excellent jewelry and accessories, lovely linens and a well-chosen collection of casual and formal handbags. The women's lingerie department is one of the best in town, with a wide selection of bras, foundation garments, robes, slips and gowns. There's a classy group of designer rooms and salons featuring, among others, Ungaro, Adolfo and Saks's famous St. John knitwear. While Saks is known as a purveyor of fashion to the very wealthy and very social, there's plenty of variety for everyone here and lots of budgetary options, including superb buys in clothing bearing Saks's own label.
Open Mon. & Thurs. 10 a.m.-9 p.m., Tues.-Wed. & Fri.-Sat., 10 a.m.-6 p.m., Sun. noon-5 p.m.

Woodward & Lothrop

1025 F St. NW
• 347-5300

5400 Wisconsin Ave.,
Chevy Chase, Md.
• (301) 654-7600

Woodies, as it is affectionately known, is another Washington institution. It's not as elegant as Garfinckel's, but it offers a very comfortable blend of upscale and downscale shopping that has been serving the city well for years. Also a favorite for china, silver and gift items, Woodies has a full range of men's and women's clothing, luggage, shoes, appliances, housewares, linens, china, silver, small appliances, furniture and lighting. The bridal department is fine, indeed, with an extensive selection of dresses and accessory items. The restaurant here is considered an undiscovered gem by many of the downtown working crowd.
Washington branch: open Mon.-Sat. 10 a.m.-8 p.m., Sun. 11 a.m.-6 p.m. Chevy Chase branch: open Mon.-Sat. 10 a.m.-9:30 p.m., Sun. 11 a.m.-6 p.m.

SHOPPING CENTERS

Fair Oaks Mall

11750 Fair Oaks,
Fairfax, Va.
• (703) 359-8303

Located at the intersection of I-66 and Route 50 West (exit 15 off I-66), Fair Oaks Mall has been operating for seven years. A complete shopping center fashioned for the upscale buyer, it boasts 180 stores, with twenty more in the works. The main department stores include Garfinckel's, Hecht's, Woodward & Lothrop, Lord & Taylor, J.C. Penney and Sears.
Open Mon.-Sat. 10 a.m.-9:30 p.m., Sun. noon-6 p.m.

The Galleria at Tysons II

2255 International Dr., McLean, Va.
• (703) 827-7700

The Galleria is the suburban mall par excellence. At no other mall, we think, can you hear the tinkling of piano music while eating Chinese fast food or pizza. The Galleria looks similar to the lobby of a hotel designed by John Portman. With Neiman-Marcus at one end and Macy's at the other, there are shops arranged around three levels, all looking into an atrium. While the accent is on fashion, there are more sporting goods stores than at most malls. Champs Sports sells absolutely everything the serious or even not-so-serious athlete could desire, from walking machines to state-of-the-art home weight-lifting equipment. There is a great selection of the boutique chains found in other malls—The Sharper Image, Kitchen Bazaar, Boston Traders, Rodier, The Limited and The White House. There's also a Custom Shop for men's shirts, Units for cotton-knit clothing, and a good Hallmark store.
Open Mon.-Sat. 10 a.m.-9:30 p.m., Sun. noon-6 p.m.

Georgetown Park Mall

3222 M St. NW
• 342-8180

Shopping at Georgetown Park is worth the trouble of weaving through the congested streets to get there. It offers a refreshing alternative to the punk, junky atmosphere that has the major streets of Georgetown in a choke hold. Indeed, it seems that the fashionable specialty stores that gave Georgetown its now overrated reputation as a rewarding place to shop have all fled to the mall. Georgetown Park has character, with a stunning interior design featuring a glass roof, lots of greenery and a good deal of charm. Garfinckel's is the mall's only major department store, but it's the diverse collection of smaller shops and elegant boutiques that make Georgetown Park so special. There is a Ralph Lauren Polo, Victoria's Secret, Williams-Sonoma and The Sharper Image. The mall boasts several good shoe stores and a number of women's clothing boutiques, some traditional in outlook, others oriented toward chic European designer fashions. Georgetown Park is a good place to shop for jewelry, menswear, children's clothes and toys. Prices hover in the upper-middle to expensive range, but a careful shopper can unearth some bargains. Japanese and Italian restaurants and a deli figure among the mall's several eateries.
Open Mon.-Fri. 10 a.m.-9 p.m., Sat. 10 a.m.-7 p.m., Sun. noon-6 p.m.

Landmark Shopping Center

5839 Duke St.,
Alexandria, Va.
• No phone

Just off I-395 at the Duke Street East exit is Landmark Shopping Center. In business for years, this open-air center has 43 stores, no movie theaters, easy access and lots of parking. You'll find a large and wonderful Sears store here, as well as branches of Woodward & Lothrop and Hecht's. *Open Mon.-Sat. 9:30 a.m.-10 p.m., Sun. noon-6 p.m.*

Mazza Gallerie

5300 Wisconsin Ave. NW
• 966-6114

Larger than Georgetown Mall, but sterile and cold by comparison, Mazza Gallerie comprises some 50 stores that draw a well-heeled—indeed, chauffeur-driven—predominantly female clientele. Predictably, then, Mazza abounds in plush designer shops, jewelers, shoe stores and specialty gift shops. The center's major stores are Neiman-Marcus and Raleigh's. Neiman's is a smaller version of its Texas namesake, with the same high-quality merchandise, the same extravagant price tags and the same uppity sales clerks. A good indoor parking garage makes access easy, and the stores will validate your ticket to allow for two free hours of parking. The Pierre Deux country French fabrics, Williams-Sonoma kitchen store, a few of the designer shops and jewelry stores and the Jane Wilner linens outlet make a trip here worthwhile.
Open Mon.-Fri. 10 a.m.-9 p.m., Sat. 10 a.m.-6 p.m., Sun. noon-5 p.m.

Montgomery Mall

7121 Democracy Blvd.,
Bethesda, Md.
• (301) 469-6000

There is little to recommend Montgomery Mall except its location, which is convenient if you happen to live in or be visiting the Maryland suburbs. Architecturally, it's nothing. There are no superstores like Nordstrom. Also, this is one of the most confusing malls in the region. It is carved into a hillside, so if you park by Garfinckel's, it is impossible to get to Sears, and losing your car means you could be on the wrong, or different, level. However, it does have a complex of movie theaters, small branches of major department store chains, and specialty shops such as Kitchen Bazaar, B. Dalton and The Limited.
Open Mon.-Fri. 10 a.m.-9:30 p.m., Sat. 10 a.m.-6:30 p.m., Sun. noon-6 p.m.

Pentagon City Fashion Center

1100 S. Hayes St.,
Arlington, Va.
• (703) 415-2400

To urbanites, who consider not having to own an automobile the mark of a civilized city, the opening of the shopping mall at Pentagon City was greeted was cheers. At last, the sort of mall one finds at Tysons or White Flint was only two stops of the Metrorail from downtown on the new Yellow Line. It was possible to shop during a lunch hour at Nordstrom, Macy's, Cache, or any of the other toney boutiques. Pentagon City does not bill itself as a full-service

mall. It wants to create an identity as the fashion center of the region. The mall itself is rather sterile, but everything you might want to put on your back is right there. If not taking the Metrorail, take Exit 9 from I-395.
Open Mon.-Sat. 10 a.m.-9 p.m., Sun. noon-5 p.m.

Potomac Mills
2700 Potomac Mills Circle,
Prince William, Va.
• (703) 643-1770

About 30 to 40 minutes outside Washington, just off I-95 at Exit 52, Potomac Mills is a mecca for shoppers who worship at the shrine of bargains and discounts. Billed as the largest off-price and outlet mall in the country, Potomac Mills brings together no fewer than 175 discount or outlet stores of every description. By far the greatest draw is Ikea—the fabulous Swedish furniture store known for its clean-lined designs, good quality and reasonable prices—followed by Waccamaw Pottery and Cohoes, which offers moderate- to high-priced men's and women's apparel and accessories. Potomac Mills also lays claim to the area's largest mall movie complex (ten theaters). Parking won't be a problem: there are 6,500 spaces outside the mall.
Open Mon.-Sat. 10 a.m.-9:30 p.m., Sun. 11 a.m.-6 p.m.

Seven Corners
6201 Arlington Blvd.
Falls Church, Va.
• (703) 532-2453

Seven Corners is probably the quickest and easiest shopping center to reach from downtown. Just head straight out Route 50, and you'll find Seven Corners at the intersection of Route 50 and Route 7. Among the 68 stores here, the largest are Woodward & Lothrop and Garfinckel's, with two levels of shopping. There's lots of parking, eight mall entrances and a good mix of stores.
Open Mon.-Sat. 10 a.m.-9:30 p.m., Sun. noon-6 p.m.

The Shops at National Place
1331 Pennsylvania Ave. NW
• 783-9090

Offering two levels of shopping in the heart in downtown, the Shops is a gem of a mall. Two of the most popular shops are Banana Republic, where the safari-style clothing is a particular favorite of news photographers and people who want to look like them, and The Sharper Image, the high-tech yuppie fantasy land. A solid contingent of women's clothing stores offer racks and stacks of fashionable, moderately priced ready-to-wear. Although some of the stores are trendy and directed to the younger shopper, there's plenty for women of all ages. The mall also includes several excellent emporiums featuring children's gifts and toys. Hungry? Several decent restaurants may be found on the lower levels, while the upper Food Hall is a junk-food paradise.
Open Mon.-Wed. & Fri.-Sat. 10 a.m.-7 p.m., Thurs. 10 a.m.-8 p.m., Sun. noon-5 p.m.

Springfield Mall

Franconia & Loisdale Rds.,
Springfield, Va.
• (703) 971-3000,
(703) 971-3600

Off I-95 South at the Franconia exit, Springfield Mall is undergoing a major renovation, intended to change its image from a family-oriented mall to a more upscale shopping center. There are about 200 different stores of all types here; the magnet stores are J. C. Penney, Montgomery Ward and Garfinckel's. You'll find about 6,000 parking spaces in this huge mall.
Open Mon.-Sat. 10 a.m.-9:30 p.m., Sun. noon-5 p.m.

Tysons Corner Shopping Center

1961 Chain Bridge Rd.,
McLean, Va.
• (703) 893-9400,
(703) 893-7720

As shopping centers go, Tysons is one of the nicest around. In addition to Bloomingdale's, Hecht's and Woodward & Lothrop, you'll find 140 other stores, including a rarity: an honest-to-gosh dime store (Woolworth's). There are small branches of Garfinckel's and Raleigh's. You'll find two sets of movie theaters, a 1,500-space parking deck with free shuttle service to the front door of the mall, plenty of ground-level parking and lots of high-quality merchandise, with a focus on fashion. Tysons Center is at the intersection of Route 7 and Route 123, right off the Capitol Beltway (I-495) at Exit 10b and 11b.
Open Mon.-Sat. 10 a.m.-9:30 p.m., Sun. noon-5 p.m.

Union Station

50 Massachusetts Ave. NE
• 289-1908

Union Station is a stop in itself. The 1907 beaux arts building had fallen into disrepair and was closed for seven years before it underwent a $160-million restoration. It now glistens, and is abuzz with people flocking to catch trains, black-tie-wearing diners heading for a party in the rotunda, patrons filling tables at trendy and expensive Adirondacks or Sfuzzi (or less expensive but equally trendy America), and shoppers . . . lots of shoppers. Like a suburban mall, Union Station has movie theaters and a food court (see listing in the Quick Bites chapter, page 87). There is no anchor department store tenant, but there are a number of the successful national chains, from The Limited and Benetton to Sam Goody for records, B. Dalton for books and Units for cotton-knit separates that all go together. In addition to the stores, located on three levels, there are also counters in the East Room, and additional stores in little nooks off that grand space. Even if you have no intentions of buying, gazing upward at the coffered vaults of the grand rotunda is worth the stop.
Open Mon.-Sat. 10 a.m.-9 p.m., Sun. noon-6 p.m.

White Flint

11301 Rockville Pike,
North Bethesda, Md.
• (301) 468-5777

The fact that White Flint prefers not to include the words "mall" or "shopping center" in its name, and insists that its address is North Bethesda instead of Rockville (as every Washingtonian knows it really is), clues you in to the fact that this ten-year-old "complex of stores" wishes to cultivate a certain upper-crust snob appeal. So be it. To get there, head straight out Wisconsin Avenue, cross the District line and keep on driving and driving. Eventually, Wisconsin turns into Rockville Pike, and White Flint will materialize. Most of the 125 stores here deal in women's fashions and accessories. The major stores include I. Magnin, Bloomingdale's, Lord & Taylor and Raleigh's. There are five movie theaters, a covered, three-level parking garage and quantities of outdoor parking spaces.
Open Mon.-Sat. 10 a.m.-9:30 p.m., Sun. noon-6 p.m.

EYEWEAR

America's Best

1000 16th St. NW
• 223-1050

America's Best gives eye exams for glasses and contact lenses and sells both at very competitive prices. With hundreds of frames in stock and a variety of options for contacts, this branch of a nationwide chain can accommodate even the pickiest customer. Appointments for exams can generally be set up within a day or two, and the turnaround time for glasses is usually a week to ten days. There are excellent sale prices here for contacts, frames and lenses, and the advertised specials change regularly. Note, however, that while other discounters may throw in such options as tinted, Photogray or oversized lenses for free, everything at America's Best is à la carte.
Open Tues. & Thurs. 9 a.m.-8 p.m., Wed. & Fri. 9 a.m.-6 p.m., Sat. 9 a.m.-5 p.m.

Embassy Opticians

1325 Connecticut Ave. NW
• 785-5700

617 Pennsylvania Ave. SE
• 544-6900

The selection of eyewear here isn't as heavily weighted toward swanky designer specs and sunglasses as at some other shops, although some fashionable lines are stocked. Embassy's drawing card is their friendly, low-key, knowledgeable service. They do their utmost to complete repairs quickly and to have new glasses ready in just a few days if you're under particular time pressure. They'll also tighten or straighten the glasses you bought there as often as necessary, for free. Custom design, tinting and handmade rimless glasses are available, and contact lenses can be fitted at the Connecticut Avenue location.

Connecticut Ave. branch: open Mon.-Fri. 9:30 a.m.-6:30 p.m., Sat. 9:30 a.m.-5 p.m. Pennsylvania Ave. branch: open Mon.-Fri. 10 a.m.-6 p.m., Sat. 10 a.m.-4 p.m.

For Eyes
2021 L St. NW
• 659-0077

1725 K St. NW
• 463-8860

3307 Lee Hwy.,
Arlington, Va.
• (703) 525-5523

You may feel as if you walked onto the set of "What's My Line" when you step into For Eyes and "sign in, please." But the crowds and the wait will be forgotten when you get an eyeful of the 600 to 800 pairs of frames, from the simplest spectacles to designer eyewear. For Eyes has amassed a faithful following by providing quality eye care at discount prices. At L Street, a doctor is on the premises, so you can go from eye exam to glasses in just one stop. Frames and lenses run from $39 to $159, bifocals cost $18 more. There's no extra charge for wire frames or for plastic, tinted, Photogray or oversized lenses. Sunscreen and anti-scratch treatments for lenses can be had for a small extra charge. Frequent specials let you pick up a pair of sunglasses or a spare pair of regular specs for less than the normal charge. Repairs are free for as long as you own a For Eyes frame, and the staff offers a special VIP service that provides glasses within a day or two, for emergencies.

Both Washington branches: open Mon.-Fri. 9:30 a.m.-6 p.m., Sat. 10 a.m.-5 p.m. Arlington branch: Mon., Wed. & Thurs. 10 a.m.-9 p.m., Tues. & Fri. 10 a.m.-6 p.m., Sat. 10 a.m.-5 p.m.

Voorthuis Opticians, Inc.
4250 Connecticut Ave. NW
• 362-7977

1122 Connecticut Ave. NW
• 833-9455

1712 I St. NW
• 333-3144

Mazza Gallerie,
5300 Wisconsin Ave. NW
• 244-7114

3301 New Mexico Ave. NW
• 363-5087

One of Washington's oldest and most prestigious opticians, Voorthuis offers everything from simple, standard frames to elegant designer eyewear. There's also an amusing selection of colorful fun frames for a change of pace. The staff is helpful and professional; the repair and follow-up service is first-rate. If you view eyeglasses as an important investment, you'll be pleased with the high quality of these lenses and frames. Prices are higher than at discount suppliers, but the variety and service are worth the money. The main office is at 4250 Connecticut Avenue NW; the other locations are smaller branch operations.

4250 Connecticut Ave. branch: open Mon.-Fri. 9 a.m.-6 p.m., Sat. 10 a.m.-5 p.m. 1122 Connecticut Ave. branch: open Mon.-Fri. 9:30 a.m.-5:30 p.m., Sat. 10 a.m.-5 p.m. I St. branch: open Mon.-Fri. 9:30 a.m.-6 p.m. Mazza Gallerie branch: open Mon.-Fri. 10 a.m.-9 p.m., Sat. 10 a.m.-6 p.m. New Mexico Ave. branch: open Mon.-Fri. 9 a.m.-5:30 p.m., Sat. 10 a.m.-5 p.m.

FLOWERS

Blackistone, Inc.
24 Kennedy St. NW
• 726-2700

Since 1898, Blackistone has been arranging the capital's flowers. Hardly the most innovative around, they are dependable, and will get the long-stemmed roses of apology there first thing in the morning. They're a member of FTD and offer charge-by-phone service that makes sending flowers easy. Other branches are in Bethesda and Rockville; both use the Washington number (726-2700) for phone orders. *Open Mon.-Fri. 9 a.m.-5 p.m., Sat. 9 a.m.-4 p.m.*

Blue Willow
1729 20th St. NW
• 234-9600

If an arrangement looks like it came from an English country garden, or there are flowers that cannot be found in any other shop as part of a centerpiece, chances are it came from Blue Willow. Master designer Patrick Doyle and his staff take pride in unusual offerings, including the containers themselves. You will not find any dumb, made-in-China baskets or glass bowls. It's more likely that the basket will be spangham moss or grapevine, and the contents will be astounding. In addition to importing blossoms from all over the world, Blue Willow has many species of orchids. While it's like a fantasy to wander in and poke around the shop, choosing a basket for your centerpiece, let the staff do the arrangement. They will put in a touch or two you hadn't considered, and that will make it dramatic and different. The minimum price is $35 for an arrangement; Blue Willow is expensive, but memorable. *Open Mon.-Sat. 9 a.m.-5 p.m.*

Greenworks, Inc.
The Willard Hotel,
1440 F St. NW
• 393-2142

2015 Florida Ave. NW
• 265-3335

Since it swept into town from Texas in 1986, Greenworks has taken Washington by storm with its spectacular, dramatic floral displays. Greenworks is floral purveyor to the fashionable Willard Hotel, and to the elaborately decorated Gannett corporate offices in Rosslyn. The stars of their displays are tropical blooms flown in from Hawaii. They do traditional arrangements or very exotic ones (the Florida Avenue branch is reputedly a bit more avant-garde); both shops carry exceptional cut flowers. In all their arrangements, Greenworks tries to include a little something that will live on, such as an African violet or houseplant. Arrangements carry a $25 minimum, with delivery service available in town and outside the beltway. Charges vary with distance, but the standard in-town charge is about $5. *Pennsylvania Ave. branch: open Mon.-Sat. 9 a.m.-6 p.m. Florida Ave. branch: open Mon.-Sat. 8:30 a.m.-6 p.m.*

Peters Flowerland
1365 Wisconsin Ave. NW
• 337-5284

1835 K St. NW
• 337-0136

1825 I St. NW
• 337-1826

Peters deserves an award for beautifying the streets of Washington. More than any other florist, Peters displays lovely bouquets of flowers for sale on the streets outside its shops—a cheerful sight for all who pass by. It's a tremendously effective sales technique, too, often encouraging a spontaneous purchase. Throughout the year, Peters carries wonderful roses, daffodils, daisies, carnations and tulips, often in mixed bouquets, plus some extraordinary seasonal offerings, all bundled up and ready to go. Most sell for $6 a bunch. There's a nice selection of flowering and foliage plants as well. The K Street Shop has a large group of inexpensive vases, if the recipient of your gift doesn't have one. Also offered: flower arrangement and delivery services. *Wisconsin Ave. branch: open Mon.-Thurs. 7:30 a.m.-10 p.m., Fri.-Sat. 7:30 a.m.-midnight, Sun. 7:30 a.m.-7 p.m. K St. & I St. branches: open Mon.-Fri. 7:30 a.m.-7 p.m., Sat. 9:30 a.m.-6 p.m.*

Le Printemps
1255 23rd St. NW
• 429-8704

If you're in the neighborhood—the burgeoning "West End" of Washington, where overzealous developers are creating another concrete canyon of buildings—this small shop, with armfuls of unusual flowers, provides a refreshing change. There are always huge bowls of colorful lilies and wonderful sprays of exotic orchids. The prices aren't low, but the flowers are very fresh and usually last several days. The shop specializes in Asian-style arrangements of silk flowers. You can provide a vase or choose one from the wide variety of brass and glass containers in the store. *Open Mon.-Fri. 8 a.m.-7:30 p.m., Sat. 10 a.m.-4 p.m., Sun. 11 a.m.-3 p.m.*

Mark Turner Flowers
666 Pennsylvania Ave. SE
• 547-2020

This Capitol Hill florist designs imaginative, yet natural, arrangements with a European flair. Mark Turner makes good use of Holland lilies, tulips and the like in stylish wedding and party arrangements. Their wedding bouquets are a real sensation: delicate and lovely, with a springlike look. You can find some nice flowering plants in this little store, but green plants are not their stock in trade. Exotic flowers can be imported on a special-order basis. The average delivery charge is in the $3.50 range, with home deliveries in the District running $2.50. *Open Mon.-Sat. 9 a.m.-5 p.m.*

Watergate Florist Ltd.
2548 Virginia Ave. NW
• 337-2545

M. A. Habid took over Watergate Florist in the spring of 1986 and has been busy ever since catering to stars, actors, diplomats, government officials and all those who want the aura of Watergate to go with their flowers. The staff is refreshingly friendly and helpful. This is most definitely a prestige emporium, and the message won't be lost on the recipients of your largess.
Open Mon.-Fri. 9 a.m.-5 p.m., Sat. 9:30 a.m.-3 p.m.

Allan Woods, Inc.
2604 Connecticut Ave. NW
• 332-3334

From this small studio and shop comes some of the most glamorous flower arrangements seen at large Washington functions. But Allan Woods also cares about the bouquet sent to a friend in the hospital or to your mother for her birthday. All of the flowers are imported directly from Holland, and the stock of elegant vases and baskets in which to send flowers is one of the best around. There are adorable stuffed animals, too, and the sales staff is efficient and friendly. While the refrigerator might look packed, chances are most of the flowers are spoken for— it's a good idea to call and discuss what you'll want if the order is a large one.
Open Mon.-Fri. 9 a.m.-7 p.m., Sat. 9 a.m.-6 p.m.

FOOD

BAKERIES

Avignon Frères
1733 Columbia Rd. NW
• 462-2050

The oldest bakery in the city, Avignon Frères has been turning out respectable breads of all varieties, French pastries of all degrees of richness and homemade donuts since 1918. Washingtonians flock here more for the warm, lively atmosphere than for fabulous food; however, breakfast includes fresh-squeezed orange juice (they squeeze the oranges in front of you), and the lunch menu features daily specials such as empanadas, South American tamals and Cuban sandwiches.
Open daily 7 a.m.-midnight.

Bakery Potomac Metro
1238 Pennsylvania Ave. SE
• 543-2960

For eight years now, partners Linda Pryor and Hamidon Diarra have been delighting neighbors and other fortunate folk who have discovered their out-of-the-way bakery. The divine fragrance of French breads and breakfast pastries draws early risers from their beds to the bakery; others stop

by for the German whole-grain breads and desserts or Hungarian delicacies like the traditional Dobostorte. Oversized croissants make a gratifying—if caloric—breakfast (you're bored with plain? Try almond or raisin). French-inspired, too, are the addictive glazed apple turnovers called chaussons aux pommes. Bakery Potomac Metro is the home of Washington's only Makronentorte, a wonderful layered concoction filled alternately with apricot and raspberry jams, covered with toasted almond slivers and glaze. It costs $32 and serves sixteen. The Trüffel torte is a celestial creation consisting chiefly of Belgian bittersweet chocolate. Grand Marnier cakes, bread sculptures and holiday sweets like Lebkuchen hearts for Valentine's Day should be ordered in advance. You may have already sampled these treats; they're servied in both Nora's and City Café.
Open Tues.-Sat. 6 a.m.-6 p.m., Sun. 7 a.m.-2 p.m.

Breads Unlimited
6914 Arlington Rd.,
Bethesda, Md.
• (301) 656-2340

Take a magazine with you to this store, in a strip mall a few blocks from Wisconsin Avenue; you're going to have to take a number and wait for service. But the wait is well worth it, for these are some of the best baked goods in the region, especially the breads. In addition to rye and pumpernickel you can really sink your teeth into, there are crusty baguettes, muffins, chewy oatmeal and crispy chocolate chip cookies, raisin rolls and cakes galore. While there is always a crowd, the numbers turn over quickly, and the service is pleasant and efficient.
Open Mon.-Fri. 8 a.m.-7 p.m., Sat. 8 a.m.-6 p.m., Sun. 8 a.m.-3 p.m.

Brenner's Bakery of Arlington
3241 Columbia Pike,
Arlington, Va.
• (703) 920-6333,
(703) 920-6334

Case after case of breads, cakes, pastries, cookies and breakfast treats are cunningly arranged to ambush even the most stoic dieter, who innocently comes by to pick up a cake the office ordered. Owners Gino Pellegrino and William Christian offer a 10-percent discount to seniors, charitable organizations and churches. Custom orders generally require two to three days' advance notice, a week for very large orders or wedding cakes. This is a good place to find that jelly doughnut you remember fondly from your childhood.
Open Tues.-Sun. 6 a.m.-8 p.m.

Pâtisserie Café Didier
3206 Grace St. NW
• 342-9083

It's the closest Washington gets to the feeling of walking into one of the Lenôtre shops in Paris. Master pastry chef Didier Schorner, formerly of New York's Tavern on the Green and Washington's now-defunct Potomac, creates a huge case of delights—from tiny meringues that melt in

your mouth and butter cookies to luscious buttercream tortes, fruit tarts, palmiers, and any sweet fancy that strikes him daily. The bûche de Noël for Christmas is almost too pretty to eat, and he will also make special occasion cakes, from wedding towers to clowns for children.
Open Tues.-Sun. 8 a.m.-7 p.m.

Tivoli
**1700 N. Moore St.,
Rosslyn, Va.
• (703) 524-8902**

Tivoli is a bright, modern deli/bakery located within steps of the busy Rosslyn metro stop. Upstairs, there is a restaurant/bar where you can stop for a meal or a drink. The deli section offers an interesting assortment of sandwiches and the usual range of delicatessen fare: salads, cheeses, cold cuts and a small selection of wines, beers and soft drinks. In the back, you'll find an impressive array of bakery items—cheesecakes, cookies, baklava, tortes and more. You can wash down these goodies with a $1.50 capuccino.
Open Mon.-Sat. 7 a.m.-8 p.m., Sun. 9:30 a.m.-4:30 p.m.

Watergate Pastry
**2534 Virginia Ave. NW
• 342-1777**

Had it been we who broke into the now-infamous Watergate complex, we would have bypassed the Democratic National Committee headquarters and headed straight for the Watergate Pastry Shop. It smells so sweet and sinful that you could easily become one of the many addicted customers who drop in daily for French pastries, coffee cakes, Danish pastry, croissants, cookies, tarts, pies, cakes, cheesecakes, truffles—or all of the above. Specialty items include wedding cakes, buttercream figures, sugar and nougatine showpieces, croque en bouche and yule logs. This is definitely one of Washington's best bakeries.
Open Mon.-Fri. 8 a.m.-7 p.m., Sat. 9 a.m.-7 p.m., Sun. 10 a.m.-5 p.m.

COFFEE & TEA

The Coffee Connection
**1627 Connecticut Ave. NW
• 483-8050**

Top-grade coffee beans, freshly blended and roasted in Norfolk, Virginia, are delivered to this shop twice weekly. No fewer than 72 coffees from all over the world are featured, as well as a large selection of regular and decaffeinated teas. While you wait for your coffee beans to be ground, inspect the displays of sleek, chic housewares. Although the shop's high volume is a virtual guarantee of freshness, some of the more exotic coffees are far more expensive here than elsewhere: we found one priced $5 a pound more than at The Daily Grind, only two doors away.
Open Mon.-Fri. 9:30 a.m.-7:30 p.m., Sat. 9:30 a.m.- 7 p.m., Sun. 11 a.m.-6 p.m.

The Daily Grind

1613 Connecticut Ave. NW
• 265-3348

This shop does all its own blending, and offers 60 varieties of Swiss water-process coffee, as well as every imaginable type of tea. The rapid turnover in this popular emporium is extra assurance of optimum freshness. Prices are competitive, from the standard blends to the most exotic, and each Thursday, a different coffee is offered as a weekly special. You can purchase a full range of spices here, too, as well as coffee-making paraphernalia and specialty kitchenware. *Open Mon.-Fri. 9:30 a.m.-6:30 p.m., Sat. 9:30 a.m.-6 p.m.*

M. E. Swing Co., Inc.

437 11th St. NW
• 628-7601

Washingtonians have been flocking to Swing's since 1916 for no-nonsense flame-roasted coffees at sensible prices. You won't find the new generation of exotic-flavored blends here, just straightforward French breakfast, Mesco, Ethiopian, Mocha Java, Colombian, Guatemalan, espresso and the like from $4.85 to $13.00 a pound. This shop also features a nice selection of loose teas from $1.60 to $1.90 a quarter-pound, while tea bags are priced at about $2 for a box of 48. You can find coffee filters, coffeemakers, tea cups and cocoa powder, but it's really the fresh coffees and teas that lure customers to this busy, friendly shop. *Open Mon.-Fri. 8:30 a.m.-6:15 p.m., Sat. 9:30 a.m.-6:15 p.m.*

Old Town Coffee, Tea & Spice

215 S. Union St.,
Alexandria, Va.
• (703) 683-0856

With a warm and charming, old-fashioned atmosphere typical of Old Town, this coffee shop does big business, not just in coffees and teas, but also in candy, chocolates, jelly beans and gourmet foods. More than 40 different coffees are on offer, with caffeine and without, and about the same number of loose teas. The kitchenware is limited to standard equipment for coffee and tea drinkers: coffee makers and accessories, teapots and coffee grinders. Yes, you can get coffee by the cup here, to carry out and enjoy as you continue your shopping. *Open Mon.-Fri. 10:30 a.m.-6:30 p.m., Sat. 10 a.m.-6 p.m., Sun. 11:30 a.m.-5:30 p.m.*

CONFECTIONS

La Bonbonnière

1724 H St. NW
• 333-6425

François Cochin, with his fabulous repertoire of French pastries and sweets, is arguably the best thing to hit Washington in this decade. Push open the glass door to his Bonbonnière, and you'll be greeted by the heavenly scents of fine truffles crafted on the premises, rich pâtisserie and

cakes. François recently added homemade ice creams and sorbets to his line, too. At holiday time, watch for his whimsical marzipan figures, and don't be surprised to find yourself elbow-to-elbow with fellow chocoholics paying $15.50 for a pound of truffles. One caution: should you present a box of said truffles to a cherished someone, rest assured that you will be implored to repeat the gesture. François will gladly ship these heart-stopping delights, but only between September and May, for the little darlings are perishable.
Open Mon.-Fri. 7 a.m.-6 p.m.

Chocolate Chocolate
1050 Connecticut Ave. NW, Washington Square
• 466-2190

An important message bears repeating—such is the firm belief of the folks at Chocolate Chocolate. These shops feature Swiss and Belgian imports. The wonderful, fresh-cream-filled Manon confections are by Newhaus. Candy Jartruffles from San Francisco are a specialty, but the bouchon (fresh buttercream and Cognac in a dark-chocolate cup) had sold out on a recent visit. That's the problem with imported chocolates. You have to wait for the next airlift.
Open Mon.-Fri. 10 a.m.-6 p.m.

Krön Chocolatier
Mazza Gallerie,
5300 Wisconsin Ave. NW
• 966-4946

Although Krön may have fallen upon hard times in other parts of the country, its Washington store continues to maintain fairly high standards. Dried fruit dipped in semi-sweet chocolate is a real treat and a perfect hostess gift. Krön's dark, intensely flavored truffles, made according to a Hungarian recipe, run about $30 a pound. Novelty items include a female torso for $60, a female leg with ribbon garter for $75, a typewriter for $15, an elephant for $15 and even a model of the Capitol for $18; all tasty, yes, but tasteful? You be the judge. Krön's also prepares chocolate-covered oreos, chocolate baskets and even chocolate fortune cookies. For your own creations, you can find cocoa powder, baking chocolate, chocolate chips, chocolate sauce and, for an amusing dessert garnish, chocolate escargots.
Open Mon.-Fri. 10 a.m.-9 p.m., Sat. 10 a.m.-6 p.m., Sun. noon-5 p.m.

ETHNIC MARKETS

Americana

1813 Columbia Rd. NW
• 265-7455

Americana is one of the Latin markets located in Adams Morgan, Washington's Hispanic and West African melting pot. The market sells crusty Latin breads, Mexican- and Argentinian-style fresh chorizos, morcilla, cheeses, dried fish, Latin American coffees (at prices far lower than at the coffee shops of nearby Dupont Circle) and the spices and herbs called for in Hispanic andsouthwestern cookery.
Open Mon.-Sat. 8:30 a.m.-7 p.m., Sun. 8:30 a.m.-5 p.m.

Las Americas

8651 16th St.,
Silver Spring, Md.
• (301) 588-0882

If you're looking for corn husks to make tamales, frozen yucca, or banana leaves from the Philippines, this huge store will be the place to find them. Las Americas specializes in Hispanic foods, but there is also more than a smattering of West Indian, African and Spanish. In addition to the canned goods, you will find fresh meats and chorizos, cheeses and a good selection of produce, both fresh and dried.
Open Mon. 10 a.m.-9 p.m., Tues.-Sat. 9 a.m.-9 p.m., Sun. 9 a.m.-9 p.m.

Da Hua Market

623 H St. NW
• 371-8888

Alas, shopping in Washington's Chinatown is not the same sensual experience as picking up produce and watching carp swim in tanks on the sidewalk of San Francisco's Stockton Street. Da Hua, which until 1988 was located under the popular Szechuan restaurant, is now a large supermarket-style shop, with speedy checkout lines and prepackaged meats. You will find aisles of canned foods, fresh meats and seafood, a few brands of Chinese sausage, and an excellent produce section for herbs and vegetables, as well as bargain prices on utensils and plates. The offerings in the freezer case are just right for a dim sum party. The Gallery Place Metrorail station is across the street.
Open Mon.-Wed. 10 a.m.-7:30 p.m., Thurs. 10 a.m.-7 p.m., Fri.-Sun. 10 a.m.-7:30 p.m.

Fu Lo Bakery & Deli

3209 N. Washington Blvd.,
Arlington, Va.
• (703) 528-5335

While many Occidentals consider desserts to be the black hole of Asian cuisines, a selection of almond cakes, coconut tartlets, honey cakes and lotus-seed cookies from Fu Lo might make converts out of many. While there is a limited selection of canned goods, this is primarily a bakery, and they also sell Chinese newspapers (printed in New York).
Open daily 9 a.m.-7 p.m.

German Deli
1331 H St. NW
• 347-5732

Washington is not the best in Wurst, and this downtown shop, with the fun and funky Mozart Café at the back of the market, is one of the best places to collect the goodies for a picnic on the nearby Mall. The hearty German breads include an excellent linseed rye and sunflower seed rye, and there is smoked eel as well as smoked meats, Wursts, hams and corned beefs. While the offerings are canned, there are a number of herrings and other fish, and don't overlook the sauerkraut and sharp mustards.
Open Mon.-Fri. 7:30 a.m.-10 p.m., Sat. 9 a.m.-10 p.m., Sun. 11 a.m.-10 p.m.

Jade Tree
350 Fortune Terrace,
 Potomac, Md.
• (301) 279-9522

Located in the Seven Locks Plaza shopping center, this small market carries such unusual items as shrink-wrapped smoked ducks and a cornucopia of fresh produce, along with canned and refrigerated products. The fresh bean curd is worth the drive from the city. They also sell Chinese newspapers and magazines.
Open Mon.-Sat. 10 a.m.-7:30 p.m., Sun. 10 a.m.-6 p.m.

Korean Korner
12225 Wilkins Ave.,
Rockville, Md.
• (301) 231-6699

This is one of the largest Asian markets in the region, organized like a huge warehouse, with speedy checkout lanes. The fresh meats are beautifully displayed, and the selection of fish and fish roes is also arranged as in a sushi bar. There are Korean and other Asian frozen prepared dishes, canned goods, and packaged soups and noodles. And don't forget the kimchee; no market with a Korean name could be without some.
Open Mon.-Sat. 10 a.m.-10 p.m., Sun. 11:30 a.m.-8 p.m.

Litteri's
517-519 Morse St. NE
• 544-0184

This store is located in a corner of the Florida Avenue wholesale market area, and finding it is not easy the first time; however, once you've left your trail of breadcrumbs, you'll come back many times for the best quality and best prices on Italian foods—both prepared and fresh—and wines and cheeses. The prosciutto from Parma is less expensive than at any other shop; the selection of frozen pastas and gnocchis is excellent; and the cold cuts and fresh mozzarella are alone worth the twenty-minute drive from downtown. Litteri's has been around since the 1930s, with good reason.
Open Mon.-Fri. 8 a.m.-5 p.m., Sat. 8 a.m.-3 p.m.

Maxim Super Market

640 University Blvd. East,
Silver Spring, Md.
• (301) 439-0110

The signs are in Vietnamese, Chinese and English, and the store is almost like a shopping center without walls. The huge market is the nucleus for an Asian fabric-store-cum-tailor, a toy store, dentist's office, and a great restaurant (from which you can also take home barbecued meats). It has the best selection of packaged foods in the region, and also fresh meats (including tripe, duck's feet, pig's heart), perfect produce, frozen foods and aisles of pots, woks and dishes. Have lunch, then wander. It's an all-weather bazaar.
Open Mon.-Sat. 9:30 a.m.-8 p.m., Sun. 9:30 a.m.-7 p.m.

Mee Wah Lung

608 H St. NW
• 737-0968

Mee Wah, in the shadow of the Chinatown arch, is an old-fashioned Chinese grocery, with tongs to reach items from the top shelves of this cramped store. The barbecued pork loin and roast ducks are made on the premises and are excellent, as is the selection of fresh produce and canned goods. It's less like a supermarket and more like a neighborhood store.
Open Mon. & Wed.-Sun. 9 a.m.-6 p.m., Tues. 9 a.m.-3 p.m.

Middle East Market

7006 Carroll Ave.,
Takoma Park, Md.
• (301) 270-5154

The countries of the Middle East should be as bountiful and as harmonious as the stock of this store, located in the center of downtown Takoma Park. There are Turkish figs, yogurt balls from Lebanon and cheeses from Yugoslavia. The sweets are enough to cause diabetes, and the spices and herbs are all you will need for any of these cuisines. The Takoma Park Metrorail station is a few blocks away.
Open Mon.-Fri. 10 a.m.-7 p.m., Sat.-Sun. 10 a.m.-5 p.m.

New Wave Seafood

3821 S. George Mason Dr.,
(Bailey's Crossroads)
Arlington, Va.
• (703) 379-9444

It is unclear if New Wave is a seafood market that also caters to the crowd at its sushi bar, or if it is a Japanese market specializing in seafood. Regardless, you can't find fresher fish—clearly what's needed for sushi. And you can sample some of it at the sushi bar before even selecting what to take home. There is always excellent salmon, tuna, swordfish, sea urchin roe, snapper, clams and lobster. And then whatever else is in season. There is a small section of rice and sauces and some dried Japanese fish, as well.
Open Mon.-Sat. 10:30 a.m.-8 p.m., Sun. 1 p.m.-7 p.m.

Vace Italian Delicatessen

3315 Connecticut Ave. NW
• 363-1999

7010 Wisconsin Ave.,
Bethesda, Md.
• (301) 654-6367

This Italian grocery and delicatessen is a longtime favorite of Cleveland Hill Park residents. While not the novelty it once was, Vace still attracts a loyal clientele with its home-made egg, spinach and tomato pastas and containers of pesto and other sauces. Many Italian-style meats and cheeses are stocked, along with several different olive oils, vinegars and familiar canned products, such as roasted sweet peppers and other items that can fill out an antipasto tray.

Connecticut Ave. branch: open Mon.-Wed. & Sat. 9 a.m.-8 p.m., Thurs.-Fri. 9 a.m.-9 p.m. Bethesda branch: open Mon.-Sat. 9:30 a.m.-7:30 p.m.

FISH & MEAT

A & B Shellfish Co., Inc.

6025 Leesburg Pike
(Bailey's Crossroads),
Arlington, Va.
• (703) 931-7200

This is a perfect place to go to treat your friends from the Midwest to the delights of East Coast living—by which we mean live Maine lobsters. Pick the size you want from the well-filled tank just inside the door. Or for a no-holds-barred blowout, try the store specialty, the New England Clambake. For $29.95, you get dinner for two, complete with its own cooking container, filled with two one-pound lobsters, twenty cherrystone clams, two fish filets, two ears of corn and a pile of red potatoes and sweet potatoes, with a little onion for flavor. These delights are available without any advance notice and might be the perfect change of pace you're looking for. Prices for the fresh fish, shrimp, clams, oysters and the like, are on the high side.

Open Mon.-Thurs. 10 a.m.-7 p.m., Fri.-Sat. 10 a.m.-8 p.m., Sun. 11 a.m.-7 p.m.

Cannon Seafood, Inc.

1065 31st St. NW
• 337-8366

762-A Walker Rd.,
Great Falls, Va.
• (703) 759-4950

For more than 40 years, Cannon's has been dishing up fresh seafood, crabs, oysters and clams in the elite neighborhoods of Georgetown and Great Falls. Most of their fish, crabs and oysters are supplied daily by their own boats to ensure the freshest possible seafood. The store features a complete line of fresh and frozen seafood from all the waters of the world, as well as green, cooked or spiced shrimp, oysters and clams shucked and prepared for the half-shell and a few exotic fishes like shark and squid. This store is a bit on the pricey side compared with the more competitive waterfront outlets, but the quality and service are superb.

Washington branch: open Mon.-Thurs. 7:30 a.m.-6 p.m., Fri. 7:30 a.m.-6:30 p.m., Sat. 8 a.m.-5:30 p.m. Great Falls branch: open Tues.-Fri. 10 a.m.-7 p.m., Sat. 9 a.m.-6 p.m.

Maine Avenue Waterfront

11th St. & Maine Ave. SW
• No phone

A collection of rustic, authentic fishing boats dispenses the most affordable, enjoyable and accessible seafood in the Washington area from its resting place on the Potomac River at the Maine Avenue waterfront. This crowded, lively area is fun to visit even if you're not interested in the wonderful fresh fish, clams, crabs, shrimp, lobster, crabmeat, bay and sea scallops, oysters and squid. But who could not be interested? There are even shops that offer ready-steamed crabs and spiced shrimp. Oysters are available in pint and quart jars, unshucked by the dozen or by the barrel for the truly addicted. The prices here are by far the best in Washington, and even better deals are available to the adventurer who buys a whole fish to clean at home; however, for the more timid, a wonderful fish cleaner holds forth in a nearby shack to do the dirty work. You may have to wait in line for a bit, however, since he's also busy cleaning the fish of fortunate Potomac River anglers. *Open daily 9 a.m.-9 p.m.*

Weisfeld's Market, Inc.

501 4th St. SE
• 547-1336

This quaint neighborhood market with an unassuming exterior has some of the best meats and fresh poultry in the Washington area, at surprisingly good prices. True carnivores will appreciate the fact that this family-owned-and-operated market sells only corn-fed Iowa beef that comes in by the truckload. It's one of the few places in town where you can get a whole Dubuque ham, and if you haven't had one, you haven't lived. Also, the butcher shop offers outstanding fresh turkeys, ducks, geese and other fine fowl on a special-order basis, and can butterfly a leg of lamb or cut a perfect roast with only a bit of notice. In this age of standardized meats, Weisfeld's ground beef is a treat, weighed and double-ground right before your eyes. Available, too, are excellent ground veal, pork and beef meatloaf mixtures and fresh chicken. There's a little of every type of standard grocery fare as well, and the wine selection is excellent for a store so tiny that it offers shoppers special mini-carts to navigate the aisles. Even then, traffic jams occur, but it's all part of the charm of this Capitol Hill gem. *Open Tues.-Sat. 8 a.m.-7:30 p.m., Sun. 8 a.m.-3:30 p.m.*

GOURMET & GOURMET CARRY-OUT

Cheese & Cheer

210 7th St. SE (across from Eastern Market)
• 547-5858

Cheese & Cheer is the official name of this tiny Capitol Hill treasure, but the regulars who frequent this ten-year-old operation simply call it "Howard's." That's because ebullient owner Howard Schweizer dominates his store in the

most delightful way, greeting virtually all his customers by their first names and even remembering what they bought the last time. In this cluttered little shop, 60-percent Brie and countless other cheeses from around the world sell for dollars less a pound than elsewhere. You'll find numerous other bargains here, too: premium wild rice, freshly made pesto all year round, pine nuts, thick-cut bacon, unsalted butter, Polish ham, smoked turkey, olive oil and sun-dried tomatoes. Check out the homemade gourmet foods like quiches, mousses, pâtés and exotic pies. Don't miss the table of cheeses and meats—an ever-changing array of items specially priced at $2.89 a pound. You will likely have to wait in line, but time passes pleasantly, because Howard often chops up samples for everyone to try. Many a shopping list has been changed in the process.
Open Mon.-Thurs. 8:30 a.m.-6:30 p.m., Sat. 8 a.m.-6 p.m., Sun. 11 a.m.-5 p.m.

Ciao
2000 Pennsylvania Ave. NW
• 296-6796

The husband-and-wife team that opened Ciao two years ago in a classy downtown office building offer great deli-style sandwiches, tasty salads and pasta treats and wickedly delicious baked goods and chocolates. Stephen Heller is the chef, and his wife, Judith Philactos, a former dancer, is the store manager. Ingredients here are all of the highest quality—the best this pair can make or buy—and it shows. The blueberry muffins are a special treat, and regular customers report they're always sold out by 10 in the morning. The homemade soups are excellent, especially the gazpacho, and the house-blended coffee, sold by the pound or by the cup, is also worth a try. On nice days, expect a line as eager sun-worshippers grab a special Ciao sandwich, some Hawaiian chips and a soda, and head outside to the bistro tables for a carry-out picnic. The couple also runs a catering service.
Open Mon.-Fri. 8 a.m.-7 p.m., Sat. 10 a.m.-6 p.m.

Columbia Plaza Gourmet
2400 Virginia Ave. NW
• 887-8240

Columbia Plaza offers the complete at-home package—food for dinner and a video rental shop, all under the same roof. It's hard to find this glitzy specialty food store. It is located in the courtyard of an apartment complex near the State Department in Foggy Bottom and close to the Kennedy Center. There is a small (but adequate) bakery, meat and cheese departments and an extremely delicious prepared-foods counter, which always has chickens happily twirling on the rôtisserie, plus numbers of salads and prepared entrées. Unlike many gourmet-to-go counters, the chef at Columbia Plaza takes into consideration that most

foods will be zapped in a microwave, so the choices are tolerant this nuking process. While this shop is not worth a trip out of your way, it is the only act in that part of the city.
Open Mon.-Fri. 7:30 a.m.-8 p.m., Sat. 10 a.m.-8 p.m., Sun. 10 a.m.-5 p.m.

Foods of Foxhall
1609 Foxhall Rd. NW
• 342-6077

You can pick up a pound of curried chicken salad at this bright and cheerful shop in one of the more exclusive residential areas, or you can get some boxed lunches to take to a Wolf Trap concert or a complete selection of hors d'oeuvres for an impromptu cocktail party. The food is well seasoned and attractively presented by Laura Murphy, who was formerly director of food and beverage at the Winterthur Museum in Wilmington, where she was accustomed to catering to the wishes of the likes of the Duponts. While there is nothing terribly innovative about eggplant caviar with tortilla chips or shrimp kebabs, they are nicely flavored, and you don't have to cook them yourself.
Open Mon.-Fri. 7 a.m.-9 p.m., Sat. 8 a.m.-7 p.m., Sun. 8 a.m.-8 p.m.

French Market
1632 Wisconsin Ave. NW
• 338-4828

The series of red-painted townhouses has gaily painted Parisian scenes in the windows, and if you call, "Bonjour" will be the greeting. The meat is the best in town, and impeccably trimmed, with roasts larded or covered with fat, homemade sausages, lamb kebabs already marinating in a heady red-wine marinade, and a case of pâtés and terrines that would rival any in the mother country. In addition, there are cheeses, a great selection of French oils and vinegars, olives and high-quality canned goods. Stop by to purchase the makings of a dinner for ten or a picnic for two. There is free delivery in the Georgetown area, which is about the only free thing. The food is glorious, but you pay dearly for it.
Open Mon.-Tues. 8:30 a.m.-6 p.m., Wed. 8:30 a.m.-1:30 p.m., Thurs.-Sat. 8:30 a.m.-6 p.m.

Helen's Too
1811 18th St. NW
• 483-4444

The food at Helen Wasserman's new gourmet shop and carry-out is simply superb. Blending Asian, French and American cuisines with her own special twist, Helen's offers a welcome change from the predictable foods found in so many area gourmet shops. Carry-out specialties change

here daily. A recent visit yielded an appealing dish of scallops with pineapple and cream, barbecue shrimp and Oriental chicken, plus a variety of fruit salads and pasta dishes. A separate bakery proposes fantastic tarts: tender pastry shells loaded to the brim with white chocolate mousse or white-chocolate-and-mocha filling, topped with fruit, and wonderful bonbons. Prices are attractive, too. A whole strawberry shortcake was selling for $25 one day, with a gorgeous chocolate cake running $17. All pastries are around $2.25. Helen's runs a fine, reasonably priced catering operation. If a menu starring curried pork with bananas, pineapple and chutney, or corn crabcakes with jalapeño tartar sauce sounds better to you than Swedish meatballs and stuffed mushroom caps, give Helen's a call.
Open Mon.-Fri. 7 a.m.-10 p.m., Sat. 9 a.m.-7 p.m., Sun. 9 a.m.-5 p.m. (Open for catering each day until 5 p.m.)

Larimer's
1727 Connecticut Ave. NW
• 332-1766,
332-3366

Larimer's is as much a Dupont Circle landmark as the fountain. It's an old-fashioned grocery store in appearance, with crowded aisles and merchandise stacked to the ceiling. But while the stock includes corn flakes and flour, this is really one of the largest specialty markets in the city, known for the superb quality of the meats, fish, cheeses and produce. There is an adequate, if not inspired, prepared-foods department and a good selection of coffees and chocolates. The wine department is a store in itself, located next door. Larimer's delivers around the city for a $3 charge, if you call by 2 p.m. that day, but before ordering blindly, it's a good idea to get to know the store.
Open Mon.-Fri. 10 a.m.-7 p.m., Sat. 9 a.m.-7 p.m., Sun. 11 a.m.-6 p.m.

Lawson's Gourmet
1350 Connecticut Ave. NW
• 775-0400

Lawson's is giving the rest of the downtown lunch trade a run for their money. First of all, there's the location. The shop, situated at the end of a flatiron building on Dupont Circle, is directly at the Metrorail stop. It is primarily a gourmet carry-out, with a good selection of cheeses and cold meats and some packaged foods. The bakery department is a highlight, with huge, moist muffins and excellent cookies, and every day, there is a good selection of cold salads perfect for desktop dining. There is also much heartier fare, appropriate to lug home on the Metro for dinner.
Open Mon.-Fri. 7:30 a.m.-8 p.m., Sat. 10 a.m.-6 p.m.

Neam's of Georgetown
3217 P St. NW
• 338-4694

This old-fashioned supermarket was the set for Meryl Streep's shopping in *Heartburn*, and the clientele is equally divided between Georgetown matrons and uniformed maids from houses whose matrons are above pushing the cart themselves. Most people just call Neam's to have food delivered, and the meats, fresh fish, produce and groceries are as impeccable as the customers. While the store is small, it always seems to have everything a person is looking for, from plump golden raisins to imported Irish bacon. There is a good selection of wines and an adequate deli.
Open Mon.-Fri. 8 a.m.-7 p.m., Sat. 8 a.m.-6 p.m.

Potomac Butter & Egg Co., Inc.
1900 Stanford Ct.,
Landover, Md.
• (301) 386-9200

For 60 years, Potomac Butter & Egg has been supplying Washington hotels, restaurants, supermarkets and a number of cash-and-carry customers with butter, eggs, meats, pâtés, frozen appetizers and some 50 to 75 different cheeses. They can sell you a whole wheel of cheese, but also offer plenty for the smaller buyer. With the advent of warehouse pricing in some supermarkets, the cost advantage of shopping here has decreased, but you'll still find prices lower than in many markets and discount stores. They offer a great selection and considerable charm in this day of mass marketing.
Open Mon.-Fri. 8 a.m.-4:30 p.m., Sat. 8:30 a.m.-2 p.m.

Provisions
218 7th St. SE
• 543-0694

Step down into the wonderful aromas and atmosphere of Provisions and you may never want to leave. Under the same management as Old Town Coffee, Tea and Spice, the shop offers 30 brands of coffees and an appealing assortment of teas. But you'll find countless other reasons to linger at Provisions. There's the wonderful assortment of cocoas, candies, gourmet foods and kitchenware, including Calphalon cookware. Then there's the marvelous selection of picnic baskets, unusual spices, flavored vinegars and mesquite chips. But don't stop there. Wander back to the spectacular deli and choose from freshly made bagels, super salads, grand sandwiches, special sodas and virtually anything else your heart desires. There's a small area of tables and chairs where you sit to nosh, or you can order your goodies to go.
Open Mon.-Fri. 10 a.m.-7 p.m., Sat. 8 a.m.-6 p.m., Sun. 10 a.m.-4 p.m.

Someplace Special (The Gourmet Giant)

1445 Chain Bridge Rd.,
McLean, Va.
• (703) 448-0800

12051 Rockville Pike,
Rockville, Md.
• (301) 881-4541

With 19,000 square feet of prime selling space, the Giant foodstore chain calls these gourmet shops "Someplace Special," and they are. The Gourmet Giant swept into McLean in November of 1982, and many Northern Virginians soon forgot what Safeway, A&P and regular Giants were; the Rockville location opened two years later. It's strictly "gourmet-to-go" here, with exceptional prepared foods perfect for busy executives, diplomats and politicians who want to entertain with the best, but appreciate a shortcut or two. Whether it's hot or cold, trendy or more traditional, if it's edible, you can find it here. Foods taste as good as they look, and no one will ever know you didn't spend all day in the kitchen. Someplace Special also sends flowers, caters, shops for you and delivers. What more could you want? If it's a roll of paper towels or a can of cat food, you'll have to go across the street to the regular Giant. This is edibles only, which can be a pain when you're in a hurry. *Open Mon.-Thurs. 10 a.m.-8 p.m., Fri.-Sat. 9 a.m.-9 p.m., Sun. 9 a.m.-7 p.m.*

Sutton Place Gourmet

3201 New Mexico Ave. NW
• 363-5800

10323 Old Georgetown Rd.,
Bethesda, Md.
• (301) 564-3100

600 Franklin St.,
Alexandria, Va.
• (703) 549-6611

A single visit will show you why true devotees lovingly refer to this one-stop gourmet paradise as "Glutton Place." Some of the finest delicacies from around the world are right at home here. One is tempted to buy everything immediately—cheeses, chocolates (including Piedmontese truffles and Michel Guérard treats), pastries, deli items, mega-sandwiches, luscious lox, crown roasts with their little frillies in place, giant shrimp, countless varieties of fresh pasta and picture-perfect fruits and vegetables. Try to stay calm and remember, you can come back as often as you please. Fauchon and Harrod's Food Hall have met their match. Sutton Place is all you could want in a classy gourmet market. You can even bring in your own skewers and have them make up the shishkebabs for your next cookout with giant, select chunks of the tenderest, juiciest meat in captivity and the crispest, most colorful vegetables. *Washington & Bethesda branches: open Mon.-Sat. 9 a.m.-9 p.m., Sun. 9 a.m.-8 p.m. Alexandria branch: open Mon.-Sat. 10 a.m.-9 p.m., Sun. 10 a.m.-8 p.m.*

Suzanne's

1735 Connecticut Ave. NW
• 483-4633

Walking into this gourmet shop, where some of the same salads and pastries are served at the restaurant and wine bar upstairs, feels like walking into a homey, friendly kitchen. That is, if your mom knew how to cook. Some of the display pieces are French antiques, and the muffins are piled in intricately woven baskets. Suzanne Reifers has kept this a bustling spot, specializing in Mediterranean foods for more than a decade, and the pastries she serves are legendary in the city. There are always some hearty soups and stews in winter and wonderful fresh salads, quiches and cheeses all year round. There is a limited supply of shelf-stable gourmet foods, but don't fret: Larimer's is just a few doors away. *Open Mon.-Fri. 8:30 a.m.-8 p.m., Sat. 8:30 a.m.-7 p.m.*

Washington Park
2331 Calvert St. NW
• 462-5566

Washington Park's gourmet provisions—fancy foods, baked goods, wines, green grocery items—brighten a corner in this already bright neighborhood. Just off Connecticut Avenue and a quick dash from the metro's Zoo exit, this relatively new entry to the carry-out market is sure to be a success. With all these refreshing and delicious things available, you just might begin to wonder: what's the use of ever cooking again? Although the dishes change regularly, special favorites include strips of chicken in a tangy red chili sauce with sesame seeds, cold green beans with whole fresh raspberries in a delicate vinaigrette, pasta primavera and seafood pasta in a cream sauce. Here, even a simple mixed fruit salad is a delicacy. An extensive selection of baked goods is on hand for the discriminating dessert-lover.
Open Mon.-Fri. 8:30 a.m.-8 p.m., Sat.-Sun. 8:30 a.m.-7 p.m.

HEALTH FOODS

Bethesda Co-op
7945 MacArthur Blvd.,
Cabin John, Md.
• (301) 320-2530

This collectively run natural-food store has been dispensing a wide variety of organic produce, natural foods, cheeses, bulk nuts, fruits, flours and coffees for ten years to the acclaim of its regulars. In addition, the store carries some packaged convenience foods, frozen foods, beer and wine. What you won't find are meats or anything with sugar or preservatives. One of the store's big attractions is a huge case of organic fruits and vegetables that, even in the dead of winter, is remarkably well stocked. The fresh cilantro sells out pretty fast, usually by noon, but you'll find an abundance of everything else you need for a Chinese stir-fry. Although the store is billed as a co-op, anyone can shop here with no "user" fee attached.
Open Mon.-Sat. 9 a.m.-8 p.m., Sun. 11 a.m.-6 p.m.

Hugo's Natural Food Market

3813-3817 Livingston St. NW
• 966-5486

Situated just three blocks from the D.C.–Maryland border, Hugo's is one of the largest natural food stores in the area, having expanded in its eight years of existence from one to its current three storefronts on Livingston Street. You'll find a large selection of produce, with a focus on organic fruits and vegetables, as well as an excellent selection of imported cheeses from all over the world. Bulk coffees, grains, fruit and nut mixtures, flours and chips are also worth a look. In addition to the foodstuffs, Hugo's is known for its large selection of vitamins, natural cosmetics and gift items. The phone number listed above will get you a live person who can provide specific information on Hugo's offerings. For directions and general information, Hugo's has a recording (966-6103).

Open Mon.-Sat. 9 a.m.-8 p.m., Sun. 10 a.m.-6 p.m.

Yes! Natural Gourmet

3425 Connecticut Ave. NW
• 363-1559

Another monster (3,000 square feet) of a health-food store, Yes! aims to be a complete grocery store, with trained staff in each section to answer questions and provide advice. The buyers chase down all the organic produce that is available, such as citrus fruits, apples, greens and vegetables, although, in the winter they occasionally find it necessary to add a few nonorganic items. The store carries hard-to-find specialty flours and bulk items such as grains, fruits, nuts and teas. Particularly noteworthy is the large bodycare shop which carries vitamins, natural cosmetics, shampoos, soaps and bath products. Among the natural cosmetics are some of the top brands from Paris and London. Also, check out the excellent deli, which carries sandwiches, soups, freshly squeezed juices and Tofutti.

Open Mon.-Fri. 9 a.m.-9 p.m., Sat. 9 a.m.-7 p.m.,Sun. 10 a.m.-6 p.m.

ICE CREAM

Bob's Famous Homemade Ice Cream

2416 Wisconsin Ave. NW
• 965-4499

236 Massachusetts Ave. NW
• 546-3860

4706 Bethesda Ave., Bethesda, Md.
• (301) 986-5911

For many years, Washington was considered a cultural backwater, and with good reason. It wasn't until 1978 that homemade ice-cream came to the nation's capital. Bob of Bob's Famous learned the ice cream business in Boston and discovered soon after moving to Washington that there was no Baileys, no Brighams—no homemade ice cream at all. Bob seized on the opportunity, and Washington has been thanking him ever since. Here, you'll find that wonderful original treat, Oreo-cookie ice cream, alongside some 150 other recipes that Bob has developed over the years. Not that there are 150 flavors available all the time. You'll have

to settle for only fifteen or sixteen different flavors on a given day. During peak season, Bob's scoops up about 1,000 gallons a week for hungry Washingtonians and tourists. The shops also feature a dozen or more toppings, and the waffle cones he imports from Denmark are half again as large as your standard sugar cone. If that's not enough to make you drop everything and head straight to the nearest location, just picture that giant cone dunked in Swiss chocolate and rolled in nuts before the Oreo-cookie ice cream goes in.
Both Washington branches: open daily noon-midnight. Bethesda branch open Sun.-Thurs. 11 a.m.-10:30 p.m., Fri.-Sat. 11 a.m.-midnight.

Cone E. Island
2000 Pennsylvania Ave. NW
• 822-8460

2816 Pennsylvania Ave. NW
• 338-6778

These ice-cream shops smell extra-wonderful, and the reason is readily apparent: they bake their own cones all day long. They also make their own ice cream. Brace yourself: it has the highest butterfat content in town, and it only costs $2.50 to create your own sundae in one of those wonderful cones. The flavors are pure yuppie—Cappuccino Kahlúa Calypso, Old South Fudge Pie, candy flavors such as Snickers, Almond Joy and Reese's Cup—and can be topped with all sorts of gooey wonders, including hot fudge, whipped cream, fresh seasonal fruits and just about everything else you can imagine. During rush hours, they're likely to sell more than 100 cones an hour. If you travel and are suffering from ice-cream withdrawal, you'll find the Cone E. Island cone mix and cone-making machines in ice-cream stores in Aspen, Fort Lauderdale, Hawaii, Singapore and Japan. They also sell to caterers or individuals for parties.
2000 Pennsylvania Ave. branch: open daily noon-midnight. 2816 Pennsylvania Ave. branch: open daily 11:30 a.m.-midnight.

WINE & LIQUOR

A & A Fine Wines and Spirits
2201 Wisconsin Ave. NW
• 337-3161

Owner Thomas Hanna has created a truly international wine store in this prime upper Georgetown location, stocking an outstanding collection of some 4,000 different varieties of wines, including some august "oldies" in a special rare wine room downstairs. The idea behind A & A is to cater not only to collectors and connoisseurs, but to everyone with an interest in wine—and give everyone the time and selection to learn more at an individual pace. Here you can find a wine for $1.33 a bottle or one that costs several hundred dollars. In addition to the wines and spirits, there's a nice selection of wine paraphernalia, from napkins for your next wine tasting to wine coasters—and even a grape cluster necklace with matching earrings. Particularly nice is the book corner, where you can find wine history books, cookbooks, guidebooks for the world's great vineyard areas, books on wine- and spirit-making and an amusing section entitled "wine fiction." Periodically, Hanna hosts wine tastings and booksigning parties. In the interest of history, we should note that A & A occupies the same space as Walter Mondale's 1984 presidential campaign headquarters. The store, however, appears to be far more successful.

Open Mon.-Thurs. 10 a.m.-8 p.m., Fri.-Sat. 10 a.m.-8:30 p.m.

Calvert-Woodley
4339 Connecticut Ave. NW
• 966-4400

Veteran hosts have been known to plan their menus for large parties around what Calvert-Woodley has for sale that week. There is always a long list of specials in *The Washington Post,* or you can wander in and rubberneck for the unadvertised gems. This is a hectic wine shop, and the sales people, if you can find someone who knows wine from Windex, are not the sort of folk to stand and chat about Chardonnays with you; however, if you want good prices, this is the place to come. For an instant party, go downstairs, where they sell a large selection of cheeses and a complete line of party snacks prepared by Albert Turgemen.

Open Mon.-Sat. 10 a.m.-8:30 p.m

Central Liquor
516-518 9th St. NW
• 737-2800

The exterior of this big, busy liquor store is a little scary, what with the plain, windowless front and the bars on the doors. But this is one of the largest volume liquor stores on the East Coast, claiming to have the "world's greatest selection at directly import prices." Prices for Central's huge inventory of wines, spirits and beers run 10 to 15 percent less than at other stores. This is not a shop for the dedicated wine collector—it's strictly a fast turnover kind of place, where wines and whiskeys frequently are direct-imported from Europe or other parts of the world, and sold without the "middleman" markup. By all means take a close look at the excellent Australian wines, some of which are

sold exclusively at Central, and most of which are values both in quality and price. Central also stocks a large number of fine Chilean wines. Weekly, you'll find a number of advertised specials and an even greater discount on case sales. The staff is knowledgeable, helpful and glad to steer you to the best value.
Open Mon.-Sat. 10 a.m.-7 p.m.

Mayflower Wines and Spirits
2115 M St. NW
• 463-7950

There's a wide array of California and French vintages here, but owner Sidney Moore's particular love is Italian wines. Her father retired from Mayflower a few years ago and returned to Italy, where he sits on the board that judges the quality of each year's production of Chianti. Serious tastings are held several times a year here, and, on Saturdays, customers can sample wines from particular regions or producers. The shop produces a monthly newsletter that waxes ecstatic about the new arrivals in the shop, details sales and includes favorite seasonal recipes. If you're a little hesitant about investing in unfamiliar wines, you might try the shop's special "six pack" approach, with six different bottles available in a sampler box each month, selling for a few dollars less than the wines' normal prices.
Open Mon.-Sat. 10 a.m.-9 p.m.

MacArthur Liquors
4877 MacArthur Blvd. NW
• 338-1433,
Fax 333-0806

Master wine merchant Addy Bassin is credited with creating an entire wine culture in Washington, and when he died in 1986, he was toasted by his customers from legendary bottles of Bordeaux and Burgundy. Bassin was one of the first wine merchants in the country to sell futures in California wines, and he amassed a collection of ports rivaled by few in the country. The shop does not boast the glamor of a Sherry-Lehmann, or even a Wide World of Wine in Washington. But true aficionadoes go there first. Not only does MacArthur, now run by Bruce Bassin, carry more than 4,500 different French and California wines (with lesser quantities and qualities of Italian and Australian), but if you must have twenty cases of a favorite, they will call the warehouse and have it delivered today.
Open Mon.-Sat. 10 a.m.-8:45 p.m.

Plain Old Pearson's
2436 Wisconsin Ave. NW
• 333-6666

As soon as the "noble experiment" of Prohibition was (thankfully) repealed, Samuel "Doc" Eisenberg started Pearson's, next to where his brother began a pharmacy. He still oversees the daily running of the business, and is a legend as the oldest retailer in Washington. Plain Old Pearson's is certainly plain on the exterior, and regulars

wonder if the floors have been polished since the store opened. While Doc began it as a liquor store to replace bathtub gin with bottles of hooch, it is now one of the most respected wine stores in the city, with great strength in both the red and white Burgundies.
Open Mon.-Sat. 10 a.m.-8:45 p.m.

Potomac Wines & Spirits
3067 M St. NW
• 333-2848

There are a lot of bottles of cheap wine that never leave their brown paper bags coming out of the door of Steve Feldman's crowded Georgetown shop, but he also carries an incredibly eclectic stock. There is the best selection of grappas in the city, next to a large case of Kosher wines. There are many finds from Australia but not much in the way of Italian. For a full-service liquor store, Potomac is excellent, with a better selection of old-fashioned booze than one finds in most shops. Feldman also stocks a United Nations of beers, including many delicious Asian brews.
Open Mon.-Sat. 9 a.m.-9 p.m.

Schneider's of Capitol Hill
300 Massachusetts Ave. NE
• 543-9300

Schneider's is a wonderful, friendly little family liquor store that has been serving Capitol Hill residents for 42 years. The shop carries some 3,000 varieties of wine, as well as a complete stock of liquor, beer and after-dinner drinks, including a particularly fine selection of Cognacs and Armagnacs. Brothers Jon and Rick Genderson are third-generation owners. They've taken wine courses, but it's reading and testing that are responsible for their outstanding knowledge of wines from all over the world. Here, you can find a credible $2.99 selection from France or a magnificent $500 collector's item. Tasting is encouraged in the store. Cases of wine are discounted 10 percent, and weekly specials are announced in Monday's *Washington Post*. The house label liquor, "Roll Call," is quite acceptable and a great conversation starter.
Open Mon.-Sat. 9 a.m.-9 p.m.

Watergate Wine & Beverage
2544 Virginia Ave. NW
• 333-0636

There's more here than you would ordinarily expect at a liquor store. Undoubtedly, the real draw for tourists and others with a fond memory of the Nixon years is the "Watergate" brand scotch, bourbon, gin and vodka, which can cause a real sensation at parties. The "Watergate" labels are available in fifths, liters and half-gallons. But the store also has a surprisingly large array of very nice gift items, including china, crystal and silver. Watergate Wine & Beverage also offers local delivery free of charge.

Open Mon.-Wed. 10:30 a.m.-7:30 p.m., Thurs.-Sat. 10:30 a.m.-8 p.m.

Wide World of Wine
4801 Massachusetts Ave. NW
• 362-9463

True wine-lovers have followed master sommelier Elliott Staren as he moved from wine shop to wine shop; all are grateful that he is now working at this spiffy new store, as serene as a glass of Sauternes and as rich as a bottle of Mouton-Rothschild. Wide World of Wine has not only one of the best selections of fine wines, but, regardless of price range, one of the best selections, period. If you want to spend thousands on Bordeaux futures, Staren will help you. But he'll also help you select a low-priced party wine.
Open Mon.-Sat. 10 a.m.-7 p.m.

GIFTS

The American Hand
2906 M St. NW
• 965-3273

The American Hand showcases fine, handmade pottery, from sturdy stoneware to amusing deco-inspired pieces and fragile, graceful porcelain. There is also a small but exclusive collection of mass-produced items, such as the Michael Graves teapots or MOMA watches, and some unusual pins and earrings. Displays change frequently, but there is always a representative selection from the wide range of pottery items created by American artists, always of the highest quality. Pottery buffs will become addicted to this shop.
Open Mon.-Sat. 11 a.m.-6 p.m., Sun 1 p.m.-5 p.m.

Appalachian Spring
1415 Wisconsin Ave. NW
• 337-5780

Union Station,
50 Massachusetts Ave. NE
• 682-0505

Appalachian Spring is a peaceful, warm and inviting American craft store that can give shoppers a needed reprieve from the bustle of Wisconsin Avenue. From pottery to jewelry, all the handcrafted objects display the finest skill. For those times when a craft fair isn't being held in the area, or when you don't have an entire Saturday or Sunday to devote to searching out a distinctive, original gift, Appalachian Spring offers a quick and sure solution.
Wisconsin Ave. branch: open Mon.-Fri. 10 a.m.-8 p.m., Sat. 10 a.m.-6 p.m., Sun. noon-6 p.m. Union Station branch: Mon.-Fri. 10 a.m.-9 p.m., Sun. noon-6 p.m.

Full Circle

317 Cameron St.,
Alexandria, Va.
• (703) 683-4500

Since 1973, Full Circle has served as a stylish showplace for craftwork by local and international artists. The pottery is particularly beautiful; you may be tempted to place a special order for several hand-thrown place settings. Variety is the keynote of this collection: you'll find Asian silk screens, silk fans, kimonos and sweaters displayed next to hand-painted boxes, rugs and wall hangings from Afghanistan, Turkey and Tunisia and original, exotic decorator fabrics. Step into the back room and feast your eyes on the stunning art and accent pieces.
Open Tues.-Sat. 10:30 a.m.-5:30 p.m.

Ginza

1721 Connecticut Ave. NW
• 331-7991

A tasteful array of Japanese decorative items, housewares and textiles fill this interesting shop. The collection of pottery and porcelain is extensive, featuring a wealth of delicate tea sets and rice bowls. Colorful Japanese kites and fans make charming presents, as do the unusual enameled earrings and other costume jewelry.
Open Mon.-Tues. & Sat. 10 a.m.-6 p.m., Wed.-Thurs. 10 a.m.-8 p.m., Fri. 10 a.m.-6:30 p.m., Sun. noon-6:30 p.m.

Little Caledonia Shop

1419 Wisconsin Ave. NW
• 333-4700

We're not quite sure why this charming, old-line Georgetown store is called Little Caledonia (is there a Scottish connection somewhere?) or why it closes at 5:50 rather than 6 p.m. But never mind. Offered here is a delightful selection of kitchen and gift items, home accessories and diminutive furniture perfect for a Georgetown or a Capitol Hill townhouse where space is at a premium. There is also an interior-design service, with thousands of fabric samples at the back of the store. Service can be frosty—or, even worse, nonexistent—so be prepared to find what you want yourself.
Open Mon.-Sat. 10 a.m.-5:50 p.m.

Little German World

1512 King St.,
Alexandria, Va.
• (703) 684-5344

Would you like to quaff your Pilsener from an authentic German stein? You'll find a handsome array to choose from at this commodious, three-year-old shop, situated on the less chic side of King Street in Old Town. With German marches, oom-pa-pa and other traditional music playing in the background, shoppers can browse among shelves of crystal Christmas ornaments (look for the colorful wooden nutcrackers, too), painted wooden candlesticks, the aforementioned beer steins, chestnut walking sticks, wooden dollhouse miniatures and small cuckoo clocks imported for the most part from Germany and Austria.

Open Tues.-Sat. 10 a.m.-6 p.m., Sun. noon-5 p.m.

Moon, Blossoms & Snow
225 Pennsylvania Ave. SE
• 543-8181

Moon, Blossoms & Snow is a showcase for contemporary American crafts. Shop owner Sharon McCarthy chooses her wares with taste and flair at the well-known and highly respected American Craft Council exhibits. Her brilliant selection includes hand-blown glasses and art nouveau oil lamps, unusual belts for women, trays and cutting boards fashioned from a combination of woods. There are wooden toys for children that you'll be tempted to keep for yourself, as well as attractive hand-dipped candles and an eclectic mix of earrings, necklaces and handmade clothes by talented American craftspeople. Those familiar with American crafts will recognize g. girvins's distinctive appliqué vests and jackets, white duck clothing, Laurel Burch accessories, Gerherdt jewelry, and Fine Line glassware. Don't overlook the one-of-a-kind Brown Bag cookie molds, kaleidoscopes, locally hand-carved Christmas ornaments, wearable art, and painted and woven scarves.

Open Mon.-Sat. 11 a.m.-6 p.m.

The Music Box Center
918 F St. NW
• 783-9399

For a quarter of a century, The Music Box Center has delighted its customers with music boxes in every conceivable shape and size, some encased in porcelain and others with intricate mechanisms, each box tinkling out a different tune. The man who lacks for nothing just might appreciate a music box that plays "Hail to the Redskins."

Open Mon.-Fri. 10 a.m.-6 p.m., Sat. 10 a.m.-3 p.m.

The Pineapple, Inc.
132 King St.,
Alexandria, Va.
• (703) 836-3639

This huge store in Old Town Alexandria offers gifts and household items in the traditional Williamsburg style. Two entire floors are filled with objects representing genteel Old Virginia: a roomful of brass table accessories, fireplace tools and candlesticks, quality linens, glassware, paper products and accent pieces. All very proper, high quality and very, very classic. There is not a single trendy thing in this shop.

Open Mon.-Wed. 10 a.m.-6 p.m., Thurs.-Sat. 10 a.m.-9 p.m., Sun. noon-5 p.m.

Santa Fe Style

1525 Wisconsin Ave. NW
• 333-3747

It was inevitable that the howling coyotes would come to prowl, even in sedate Georgetown. Everything in the shop—decorated to within an inch of its life to look like a hacienda—looks as if it came from a movie set in the desert. There are candlesticks made from bent branding irons, Christmas wreaths of green cactus pads with red chile peppers, terra-cotta pottery, Indian blankets, leather throw rugs. You get the picture. The cute little items are certainly more expensive than they are in Santa Fe or Taos, but, then again, you don't have to pay the plane fare.
Open Mon.-Sat. 10 a.m.-6 p.m., Sun. noon-5 p.m.

Save the Children International Craft Center

2803 M St. NW
• 342-8096

An ever-changing selection of striking gifts and decorative objects from around the world are featured in this shop. The wares are produced in projects sponsored by the Save the Children Federation. It hopes to foster community development by helping native craftspeople make a living and at the same time to preserve old artistic techniques. The handsome window displays always highlight a particularly exotic piece. Wooden toys, carvings, mirrors, jewelry, wallhangings and some small rugs are always in stock, and there is usually a small collection of clothing in cotton, wool or other natural fabrics. The prices for all this wonderful stuff are wonderfully moderate.
Open Mon.-Fri. 11 a.m.-6 p.m., Sat. noon-6 p.m.

The Sharper Image

The Shops at National Place,
1331 Pennsylvania Ave. NW
• 626-6340

Georgetown Park Mall,
3222 M St. NW
• 337-9361

Tysons Corner,
1961 Chain Bridge Rd.,
McLean, Va.
• (703) 734-9405

White Flint,
11301 Rockville Pike,
North Bethesda, Md.
• (301) 881-0224

A high-tech playground for adults, trading in such necessities as table-top pool tables, portable home solariums for a year-round tan, and sonic massagers that send waves of vibrating energy deep into tired muscles. Or perhaps your taste runs to items like a pocket-sized radar detectoror a bathroom scale with a voice and—ugh!—a memory. This coast-to-coast chain is guaranteed to bring out the child in anyone. If you don't see what you want, a full catalog shopping service (800-344-4444) operates 24 hours a day. Fidelity is rewarded with a Frequent Buyer Program that lets you earn points toward gift certificates with every dollar you spend.
The Shops branch: open Mon.-Wed. & Fri.-Sat. 10 a.m.-7 p.m., Thurs. 10 a.m.-8 p.m., Sun. noon-5 p.m. Georgetown Park Mall branch: open Mon.-Fri.10 a.m.-9 p.m., Sat. 9 a.m.-7 p.m., Sun. noon-6 p.m. McLean & North Bethesda branches: Mon.-Sat. 10 a.m.-9:30 p.m., Sun. 11 a.m.-6 p.m.

HOME

FABRICS

Laura Ashley
3213 M St. NW
• 338-5481

The tiny prints, cheerful flowers and beautiful colors are Laura Ashley trademarks. Romantic decorating materials are on hand, of course: wallpaper, upholstery fabrics, printed wallpaper borders, matching lamp shades and other accessory items. You'll also find matching sheets and pillow cases and other coordinates for the home. There's a large collection of nostalgic clothing that is adorable on children, but adults should take a critical look in the mirror before indulging in the rustically styled (but very expensive) outfits. The look is emphatically not for everyone. Other branches: Mazza Gallerie, White Flint and Fair Oaks mall. *Open Mon.-Fri. 10 a.m.-6 p.m., Sat. 10 a.m.-6 p.m., Sun. noon-5 p.m.*

Couture Fabrics of Alexandria
320 King St.,
Alexandria, Va.
• (703) 548-7709

This stylish emporium specializes in fancy dress-fabrics. Here, you can locate shimmering lamé for a slinky gold or silver evening dress, rhinestone or beaded fabric for festive dressing, and even leatherlike fabrics for jackets or pants. There are some lovely woolens here of all different weights, designs and textures, as well as some colorful wool blends. No wash-and-wear cottons; this shop caters to people who seek fine fabrics for high fashion or classic dress design. *Open Mon.-Wed. & Fri.-Sat. 9:30 a.m.-5:30 p.m., Thurs. 9:30 a.m.-9 p.m., Sun. 1 p.m.-5 p.m.*

G Street Fabrics
11854 Rockville Pike,
Rockville, Md.
• (301) 231-8998

When G Street Fabrics went the way of so many downtown businesses and moved from its inner city location to the suburbs, the increase in space made the grumbles cease. If you're sewing—or having something sewn for you—anything from a skirt for a table to a dress for yourself, this is the place to go. They have a huge selection of everything from the most inexpensive cotton linings to tapestries for chairs that run twice the price at designer shops in town. The staff is incredibly helpful and knowledgeable. Sewing classes are offered, and if you want to give your clothes a personal touch, take a look at the button department. *Open Mon.-Fri. 10 a.m.-9 p.m., Sat. 10 a.m.-6 p.m., Sun. noon-5 p.m.*

Liberty of London
Georgetown Park Mall,
3222 M St. NW
• 338-3711

This branch of the old-line British store seems to carry fewer of the famous scarves and ties than might be expected, but the fabric department is abundantly stocked with Liberty's signature paisley, floral and geometric prints. A few finished dresses and sweaters are available, mostly on the dowdy side, but there is also a wide selection of unfinished skirts in various fabrics, easy for even a less-than-accomplished seamstress to run up in record time. The skirts are gathered at the waist, with an open seam on the left side; all one need do is trim the waist to fit, sew up the seam, and hem. Liberty makes some lovely fabric-covered picture frames, guest books and other gift items; upholstery fabrics are available by special order from catalogs.
Open Mon.-Fri. 10 a.m.-9 p.m., Sat. 10 a.m.-7 p.m., Sun. noon-6 p.m.

Pierre Deux
Mazza Gallerie,
5300 Wisconsin Ave. NW
• 244-6226

Some shops don't ever have to advertise, and this is one. For public relations, they "do charity," such as providing the linens for a White House dinner. Blond-wood antiques and reproductions and those unmistakable eighteenth-century Provençal prints reign supreme here. Attractive saleswomen dressed in floral print chemises and skirts can help you pick out just the right quilted handbag that will likely go with nothing else you own, but what the heck? The home furnishings section is positively inspiring, and the children's clothes and toys are truly precious. Prices are in line with the upscale location and merchandise.
Open Mon.-Fri. 10 a.m.-9 p.m., Sat. 10 a.m.-6 p.m., Sun. noon-5 p.m.

FURNITURE

Exceptional furniture stores and interior shops are relatively scarce in Washington. For those who cannot or do not wish to go the antique route, some of the best-quality furniture selections can be found in the local department stores. Washingtonians often rely on interior decorators to handle their design chores, from choosing the smallest accessory touch to supervising a total remake of their living quarters. They'll seek out antiques, Oriental rugs or specialty furniture, and they have access to huge catalogs of wallpaper, fabrics, paint and the like. Most important, only interior designers and their clients are admitted to the fabulous Design Center in southwest Washington, where all the fabric and furniture companies maintain showrooms.

Colony House Furniture

1700 Lee Hwy.,
Rosslyn, Va.
• (703) 524-1700

Don't be put off by the grimy exterior of this store or by the fact that the traffic from nearby Route 66 seems to be threatening your very existence. Once through the doors of this outstanding furniture store, you won't think about anything but where to put this or that wonderful sofa, side chair, bedroom set or accessory piece. In a city that lacks top-drawer furniture stores, Colony House is a delightful exception. There is a particularly impressive selection of reproduction eighteenth-century dining room tables and chairs. Real wood, folks, no veneers. The store's display technique is especially fetching, giving a real sense of what the furniture would look like in your home, complete with cocktails on the coffee tables. The occasional tables are scaled to smaller apartments or townhouses. A good example is a flip-top cocktail table that can be small enough not to intrude when you don't need it, and big enough to do the job when you do. The second floor is filled with stately four-poster beds and a nice collection of colonial dining and casual kitchen furniture. There is an interior design service on the premises.
Open Mon.-Fri. 9 a.m.-9 p.m., Sat. 9 a.m.-6 p.m.

Conran's

Georgetown Park Mall,
3227 Grace St. NW
• 298-8300

10400 Old Georgetown Rd.,
Bethesda, Md.
• (301) 564-9590

Here, you'll find a nice selection of basic furniture for people who don't want to spend a fortune on home decoration. Conran's specializes in clean lines, without a great deal of pizzazz or daring. It's a modern look, without any frills or fancy touches in fabric or design. You can find lighting, rugs, very nice leather sofas and chairs, and a full contingent of kitchenware and housewares, from laundry hampers to wine glasses. Conran's chief virtue is its broad spectrum of merchandise, which allows customers to outfit an entire house or apartment in a single day, if need be, with functional, attractive furnishings.
Washington branch: open Mon.-Fri. 10 a.m.-9 p.m., Sat. 10 a.m.-7 p.m., Sun. noon-6 p.m. Bethesda branch: open Mon.-Fri. 10 a.m.-9 p.m., Sat. 10 a.m.-6 p.m., Sun. noon-5 p.m.

Park Place

2251 Wisconsin Ave. NW
• 342-6294

Few stores in the Washington area specialize in porch, patio and garden furniture, but at Park Place, you can find beguiling stone fountains or stunning, giant light-clusters to illuminate a swimming pool or line the driveway to your estate. Even the less adventurous or well-heeled will admire the furniture; in addition to teak, oak and wrought-iron pieces, Park Place carries the fabled Weatherend Estate Furniture, designed in Rockport, Maine, and made from 100-percent Honduras mahogany—it may just be the best in the world. Owner C. Philip Mitchell is a great believer

in the delights of porches, witness his connoisseur's selection of lounging furniture. But it is the outstanding beveled leaded glass that is the shop's major claim to fame. From doors to transoms to windows, Park Place carries more than 100 elegant beveled-glass designs (others are available by special order). An extensive selection of crown moldings and ceiling medallions is also on view here. Anyone seeking exceptional glass design, stylish interior accents, or a front porch swing like Grandma once had, should stop in here. Despite the Georgetown address, you'll find lots of free parking in the rear of the shop.
Open Mon.-Wed. & Fri. 10 a.m.-6 p.m., Thurs. 10 a.m.-9 p.m., Sat. 10 a.m.-5 p.m., Sun. noon-5 p.m.

Scan Contemporary Furnishings
**Loehmann's Plaza,
7311 Arlington Blvd.,
Falls Church, Va.
• (703) 573-0100**

For 26 years, Scan has been offering clean-lined Scandinavian designs in wood and leather. Particularly famous for their teak, rosewood and oak platform beds and bedroom accessory pieces, Scan has some attractively priced sofas, chairs and dining room furniture, as well as a large collection of stereo cabinets and wall storage units. Special purchases are worth watching for. Most pieces are already assembled, others are not, but the latter come with easy mounting instructions. The Virginia store is the largest in the area, and has a floor sample of everything that is available.
Open Mon.-Fri. 10 a.m.-9 p.m., Sat. 10 a.m.-6 p.m., Sun. noon-5 p.m.

Theodore's Contemporary Interiors
**2233 Wisconsin Ave. NW
• 333-2300**

If you appreciate the clean, uncluttered lines of contemporary furniture, you'll find much to like at Theodore's. For nearly two decades, Theodore's has led the field in modern design hereabouts. This Georgetown store, with free parking in the rear, has a light, cool, open feeling wholly in tune with the furniture and accessories on display. We especially liked a luscious upholstered bed, and very nearly succumbed to a stunning black-lacquered stereo cabinet. The knowledgeable sales personnel willingly offer design hints and discuss options in a friendly, unaggressive way.
Open Mon. & Thurs. 10 a.m.-9 p.m., Tues.-Wed. & Fri.-Sat. 10 a.m.-6 p.m.

Uzzolo
**1718 Connecticut Ave. NW
• 328-0900**

Specializing in high-tech, space-age design, Uzzolo is a rather austere enclave, where black, white and chrome figure prominently in the displays. The first floor features high-priced, contemporary leather sofas and chairs, as well as tables of abstract design in a variety of materials. The

stark, stripped-down lamps seem to glower rather than glow, but there is wit and flair in the abstract or asymmetrical accent pieces, like vases and candlesticks. Some of the prices may astonish you. The bottom floor is devoted to more reasonably priced, cleanly designed kitchenware and small appliances. The sturdy, colorful sets of dishes and nice glassware are well worth your attention.
Open Mon.-Sat. 11 a.m.-7 p.m., Sun. noon-6 p.m.

The Wicker Shoppe

210 North Lee St., Alexandria, Va.
• (703) 548-7773

A tremendous selection of quality wicker furniture for every room in the house is the Wicker Shoppe's stock in trade. The pretty kitchen and dining tables, sofas, chairs, loveseats, coffee tables and bedroom furnishings are just the thing for apartment-dwellers with limited space and budgets. Moreover, the airy look of white or painted wicker with colorful pillows and cushions goes a long way to lighten a room that could really use more windows. A worthwhile collection of cane furniture is also offered, as well as some charming baskets, lamps and accessories. Prices are attractive, and periodic sales reductions make them even more so.
Open Mon.-Wed. &Fri.-Sat. 10 a.m.-6 p.m., Thurs. 10 a.m.-8 p.m., Sun. noon-5 p.m.

KITCHEN & HOUSEWARES

Brookstone Co.

1140 Connecticut Ave. NW
• 293-9290

Union Station,
50 Massachusetts Ave. NE
• 289-3553

Brookstone may just be one of Washington's best-kept secrets. In addition to offering clever and original items for the home, interesting-looking male customers outnumber females by about ten to one, in a town where the overall men-to-women ratio seems to some to be almost the exact opposite. As for the merchandise, well, that's interesting-looking, too. Customers pick up a clipboard and pen, then wander around the displays (handling the merchandise is positively encouraged), noting whatever strikes their fancy. We were struck, so to speak, by the plastic rock with a secret key compartment; the huge plastic owl, with sparkly eyes that ward off garden pests, which is a hoot; the specially contoured garden tools to keep green thumbs from wilting; and the fire-starter sticks. The staff of this agreeable shop is friendly and helpful.
Connecticut Ave. branch: open Mon.-Wed. & Fri. 10 a.m.-7 p.m., Thurs. 10 a.m.-8 p.m., Sat. 10 a.m.-6 p.m. Union Station branch: open Mon.-Sat. 10 a.m.-9 p.m., Sun. noon-6 p.m.

Hoffritz

Union Station,
50 Massachusetts Ave. NE
• 842-2728

If sharp knives and custom cutlery are what you're after, Hoffritz is the place to go, for anything from steak knives to cleavers, in stainless or carbon steel. Although the store features numerous name-brand knives, such as Sabatier, its own brand is frequently cheaper and of equal or better quality. The store also sharpens knives, giving a $3 discount per knife for its own brand. The store won't sharpen knives worth more than $100, any knife other than a kitchen knife over ten inches long, swords or hunting knives. In addition to cutlery, Hoffritz offers a good selection of manicure implements and pocket knives.
Open Mon.-Sat. 10 a.m.-9 p.m., Sun. noon-6 p.m.

Kitchen Bazaar

4401 Connecticut Ave. NW
• 244-1550

Kitchen Bazaar is a very successful supplier to cooks in the nation's capital, with this flagship location complemented by others at almost every major shopping mall, including Tysons II Galleria and Montgomery Mall. Slimshakers, Cuisinarts, Sabatier knives, assorted garlic presses, pots, pans, bowls, bakeware, crumb vacs, rolling pins, cookbooks, coffee makers, pasta makers, Donvier ice-cream machines—there's everything you'd ever want for your kitchen, and more. By no means a discount store, Kitchen Bazaar does have frequent sales, announced in their newsletter, *The Kitchen Bazaar Times*, sent regularly to customers on the mailing list. The stores also offer cooking demonstrations by famous visiting cookbook authors, and Cuisinart and Simac classes for budding chefs. Judging by the crowds, all of Washington cooks—or wants to look as though it does.
Open Mon.-Wed. 10 a.m.-7 p.m., Thurs.-Fri. 10 a.m.-9 p.m., Sat. 10 a.m.-6 p.m., Sun. 11 a.m.-5 p.m.

Reliable Home Appliances

737 15th St. NW
• 737-2537

Here, you'll find televisions, stereo components, dishwashers, microwaves, refrigerators, blenders, food processors and countless other appliances for some of the best prices in town. The downtown store—small, low-ceilinged and jam-packed with merchandise—is staffed by knowledgeable and helpful salespeople who will go through the specs with you, discuss warranties and just plain help. If you don't mind shopping with the spec books and not the models themselves, this is your kind of place. Other cost-conscious shoppers visit showrooms around town before they stop in at Reliable to buy. Bring your checkbook or cash: no credit cards here (although credit is available with an approved application). Eight locations in the Washington area.
Open Mon.-Wed. & Fri. 10 a.m.-7 p.m., Thurs. 10 a.m.-8:30 p.m., Sat. 9 a.m.-6 p.m.

Williams-Sonoma

Mazza Gallerie,
5300 Wisconsin Ave. NW
• 244-4800

Georgetown Park Mall,
3222 M St. NW
• 965-3422

Long known in the Washington area from its catalog, this San Francisco shrine to the New Hedonism finally made it east in 1985. This wonderful store is the kitchen equivalent of *The New York Times*—all the equipment that's fit to stock. During America's cooking revolution, while Julia Child and Craig Claiborne were starting to produce recipes and cookbooks, Chuck Williams was importing the equipment necessary to produce the creations. He started in the 1950s with a hardware store in Sonoma, California, then moved to San Francisco in 1958. He scoured Europe for sauté and crêpe pans, fish poachers, asparagus steamers, pizelle irons, garlic keepers and all the paraphernalia cherished by the serious cook. His enterprise has grown to include a chain of Williams-Sonoma shops and a full-color housewares catalog which arrives in millions of American homes quarterly. If you're not already on the mailing list, waste no time. The Washington Williams-Sonoma branch stocks more than 4,000 items. The store also offers demonstrations by cookbook authors and "basics" classes for Cuisinart-users. Don't forget to pick up some pop-up sponges from France. *Mazza Gallerie branch: open Mon.-Fri. 10 a.m.-9 p.m., Sat. 10 a.m.-6 p.m., Sun. noon-5 p.m. Georgetown Park Mall branch: open Mon.-Fri. 10 a.m.-9 p.m., Sat. 10 a.m.-7 p.m., Sun. noon-6 p.m.*

KNIFE & SCISSORS SHARPENERS

A number of neighborhood hardware stores offer this service, but gone are the days when the itinerant sharpener wheeled his stone through the streets, calling for housewives to bring out their dull blades and pinking shears.

Brown's Lock & Key

5145-B Duke St.,
Alexandria, Va.
• (703) 370-6170

This shop, across from the Cameron Station PX (where retired military personnel stock up on subsidized groceries), says it will sharpen anything with an edge, including construction tools. A job can take up to two days. *Open Mon.-Fri. 8 a.m.-6 p.m., Sat. 9 a.m.-2 p.m.*

Kitchen Bazaar

4401 Connecticut Ave. NW
• 244-1550

This branch (the original) of the estimable cookware stores sharpens knives (no scissors) once a week, when the spirit moves the stock-room manager. That usually means midweek—and it usually means one trip to leave the knives and another to pick them up. The cost is about 30 cents per blade-inch. No serrated or hollow-ground knives accepted. *Open Mon.-Wed. 10 a.m.-6 p.m., Thurs.-Fri. 10 a.m.-9 p.m., Sat. 10 a.m.-6 p.m., Sun. noon-5 p.m.*

LIGHTING

Dominion Electric Supply Co.

5053 Lee Hwy.,
Arlington, Va.
• (703) 536-4400

The lack of weekend hours is absolutely abominable, but if you can overcome that major drawback, Dominion is worth a visit for lighting fixtures of any description. The store carries nearly 70 brands of top quality lighting at unbeatable prices: discounts here run about 40 percent less than list. You'll find a spectacular display of chandeliers, from the most glamorous and traditional to the most modern and flashy, in sizes that could fit discreetly over a dining table or jazz up a hotel lobby. A good selection of Tiffany-style shades are on display, and you'll find a full array of track lighting and outdoor patio fixtures.
Open Mon.-Fri. 7:30 a.m.-5 p.m.

Fan Fair

2251 Wisconsin Ave. NW
• 342-6290

Fan Fair is one of the largest-volume ceiling fan stores in the country, specializing in Casablanca and Hunter ceiling fans and the lighting fixtures that go with them. But don't think that just because this store does a lot of business, you'll get shortchanged on service. The staff here is informed, helpful and eager to discuss your needs, to make sure you get precisely what you're looking for (and that the fan you choose will do what you want it to). The prices are good here, and even better during the periodic sales. There's free parking at the rear of the store, which shares a shop location with Park Place (see listing in the "Furniture" section, page 235).
Open Mon.-Wed. & Fri. 10 a.m.-6 p.m., Thurs. 10 a.m.-9 p.m., Sat. 10 a.m.-5 p.m., Sun. noon-5 p.m.

The Lamp & Shade Center, Inc.

5714 Connecticut Ave. NW
• 362-4312

6533 Arlington Blvd.,
Falls Church, Va.
• (703) 536-6220

7022 Commerce St.,
Springfield, Md.
• (301) 569-8444

If you can't find the light fixture, chandelier, table lamp or floor lamp you're looking for here, it isn't made. These stores feature a huge assortment of lamps, lights and shades with a case of every shape and size, from the small and simple bedroom lamp for under $30 to the elegant $4,000-plus crystal chandelier, as well as a stunning group of shades. The stock can fill any decorating bill, from traditional and classic to ultramodern and art deco. Sale prices are always outstanding. You'll also find a full selection of those beautiful Casablanca ceiling fans for your gin joint.
Washington branch: open Mon.-Sat. 9:30 a.m.-6 p.m. Falls Church & Springfield branches: open Mon. & Thurs.-Fri. 10 a.m.-9 p.m., Tues.-Wed. & Sat. 10 a.m.-6 p.m., Sun. noon-5 p.m.

Reed Electric Co.

1611 Wisconsin Ave. NW
• 338-7521

Reed Electric has handled Washington's lighting needs since 1949. With free parking off Wisconsin Avenue, and a contracting department through which you can arrange for installation of fixtures and ceiling fans, this store is a real gem. The stock boasts more than 500 types of light bulbs, track lighting, silk lampshades (in a wide range of colors, shapes and sizes) lamps, picture lights, sconces, desk lamps and ceiling fans. You're likely to find just what you need. *Open Mon.-Fri. 8:30 a.m.-8 p.m., Sat. 9:30 a.m.-5 p.m., Sun. noon-5 p.m.*

LINENS

Descamps

3222 M St. NW
• 965-0913

While Washington does not sell the total extravagance of Porthault, it does just fine with the French-style Primrose Bordier by Descamps. The bed and bath linens are all pure cotton, in beautiful prints and vibrant solids. One warning: They have to be ironed, which means that the laundry bills are as high as the original cost. *Open Mon.-Sat. 10 a.m.-9 p.m., Sun. noon-6 p.m.*

In Detail

Georgetown Park,
3222 M St. NW
• 965-5029

White Flint,
11301 Rockville Pike,
North Bethesda, Md.
• (301) 231-8146

The Galleria at Tysons II,
1775 M International Dr.,
McLean, Va.
• (703) 734-1305

While the prices are certainly not what you find at The Company Store outlet, you also don't have to go to LaCrosse, Wisconsin, to shop. In Detail is better known from its mail-order catalog than its stores, which opened in the Washington area during the past year. They carry luxury linens for bath and bed, as well as the comforters and pillows to go underneath the linens. You'll also find bath accessories, such as soap dishes. Look for the frequent sales. *Washington branch: open Mon.-Fri. 10 a.m.-9 p.m., Sat. 10 a.m.-7 p.m., Sun. noon-6 p.m. North Bethesda branch: open Mon.-Sat. 10 a.m.-9:30 p.m., Sun. noon-6 p.m. McLean branch: open Mon.-Sat. 10 a.m.-9:30 p.m., Sun. 11 a.m.-6 p.m.*

Linens 'n Things

Loehmann's Plaza,
7241 Arlington Blvd.,
Falls Church, Va.
• (703) 573-1333

Let's face it, linens are expensive, and unless you're entertaining Queen Elizabeth II, you might wish to spend a little less for your sheets and towels. Linens 'n Things lets the budget-conscious shopper fill a linen closet at bargain prices. So maybe you won't find the latest designer sheet, but for 25 to 50 percent less than at major department stores, who cares? You'll find a wide selection of towels, blankets, comforters, shower curtains and a small selection of table linens here as well, also at attractive prices. You'll find branches in a number of off-price suburban shopping areas, including Fairfax, Springfield, Woodbridge and Po-

tomac Mills.
Open Mon.-Sat. 10 a.m.-9 p.m., Sun. 11 a.m.-5 p.m.

Walpole's
1722 Connecticut Ave. NW
• 667-2849

Walpole's is worth a stop just to inhale the wonderful smells of bath products, soaps and potpourri. Moreover, this is also one of the best stores in town for expensive, exquisite linens for kitchen, bedroom and bath. Walpole's is a place where you can still find old-fashioned hand-embroidered handkerchiefs and towels, tablecloths and kitchen towels. Some irregular and sale items are available year-round, and the three major yearly sales should not be missed. If you're shopping at the Mazza Gallerie, visit the other Walpole's branch just across the District line at Wisconsin and Western avenues, or the one in the Seven Corners Shopping Center in Fairfax, Virginia.
Open Mon.-Sat. 10 a.m.-6 p.m.

Jane Wilner
Mazza Gallerie,
5300 Wisconsin Ave. NW
• 966-1484

Jane Wilner provides distinctive linens of all types. If her custom bed and table linens, shower curtains and towels look as if they came right off the pages of *House and Garden* or *House Beautiful*, it's because they probably did. The store stocks European-look linens at reasonable (for the quality) prices. Custom orders require at least a 50 percent deposit and take three weeks. The staff specializes in personal service and will gladly share a wealth of creative decorating ideas.
Open Mon.-Fri. 10 a.m.-9 p.m., Sat. 10 a.m.-6 p.m., Sun. noon-5 p.m.

ORIENTAL RUGS

Parvizian, Inc.
7034 Wisconsin Ave.,
Chevy Chase, Md.
• (301) 654-8989

The first price tag you spy may read $49,000, but don't gasp and rush out; a member of Parvizian's courteous sales staff will happily show you something a mite less sumptuous—unless, of course, sumptuous is just what you're after. This elegant and understated emporium specializes in gorgeous Persian rugs from Iran as well as Chinese silk and Romanian rugs in an imposing array of sizes, styles, colors and prices. A chat with the helpful and knowledgeable personnel will reveal that "special sales" can reduce the asking price of a carpet by—literally—many thousands of dollars. It will also be pointed out that a used rug might fit your budget or decorating needs better than a new one. Some rug stores keep their carpets all tightly wrapped, making undecided shoppers feel awkward or guilty about asking someone to unroll them. At Parvizian, virtually all the rugs are stored flat, by size, for easy access. Here, they understand that sometimes something that looks perfect in the shop just doesn't work once you get it home. They'll let you take the carpet home for a day to make sure it's right, then happily exchange it if it isn't. This impressive store also offers unusual wood-inlay furniture.

Open Tues.-Wed. & Fri.-Sat. 9:30 a.m.-6 p.m., Mon. & Thurs. 9:30 a.m.-9 p.m., Sun. noon-5 p.m.

Pasarad
1351 Connecticut Ave. NW
• 659-3888

The display windows of this large store are always hung with a seductive array of Persian rugs, which make up the bulk of its wares. Carpets from India, Pakistan and China are also stocked, however, and there is a very nice selection of runners and entrance hall rugs. Some of the larger carpets would be more suited to the luxurious spaces of Washington's embassies than to most homes, but you can also find a good collection of smaller rugs in unusual sizes that may help solve the decorating dilemmas encountered in townhouses and small condominiums.

Open Mon.-Fri. 9:30 a.m.-7 p.m., Sat. 9 a.m.-7 p.m., Sun. noon-5 p.m.

Trocadero Oriental Rug & Textile Art
1501 Connecticut Ave. NW
• 328-8440

An interesting selection of antique Middle Eastern rugs, as well as pillows and cushions with woven wool covers, is to be found here. There is also a small collection of textiles from other parts of the world, including wonderful fabric bags from Guatemala.

Open Mon.-Fri. 10:30 a.m.-6:30 p.m., Sat. 10 a.m.-6 p.m., Sun. 1 p.m.-5 p.m.

IMAGE & SOUND

CAMERA STORES & PHOTO LABS

If you're looking for bargains on cameras or accessories, go to New York. Nothing in Washington can match the prices or inventories available from the big New York outlets, such as 47th Street Photo. Still, there are plenty of camera shops in town, although the emphasis is clearly on fast processing rather than on equipment discounts.

Chrome

3247 Q St. NW
• 333-3270

You didn't take all those pictures to have a lab ruin the film, and you never have to worry about that with Chrome. They are about the best in the city, and a lot of professionals use them for the processing of transparency film.
Open Mon.-Thurs. 9 a.m.-7 p.m., Fri. 9 a.m.-6:30 p.m., Sat. 10 a.m.-2 p.m.

Colorfax Photo Labs

1667 K St. NW
• 622-4300

This is a good place for speedy film processing, reprints and enlargements. An 11-by-14 color enlargement will cost you $12.95 and will be ready in two to three days. These small shops are located throughout the city and suburbs, 37 locations in all.
Open Mon.-Fri. 9 a.m.-6 p.m. (Some branches also open Sat. 10 a.m.-2 p.m.)

Fuller & d'Albert, Inc.

3170 Campbell Dr., Fairfax, Va.
• (703) 591-8000

As far as we can determine, this is decidedly the best-equipped camera outlet in the Washington area. Don't be deceived by the industrial setting—there are treasures in this nondescript brick building. Full lines of professional and serious amateur camera and darkroom equipment are offered, ranging from Nikon to Hasselblad. Most of an entire wall is filled with black-and-white photographic paper, and there are separate rooms for specialized equipment. The store has its own large darkroom, with plenty of state-of-the-art equipment. Seminars are held frequently by experts. Prices on just about everything run from 10 percent to 30 percent below the competition.
Open Mon.-Fri. 9 a.m.-6 p.m., Sat. 9 a.m.-5 p.m.

Image

1919 Pennsylvania Ave. NW
• 833-1550

Image is a custom lab that does a variety of quality photographic work in both color and black and white. Special corrective processing is available (for instance: you shot your roll at the wrong film speed). Prices are moderate. A hand-printed 11-by-14 enlargement runs about $30. Tack on another $5 if you want a print from a slide, to cover the cost of an internegative. The staff is knowledgeable, the service reasonably fast. You can also have movies put on videotape.
Open Mon.-Fri. 9 a.m.-6 p.m.

Penn Camera

915 E St. NW
• 347-5777

If you can't make it out to Fuller & d'Albert in Virgina, then, by all means, come here. This shop, a few blocks from the Metro Center subway station, is crammed with equipment and supplies, much of it high-quality merchandise, usually offered on a slight (about 10-percent) discount. Well stocked with Nikon, Canon and Olympus products. The staff is well-informed and helpful. Here you can find a good inventory of used 35mm bodies and lenses.
Open Mon.-Fri. 9 a.m.-6 p.m., Sat. 10 a.m.-5 p.m.

Pro Photos Repair & Sales

1919 Pennsylvania Ave. NW
• 223-1292

This tiny shop, two flights over "Image," offers top-notch, speedy processing and repair service. Used by professionals for rush work, its shelves bulge with darkroom equipment and items that aren't stocked in most other area camera stores. If you can't find what you want here, the staff will tell you where you can, or will special-order it for you.
Open Mon.-Fri. 9 a.m.-6 p.m., Sat. 9 a.m.-3 p.m.

Ritz Camera Centers

1120 20th St. NW
• 775-9053

These shops are all over the city. They offer quick on-premises processing—one hour is their boast—for color snapshots, with an oversize 4-by-6 print the standard. Ritz also does a mail-order business, advertising in national photographic publications, and hawks its own line of discount lenses and other accessories. Coupons are returned with processing for reduced-price enlargements, frames and album pages. However, more complicated orders take two weeks or longer. Also, the shops do not carry much equipment that would interest the serious photographer. But it's fun to stand and watch continuing strips of other folk's photos come rolling out of the Ritz processing machines.
Open Mon.-Fri. 8:30 a.m.-6 p.m.

RECORD STORES

The Birchmere

3901 Mt. Vernon Ave.,
Alexandria, Va.
• (703) 549-5919

This unusual record shop, in the basement of the area's most popular bluegrass nightclub, features an outstanding selection of country, folk and acoustic music. We know for a fact that a publicity-shy aficionado, who has one of the largest private collections of pop albums in the country, sells extras from that trove here on a consignment basis.
Opens 7 p.m. (days & closing times vary).

Compact Discovery

8223 Georgia Ave.,
Silver Spring, Md.
• (301) 587-1963

One of the first of a new breed, this is a shop devoted solely to compact discs. Located two blocks from the Silver Spring subway stop, it is a modest store with unpainted plywood bins and shelves. You won't find many bargains among new CDs. The value of this place is the large assortment of used CDs for sale, usually for under $10. Unlike records, previously owned CDs should sound as good as new ones. If in doubt, you can inspect the shiny metallic surfaces in the store for gouges or imperfections. Should you have CDs to part with, they fetch $5 each, toward other purchases.
Open Mon.-Tues. 11 a.m.-6 p.m., Wed.-Fri. 11 a.m.-8 p.m., Sat. 10 a.m.-6 p.m., Sun. noon-5 p.m.

Olsson's Books & Records

1307 19th St. NW
• 785-1133

106 S. Union St.,
Alexandria, Va.
• (703) 684-0077

7647 Old Georgetown Rd.,
Bethesda, Md.
• (301) 652-3336

This place is for the shopper who can't decide between books and records. Browse through one section, then the other—there are plenty of choices in both categories. Olsson's, formerly the Book and Record Annex, has an especially good collection of classical records and compact discs. Often, you can find selections for a dollar or two below prices at the discount chains. There are five other locations in the city, including 1200 F Street (347-3686) and 1239 Wisconsin Avenue in Georgetown (338-9544).
Open Mon.-Thurs. 10 a.m.-11 p.m., Fri.-Sat. 10 a.m.-midnight, Sun. noon-6 p.m.

Orpheus Records

3249 M St. NW
• 337-7970

This mainly vinyl store in the heart of Georgetown is for serious and whimsical collectors alike. Its bins brim with long-forgotten LPs you just can't find anywhere else. (Example: the definitive collection of "Louie-Louie," ten separate interpretations.) They welcome trade-ins and do a brisk business in used records. There are separate bins for collectibles, with many precious old Riverside and Prestige jazz classics available. Many good bargains, with most records selling for $3.99 or $4.99. Some cassettes and compact discs.
Open Mon.-Sat. 11 a.m.-11 p.m., Sun. noon-8 p.m.

Record Mart

217 King St.,
Alexandria, Va.
• (703) 683-4583

This always-busy little shop, up a narrow flight of steps, specializes in hard-to-find titles, both new and secondhand. The blues section is outstanding, and bargains abound. And since our last edition, the store has built a compact-disc collection of 500 titles.
Open Mon. & Wed.-Sat. 11 a.m.-9 p.m., Tues. 11 a.m.-7 p.m., Sun. noon-6 p.m.

Serenade Record Shop

1710 Pennsylvania Ave. NW
• 638-5580

1800 M St. NW
452-0075

Just a block from the White House, this well-stocked establishment has a little bit of everything, but specializes in hard-to-get Latin American and European popular albums—many available on compact disc. Prices are competitive, with plenty of sales on selected recordings. There's also a wide selection of audio accessories and blank tapes (nice to know if you work in the White House). There is also an entrance at 1713 G Street NW so you can slip out the back after browsing through the front. Serenade counts this as an additional shop, even advertising a separate phone number, but we know better.
Pennsylvania Ave. branch: open Mon.-Fri. 9:30 a.m.-6:30 p.m., Sat. 9:30 a.m.-6 p.m. M St. branch: open Mon.-Thurs. 9:30 a.m.-7 p.m., Fri. 9:30 a.m.-6:30 p.m., Sat. 9:30 a.m.-6 p.m.

Tower Records

2000 Pennsylvania Ave. NW
• 331-2400

There is a force that lures us into this sprawling audio mecca—clearly the record store by which all others in Washington must be judged—whenever we get within three blocks. Resisting its siren song is usually futile, for the place is open day and night, seven days a week, 365 days a year. Once inside, all restraint evaporates and our arms quickly begin filling up with purchases. This spacious two-floor emporium has separate rooms for rock, jazz and classical, each enlivened with background music. There's also a video rental and sales shop and a wide offering of audio accessories. Even if some of them resemble extras from *The Rocky Horror Picture Show*, the salespeople are cheerful and helpful. Prices are often 10 to 20 percent below those of other outlets, with plenty of bargains on rock classics.
Open daily 9 a.m.-midnight

STEREO EQUIPMENT

Audio Associates

837-A Rockville Pike,
Rockville, Md.
• (301) 762-3701

There is a lot of high-quality equipment here, enough to please most discerning audiophiles, including product lines from ADS, AIWA, Alpine, B&O, Denon, Genesis, Yamaha, Tandberg and Sherwood. This store is not for those on a tight budget, although prices are reasonable. The staff is pleasant, knowledgeable and low-key. Even if you don't buy anything, just listening may change your attitude toward speaker systems. You are invited to bring along a favorite record or CD to help in speaker comparisons.
Open Mon.-Tues. & Thurs.-Fri. 11 a.m.-9 p.m., Wed. & Sat. 10 a.m.-6 p.m.

Circuit City

1905 Chain Bridge Rd.,
Tysons Corner, Va.
• (703) 893-6112

Branches keep sprouting in the suburbs (at least fifteen at last count) for this supermarket of audio and video equipment. Its shelves are predominantly packed with the dependable, midprice Japanese imports that have done so much to exacerbate the United States trade deficit: Sanyo, Technics, Sony, Sharp and Sansui. There are also many phones and electronic typewriters. The discount prices are hard to beat, especially if you keep an eye out for the frequent sales. If you buy an item, then find it sold locally for less, the store will refund the difference—plus an extra 10-percent off. There are long lines at the checkout counters on weekends, so try to shop during off-hours—or, order by phone and have merchandise shipped to you.
Open Mon.-Fri. 11 a.m.-9 p.m., Sat. 9 a.m.-10 p.m., Sun. 11 a.m.-6 p.m.

Luskins

812 F St. NW
• 638-1655,
621-8400 (phone orders)

Luskins's motto is "the cheapest guy in town," but like most other stereo discount chains, nearly all of the branches (there are fifteen other locations) are in the suburbs; however, we did discover one downtown address. Luskins offers good prices on compact-disc players, televisions, tape decks, car stereos and VCRs. They promise to beat any local dealer's advertised price by 10 percent. Also in stock: smoke detectors, electronic keyboards, cordless phones and so on.
Open Mon.-Sat. 10 a.m.-6 p.m.

Myer-Emco

2139 Wisconsin Ave., NW
• 342-9200

This store carries products a notch above the usual mass-produced audio components, sometimes at a slight discount. Featured brands include Harmon/Kardon, Luxman, Yamaha, Polk and Nakamichi. Home delivery and installation on major purchases are available, if desired. Each store has a well-equipped audio lab for repairs and warranty work, as well as a full line of video equipment. Three other locations: 3511 Carlin Springs Rd., Bailey's Crossroads, Virginia (703-379-8800); 1161 Old Georgetown Rd., Rockville, Maryland (301-468-2000); 11000 Baltimore Blvd., Beltsville, Maryland (301-595-7900).
Open Mon.-Fri. noon-9 p.m., Sat. 10 a.m.-6 p.m., Sun. noon-5 p.m.

Reliable Home Appliances

737 15th St. NW
• 737-2537

Prices on stereo equipment just don't get any better. Ambience doesn't get much worse. If you know exactly what you want (and we mean *exactly*, and they happen to have the item in stock, you're in business. No-frills "RHA" stores are jammed with stacks of cartons, with audio and video equipment sharing space with toasters, dryers and microwave ovens. Efficient, but usually harried, clerks are

busily thumbing through loose-leaf catalogs in search of prices and inventory lists, and there are always ten people ahead of you. But the bargains are usually worth the hassle. Featured is equipment by Pioneer, Audio Technica, Technics, Akai, Jensen, Teac and Sanyo. Don't expect much follow-up service or advice. You buy it, you hook it up. Three branches in Maryland, two more in Virginia.
Open Mon.-Wed. & Fri. 10 a.m.-7 p.m., Thurs. 10 a.m.-8:30 p.m., Sat. 9 a.m.-6 p.m.

VIDEO SHOPS

Erol's
6428 Georgia Ave. NW
• 722-4700

155 Maryland Ave. NE
• 399-3377

Erol's started as a cut-rate television warehouse outlet. Over the past decade, it has ridden the crest of the VCR revolution, and now these shops are as common as 7-Eleven convenience outlets (where, incidentally, you can now also rent video tapes). Erol's has 85 tape-rental stores in the area, with thirteen that also rent video cameras and playback equipment. A one-year membership normally costs $25, much less during frequent promotional sales. The stores are well stocked with current mainstream titles, but don't expect to find films more than three years old. The stores are efficiently run, with large staffs and computerized check-out equipment, enabling long lines to be processed with dispatch. Wide selections are available in both VHS and Beta. With a membership card, tapes cost $2.50 the first night, $2 each additional night. The shop nearest downtown that rents video cameras is at 3610 Columbia Pike in Arlington, Virginia (703-521-3510).
Open Sun.-Fri. 11 a.m.-10 p.m., Sat. 10 a.m.-10 p.m.

International Video Club
2414 18th St. NW
• 387-5100

This is the city's best-stocked video store and certainly is the best source of foreign-language tapes, with separate sections for French, Spanish, Italian, Arabic and Indian-Pakistani movies. It claims to carry 8,000 titles, about half of them in English. (Spanish runs a close second.) The place is well ordered and airy, with tapes on bright-red and green shelves, categorized both by language and by subject. A special back room is set up for "adult films" in various languages. The place is always busy, but there is a large staff behind the counter to help. A year-long membership costs $25 ($69 for lifetime). Regular movies are $2.50 the first day, $1.50 each day thereafter—although on Fridays, you can rent them for three days and pay only $4. Adult titles and some foreign tapes rent for slightly more.
Open daily 11 a.m.-9 p.m.

LEATHER & LUGGAGE

Camalier & Buckley
1141 Connecticut Ave. NW
• 783-1431

Camalier & Buckley is pure upper-crust England—dignified and reserved—and it absolutely radiates an aura of major-league old money. This is one of the nicest leather stores in Washington. Its luggage and leather goods for men and women, and accessory items for the home and office, are traditional and high quality. Don't expect to unearth any bargains here. You'll also find branch stores at Montgomery Mall (Bethesda, Maryland), Seven Corners Center (Falls Church, Virginia).
Open Mon.-Wed. & Fri.-Sat. 9:30 a.m.-6 p.m., Thurs. 9:30 a.m.-7 p.m

The Complement
1652 K St. NW
• 833-2295

1984 M St. NW
• 296-4494

The Complement offers a wide selection of brand-name luggage and always seems to be having a sale. You'll find Hartman, American Tourister, Amelia Earhart, Lark and many other top manufacturers represented here. You will also find an interesting choice of women's handbags and briefcases, as well as small leather articles for men and women. There are numerous branch stores in most major shopping centers in Maryland and Virginia, including White Flint (in Rockville, Maryland) and Seven Corners Center (in Falls Church, Virginia).
K St. branch: open Mon.-Wed. & Fri. 9:30 a.m.-6 p.m., Thurs. 9:30 a.m.-7 p.m., Sat. 10 a.m.-5 p.m. M St. branch: open Mon.-Fri. 9:30 a.m.-8 p.m., Sat. 9:30 a.m.-67 p.m.

Georgetown Leather Design
Mazza Gallerie,
5300 Wisconsin Ave. NW
• 363-9710

3265 M St. NW
• 333-9333

1150 Connecticut Ave. NW
• 223-1855

No surprises at this overrated emporium. Georgetown Leather features leather, leather, leather, from cigarette cases to wallets to briefcases to handbags to shoes and boots. There are also long leather trench coats for both men and women. This is not the place to come for luggage, and we found the selection of clothing and other items disappointing.
Mazza Gallerie branch: open Mon.-Fri. 10 a.m.-9 p.m., Sat. 10 a.m.-6 p.m., Sun. noon-5 p.m. M St. branch: open Mon.-Sat. 10 a.m.-8 p.m., Thurs. 10 a.m.-8 p.m., Sun. noon-6 p.m. Connecticut Ave. branch: open Mon.-Sat. 10 a.m.-6 p.m., Thurs. 10 a.m.-7 p.m.

Gucci

600 New Hampshire
Ave. NW
• 965-1700

5504 Wisconsin Ave.,
Chevy Chase, Md.
• (301) 951-4400

Gucci made saddles for the Italian army during World War I. The Gucci empire has since grown steadily into one of the best-known and most recognizable signature leather suppliers in the world. The stores offer that "Double G" look in pricey handbags, luggage, briefcases, belts, small leather goods, shoes and slippers. You'll also find some luxurious gift items such as scarves, picture frames, ashtrays, Pimm's cups, umbrellas, watches, pens, key rings and clocks. There is also a small ready-to-wear selection for men and women.

Washington branch: open Mon.-Sat. 10 a.m.-6 p.m. Chevy Chase branch: open Mon.-Wed. & Fri.-Sat. 10 a.m.-6 p.m., Thurs. 10 a.m.-7:30 p.m.

Louis Vuitton

Washington Square,
1028 Connecticut Ave. NW
• 296-6838

Open three years, this is the only Vuitton boutique in Washington, although several of the better department stores carry a limited number of Vuitton items. The store is elegant, and here you'll find the real thing in those familiar signature items so often copied. Vuitton's new leather line with briefcases, handbags and travel bags (no luggage) in a nice bright blue, a great green, black and rust is fully stocked in the downtown store. Polite and pleasant sales people, so unlike their New York counterparts, cater to a primarily business clientele. If price is no object, but Vuitton is, hurry on in.

Open Mon.-Sat. 10 a.m.-6 p.m.

MENSWEAR

CLOTHES

Washington's male population is distinguished by its lack of style, and its pride therein. Major department and specialty stores such as Garfinckel's, Hecht's, Woodward & Lothrop, Neiman-Marcus and Nordstrom have extensive menswear departments. These listings are for shops that concentrate on outfitting the capital male. Other (trendy) shops come and go quickly; to catch them, wander north on Wisconsin Avenue above M Street.

Arthur A. Adler
1805 L St. NW
• 872-8850

When President Bush saw in *The Washington Post* that Arthur A. Adler was having a sale, he jumped into his limousine and went shopping, as he has done often since moving to Washington. This is perhaps the city's finest purveyor of traditional, natural-shoulder clothing. Southwick and Norman Hilton are among its brands.
Open Mon.-Wed. & Fri.-Sat. 9:30 a.m.-6 p.m., Thurs. 9:30 a.m.-7 p.m.

Jos. A. Bank
1118 19th St. NW
• 466-2282

Look inside the suit coats of some of the best-known bureaucrats and businessmen in Washington, and there'll be a label from this walk-up, pay-less store. Traditional, Brooks Brothers—style clothing for a good bit less money is the hallmark of this frill-free establishment. If you want the wood paneling, go and pay Brooks Brothers prices.
Open Mon.-Wed. & Fri. 9 a.m.-6 p.m., Thurs. 9 a.m.-8 p.m., Sat. 9 a.m.-5:30 p.m.

Britches of Georgetowne
1247 Wisconsin Ave. NW
• 338-3330

1219 Connecticut Ave. NW
• 347-8994

The motto here is tweediness with a twist. Since the late 1960s, this shop has catered to serious Washington dressers who were ready to move beyond blue serge, but not too far. Britches has never seen a piece of double knit it liked. Sometimes, the shop clerks need to be reminded that they are not of royal blood, so be warned. About five doors closer to M Street is Britches Great Outdoors, a separate shop for reasonable casual wear. (And there are also Britches for Women and Great Outdoors for Women, too.)
Wisconsin Ave. branch: open Mon.-Fri. 10 a.m.-9 p.m., Sat. 10 a.m.-6 p.m., Sun. noon-6 p.m. Connecticut Ave. branch: open Mon.-Wed. & Fri.-Sat. 10 a.m.-6 p.m., Thurs. 10 a.m.-8 p.m.

Brooks Brothers
1840 L St. NW
• 659-4650

Some elder statesmen get misty-eyed thinking about the good old days, when there was no Brooks Brothers in their home cities, and the salesmen would come to town with trunk shows; however, Brooks is as much a part of corporate America as the stock market now. Straight-arrow conservatism since near the time of the *Mayflower,* or so one might think from the rectitudinous retailing that goes on within these sometimes stuffy precincts. A Brooks Brothers' label near their heart gives some businessmen the courage they need to go to the merger mat with the likes of T. Boone Pickens or Carl Icahn. If you're looking for trendy designers, don't bother coming here; almost everything is house brand, but what a brand.
Open Mon.-Wed. & Fri.-Sat. 9:30 a.m.-6 p.m., Thurs. 9:30 a.m.-8 p.m.

Georgetown University Shop

Chevy Chase Center,
Chevy Chase, Md.
• (301) 656-4004

Here, madras is considered daring. This shop loved the late 1950s and early 1960s so much, it stayed there. When some of its older patrons gather around the front counter, this place feels like a Kennedy cabinet meeting. Even if the look is dated, keep an eye out for this shop's box-sales on socks, shirts and underwear.

Open Mon.-Wed. & Fri.-Sat. 10 a.m.-6 p.m., Thurs. 10 a.m.-8 p.m.

Polo Shop

1220 Connecticut Ave. NW
• 463-7460

Georgetown Park Mall,
3222 M St. NW
• 965-0904

These are the Washington outlets for the empire created by Ralph Lauren, a designer who appropriated a great idea (the Lacoste tennis shirt) and decided its success meant he might as well stitch up a full line for men, not to mention a line for women as well as sheets, towels and luggage. It is a look that you now recognize anywhere, and it's what the Brooks Brothers man wants to wear in his casual time.

Connecticut Ave. branch: open Mon.-Wed. & Fri.-Sat. 10 a.m.-6 p.m., Thurs. 10 a.m.-8 p.m. Georgetown Park Mall branch: open Mon.-Fri. 10 a.m.-9 p.m., Sat. 10 a.m.-7 p.m., Sun. noon-6 p.m.

Raleighs

1133 Connecticut Ave. NW
• 833-0120

An old-line clothing store, Raleighs specializes in men's styles that are guaranteed not to shock Aunt Mabel over Sunday lunch at the club. This is where your mother would take you for your first suit, or where you might deal with the same salesman for years on end (although that part of Raleighs' steadfast charm seems to be fading). Also changing is its location: by the end of 1990, its old store across Connecticut Avenue will have been rebuilt, and Raleighs and its faithful retinue will have moved back in.

Open Mon.-Wed. & Fri.-Sat. 9 a.m.-6 p.m., Thurs. 9 a.m.-8 p.m.

Steven-Windsor

1730 K St. NW
• 293-2770

Not every man has a perfect body, and some men are just too tall for the suits found at most shops. This is the downtown branch of the Washington area's leading chain of stores for big and tall men. It is not exactly a repository of all the best in natural fibers, but the offerings are fairly stylish for the generally forgotten figure. Several suburban locations, including Old Town Alexandria, Willston Center in Virginia, and Rockville Pike in Maryland—as well as some malls.

Open Mon.-Wed. & Fri.-Sat. 9:30 a.m.-6 p.m., Thurs. 9:30 a.m.-8 p.m.

Syms

1000 E. Broad St.,
Falls Church, Va.
• (703) 241-8500

11840 Rockville Pike,
Rockville, Md.
• (301) 984-3335

In one weekend, the same Bill Blass suit was spotted at Syms for $175 and at Saks Fifth Avenue for $475. You begin to see what Syms means by its slogan, "An educated consumer is our best customer." Just watch out for garments that may be a season or two out of date. The selection, especially in the standard sizes, is as staggering as the lack of merchandising amenities. For instance, no national credit cards are honored, but a personal check will be accepted with proper credit identification. Dressing rooms feel more like locker rooms, and the alterations offered are minimal. So, save $300 on a suit and find a good tailor. Even further price reductions occur around the holidays.
Open Tues.-Fri. 10 a.m.-9 p.m., Sat. 10 a.m.-6:30 p.m., Sun. 11:30 a.m.-5:30 p.m.

SHOES

Bally of Switzerland

1020 Connecticut Ave. NW
• 429-0604

Don't press the "of Switzerland" business too hard; there is a lot of pricy stuff here from south of the Alps. Less exclusive—and, some say, less dependable—than when they first hit America several decades ago, Bally is still the shoe of choice for many of the better-shod soles in the capital.
Open Mon.-Sat. 9:30 a.m.-6 p.m.

Boyce & Lewis Shoes

1706 I St. NW
• 638-6092

Return with us now to those thrilling days of yesteryear—The Smithsonian should take over this delightful throwback, which has the feel of a shoe store from just after World War II. The approach to service and style is also no-nonsense: E. T. Wright arch-preserver shoes are the stock-in-trade of these orthopedic specialists with the motto "No foot too hard to fit." There are a few Sebago models for the really daring.
Open Mon.-Sat. 9:30 a.m.-5:45 p.m.

Florsheim

1218 Connecticut Ave. NW
• 223-0975

The name says it all. Solid, middle-of-the-road footwear is still Florsheim's specialty, although the odd color and outré style creeps into the line here and there.
Open Mon.-Sat. 9 a.m.-6 p.m.

Hahn's

14th & G Sts. NW
• 783-1080

This is the downtown branch of a chain that carries a selection of brands: Bass, Florsheim, Rocksport, Weejuns, etc. The salesmen can seem a little aloof, but that's far from the worst thing that can be said about customer service these days.
Open Mon.-Sat. 9:30 a.m.-6 p.m

Johnston &
Murphy
1814 M St. NW
• 429-9053

1718 G St. NW
• 789-4000

With the exception of a few sportier models from other makers, both stores carry only classic Johnston & Murphy lines. Having said that, within those confines are special sizes at both ends of the spectrum, including sizes up to fifteen-AA, which must look more like a bedslat than a foot. *Open Mon.-Fri. 9:30 a.m.-6 p.m., Sat. 10 a.m.-5:30 p.m.*

TAILORS

Many cleaners provide minor repair service, but the operations listed here deal with suits and such, as well as major sartorial overhauls.

Art Custom Tailor
1725 Wisconsin Ave. NW
• 337-4800

After dressing some of the nation's most powerful and puffed-up for a quarter century, the attitude here can be as "haute" as the craftmanship—and the price. This upper Georgetown tailor is 26 years old; it uses only 100-percent English wools for men's suits, which start at $1,100. Cashmere, mohair? Dig deeper: $2,500. A suit can be whipped up in two weeks. If you want a few suits, you could fly to Hong Kong or Singapore and get them made for less. If Art Custom Tailor made it, you can bring it in for tune-ups, but otherwise, no alterations or repairs. *Open Mon.-Fri. 9 a.m.-6 p.m., Sat. 9 a.m.-5 p.m.*

Jos. A. Wilner &
Co.
1714 L St. NW
• 223-0448

Heading toward its centennial, Wilner has dressed politicians and celebrities, as well as the regular stiffs who work in nearby downtown offices. The shop does made-to-measure as well as repairs. Suits in four to five weeks for $475 and up are promised. Wools, blends and silks—domestics and imports—can go into the finished products, which are a combination of hand and machine work. *Open Mon.-Fri. 9 a.m.-5 p.m., Sat. 9 a.m.-4 p.m.*

SPORTING GOODS

Bicycle Pro Shop
3413 M St. NW
• 337-0311

This delightfully cluttered shop, near Key Bridge in Georgetown, sells men's, women's and children's bicycles of three-, five-, ten- and twelve-speed varieties, including racing and touring bikes and accessories. Prices start at around $169. Quality merchandise, including Sentinel,

Bianchi, Cannondale, Kent and Pinto, is featured. They have a large warehouse, so most items can be produced quickly.
Open Mon.-Wed. & Fri. 10 a.m.-6 p.m., Thurs. 10 a.m.-7 p.m., Sat. 10 a.m.-5 p.m.

Champs Sports
The Galleria at Tysons II,
2255 International Dr.,
McLean, Va.
• (703) 448-7486

This is a candy store for jock adults. If it concerns the toning of the muscles, they'll have it here. If you want to select a treadmill, then the helpful—if slightly too healthy-looking—staff will then take you for the perfect attire and correct shoes. There is every piece of paraphernalia the athlete could want, and a good selection of stylish clothing for those who want to go shopping on Saturday looking like an athlete.
Open Mon.-Sat. 10 a.m.-9:30 p.m., Sun. noon-6 p.m.

Eddie Bauer, Inc.
1800 M St. NW
• 331-8009

This large mail-order sporting goods operation has three outlets in the area. This downtown store has two floors, packed with the same camping and hiking equipment and rugged clothes that fill the famous Bauer catalog. If you can't find what you want, you can fill out a card in the store and place an order. The staff is friendly and helpful, and lets you browse to your heart's content. What more can be asked of an establishment that displays kayaks alongside cured smoked salmon and $6 varnished wooden yo-yos? Other locations: Tyson's Corner Shopping Center, McLean, Virginia (703-893-4483); and 11301 Rockville Pike, Bethesda, Maryland (301-231-8383).
Open Mon.-Fri. 10 a.m.-7 p.m., Sat. 10 a.m.-6 p.m, Sun. noon-5 p.m.

Herman's World of Sporting Goods
4350 Jennifer St. NW
• 537-1388

This shop, across from Mazza Gallerie, and the one at Springfield Mall in nearby Springfield, Virginia (703-971-8303), with their two floors and wide selection, are the best of the eleven Herman's stores in the Washington area. There are togs ranging from the unexciting—sweatsuits, running shoes, tennis outfits—to nifty designer duds that will make you look great even if your physique isn't up to par. Children's sportswear is often discounted substantially.
Open Mon.-Fri. 10 a.m.-9 p.m., Sat. 10 a.m.-8 p.m., Sun. noon-5 p.m.

Hudson Trail Outfitters, Ltd.
4437 Wisconsin Ave. NW
• 363-9810

Hiking, camping, caving, backpacking, climbing, canoeing, mountaineering, kayaking and cross-country skiing equipment are all featured here. Climbing ropes and sleeping bags, compasses and thermal underwear are available for those who want to face the wilderness functionally and stylishly equipped. There are thirteen other locations; at two of them—10560 Metropolitan Avenue, Kensington, Maryland (301-949-2515) and at Fairfax Circle in Fairfax, Virginia (703-591-2950)—they also rent canoes and fishing boats.
Open Mon.-Wed. & Fri.-Sat. 10 a.m.-7 p.m., Thurs. 10 a.m.-8 p.m., Sun. noon-5 p.m.

Irving's Sport Shops
10th & E Sts. NW
• 393-2626

1203 Connecticut Ave. NW
• 393-2626

A good all-around shop for sporting goods, with a separate, well-stocked shoe department, Irving's also has a complete selection of boxing equipment. You will also find exercise machines, fishing gear, sleeping bags, golfing equipment, rowing machines and warming jackets. Prices are competitive. Another location: 1111 20th St. NW (466-8830).
Open Mon.-Sat. 10 a.m.-6 p.m.

Dan Kain Trophies, Inc.
3100 N. Washington Blvd., Arlington, Va.
• (703) 525-8100

This corner shop sells quantities of sports trophies, but its most exclusive offerings are the "sports fantasy" tapes you can order here. Veteran Washington sportscaster Nat Allbright, with his gravelly radio voice, will put you in the middle of the action. He charges $50 for a half-hour cassette. You can hit that ninth-inning grand slam, run a Super Bowl touchdown or win the Master's Tournament. You name the sport, the event, or let him help you pick. Allbright got his start before a broadcast mike 35 years ago, recreating Brooklyn Dodgers play-by-plays from teletype dispatches for Washington-area fans. (Ronald Reagan got a similiar start in show-biz on an Iowa station.) You can order tapes in the shop, or call him directly at 703-524-1341. "The bases are loaded in this final game of the World Series. Harvey Gundersmutz, mild-mannered government accountant turned baseball legend, is at bat—two down, top of the ninth, two strikes, three balls. The stadium is hushed. He swings. It's going, going. . . ." You get the idea.
Open Mon.-Tues. & Thurs.-Fri. 9 a.m.-5:30 p.m., Wed. 9 a.m.-8 p.m., Sat. 9 a.m.-4 p.m.

Racquet & Jog
International Square, 915 19th St. NW
• 861-6939

Specialists in racquet sports and serious running equipment, this shop also features Gore-tex suits, warm-up jackets and one-day racquet stringing. There are separate

displays for soccer, workout, running, racquetball and aerobic shoes. That's what we mean by serious.
Open Mon.-Fri. 9:30 a.m.-6:30 p.m., Sat. 10 a.m.-5 p.m.

Spinnaker 'n Spoke
George Washington Pkwy.,
Alexandria, Va.
• (703) 548-9027

This tiny shop, on the Washington—to—Mount Vernon bicycle path at the Washington Sailing Marina, is really for yuppies. The merchandise is trendy and high-priced, not to mention attractively displayed. The shop and the neighboring "Potomac Landing" restaurant replaced a rough-and-tumble café and marina office, so the local sailors are still upset. The store is said to have actually displayed a copy of Tennessee Williams's *Small Craft Warnings* in its boating book section, but that may have been someone's idea of a good joke. It does carry some well-made items, and may be worth visiting if only because this is where *Stars & Stripes* skipper, Dennis Conner, filmed a Wheaties commercial a week after recapturing the America's Cup.
Open daily 9 a.m.-6 p.m.

Tennis & Fitness Sports Discounters
3621 Columbia Pike,
Arlington, Va.
• (703) 920-6962

Owner Bert Jose offers a full range of racquets for tennis, squash and racquetball, and if you can find what you want cheaper elsewhere, he will match or beat the price. You can also find a complete line of clothes, shoes, balls and sports accessories—all major brands—at substantially less than at the other area sports shops. Rapid racquet stringing and repair are other specialties of this great operation, which provides shopping-by-phone service and home or office delivery, as well as private and group tennis lessons. The latter can give a beginner a real shot at a decent game and bring more experienced players to top form.
Open Mon.-Sat. 10 a.m.-7 p.m., Sun. noon-5 p.m.

Washington Golf Centers
9309 Georgia Ave.,
Silver Springs, Md.
• (301) 587-4653

This store sells everything most golfers find indispensable: clubs, bags, balls, shoes, clothing and accessories. Name brands include Wilson, Spaulding, McGregor, Hope, Dunlop and Titleist. Merchandise is often sold at discounts of 25 percent or more, with frequent holiday sales. They have a computerized swing analyzer and club-fitting services, as well as doing repairs. Four other locations.
Open Mon.-Thurs. 10 a.m.-8 p.m., Fri.-Sat. 10 a.m.-6 p.m., Sun. noon-4 p.m.

TOBACCONISTS

John Crouch Tobacconist
128 King St.,
Alexandria, Va.
• (703) 548-2900

This store is open literally every day, with the exception of Christmas Day, to meet the specialty tobacco needs of its loyal customers. Most tobacco shops these days buy tobacco in bulk from large houses. John Crouch hasn't yielded to that temptation and still does a large proportion of its own blending. If you're shopping for a special gift to please a discriminating pipe smoker, you'll find an exceptional variety of wonderful-smelling pipe tobaccos here. But the staff will steer you off a higher-priced blend if you're buying for someone who regularly smokes a commercial brand because, in all probability, that pipe puffer just won't like the fancy stuff. You can also find an excellent selection of quality pipes, and some real bargains in the group of top-line "seconds." The shop also specializes in a wide array of beer steins and some really super Russell Green River Cutlery, from a New England concern that has been making quality knives since 1834.
Open Mon.-Thurs. 10 a.m.-10 p.m., Sun. 11 a.m.-8 p.m.

Earthworks Tobacco & Snuff
1724 20th St. NW
• 332-4323

This incredible shop, near Dupont Circle, considered one of the best tobacconists in the country, is worth a stop even if you're not a pipe smoker or a snuff sniffer. The museumlike atmosphere comes from the delightful collection of tobacco antiquities, from pipes and humidors to seventeenth- and eighteenth-century snuff boxes. The shop is reputed for its impressive selection of Meerschaum pipes, including some true collector's items, and it carries 100 different brand names of briar pipes from all over the world. You'll find more than 200 foreign pipe-tobacco blends, both tinned and bulk varieties. For those not interested in pipes, Earthworks offers a good choice of cigars, the largest collection of imported cigarettes on the East Coast and a huge "snuff bar," with about 200 varieties of sniffing stuff from Europe. The "snuff bar" is particularly popular with European visitors and the diplomatic crowd.
Open Mon.-Fri. 10 a.m.-8 p.m., Sat. 10 a.m.-7 p.m.

Georgetown Tobacco
3144 M St. NW
• 338-5100

Personalized service is the big selling point of this tobacconist, which has such a loyal following that a good bit of its business is conducted through mail-order sales to such exotic locales as New Zealand, Singapore, New Guinea and

Japan. The rich aroma that greets you when you step in the door is from the leaves of Maryland tobacco hanging from the ceiling (for a realistic decorator touch). In addition to an admirable array of bulk pipe tobaccos, pipes, and tobacco accessories from pipe-carrying cases to cigarette lighters, this shop boasts three special humidor rooms that are jammed with, literally, thousands of cigars from all over the world. Customers are frequently on a first-name basis with the staff, which prides itself on doing more than just selling a product. The strategy works. In Georgetown, where stores come and go almost as quickly as tourist buses, this shop is in its 23rd year and still going strong.
Open Mon.-Sat. 10 a.m.-9 p.m., Sun. noon-8 p.m.

WHERE TO FIND: RENTALS & SERVICES

BABYSITTERS

Washington has a higher proportion of working mothers than does any other U.S. metropolitan area, so it's no surprise that babysitters and child-care services are in short supply. Most daycare centers have long waiting lists. Moreover, while there are quite a few agencies that will help you find a permanent nanny, only a handful can come up with a temporary sitter. If you're staying at a hotel, the concierge should be able to arrange a service for you. Check the "sitting services" section of the Yellow Pages, too. Chevy Chase Babysitters (301-944-8344) and Babysitting Services (Maryland only, 301-776-5511) are good bets. Or try one of the following listings:

Child's Play
16th & K Sts. NW
• 785-0211

This child-care center, just two blocks from the White House, does the majority of its business as a full-time daycare center, charging $742 a month for infants and toddlers (2 to 24 months) and $583 a month for preschoolers (ages 2 through kindergarten). There's an extended morning program that begins at 7:30 a.m., for an additional $5 a day. Call Susan Block, the director, for details.
Open Mon.-Fri. 8 a.m.-6 p.m.

Family & Nursing Care

8555 16th St., Ste. 404,
Silver Spring, Md.
• (301) 588-8200

While this service began primarily to provide in-home nursing services, the focus is now on providing child care. The rates vary, according to the number of children and their ages, and all babysitters go through a five-step screening process. The services are available 24 hours a day, and the agency is both licensed and bonded.
Open daily 24 hours.

BALLOON RIDES

Balloon-a-tics

7713 Lake Dr.,
Manassas, Va.
• (703) 361-4725

If hot air indeed powers Washington, you might as well take advantage of its resources with a hot-air-balloon ride. Glide soundlessly over wooded glens, subdivisions and shopping centers. Peer into backyards. Waft over traffic jams. For a romantic flight for two, a free bottle of Champagne is standard fare. Doesn't that beat the brunch at Clyde's? The basic ride lasts an hour and a half and costs $300 per couple.
Hours vary; leave message on tape.

BOATS

One doesn't usually think of the Potomac in terms of pleasure boating, but it has an outstanding and largely under-utilized source of aquatic pleasures that range from canoeing on the C&O Canal in Georgetown and sailing alongside National Airport to water skiing near Mount Vernon. The Potomac, narrow and rocky above Washington, changes character dramatically as it passes beside the city, becoming tidal, and gradually spreading out as it winds its way south 100 miles to the Chesapeake Bay. Not far below Mount Vernon, the Potomac is more than a mile wide, deep, and has wooded shores on both the Maryland and Virginia sides. Although boating in the close-in areas has been hampered somewhat in recent years by the spread of aquatic weeds, there are a half dozen full-size marinas on the river within twenty miles of Washington.

Annapolis Boat Rentals, Inc.

601 6th St.,
Annapolis, Md.
• (301) 267-7205

If you're the type you goes in for more serious boating, by all means go to Chesapeake Bay. Here, you can rent sailboats by the hour or by the day, with instruction available. Call for details.

Fletcher's Boat House
4940 Canal Rd. NW
• 244-0461

On the C&O towpath, about three miles above George-town, Fletcher's rents canoes and rowboats for use on the canal, as well as bicycles for the towpath. You can also rent canoes at Jack's Boat House, 3500 K Street NW, under the Key Bridge in Georgetown (337-9642).
Open Mar.-Oct. daily 9 a.m.-dark.

Tidal Boat House
1501 Maine Ave. SW
• 484-0206

They take more energy to move than one would think, but these light-blue paddle boats—two can paddle at once—are just plain fun. You can splash your way across the Tidal Basin right in front of the Jefferson Memorial and the cherry trees.
Open daily 11 a.m.-dusk.

Washington Boat Lines, Inc.
6th & Water Sts. SW
• 554-8000

You can rent large, fully crewed yachts and tour boats here for private parties, group tours and cruises—for groups of up to 900. Now, that's a boatload!

Washington Sailing Marina
George Washington Pkwy.,
Alexandria, Va.
• (703) 548-9027

This is one of the three marinas in the area operated by concessioners for the National Park Service. Here you can rent a one-person sunfish, or a somewhat larger day sailer and take comfort in the knowledge that if you get blown away or capsize, someone will rush out in a motorboat to rescue you. There are also a restaurant and a store on the premises. Conveniently located just south of National Airport. A few miles farther south, at Belle Haven Marina (768-0018), you can rent larger boats (up to 22 feet) and take sailing lessons. Boats are also available at the third Park Service marina, located at Buzzard Point, 2200 1st Street SW (488-8400).
Open daily 9 a.m.-6 p.m. (slightly later in summer).

BODYGUARDS

Commando K-9 Detectives, Inc.
6901 Sheriff Rd.
Landover, Md.
• (301) 386-5994

You never know when someone's out to get you. With a name like Commando, you sense up front that this place means business. They offer "unconditional" 24-hour ser-vice, with man-and-dog teams if necessary—anywhere in the Washington metropolitan area. Armed bodyguards will protect you and your residence. They also provide security for special events. The next church bake sale, perhaps?
Open daily 24 hours (phone for information).

CARS

Unless you're traveling out to the suburbs, it's easier to get around Washington using cabs and the Metrorail than trying to drive. Downtown parking lots will charge up to $5 per hour, and hotel valet parking for one night is more than a round trip from National Airport to downtown. All of the major car rental companies have offices downtown, as well as at all the airports, and a few other locations. For starters, try Avis (800-331-1212), Thrifty (800-367-2227), Budget (800-527-0700), Hertz (800-654-3131) or National (800-328-4567). All are open daily 24 hours.

CHEFS, BARTENDERS, WAITERS

FoodTemps
7315 Wisconsin Ave.,
Bethesda, Md.
• (301) 907-9090

It must be a special dinner, but you really don't want to hire a caterer, or you want to cook part of it yourself, but then have someone competent in the kitchen to finish the food. These are the times to call Food Temps. In addition to providing professional personnel to restaurants when a chef is on vacation or a flu is sweeping the kitchen, they will also place chefs in private homes. It's like having your own cook, and you can complete the elegance with well-trained butlers and bartenders, if desired.
Open Mon.-Fri. 9 a.m.-7 p.m.

Student Placement Office of Georgetown University
G03 White Gravenor,
37th & O Sts. NW
• 687-4187

Not all college students were born with silver spoons in their mouths and a trust fund in their bank accounts. Georgetown University keeps a book of job offerings, and you can hire students for almost all legal activities, from bartending and waiting dinner parties to moving furniture and raking leaves. You set the hourly wage, and the students call if they are interested in the job.
Open Mon.-Fri. 8:30 a.m.-5 p.m.

CLOWNS

This town can understand and appreciate clowns more than most. At Town Clowns (745-7393), a costumed performer will deliver chocolates or cookies; Dubrow the Magician (789-2800) offers magic shows for all occasions; The Partyman (979-6291) has clowns as well as magicians and balloons; Myklar the Ordinary (839-3363) deals in sophisticated magic and comedy.

COSTUMES

Backstage Rental & Sales
2101 P St. NW
• 775-1488

This store, two blocks from the Dupont Circle subway stop, is jam-packed with theater memorabilia, and offers hundreds of costumes for rent. Several thick photo albums display color pictures of all the selections. This is the place to come, whether you've got a role in a Wagnerian opera, are headed for a Halloween costume party, or want to apply for a job at Tower Records and want to look like the other employees. Most costumes rent for $30 to $40. The store also sells theater books, old movie posters, masks and Groucho noses.
Open Mon.-Wed. & Fri.-Sat. 10 a.m.-6 p.m., Thurs. 10 a.m.-8 p.m.

A. T. Jones & Sons
708 N. Howard St.,
Baltimore, Md.
• (301) 728-7087

Since 1868, Jones & Sons has been dressing people in costumes, from the magnificent to the absurd, in grand style. Thousands of costumes are crammed into this wonderful store, which quite honestly boasts the largest selection of costumes outside Hollywood. Professional theaters and operas depend on this costumer, whose specialty is musicals. This is also the costumer of choice for The Gridiron Club, the group of Washington journalists who couldn't put on its white-tie spring dinner and show without the skill and creativity of A.T. Jones. A limited variety of props is also available. The average costume runs from $60 to $70—and is worth every penny!
Open Mon.-Fri. 9 a.m.-4 p.m., Sat. (Oct. only) 9 a.m.-4 p.m.

Stein's Theatrical & Dance Center
3100 Clarendon Blvd.
Arlington, Va.
• (703) 522-2660

Costumes rentals and masks of all sorts. It houses a vast selection of costumes and other theatrical clothing. Be a barbarian woman for $40, a medieval queen for $45, a French maid for $35, Sherlock Holmes for $35. Plenty of noses, too. And a Tip O'Neill mask can be had for $18.
Open Mon.-Fri. 10 a.m.-7 p.m., Sat. 10 a.m.-6 p.m.

FORMAL WEAR

Given the capital's fast-paced social whirl, it's no wonder that formal wear can be easily rented throughout the area. The listings take up five of the Yellow Pages, and frequently, major downtown hotels have special arrangements with rental outlets. After Hours, 2715 Wilson Boulevard, Arlington, Virginia (703-522-6455), does not require advance notice; Friendly Formals, 1220 L Street NW (842-5132), offers discounts for students and weddings; Bethesda Custom Tailors, 7836 Wisconsin Avenue, Bethesda, Maryland (301-656-2077), specializes in rush service. Or, let your fingers do the walking.

HOUSE, PLANT & PET SITTERS

Pets 'n Plants
3817 Jennifer St. NW
• 362-2911

This service will take care of pets, plants and houses, or any combination of the above, anywhere in the metropolitan area. Sitters come into your home at least once a day, take out the trash, rotate lights, feed and exercise pets and even give your ailing dog or cat its medicine. They also water plants, and plant service comes free if you have a pet. Dale Thompson, who manages the service, says seven days' advance notice is appreciated. No attack dogs or snakes, she pleads.

Sit-a-Pet
Arlington, Va.
• (703) 243-3311

Sit-a-Pet charges $12 per pet per day, anywhere in the area, $18 for two visits a day; sitters will even look after snakes if you insist. They also care for plants and bring in the mail and papers. Owner Martha Grisanti bills the service as the preferable alternative to kennel care. Their motto: "There's no place like home."

ICE SKATING

Pershing Park
15th St. & Pennsylvania Ave. NW
• 737-6938

This entire outdoor 100-by-75-foot ice surface, nestled between the Willard Hotel and the Treasury Department, is available for parties or other festivities at $100 an hour on Monday, Tuesday, or Wednesday nights during winter months. The ice is manufactured. Other frosty days and nights, you can skate there for $3.50 (skate rentals are $1.75). Or buy a glass of wine from the concession stand and sit and watch others doing it.

LIMOUSINES

Classy Chassis
8456 Ardwick-Ardmore Rd.
Landover, Md.
• (301) 322-1913

There are so many limo services in Washington that its hard to distinguish one from the next. Classy Chassis is a world apart, however. They offer such classic touring cars as a 1935 Rolls Royce, a 1946 Cadillac and a 1954 Rolls Royce Silver Race—with chauffeurs attired in the sartorial splendor you would expect for such a set of wheels as these.

Diplomat Limousine Service
110 S. Floyd St.,
Alexandria, Va.
• (703) 461-6800

This is your basic, formal limousine service, available 24 hours a day, on short notice if needed. They'll pick you up and drop you off at the airport, if you wish. The no-frills limo (isn't that a contradiction in terms?) rents for $30 an hour, stretch limos for $40 an hour.

Top Centre Ticket & Limousine Service
2000 Pennsylvania Ave. NW
• 452-9040

These limos come with theater tickets, or is it the other way around? With one phone call, you can arrange for prime seats at concerts, the theater or sporting events—then be taken there in grand style. This service boasts that it has Washington's only "Stretch Corvette."

ORCHESTRAS & MUSICIANS

Dave Burns Music
1712 19th St. NW
• 462-2129

The Dave Burns "Hot Mustard Band" is an old-time big dance band, offering "sophisticated swing." It's available for receptions, parties and other events, large and small.

PLANES

Gibson Aviation, Inc.
330 Aviation Way,
Frederick, Md.
• (301) 831-4600

If you need to make a fast getaway, and in this town that need may arise more often than elsewhere, give Gibson a ring. They boast 24-hour service, "immediate dispatch," and will whisk you away to places as distant as Bermuda, the Caribbean, Central America and South America. Their fleet includes Learjets, Citation jets, Bell Jet Ranger helicopters and Beechcraft King Airs.

ROOMMATES

Roommates Preferred
904 Pennsylvania Ave. SE
• 547-4666

Betsy Neal has been running this roommate referral service since 1973, and while other similar services have come and gone, her business seems to be booming. She still makes matches via close personal scrutiny of applicants. This is not a dating service, after all, and picking the right roommate is too important a task to be left to a computer. She interviews all applicants, who pay a one-time $50 fee for the service, and fill out a seven-page application listing preferences and habits. There's a two-month trial period: if you don't like your roommate, you get to select another one free. After that, you're on your own.

SECRETARIAL SERVICES

My Other Secretary
1133 15th St. NW,
Ste. 1010
• 429-1997

Personalized secretarial services are offered, including around-the-clock "emergency" service. They will pick up and deliver documents, do word processing, typing, tape transcription and shorthand.

TROLLEY

Rent-a-Trolley
Old Town Trolley Tours,
3150 V St. NE
• 269-3020

It's been a quarter century since trolleys clanged through the streets of Washington. Now, however, you can charter this ersatz trolley, which rides on rubber wheels for special tours, club outings, even weddings. It costs $125 an hour, with a two-hour minimum. But you could just ride one of the daily tours for $14 ($5 for children).
Open daily 9 a.m.-5 p.m.

UNUSUAL EQUIPMENT

A-Plus Rental Center
7701 Fullerton Rd.,
Springfield, Va.
• (703) 451-6060

This store is crammed with things to rent, its metal shelves overflowing. You could, probably, even rent the metal shelves. They have an entire section of party rentals, from large tents and canopies to crystal punch bowls, silverware and Champagne glasses. Also available are trailer hitches, power tools and floor waxers.
Open Mon.-Sat. 7:30 a.m.-6 p.m.

Rent-a-Crane
7905 Hill Park Ct.,
Lorton, Va.
• (703) 971-5500

No lifting job is too big. If you need a crane—and goodness knows, we all find ourselves in a situation now and then where a crane would come in handy—this is for you.
Open Mon.-Fri. 6 a.m.-5:30 p.m.

WOMENSWEAR

ACCESSORIES

HANDBAGS

Helen's Handbags
Wintergreen Plaza,
831G Rockville Pike,
Rockville, Md.
• (301) 424-5600

Helen and her husband do the buying for their two shops, known for their huge selections—more than 10,000 bags. You can pick from stylish casual, office and evening bags in a wide range of prices, as well as small leather goods such as wallets, eyeglass and cigarette cases, costume jewelry, briefcases and a few belts. Gucci it's not, but then neither are the prices. The other location is with the rest of the discount world at Potomac Mills Mall in Woodbridge, Virginia (703-490-1260).
Open Tues.-Fri. 10 a.m.-9 p.m., Sat. 10 a.m.-6 p.m., Sun. noon-5 p.m.

HATS

High Hatter
1746 L St. NW
• 223-4287

Even women who think they look silly in hats should be able to find something flattering in this shop, where lace-covered walls and a floral carpet evoke memories of Victorian-era millinery shops. Feathers, ribbons and veils adorn the profusion of hats here, many of which are small and softly feminine. There are snazzy, streamlined designs to complement tailored suits and coats, wedding headgear for brides-to-be and amusing fur hats in season. A selection of conservative hats for men is stocked. Prices are reasonable.
Open Mon.-Fri. 10 a.m.-6 p.m., Thurs. 10 a.m.-7 p.m., Sat. 11 a.m.-4 p.m.

Vivace
The Shops at National Place,
1331 Pennsylvania Ave. NW
• 737-0657

Feathers, veils and fake gems are the basis of many of the eye-catching hats packed chock-a-block in this shop. A few sensible styles, such as berets, can be found, but most of the hats are decidedly dressy and meant to make a lasting impression. Such fine work commands stiffish prices.
Open Mon.-Wed. & Fri.-Sat. 10 a.m.-7 p.m., Thurs. 10 a.m.-8 p.m., Sun. noon-5 p.m.

CLOTHES

Earl Allen

1825 I St. NW
• 466-3437

3109 M St. NW
• 338-1678

Earl Allen has a split fashion personality, but that's great for the Washington woman. Professional women who want low-key, yet fashionable, outfits appreciate Earl Allen's tasteful collection of separates and dresses (dress prices start at about $100). But then there are the times for more glamour, and the handsome Italian sweaters and eye-catching accessories fit the bill. The I Street location houses a smaller selection, but opens early for working women who want to shop before heading to the office.
I St. branch: open Mon.-Fri. 7:30 a.m.-7 p.m. M St. branch: open Mon.-Fri. 10 a.m.-7 p.m., Sat. 9:30 a.m.-6 p.m., Sun. 11 a.m.-5 p.m.

La Boutique Française

Mazza Gallerie,
5300 Wisconsin Ave. NW
• 362-3762

Yes, the dresses, suits and blouses are lovely. Yes, the fabrics are unusual. Yes, the alterations are impeccably done. Yes, the fashion is high, and the clothes are amusing. But there's something chilling about a salesperson who screams at full volume and rushes across the store to grab a hanger out of a customer's hands. There are other stores nearby, with clothes every bit as nice, minus the abusive sales personnel.
Open Mon.-Fri. 10 a.m.-9 p.m., Sat. 10 a.m.-6 p.m., Sun. noon-5 p.m.

Burberry's of London

1155 Connecticut Ave. NW
• 463-3000

It's classic everything here, from the raincoat to the wool blanket to the suitcase to the golf bag to the umbrella. The signature plaid is all over, including on the sales personnel, who are as crisp and British as Bath Oliver biscuits. Shop here for the prim blazer, skirt and sweater to take on horse-country weekends, or if you just want something, anything, that is easily recognizable as being very expensive. The quality is utterly irreproachable, and prices are predictably high (witness the $285 cashmere-and-silk scarf). The store offers a full selection of menswear.
Open Mon.-Wed. & Fri.-Sat. 9:30 a.m.-6 p.m., Thurs. 9:30 a.m.-7 p.m.

Cache

Georgetown Park Mall,
3222 M St. NW
• 342-0146

The Galleria at Tysons II,
2255 International Dr.,
McLean, Va.
• (703) 848-8919

White Flint,
11301 Rockville Pike,
North Bethesda, Md.
• (301) 984-3473

There is a certain look to Cache's private label clothes. They are for the adult woman who really wants to make a dramatic statement. The oversized tops are usually encrusted with *faux* jewels or nail studs, T-shirts can be embellished with sequins, and everything seems to go together with long, flared skirts. It's not a look that anyone else carries, and if you like the clothes, you'll become an addict. In addition, the shops carry a large selection of moderately priced, glitzy evening wear and some costume jewelry that seems to be made for the clothes.
Washington branch: open Mon.-Fri. 10 a.m.-9 p.m., Sat. 10 a.m.-7 p.m., Sun. noon-6 p.m. McLean branch: open Mon.-Sat. 10 a.m.-9:30 p.m., Sun. noon-6 p.m. North Bethesda branch: open Mon.-Sat. 10 a.m.-9:30 p.m., Sun. noon-5 p.m.

Jackie Chalkley

Foxhall Square,
3301 New Mexico Ave. NW
• 686-8882

The Willard Collection,
The Willard Hotel, Ste. 130,
1455 Pennsylvania Ave. NW
• 638-3060

Jackie Chalkley runs two noteworthy stores that currently represent more than 400 designers of handmade decorative arts, limited edition clothing and fashion accessories (the earring collection is spectacular). Both locations regularly host a series of one-person and group exhibitions of clay, glass and wood objects and wearable art. December's show always stars a wonderful assortment of toys for adults, and inspires many a weary Christmas shopper with exciting gift ideas. Both stores offer total wardrobe planning with an assist from an experienced, professional staff. The Willard store is an architectural gem, as well. The interior, designed by Milo Hoots, was honored by the American Society of Interior Designers as the best commercial design of 1986.
New Mexico Ave. branch: open Mon.-Sat. 10 a.m.-5:30 p.m. Willard branch: open Mon.-Sat. 10 a.m.-6 p.m.

Colette of the Watergate

2516 Virginia Ave. NW
• 333-7200

Colette's Virginia Avenue shop is a kind of "everything" boutique, carrying lingerie as well as day and evening wear, and accessories for whatever you're trying to brighten up or highlight. About the only thing you won't find is shoes. Colette is considerably less expensive and chic than the other Watergate boutiques. Nonetheless, it has a friendly, service-oriented staff and two dressmakers on the premises.
Open Mon.-Sat. 9:30 a.m.-6 p.m.

Claire Dratch

1224 Connecticut Ave. NW
• 466-6500

7615 Wisconsin Ave.,
Bethesda, Md.
• (301) 656-8000

Claire Dratch dresses women unafraid to make a bold fashion statement. Her striking evening clothes run to fur, feathers, bangles and beads; the casual clothing is just as memorable, if less sumptuous. Spectacular costume jewelry and accessories. Prices are understandably high for the most magnificent pieces (watch for the sales). The Bethesda store offers a full selection of bridal wear, evening gowns and other formal clothes.
Washington branch: open Mon.-Wed. & Fri.-Sat. 10 a.m.-6 p.m., Thurs. 10 a.m.-7 p.m. Bethesda branch: open Mon.-Wed. & Fri.-Sat. 9:30 a.m.-5 p.m., Thurs. 9:30 a.m.-9 p.m.

Fine Design

50 Massachusetts Ave. NE
• 682-0167

Specializing in great cotton clothing, from sweaters to shorts, Fine Design combines excellent quality with attractive prices. Owner Ellen Fine herself designs a line of casualwear and sportswear for the store, which has branches in New York, Boston, Baltimore and St. Louis.
Open Mon.-Fri. 9 a.m.-9 p.m., Sat. 10 a.m.-9 p.m., Sun. 11 a.m.-6 p.m.

The Forecast

218 7th St. SE
• 547-7337

The greatest selection of socks, patterned hose, tights and leg warmers in the city is right here, as well as a host of marvelous accessories, from scarves and bags to silk ties and belts. Head to the back of the store for stunning sweaters and a small, but select, group of high-fashion dresses and casual wear. Affordable.
Open Mon.-Fri. 11 a.m.-7 p.m., Sat. 10 a.m.-6 p.m.

The Forgotten Woman

Mazza Gallerie,
5300 Wisconsin Ave. NW
• 363-0828

How delightful to visit a store where large doesn't imply odd or ugly. Part of a very successful chain offering fashionable clothes for the larger woman, this store calls a size 16 a "two" and size 24 a "six." The clothes are every bit as nice as any your smaller friends wear. You'll find everything from sportswear to suede suits and formal wear, and while the prices are not low, they aren't out of line.
Open Mon.-Fri. 10 a.m.-8 p.m., Sat. 10 a.m.-6 p.m., Sun. noon-5 p.m.

Great Gatsby

218 N. Lee St.,
Alexandria, Va.
• (703) 683-0094

This charming store began as a purveyor of genuine antique clothing. Because of the scarcity of high-quality garments, as well as the difficulty of cleaning and caring for such apparel, Great Gatsby now specializes in beautiful, presumably much more durable, reproductions of ultra-feminine, romantic dresses and blouses in Victorian and early twentieth-century styles. Although the prices are on the high

side, this shop is the perfect place to search for an unusual wedding gown, prom dress or lacy blouse for evening wear. A small selection of reproduction antique jewelry will provide the appropriate finishing touch.
Open Mon.-Sat. 10 a.m.-5:30 p.m.

Harriet Kassman
4400 Jennifer St. NW
• 363-1870

The Willard Hotel,
1455 Pennsylvania Ave. NW
• 393-2276

This is where those women who have such a sophisticated European look (and can spend mucho bucks) shop. If you want an Umberto Ginorchietti hand-knit Italian sweater, Harriet will have one for a mere $990. The shops carry a lot of designers not found elsewhere in town, plus some, such as Chita B and Ellen Tracy, that are the same as at Woodie's. The selection is exciting, especially for the thin woman (size six or under), but the sales staff can be a bit pushy. Both shops are located near, but not in, shopping malls: The Jennifer Street location is across from the side door of Mazza Gallerie; the Willard Hotel branch is around the corner from The Shops at National Place.
Jennifer St. branch: open Mon.-Wed. 10 a.m.-6 p.m., Thurs. 10 a.m.-9 p.m., Fri.-Sat. 10 a.m.-6 p.m. Willard branch: open Mon.-Sat. 10 a.m.-6 p.m.

Guy Laroche Boutique
The Watergate,
600 New Hampshire Ave. NW
• 333-8702

Guy Laroche ready-to-wear is for real-life situations, not just for parties (though his dressy clothes are great, too). Laroche is certainly the most wearable of the French designers, and he is well served here by a sales staff ready to coordinate the current collection with pieces from seasons past—a practice that brings customers back year after year. The Laroche collection is made in France, except for the sweaters, which are from Italy. The wool challis blouses are machine washable, as are most of the summer clothes, which stay crisp-looking even in heat and humidity.
Open Mon.-Sat. 10 a.m.-6 p.m.

Loehmann's
Loehmann's Plaza,
7241 Arlington Blvd.,
Falls Church, Va.
• (703) 573-1510

Loehmann's Plaza,
Randolph Rd. &
Nicholson Ln.,
Rockville, Md.
• (301) 770-0030

New women's clothing discounters seem to pop up every few months, but none can match the range of stock offered by this grand old chain. Not all of the merchandise is of great quality, but there still seems to be more truly high-style designer apparel available here—both in the designer collections of The Back Room and on the regular racks—than at any of its imitators. The best buys are cothes with the Back Room orange tags, but hanging in the main room. That frequently means that the clothing has been marked down from its original discounts, and significantly so.
Open Mon.-Fri. 10 a.m.-9 p.m., Sat. 10 a.m.-5:30 p.m., Sun. noon-6 p.m.(both locations).

Lynelle
1800 M St.
• 223-4222

If you're in the neighborhood of the Cleveland Park metro station, Lynelle's is worth a stop. On the second floor of an aging building, the premises are, shall we say, utilitarian. Proprietress Lynda Rosenberg takes customers firmly in hand and advises them on how to spruce up their wardrobes with selections from her stock of moderately priced sportswear and the attractive daytime dresses that she prefers to the ubiquitous, predictable suits that so many career women swear by.
Open Mon.-Sat. 10 a.m.-6 p.m.

Marie Claire
1330 Connecticut Ave. NW
• 466-2680

Unusual European imports get top billing here. This store caters to affluent young shoppers, and if you don't meet the sales help's idea of a Marie Claire girl, you may find the service a little on the chilly side. But persevere, for these fashions are the last word in chic, and there's a glittering assortment of belts and accessories. Prices range from $100 to $1,000: dresses average around $300, blouses around $200 and suits about $400. Cruise wear, evening clothes and well-tailored suits can all be found here, with the stock changing over for the coming season about two to three months in advance.
Open Mon.-Wed. & Fri.-Sat. 10 a.m.-6 p.m., Thurs. 10 a.m.-7 p.m.

Marie Coreen
Mazza Gallerie,
5300 Wisconsin Ave. NW
• 537-1666

White Flint
11301 Rockville Pike
Bethesda, Md.
• (301) 984-9666

The dapper linen suits and silk shirts, the dazzling evening wear and the showstopping bridal gowns on display here are the creations of owner Marie Choe. Each garment has a special touch that sets it apart; the fabrics and tailoring are matchless. Whether it's something special for a cruise, something unforgettable for a black-tie bash or the perfect business suit, Marie has it. If it doesn't fit, she'll alter it. If it is the wrong color, she'll make what you want—Truly amazing!
Open Mon.-Fri. 10 a.m.-9 p.m., Sat. 10 a.m.-6 p.m.

Rizik Brothers, Inc.
1260 Connecticut Ave. NW
• 223-4050

Rizik's offers a fine selection of classic, well-tailored clothing and accessories for business wear and gala evenings. The bridal department is the store's special pride: Rizik's boasts of being able to clothe the entire bridal party in either traditional or contemporary styles up to size twenty. Start out with plenty of lead time, because orders take three months, plus one month for fittings and adjustments. The foreign embassy workers who shop here give high marks to the multilingual staff.
Open Mon.-Wed. & Fri.-Sat. 9 a.m.-6 p.m., Thurs. 9 a.m.-8 p.m.

Lillie Rubin

Mazza Gallerie,
5300 Wisconsin Ave. NW
• 364-1533

While Lillie Rubin could hardly be considered bargain shopping, if you are looking for glitzy evening clothes that will look like you spent a lot more money than you actually did, this is the place to shop. Lillie Rubin does not sell many classics. Most of the daytime and evening clothes are this season's styles that will hit the thrift-shop racks by next year. The designs and the fabrics are not what they used to be, especially in the evening wear collection. Others must share our impression, for the shop sits virtually empty on busy Saturday afternoons in a very popular shopping mall. The sales staff is a bit stuffy.

Open Mon.-Fri. 10 a.m.-9 p.m., Sat. 10 a.m.-6 p.m., Sun. noon-5 p.m.

Saint Laurent Rive Gauche

600 New Hampshire Ave. NW
• 965-3555

5516 Wisconsin Ave.,
Chevy Chase, Md.
• (301) 656-8868

A very chic shop for a chic clientele—women who relish the prospect of replacing their wardrobes with each shift in the winds of fashion. The entire current collection is available: high-fashion daytime suits and separates, smart coats and festive evening wear. The sales staff willingly helps customers mix, match and accessorize these urbane and expensive clothes.

Washington branch: open Mon.-Sat. 10 a.m.-6 p.m. Chevy Chase branch: open Mon.-Wed. & Fri.-Sat. 10 a.m.-6 p.m., Thurs. 10 a.m.-9 p.m.

Saks-Jandel

5510 Wisconsin Ave.,
Chevy Chase, Md.
• (301) 652-2250

This shop features opulent displays of the most dashing and costly designer fashions by Maud Frizon, Valentino, Claude Montana, Angelo Tarlazzi, Saint Laurent, La Maison Blue, Calvin Klein, Cerruti, Ungaro, Missoni, Givenchy, Norma Walters and countless others. The impressive costume jewelry by Marlene Stone could easily pass for the real thing, and no wonder—the pieces are fashioned of eighteen-karat gold and semiprecious stones. Prices? Well, they range from seemly to outrageous. Customers are young, old and in-between, but you can bet they all have money. Do watch for the sales, when the prices are only astronomical.

Open Mon.-Wed. & Fri. 10 a.m.-6 p.m., Thurs. 10 a.m.-9 p.m., Sat. 10 a.m.-6 p.m.

Saks-Watergate

2522 Virginia Ave. NW
• 337-4200

Saks-Watergate is a bright and cheerful boutique, featuring American designers. The Europeans are there in force as well, and the obliging staff is glad to pull items from the more extensive collections at the Chevy Chase store if you can't find your heart's desire here. With three seamstresses on the premises, you can count on efficient service and special help.

Open Mon.-Sat. 10 a.m.-6 p.m.

Sym's

11840 Rockville Pike,
Rockville, Md.
• (301) 984-3335

1000 E. Broad St.,
Falls Church, Va.
• (703) 241-8500

The variety of merchandise sold at this discount women's (and men's) clothing chain has increased, apparently at the expense of quality. It seems harder these days to find nice skirts and dresses. While the array of blouses, sportswear and coats is all right, the best finds here are often accessories, such as purses, shoes, belts and nylons. Discounted luggage, linens, umbrellas and other small items also are available.
Open Tues.-Fri. 10 a.m.-9 p.m., Sat. 10 a.m.-6:30 p.m., Sun. 11:30 a.m.-5:30 p.m. (both branches).

Talbot's

1225 Connecticut Ave. NW
• 887-6973

4801 Massachusetts Ave. NW
• 966-2205

White Flint,
11301 Rockville Pike,
Rockville, Md.
• (301) 984-8577

If you're still wearing circle pins and Peter Pan collar blouses, Talbot's is the place to shop. This is a familiar purveyor of well-made classic sportswear and dresses. The low-key, conservative styles change little from year to year; rather, the emphasis is on long-lasting, quality merchandise in good fabrics. Talbot's is always a good bet for sweaters; there's also a nice selection of accessories and a newly expanded line for "petites." Prices are fair, and the service is generally cheerful and helpful.
Connecticut Ave. branch: open Mon.-Wed. & Fri. 10 a.m.-6 p.m., Thurs. 10 a.m.-8 p.m. Massachusetts Ave. branch: Mon.-Wed. & Fri. 10 a.m.- 6 p.m., Thurs. 10 a.m.-8 p.m., Sat. 10 a.m.-6 p.m. White Flint branch: open Mon.-Sat. 10 a.m.-9:30 p.m., Sun. noon-6 p.m.

Ann Taylor

1720 K St. NW
• 466-3544

Mazza Gallerie,
5300 Wisconsin Ave. NW
• 244-1940

Contemporary, but not flamboyant, Ann Taylor separates and daytime dresses combine good fabrics, cut and workmanship. You'll find plenty of chic basics around which to build a season's wardrobe, but to our minds, the prices seem a trifle high. There's a wide selection here of the attractive, but overpriced, Joan and David line of low- and midheeled shoes.
K St. branch: open Mon.-Wed. & Fri. 10 a.m.-7 p.m., Thurs. 10 a.m.-8 p.m., Sat. noon-5 p.m. Mazza Gallerie branch: open Mon.-Fri. 10 a.m.-9 p.m., Sat. 10 a.m.-6 p.m., Sun. noon-5 p.m.

Valentino

The Watergate,
600 New Hampshire
Ave. NW
• 333-8700

Valentino's clothes may well be the ultimate in chic. This Watergate boutique has a look of understated elegance that complements Valentino's deceptively simple designs and opulent fabrics. As is the case with most Watergate boutiques, Valentino's has an excellent alterations staff. You'll find a full range of daytime and evening wear in sizes four to fourteen, and a bank in the neighborhood to mortgage your house so you can pay for them.
Open Mon.-Sat. 10 a.m.-6 p.m.

Frankie Welch of Virginia

305 Cameron St.,
Alexandria, Va.
• (703) 549-0104

Frankie Welch, a Virginia designer, found fame and fortune dressing the political wives of Washington, from the White House to Capitol Hill. Stylish, but not daring, this is "appropriate" clothing for business and evening wear (virtually no pants). Most dresses fall in the $200 range, but can rise several hundreds of dollars higher. Among the accessories, you will, of course, find the Frankie Welch signature scarves. For the last few years, Frankie has been spending her time designing textiles, while daughter Genie minds the store.
Open Mon.-Wed. & Fri.-Sat. 10 a.m.-6 p.m., Thurs. 10 a.m.-7 p.m., Sun. noon-5 p.m.

The White House

Georgetown Park Mall,
3222 M St. NW
• 965-4419

Union Station,
50 Massachusetts Ave. NE
• 289-1639

The Galleria at Tysons II,
2255 International Dr.,
McLean, Va.
• (703) 883-2580

If you've gotta have a gimmick, then this one is certainly right for Washington. Everything at The White House—surprise of surprises—is white, or cream. There is some beautiful lingerie, sweaters, accessories, sneakers, tennis togs, and filmy dresses in summer. Walking past the shop, it looks rather antiseptic and monochromatic, and then you realize that's the way it is supposed to look.
Georgetown Park Mall branch: open Mon.-Sat. 10 a.m.-7 p.m., Sun. noon-5 p.m. Union Station branch: open Mon.-Sat. 10 a.m.-9 p.m., Sun. noon-6 p.m. McLean branch: open Mon.-Sat. 10 a.m.-9:30 p.m., Sun. 11 a.m.-6 p.m.

FRAGRANCE

All of the department stores in the Washington area have extensive fragrance and cosmetic departments. The downtown Garfinckel's and Neiman-Marcus at Mazza Gallerie each have about a third of a floor devoted to scents, and at Bloomingdale's and Macy's you may be accosted by out-of-work actors spraying passersby on their way to the perfume counter.

Crabtree & Evelyn

Georgetown Park,
3222 M St. NW
• 342-1934

Crabtree & Evelyn brings a bit of Victorian charm to Washington. Their recipes for soaps, toiletries, jams, chutneys and such date back to the 1800s and early 1900s when the English relied on their gardens to furnish foods and fragrances. The attractive soap-scented stores are an ideal source for hostess gifts. We're quite fond of the triple-milled soaps, glycerin soaps in fruit and floral fragrances, bath gels, and potpourri in sachets, bulk and room sprays. The store offers special men's and children's lines, and can create custom-filled gift baskets, ranging in price from $5 to $100. Also, don't overlook the excellent vinegars and jams
Open Mon.-Fri. 10 a.m.-10 p.m., Sat. 10 a.m.-7 p.m., Sun. noon-6 p.m.

Gallery de Parfum, Inc.

3251 Prospect St. NW
• 965-5090

1130 Connecticut Ave. NW
• 659-0909

Georgetown's Gallery de Parfum offers complete lines of all European and American designer fragrances: perfumes, eau de toilettes, body gels, lotions and the like for men and women. Christian Dior skincare and makeup lines are featured. The Gallery recently opened an attractive second branch on Connecticut Avenue, with a selection of fragrances unmatched by any store in the area. *Prospect St. branch open Mon.-Sat. 10 a.m.-6 p.m., Sun. noon-5 p.m. Connecticut Ave. branch open Mon.-Sat. 10 a.m.-6:30 p.m.*

Royal Windsor

The Shops at National Place,
1331 Pennsylvania Ave. NW
• 737-3750

Royal Windsor's particular strengths are its appealing selection of imported soaps—cucumber, oatmeal, apricot, buttermilk, glycerin—and the prettily packaged toiletries that can dress up a bathroom or bedroom. The young staff seems to lack any real knowledge of the relative merits of the different products (no one knew, for example, if the soaps are hand-milled), but they are helpful and full of good will. *Open Mon.-Wed. & Fri.-Sat. 10 a.m.-7 p.m., Thurs. 10 a.m.-8 p.m., Sun. noon-5 p.m.*

FURS

Fred the Furrier

7220 Wisconsin Ave.,
Bethesda, Md.
• (301) 654-0555

You've probably seen him in the newspaper or on television, this Fred Schwartz, alias Fred the Furrier, talking to you, up close and personal, about the glory of fur. That's him telling Ann and Jennifer that it's time to come in from the cold and wrap up in one of his sables, foxes, minks or beavers. Fred the Furrier is in touch with women's secret fur fantasies, and as a result, his business is booming. No more need one grab the shuttle to New York to find Fred, for he recently invaded Washington, moving in on what *The Washington Post* lovingly labeled "Gold Card Row," on Wisconsin Avenue between Mazza Gallerie and White Flint. Good old Fred sells divine furs at far less than most of his snooty Washington counterparts. *Open Mon.-Wed. & Fri. 10 a.m.-7 p.m., Thurs. 10 a.m.-9 p.m., Sat. 10 a.m.-6 p.m.*

Gartenhaus

6950 Wisconsin Ave.,
Chevy Chase, Md.
• (301) 656-2800

Yes, darling, if the label on your fur is as important to you as the pelts, you're at the right place. But mind: There is no such thing as casual browsing here. Two sales clerks, who look as if they just stepped off the runway at a Paris fashion show, rush at you the minute you step through the door, just to be sure you don't maul the merchandise (was

it our blue jeans?). Still, this is one of the top, top furriers in Washington, and you will find only the highest-quality, most luxurious furs here. In addition to the exclusive furs at this exclusive store with very exclusive prices, Gartenhaus has an extensive selection of fur hats, muffs, ear muffs, fur-lined gloves and other accessories.
Open Mon.-Wed. & Fri.-Sat. 10 a.m.-6 p.m., Thurs. 10 a.m.-9 p.m.

Miller's
1304 G St. NW
• 628-5628

This is the opposite end of the spectrum from Saks-Jandel and Gartenhaus, but don't sell Miller's short. For the woman who wants a fur, but can't afford a huge investment, Miller's may be just the place, especially for first-time buyers. You won't find any $50,000-and-up furs, but you wouldn't be here if you could. Miller's purpose is to satisfy the fur lust of the woman on a budget. There's a small selection of designer furs from Bill Blass, Adolfo, Guy Laroche and the like. Miller's has been selling furs in Washington since 1921. So let the snobs sniff at the label while you chuckle all the way to the bank.
Open Mon.-Sat. 9:30 a.m.-5:30 p.m.

Rosendorf/Evans
1750 K St. NW
• 833-9100

This shop serves the woman who's ready to spend a substantial sum for mink, fox or beaver, but not the staggering prices commanded by the city's most exclusive fur salons. Rosendorf/Evans is a dependable supplier with a reputation for quality design and alterations. The warm, helpful sales staff takes a personal interest in finding the ideal fur for you and your budget. Follow-up services are first-class. You'll find a wide selection of fur jackets as well as full-length furs of all persuasions. Appraisals are also performed. There are branch locations, with longer hours, at both Tyson's Corner in McLean, Virginia (893-3680) and Montgomery Mall in Bethesda, Maryland (469-6888).
Open Mon.-Sat. 9:30 a.m.-6 p.m.

Saks-Jandel Furs
5514 Wisconsin Ave.,
Chevy Chase, Md.
• (301) 652-2250

Saks-Jandel sells opulent Russian sable, marvelous minks, crystal fox, natural golden island fox—and a magnificent, pure white masterpiece made of Russian lynx bellies that sports a $175,000 price tag. The clientele is distinguished. Don't be surprised to see a customer arrive with a Secret Service escort. But Saks-Jandel accommodates every shopper with attentive, knowledgeable service, and its management swears that it is the basic fur buyers, rather than the Sue Ellen Ewings of the world, who account for most of the sales. Saks-Jandel furs appear frequently in *Vogue*, and many command astronomical sums, but what you buy will wrap you in an aura of absolute luxury.

Open Mon.-Wed. & Fri.-Sat. 10 a.m.-6 p.m., Thurs. 10 a.m.-9 p.m.

JEWELRY

FINE JEWELRY

Boone & Sons, Inc.
1730 K St. NW
• 785-4653

5530 Wisconsin Ave.,
Chevy Chase, Md.
• (301) 657-2144

1384 Chain Bridge Rd.,
McLean, Va.
• (703) 734-3997

Boone's specializes in diamond jewelry, and has a large selection of diamond solitaires and wedding bands. Estate diamonds are a specialty, and a display window is always devoted to "sales" of diamond rings and other estate jewelry in their original settings. Interesting deals abound on the diamonds and other precious stones. The sales personnel is knowledgeable and generally quite obliging. Boone & Sons does excellent appraisal work as well.

Washington branch: open Mon.-Fri. 10 a.m.-6 p.m. Chevy Chase branch: open Mon.-Wed. & Fri.-Sat. 10 a.m.-6 p.m., Thurs. 10 a.m.-9 p.m. McLean branch open Mon.-Sat. 10 a.m.-6 p.m.

J. E. Caldwell Co.
1140 Connecticut Ave. NW
• 466-6780

White Flint,
Rockville, Md.
• (301) 770-1490

Fair Oaks Mall,
Gaithersburg, Md.
• (301) 352-0881

This store features a vast display space for fine jewelry, flatware, china and crystal. Caldwell's seems to have just about everything—from a glittering display of diamond necklaces and jeweled Rolex watches to Waterford crystal and Royal Doulton china. There is a large array of other pricey gift items like brass desk accessories, music boxes and lacquered Russian boxes. If you don't have a lot of time to shop around, this is the place to start.

Open Mon.-Sat. 9:30 a.m.-5:30 p.m.

Collector's Cabinet
1023 Connecticut Ave. NW
• 785-4480

An eccentric mix of stuffed animals, exotic seashells and lovely jewelry fashioned from semiprecious stones and minerals fills this shop. Malachite, tiger's eye, lapis, sodalite, rhodolite, amber and several other less familiar substances provide the basis for the wide array of beads, rings, earrings and necklaces. The stones are usually paired with silver, but an increasing number are set in fourteen-carat gold. A limited number of gem stones are also featured, including some fine amethysts and aquamarines.

Open Mon.-Fri. 10 a.m.-6 p.m., Sat. 10:30 a.m.-4:30 p.m.

Pampillonia

1213 Connecticut Ave. NW
• 628-6305

Mazza Gallerie,
5300 Wisconsin Ave. NW
• 363-6305

This jeweler boasts that it was founded in 1883 and served as jeweler to King Victor Emmanuel of Italy. Pampillonia offers both stunning estate jewels and dazzling, clean-lined contemporary pieces. Besides striking necklaces that display large individual gems to maximum advantage, there is an extensive selection of jeweled bands, available in several widths, and an elegant array of pavé diamond earrings and rings. Pampillonia emphasizes high-quality, eighteen-carat designs, particularly from Italy and Switzerland, that are handmade, in the European tradition. The stores also create custom pieces, and handle resetting and repairs.
Connecticut Ave. branch: open Mon.-Fri. 9:30 a.m.-5 p.m. Mazza Gallerie branch: open Mon.-Fri. 10 a.m.-8:30 p.m., Sat. 10 a.m.-5:30 p.m.

Rubesch's, Inc.

119 S. Royal St.,
Alexandria, Va.
• (703) 548-0659

This small jeweler, located on a quiet side street in Old Town Alexandria, is a three-generation family firm whose musty, old-fashioned premises would not be at all out of place in an old neighborhood of London. This gold- and silversmith features lovely antique silver and jewelry, and makes custom jewelry as well. Longtime customers value Rubesch's skillful repairs, and trust them to replate silver, redesign jewelry, restring pearls and perform appraisals.
Open Tues. & Thurs.-Fri. 10 a.m.-6 p.m., Wed. 10 a.m.-7 p.m., Sat. 10 a.m.-4 p.m.

The Silver Parrot, Ltd.

113 King St.,
Alexandria, Va.
• (703) 549-8530

Some of the area's most sophisticated and exciting designs in silver jewelry are to be found in this narrow, crowded shop on the busy main drag of Old Town Alexandria. There are some lovely pieces in art deco and art nouveau styles, as well as striking, abstract, modern earrings and bracelets. Lapis, onyx and amethysts figure in the most interesting contemporary designs. Prices aren't low, but the quality is very good. Custom design and repairs are also available.
Open Mon.-Thurs. 10 a.m.-10 p.m., Fri.-Sat. 10 a.m.-11 p.m., Sun. 11 a.m.-8 p.m.

Tiny Jewel Box

1143 Connecticut Ave. NW
• 393-2747

If you're in the market for antique jewelry, don't overlook this store. The most exciting items on display are important necklaces, earrings, pearls and beads. While some of the Victorian-era pieces—garnet-encrusted necklaces and earrings, for example—may not be to everyone's taste, the quality of the merchandise here is always high. Major items are usually expensive, but many of the earrings and jeweled bands fit less-than-princely budgets. The service, although hardly effusive, is always knowledgeable.
Open Mon.-Fri. 9:30 a.m.-5 p.m.

COSTUME JEWELRY

Beadazzled
1522 Connecticut Ave. NW
• 265-2323

If you see some stunning beads on Washington women that seem to be made to match their clothes, chances are they came from Beadazzled. In the front room of the shop, located in a townhouse just above Dupont Circle, there are counters of beads from which to pick and choose to custom design a necklace. In the back room are some necklaces already designed by local craftspeople. The shop will also take your own necklaces and restring them with some new beads; or, take its class in bead-stringing and do it yourself. *Open Tues.-Sat. 11 a.m-6 p.m., Sun. noon-4 p.m.*

Esclusivo
The Shops at National Place,
1331 Pennsylvania Ave. NW
• 737-9393

Georgetown Park Mall,
3222 M St. NW
• 333-6886

Large earrings, chunky bracelets and flamboyant necklaces are the mainstays at this shop. There are some handsome and expensive reproductions of fine jewelry, including the Christian Dior line, as well as abstract contemporary designs in a variety of metals by Alexis Kirk. A selection of less expensive costume jewelry is calculated to attract the teenage and young adult shopper.
Pennsylvania Ave. branch: open Mon.-Wed. & Fri.-Sat. 10 a.m.-7 p.m., Thurs. 10 a.m.-8 p.m., Sun. noon-5 p.m. Georgetown Park mall branch: open Mon.-Fri. 10 a.m.-9 p.m., Sat. 10 a.m.-7 p.m., Sun. noon-6 p.m.

Tabandeh
Mazza Gallerie,
5300 Wisconsin Ave. NW
• 244-0777

The display windows of this glittering boutique on the lower level of Mazza Gallerie are laden with outrageous costume jewelry—none of it for the faint-of-heart. Most pieces are large and chunky, and feature massive *faux* precious stones. Inside are trays of large, somewhat more restrained, costume jewelry, with an occasional understated piece. Most of the earrings are too large for pierced ears, but the clips have nice little pads to make them comfy. Despite the florid designs, the jewelry doesn't look cheap— and it isn't. Tabandeh is a fun place to browse, and the staff is pleasant and outgoing.
Open Mon.-Fri. 10 a.m.-9 p.m., Sat. 10 a.m.-6 p.m.

Ylang Ylang
Mazza Gallerie,
5300 Wisconsin NW
• 966-1199

A vaguely decadent air pervades this shop, which is largely devoted to dangly, spangly earrings, necklaces and bracelets. Some of the earrings and bracelets are definitely in contention for the "largest in their class" honors—the earrings can run to four inches in length and three in width.

The wares could also probably take the prize for the gaudiest use of fake stones. The store, which is run by a European company, advertises that its collection changes twice yearly. Prices seem unduly extravagant.
Open Mon.-Fri. 10 a.m.-9 p.m., Sat. 10 a.m.-6 p.m.

JEWELRY REPAIR

In the downtown area, jewelers (other than those already mentioned) that are good bets for repairs include:

Benson's Jewelers
1319 F St. NW (2nd Fl.)
• 628-1838
Open Mon.-Sat. 9:30 a.m.-5 p.m.

Compton Jewelers
1709 G St. NW
• 393-2570
Open Mon.-Fri. 9 a.m.-5 p.m.

Woodward & Lothrop
1025 F St. NW
• 347-5300
Open Mon.-Sat. 10 a.m.-8 p.m., Sun. 11 a.m.-6 p.m.

LINGERIE

Les Gals
1919 K St. NW
• 463-6124

1000 Vermont Ave. NW
• 371-0289

1037 Connecticut Ave. NW
• 659-9831

Just put a run in your hose? Need to replace that bra right away? Slip hanging? About to be rushed to the hospital and need all of the above? Then Les Gals is the place for you. Nothing fancy here, but a quick fix for hosiery, lingerie, active wear and accessories. The K Street and Vermont Avenue stores both carry a selection of casual, go-to-work dresses from Liz Claiborne, and shoes by Liz Claiborne, Perry Ellis and Evan Picone. The Connecticut Avenue store is smaller, dealing only in lingerie items, including hard-to-find items and sizes.
K St. & Vermont Ave. branches: open Mon.-Fri. 10 a.m.-6:30 p.m., Sat. 11 a.m.-5:30 p.m. Connecticut Ave. branch: open Mon.-Fri. 9:30 a.m.-6 p.m., Sat. (except July &Aug.) 10:30a.m.-4:30 p.m.

Victoria's Secret

The Shops at National Place,
1331 Pennsylvania Ave. NW
• 347-3535

Georgetown Park Mall,
3222 M St. NW
• 965-5457

1050 Connecticut Ave. NW
• 293-7530

The Victoria's Secret chain is just a little naughty. With two shops in downtown Washington, the store caters to the women who wear slinky lingerie and men who are shopping for sexy gifts. You'll find everything from garter belts in black, red and innocent white to peignoir sets in primary colors and pastels. There are silks, satins, cottons and lace, sizzling little boxer shorts for the ladies and revealing bikinis for men. Ask to be put on the mailing list so you can receive catalogs (with lots of racy pictures) several times a year; the catalogs offer items not stocked in the stores. *The Shops branch: open Mon.-Wed. & Fri. 10 a.m.-7 p.m., Thurs. 10 a.m.-8 p.m., Sun. noon-5 p.m. Georgetown Park Mall branch: open Mon.-Sat. 10 a.m.-9 p.m., Sun. noon-6 p.m. Connecticut Ave. branch: open Mon.-Wed. & Fri.-Sat. 10 a.m.-6:30 p.m., Thurs. 10 a.m.-7 p.m.*

SHOES

Andre Bellini

White Flint,
11301 Rockville Pike,
Rockville, Md.
• (301) 231-9144

High-style Italian designer imports are the focus of this spacious, mirrored salon. There is a wide selection of styles, colors and leathers, particularly colorful combinations of leathers and skins. A wider-than-usual collection of elegant evening shoes is on hand, along with expensive, but interesting, leather belts and purses. The sales are terrific. *Open Mon.-Sat. 10 a.m.-9:30 p.m., Sun. noon-6 p.m.*

Bally of Switzerland

1022 Connecticut Ave. NW
• 429-0604

The European origin of these shoes is evident in the unusual textures and colors and the juxtaposition of colored leathers in elegant designs. The store stocks the Bally and Pancaldi labels, which consistently have more flair than many more familiar designer brands available in Washington. There are also some comfortable, stylish walking shoes and coordinated purses. Prices are high, starting at about $130 for flats and $150 for heels, but such prices are often charged elsewhere, without the special detailing found here. *Open Mon.-Wed. & Fri.-Sat. 9:30 a.m.-6 p.m., Thurs. 9:30 a.m.-7 p.m.*

Bootlegger

1142 Connecticut Ave. NW
• 785-2863

A strange mélange of unexciting, but good-quality, shoes for the working woman co-exists uneasily here with shelves of shoes and ankle boots in punk-rocker styles heavy on black leather, metal and laces. There's usually a pretty good selection of boots and good seasonal sales. There are two other Bootlegger locations in Washington and five in surrounding suburbs. *Open Mon.-Fri. 9 a.m.-7 p.m., Sat. 10 a.m.-6 p.m.*

Hahn's

1776 K St. NW
• 833-1567

Hahn's outlets (nearly twenty in the metropolitan area) offer footwear and purses in the midprice range. Hahn's is a good place to shop for casual weekend shoes, and is also valuable if a heel comes off, a strap breaks or your feet are killing you and you need to find a decent pair of replacement shoes in a hurry. Recently, however, a *faux*-reptile pair we purchased to relieve aching feet wore out before the credit card bill arrived!
Open Mon.-Sat. 9:30 a.m.-6 p.m.

Hess

2000 Pennsylvania Ave. NW
• 887-9172

Georgetown Park Mall,
3222 M St. NW
• 333-7043

Hess emphasizes classic, well-made designer imports in predominantly safe styles. The prices are what you'd expect for such well-known brands as Bruno Magli, Charles Jourdan and Ferragamo, as well as Anne Klein, Evan Picone and Perry Ellis. If you're looking for a little more pizzazz, check out the Georgetown Park Mall and White Flint locations. All branches stage good sales throughout the year.
Pennsylvania Ave. branch: open Mon.-Sat. 10 a.m.-7 p.m. Georgetown Park Mall branch: open daily 10 a.m.-9 p.m.

Shoe Loft

11832 Rockville Pike,
Rockville, Md.
• (301) 231-9060

This no-frills discount store stacks boxes of each style so that you can see immediately if they have your size. The discounts aren't huge, but the shop's strong point is the quality of the selection it offers. Brands include Joan and David, Emme Uno, Liz Claiborne, Sesto Meucci, Pallizzio and many more, all at less than you would pay at a regular outlet.
Open Mon.-Fri. 10 a.m.-9 p.m., Sat. 10 a.m.-6 p.m., Sun. noon-5 p.m.

Shoe Scene

1330 Connecticut Ave. NW
• 659-2194

This spacious store stocks a wide selection of footwear from such familiar manufacturers as Sesto Meucci, Evan Picone, Liz Claiborne, 9-West, Bandolino and Jazz. There's generally a good selection of boots (in season), including some moderately priced boots in rubber and vinyl besides the usual expensive leather models. An extensive rack of sale shoes draws many customers to the back of the shop, and two-for-one sales are a frequent feature.
Open Mon.-Fri. 10 a.m.-6:30 p.m., Sat. 10 a.m.-6 p.m.

Shoe Stop of Bethesda

Wildwood Shopping Center,
10251 Old Georgetown Rd.,
Bethesda, Md.
• (301) 530-3400

One of the best places to shop for designer shoes, outside the expensive apartment stores, is this small discount shop deep in Bethesda (about a mile past the National Institutes Health). Unlike many discount emporiums, this one stocks only high-quality, designer brands. The low prices for evening shoes can help assuage one's guilt over buying a

pair to go with just one dressy outfit. The occasional sales are sensational. Look here for labels such as Charles Jourdan, Seducta, Bruno Magli, Ferragamo, Petri and other imports from France, Italy, Brazil and Hong Kong. As is usually the case with imports, there is an especially nice selection for women with elegant, narrow feet.
Open Mon.-Wed. & Fri. 10 a.m.-8 p.m., Thurs. 10 a.m.-9 p.m., Sat. 10 a.m.-6 p.m., Sun. 10 a.m.-5 p.m.

Shoe Town
**Loehmann's Plaza,
7239 Arlington Blvd.,
Falls Church, Va.
• (703) 560-6960**

The merchandise at this shoe discounter, the forerunner of many, more recent imitators, runs the gamut from casual loafers to chic European creations. The yards of racks for each size may seem overwhelming, but persistence pays off. A second branch, in Rockville, Maryland, at the intersection of Randolph Road and Nicholson Lane (231-9258), keeps the same hours.
Open Mon.-Sat. 10 a.m.-9 p.m., Sun. noon-6 p.m.

Shoes by Lara
**922 19th St. NW
• 659-9420**

It's not often that one finds a discount store in a prime downtown location. You'll find Bandolino, Joan and David, Polly Bergen, Charles Jourdan, Andrew Geller and many other fine shoes at rock-bottom prices. The new arrivals are stacked on tables in the center of the room, and then there are sections arranged by sizes along the walls. This may not be the place to go if you must have a pair of blue suede shoes today, but if you keep dropping by, you can find real bargains on top shoes, many of them priced at $20 per pair.
Open Mon.-Fri. 9:30 a.m.-7 p.m., Sat. 10 a.m.-6 p.m.

Storm's Shoes
**435 11th St. NW
• 347-6672**

For someone with foot problems, style must often take a back seat. But this is the place orthopedists recommend for their female patients who want a little flair as well as comfort and proper fit. In business for more than 50 years, this shop also stocks extra-wide shoes and hard-to-find sizes up to twelve.
Open Mon.-Sat. 9:30 a.m.-6 p.m.

SIGHTS

INTRODUCTION

When visiting Washington, you'll probably feel like you're back in grade school, on a long class field trip. You'll parade from museum to museum, from landmark to landmark, acquiring more historical trivia than can possibly be assimilated and fearing, in the back of your mind, that there's sure to be a quiz when it's all over.

The important thing is not to be overwhelmed. It's true that Washington has more must-see landmarks than any other American city—the Lincoln Memorial and Vietnam Veterans Memorial at night, the White House and the Capitol, the Smithsonian museums and the National Gallery of Art, to name a few. So start with the realization that you can't see everything, and once you've freed yourself of that burden, you can be selective and linger over some of the city's treasures. You'll find yourself discovering things about American life and culture and history that stay with you long after you mail your postcards.

Most of the major galleries, museums and tourist attractions lengthen their hours during peak seasons in the spring and summer, and the only times you will find them closed are on major national holidays. If you're in Washington around Thanksgiving or Christmas or the like, it is wise to call ahead to see whether the place you wish to visit is closed or operating on a shortened holiday schedule.

ARTS

ART MUSEUMS

National Gallery of Art West Building
6th St. between Constitution Ave. & Madison Dr. NW
737-4215

National Gallery of Art East Building
4th St. between Constitution Ave. & Madison Dr. NW
• 737-4215

The next time someone at a cocktail party haughtily informs you that outside of New York and Los Angeles, America is a cultural vacuum, remind them that in Washington, art is both grand and patriotic. This capital city boasts more museums and exhibition space per square mile than anywhere else in the world, and on the mall that sweeps down from the Capitol Dome to the Washington Monument, the National Gallery of Art is the flagship of the fleet.

Proposed as a gift to the nation by financier Paul Mellon, the NGA was founded by an Act of Congress in 1937. Mellon not only donated his incomparable art collection, he also provided the money to erect an elegant neoclassical building by architect John Russell Pope. The spectacular

East Building by I. M. Pei joined the complex in 1978, and together they house some of the greatest art in the world.

Fashionable Washingtonians meet their dates on the second-floor balcony of the East Building. There, caressed by the soft breeze created by the massive but gentle sway of the Alexander Calder mobile overhead, waiting is a pleasure. The view takes in the vast expanse of this building that some have criticized for being less a gallery for displaying art than an artwork itself. Most of the exhibitions take place in smaller side galleries where the scale is more conducive to aesthetic musing. In one, you'll find small Impressionist paintings, in another, abstract expressionist Barnett Newman's fifteen-painting cycle, *Stations of the Cross*. The main lobby is left to colossal artworks, many of which—such as the Calder, the tapestry by Joan Miró, and the Anthony Caro sculpture of rusted iron—were commissioned directly from the artists for the building.

The older West Building, for the most part, displays pre-twentieth-century art. In recent years, the NGA has managed to stage one blockbuster exhibition after another. Shows such as "The Treasure Houses of Britain" (1986) and "Matisse: The Early Years" (1987) have commanded critical and popular response that make for long lines outside the museum. However, if crowds make you nervous, don't slight the permanent collections of the west wing that usually remain cool and empty even during the "hottest" show.

In the marble-floored galleries are masterpieces by Rembrandt, Van Eyck and El Greco. For a real treat, find the only painting by Leonardo da Vinci outside Europe, *The Ginevra de Benci*. The works of early Renaissance masters, Sasseta in particular, abound. If you like postmodern colors, the distinctive greens and pinks of these paintings will delight and surprise you.

If you begin to sag with museum fatigue, visit one of the lovely atriums between the galleries. There, in peace and quiet broken only by the splash of a fountain, you can rest your eyes—and your feet—and ponder the creative wonder of it all. On Sunday evenings at 8 in the East Garden Court, the museum offers concerts performed by the National Gallery Orchestra that often feature the work of young composers and performers. These concerts, like the entire museum itself, are always free. Tell that to your New York museum snob.

Open Mon.-Sat. 10 a.m.-5 p.m., Sun. 11 a.m.-6 p.m. Closed Christmas & New Year's. Admission free.

National Museum of American Art

Smithsonian Institution,
Gallery Pl. NW (8th & G Sts.)
• 357-2700

The National Museum of American Art is the present name of the country's oldest art collection. Originally it was called the National Gallery of Art, but when Paul Mellon requested that distinction for his gift to the nation, the Smithsonian accommodated his request and renamed its art museum the National Collection of Fine Arts. Since 1983, however, it's been the NMAA.

Although plans are in the works for expansion to a nearby building, it currently shares the Old Patent Building with the National Portrait Gallery. Erected in the middle of the last century to house the administration of a growing collection of American inventions, it was designed as a replica of the Parthenon. During the Civil War, it was put to use as a hospital and a morgue following the nearby battle of Antietam. Clara Barton and Walt Whitman ministered to the wounded and dying in rooms that now display some of the nation's finest art.

In a rapidly expanding area of downtown Washington that includes Chinatown and the D.C. Convention Center, Gallery Place is an exciting and busy area near a subway stop of the same name.

Recently refurbished, the museum's galleries boast rare treasures by American artists. Although not a "masterpiece museum" like its cousin, the National Gallery of Art on the mall, the NMAA admits a wider range of aesthetic achievement. In the new installations, the museum has taken pains to highlight its special collections. Selections of George Catlin's 455-painting gallery depicting Native Americans are always on display. Appropriately nearby are the majestic paintings of the Grand Canyon by Thomas Moran, other American landscapes by, among others, Albert Bierstadt, and the cowboy bronzes of Frederick Remington. The museum has a large collection of miniatures, and a recently acquired collection of American folk art.

On the third floor, you'll find the museum's unusual and impressive collection—it's the country's largest—of paintings and sculpture by artists who worked for the New Deal's 1930s Fine Art project. Look carefully for early examples of work by Jackson Pollock, Clifford Still and Franz Kline. For a real laugh at American mores, don't miss the three paintings by Paul Cadmus titled *Scenes From Suburban Life*. No surprise that the post office for which these wittily acerbic compositions were intended turned them down.

Do visit the Lincoln Gallery, also on the third floor. Just a short distance from Ford's Theater, where Abraham Lincoln was shot, this room served as the site of Lincoln's 1864 inaugural ball. Now it holds the energetic work of this century's most important American artists. In addition to large works by Franz Kline, Clifford Still, Robert Rauschenberg and Isamu Noguchi, there is an impressive array of paintings by artists such as Morris Louis and Gene Davis, who were part of the Washington Color School.

Temporary exhibitions on a wide range of American artists can be seen throughout the building, which also houses a 50,000-volume library and the Archives of American Art.

Open daily 10 a.m.-5:30 p.m. Closed Christmas. Admission free.

National Portrait Gallery

Smithsonian Institution, Gallery Pl. NW (F & 8th Sts.) • 357-2920

On the south side of Gallery Place is a museum where the subject of the artwork is more important than the artist. At the National Portrait Gallery, both the famous and the infamous people who make up the nation's history can be seen in a variety of media. Portraits of the presidents from the first to the current White House resident are displayed in the second-floor galleries. Lest you think that history is dull, you'll be reminded that portraits come in various forms. Particularly interesting is the NPG's collection of *Time* magazine covers, the caricatures that portray popular and political figures and an impressive collection of photographic portraits. If you must search out famous artists rather than their sitters, the NPG offers important works by John Singleton Copley, Charles Willson Peale, John Singer Sargent and Augustus St. Gaudens. One of the best and most unusual is a portrait of American Impressionist painter Mary Cassatt, painted by her friend and admirer, Edward Degas.

Probably the most famous American portraits, Gilbert Stuart's canvases of George and Martha Washington, hang at the NPG for five years in a decade. (After several years of haggling over ownership, an agreement was reached with the Boston Museum of Fine Arts, where they hang during the alternate five years). Don't be surprised to find out that only the heads of our first president and his first lady were painted by Stuart. Stuart, who was the most famous and sought-after portraitist of his era, usually completed only the faces of his sitters, leaving the time-consuming and less interesting bodies to his assistants.

Open daily 10 a.m.-5:30 p.m. Closed Christmas. Admission free.

AND ALSO...

B'nai B'rith Klutznick Museum
1640 Rhode Island Ave. NW
• 857-6583

Predominantly a history museum, the gallery offers a range of material from 1,000-year-old coins to modern art. Although the emphasis is on early Jewish-American settlements, the collections introduce the visitor to Jewish history, and occasional exhibitions emphasize specific topics, such as archaeology or the work of a particular artist. *Open Sun.-Fri. 10 a.m.-5 p.m. Closed Jewish holidays. Admission free.*

The Corcoran Gallery of Art
17th St. & New York Ave. NW
• 638-3211

When the museum canceled a scheduled showing of late photographer Robert Mapplethorpe's far-out works last year, it became an unwilling pawn in the debate over art censorship. Several resignations were handed in and the reverberations from the fallout are still rumbling. Still, as one of Washington's few privately funded museums, the Corcoran Gallery of Art holds a special place as the city's own museum. An association with the Corcoran Art School (one of the nation's oldest) gives the Corcoran Gallery a lively presence in the Washington cultural arena. Its collection—predominantly work by nineteenth- and twentieth-century American artists—boasts some of the finest examples of area talent, and in the past, exhibitions have been geared to more experimental artists. Every two years, the Corcoran hosts an exhibition that focuses on an important theme or region of contemporary American art.

The basis of the current collection came from banker and art collector William Wilson Corcoran, whose pictures were originally housed in the mansion now used to hold the Renwick Gallery (Pennsylvania Avenue at 17th Street NW). Later, Corcoran's collection of early American portraiture, Hudson River school paintings and nineteenth-century sculpture—including a copy of Hiram Powers's controversial nude sculpture, *The Greek Slave*—was moved to its current home, the beaux arts building that was Frank Lloyd Wright's favorite building in Washington. *Open Tues.-Wed. & Fri.-Sat. 10 a.m.-4:30 p.m., Thurs. 10 a.m.-9 p.m. Admission free.*

The Dumbarton Collections
1703 32nd St. NW
• 342-3200

The Robert Woods Bliss Collection of pre-Columbian and Byzantine art that makes up the Dumbarton Collections is housed in a 1963 addition, designed by Phillip Johnson, to the original Dumbarton mansion. A grouping of nine domed glass cylinders, the building displays excellent collections that include jewelry, sculpture, mosaics and pottery. Robert Woods Bliss was ambassador to Argentina when he bought the early nineteenth-century Dumbarton House and began its restoration. His wife, with the help of landscape architect Beatrix Farrand, created the plan for the vast gardens that surround the present museum. The gardens are so spectacular that the museum's recorded information number will tell you what is in bloom as well as what exhibitions are featured inside. Harvard University, which was the recipient of the Woods property, maintains the entire complex, which also houses a center for the study of Byzantine art.

Open Tues.-Sun. 2 p.m.-5 p.m. Admission free.

The Freer Gallery of Art

Smithsonian Institution, Jefferson Dr. & 12 St. SW
• 357-1300

The Freer, which houses Asian and Near Eastern art and a major collection by James McNeill Whistler, is closed for a massive renovation to expand its art-conservation and storage facilities. It is scheduled to reopen in 1992.

The Hirshhorn Museum and Sculpture Garden

Smithsonian Institution, Independence Ave. & 7th St. SW
• 357-1300

This museum is a modern art lover's delight. The Hirshhorn was controversial when it was built—Congress didn't want any of the large contemporary sculpture to overflow onto the Mall and spoil the view from the Capitol—but since has embarked on a new era of exhibition and collection. Joseph Hirshhorn, the self-made millionaire whose art collecting went along the lines of "I'll take ten!" gave his collection and an endowment to the nation in the early 1970s. Today, a new generation of curators add prime examples of modern art from Europe and America to works by Auguste Rodin, Brancusi, Winslow Homer, Mary Cassatt, Josef Albers, Francis Bacon, Jim Dine, Frank Stella and Ellsworth Kelly, to name just a few. In galleries that are easy to traverse, you'll see some of the very best works by contemporary artists as well as established modern masters.

The newly landscaped sculpture garden on the Mall side of the museum is a lovely place to spend time. Don't miss the *Burghers of Calais* by Rodin and several sculptures by Henry Moore. Closer to the museum, in the center of the "doughnut," is a soaring fountain that makes sculpture-watching bliss on a hot summer day.

Films by independent producers and artists are shown on most Thursday and Friday evenings. Several times a year, the Hirshhorn sponsors festivals of the very best work by young filmmakers. Admission is free, but call ahead for details. These programs are not held in the summer.

Open daily 10 a.m.-5:30 p.m. (winter), 10 a.m.-5:30 p.m. (summer). Closed Christmas. Admission free.

National Building Museum

F St. between 4th & 5th Sts. NW
• 272-2448

Although the gallery space for exhibitions in this new Washington museum is minimal, the edifice in itself is a monument to building in America. One of the oldest buildings in Washington, it housed the agency that administered pensions for Civil War veterans. A copy of Rome's Palazzo Farnese, the Old Pension Building, as it is known, had room for 1,500 clerks, who in pre-air-conditioned days enjoyed the cool effect of the fountain that plays in what still is Washington's largest indoor space. Tap the columns—they're really plaster, painted to look like marble. The exhibition on view details the construction and restoration of this Washington landmark. The permanent collection includes architectural drawings and models of America's most important buildings.
Open Mon.-Sat. 10 a.m.-4 p.m., Sun. noon-4 p.m. Admission free.

National Museum of African Art

Smithsonian Institution,
The Quadrangle,
950 Independence Ave. SW
• 357-4600, 357-2700

In September 1987, the National Museum of African Art, along with the Arthur Sackler Collection of Asian and Near Eastern Art and a new International Center, moved into a mostly underground, 4.2-acre complex called The Quadrangle. (Above the Quandrangle grows the Enid A. Haupt Garden, a jungle of blossoms that includes a Victorian parterre filled with magnolia trees, tea roses and nineteenth-century garden furniture. Best, though, is the sky-high fountain spurting from the middle of the walkway: perfect to stroll through on a hot Washington day.) Created in 1964, the museum had been situated in several houses on Capitol Hill, one of which had been occupied by abolitionist and former slave Frederick Douglass. In addition to consolidating the Smithsonian's collections of non-Western art (The Freer Gallery of Eastern Art will be right next door), the move allows the Museum of African Art to show a wider range of its important and unique collection. The new gallery's use of light and innovative installations recalls both the cultural context and evocative spirituality of many of these beautiful objects.
Open daily 10 a.m.-5:30 p.m. Closed Christmas. Admission free.

The National Museum of Women in the Arts

801 13th St. NW
• 783-5000

Opened in April 1987, this museum is the fulfillment of patroness Wilhelmina Holladay's dream to have the work of women artists seen, acknowledged and enjoyed. Her collection of more than 200 works of art by women spans 350 years of the European and American tradition. It is motivated and arranged less as a historical overview than as a tribute to women's contribution to the arts. Although the museum has its detractors who insist that the idea of a women's museum is a reactionary one, the existence of this collection will at least force the public to consider the merits of a separate showing of women's art. The 1907 structure that houses the new museum is in a quickly changing area of downtown Washington. Once a Masonic Temple, the newly restored building stands alone as a gilded lily in the midst of construction and traffic congestion. *Open Mon.-Sat. 10 a.m.-5 p.m., Sun. noon-5 p.m. Admission charge.*

Octagon House
1799 New York Ave. NW
• 638-3105

In fact a hexagon, Octagon House was saved from the wrecker's ball in 1899 by the American Institute of Architects, which used the building as headquarters until 1949, when it moved to a new location next door. Now restored to its eighteenth-century Federal-style splendor (it was designed by the first architect of the Capitol, William Thornton, and served as James and Dolley Madison's home during the winter of 1814–1815), it is sometimes used as an exhibition space. There, small but beautifully displayed and thoroughly researched exhibitions of drawings and models by the world's greatest architects, both past and present, are a treat. Its small, walled garden is one of the quietest and nicest in Washington. *Open Tues.-Fri. 10 a.m.-4 p.m., Sat.-Sun. noon-4 p.m. Admission charge.*

Phillips Collection
1600 21st St. NW
• 387-0961

There are more than a few people who would narrow the important art in Washington down to one painting— Renoir's large and colorful *Boating Party*. You can almost taste the wine and feel the afternoon sun on the canvas. When Duncan and Marjorie Phillips opened their brownstone home off Dupont Circle to the public in 1921, the *Boating Party* and hundreds of other works became the basis for the first museum in Washington devoted to the display of modern art.

The Phillipses continually added to their collection. Works by American modernists such as Arthur Dove, John Marin and Georgia O'Keeffe soon joined those by Cézanne, Monet, Klee and Van Gogh. Later, the Phillipses added works by Rothko, Franz Kline and Phillip Guston. In 1960, the original home was expanded, and a 1984 restoration has beautifully refurbished the galleries. On Sunday afternoons, the Phillips Collection sponsors concerts in what once served as Marjorie Phillips's music room. *Open Tues.-Sat. 10 a.m.-5 p.m., Sun. 2 p.m.-7 p.m. Donation requested.*

Renwick Gallery

National Museum of
American Art,
Pennsylvania Ave. & 17th St.
NW
• 357-1300

Although recent years have seen the Renwick used as something of a *Kunsthalle* by the Smithsonian for a variety of exhibitions, from nineteenth-century Russian paintings to American art deco, it has finally been decided to focus the Renwick's efforts on the collection and display of American crafts. Plans call for a full schedule of exhibitions that will highlight the best traditional and contemporary work by American artists in this field.

Designed in 1859 by James Renwick, the building was originally constructed to house the collection of William Wilson Corcoran. When the Corcoran Museum moved to its current location, the mansion was turned over to the government, which used it over the years for office space. President Lyndon Johnson presented it to the Smithsonian, which restored the structure to its former glory. Today you can climb the Grand Staircase to the Grand Salon and enjoy a painting gallery—hung floor to ceiling—in the plush extravagance of satin banquettes and velvet curtains, creating an atmosphere that would have pleased Corcoran. The Renwick is located next door to Blair House, the government's official guest house, so you may have to elbow your way past a sheikh's bodyguard to enter, but the gallery is worth it.
Open daily 10 a.m.-5:30 p.m. Closed Christmas. Admission free.

The Arthur M. Sackler Gallery

Smithsonian Institution,
The Quadrangle,
Jefferson Dr. between 11th &
12th Sts. NW
• 357-2700

One of the Smithsonian's greatest coups of recent years was the acquisition of Arthur Sackler's immense and vastly important collection of more than 1,000 art objects from both the Near East and East Asia. The collection, which consists predominantly of Chinese art, is now housed in an unusual templelike structure which has you descend through sleek passages lined with granite, brass and wood to the underground levels, where the artifacts are beautifully juxtaposed in modern splendor. In conjunction with the museum, a study center, including a research library containing more than 50,000 slides, is open to the public.
Open daily 10 a.m.-5:30 p.m. Closed Christmas. Admission free.

Textile Museum

2320 S St. NW
• 667-0441

Just as was the case with the Phillips Collection a few blocks away, the Textile Museum has its original roots in a family hobby. In 1925, George H. Myers turned his home—and his lifelong collection of rugs, blankets, fabrics and garments—into this small but fascinating museum. Its continuing series of exhibitions of textiles from all over the world, as well as special displays of the permanent collection—

from Turkish rugs to eyelet lace—prove that Washington is as capable of finesse as grandeur. The building is by John Russell Pope, who was also the architect of the National Gallery of Art and the Jefferson Memorial.
Open Tues.-Sat. 10 a.m.-5 p.m., Sun. 1 p.m.-5 p.m. $3 donation requested.

The Washington Project for the Arts
400 7th St. NW
• 347-4813

If you really want to know what's happening on Washington's art scene, make a trip to the Washington Project for the Arts gallery. Halfway between the National Gallery of Art and the National Museum of American Art, the WPA, now housed in a space that used to host a dimestore, is the center for avant-garde activity in Washington (and is the gallery which finally exhibited the Mapplethorpe show). In conjunction with its adjoining bookstore, the WPA offers exhibitions of artists from all over the country. You might see paintings, sculptures, videos, photography, handmade books or combinations thereof. Performance artists also are presented. Call ahead for occasional evening schedules.
Open Tues.-Fri. 10 a.m.-5 p.m., Sat. 11 a.m.-5 p.m. Admission free.

GALLERIES

Adams Davidson Galleries
3233 P St. NW
• 965-3800

Here you'll find nineteenth-century American oils, watercolors and drawings. If you saw something you really liked at one of the museums, you might want to stop here and see if there is another one just right for your house. These smaller-sized examples of Hudson River school and American Impressionist painters would be easy to live with.
Open Tues.-Fri. 10 a.m.-5 p.m., Sat. noon-6 p.m.

David Adamson Gallery
406 7th St. NW
• 628-0257

Having recently moved from Gallery Row to his new digs in Kalorama, David Adamson has again set up shop, showing off his paintings and prints of contemporary realism.
Open Tues.-Sat. 11 a.m.-5 p.m.

Addison/Ripley Gallery Ltd.
9 Hillyer Ct. NW
• 328-2332

Located just behind the Phillips Collection, this gallery occupies what used to be a stable for the Townsend Mansion that looms off to your left (it's currently the exclusive, all-male Cosmos Club). Now the walls are filled with contemporary art from the United States and Europe. On the third floor of the building is the Foundry Gallery, which most often features the work of Washington artists.
Open Tues.-Sat. 11 a.m.-5 p.m.

Anton Gallery
2108 R St. NW
• 328-0828

Until recently one of the few galleries on Capitol Hill, Anton has moved closer to the action. Its usually stimulating shows are an appropriate addition to R Street's gallery activity. Anton shares its building with the city's only cooperative gallery, Studio Gallery, which exhibits only the work of its members. They staff the gallery as well, so you may get to discuss the work with the artists themselves. *Open Tues.-Sat. noon-5 p.m.*

Franz Bader Gallery
1701 Pennsylvania Ave. NW
• 659-5515

Franz Bader was one of the first dealers to show modern art in Washington. Although he no longer owns the gallery that bears his name, his interest in contemporary art continues to be honored by the current staff. The gallery also maintains one of the best art bookstores in Washington. *Open Tues.-Sat. 10 a.m.-5 p.m.*

Baumgartner Galleries
2016 R St. NW
• 232-6320

Contemporary artists from Europe and America are the galleries' mainstay. If you're a fan of the Swiss artist Friedensreich Hundertwasser, you can ask to see a wide range of his work here. Other names may not be as well known, but the quality of the art is always high. *Open Tues.-Sat. 11 a.m.-6 p.m.*

Capricorn Galleries
4849 Rugby Ave.,
Bethesda
• 657-3477

Although in the Maryland suburbs, this gallery is worth the trip if you're a fan of contemporary realist painting and drawings. The gallery shows some of the best work by national and local artists. *Open Tues.-Sat. 10 a.m.-5 p.m., Sun. 1 p.m.-5 p.m.; by appt. after 5 p.m.*

Carega/Foxley/ Leach Gallery
1732 Connecticut Ave. NW
• 462-8462

This new gallery specializes in contemporary art by regional American artists. Shows might survey the work of artists from the Midwest, Los Angeles or Florida. The idea and the artwork are innovative, so expect to see work by new and unfamiliar artists. *Open Tues.-Sat. 11 a.m.-5 p.m.*

Kathleen Ewing Gallery
1609 Connecticut Ave. NW,
Ste. 200
• 328-0955

Washington galleries make it easy for you to enjoy photography. Across the street from Jones Troyer Fitzpatrick is Kathleen Ewing's gallery where you'll view the work of local photographers, though you're just as likely to see a show of photographs by young British photographers or room-sized installations that use both photographs and paintings. Feel free to ask questions; the staff is especially ready to satisfy new devotees of the art of photography. *Open Wed.-Fri. 11 a.m.-6 p.m.,Sat. 11 a.m.-5 p.m.*

Fendrick Gallery
3059 M St. NW
• 338-4544

The Fendrick Gallery is one of Washington's longest-running contemporary art galleries, but there is nothing dated here. The best shows include crafts that are really artworks, especially the fantastic ironwork of Albert Paley and Wendell Castle's furniture. Or the gallery could be filled with larger-than-life papier-mâché sculptures of animals by Joan Danziger. Always entertaining.
Open Tues.-Sat. 10 a.m.-6 p.m.

Fondo del Sol Visual Art & Media Center
2112 R St. NW
• 265-9235

Devoted to work by Hispanic and Native American artists, Fondo del Sol is part gallery, part meeting place, part information center. You might encounter a real car covered with buttons and tin foil, with a pink flamingo for a hood ornament, or traditional sculpture from Trinidad. Several Sundays during the summer, the street in front of the gallery is given over to Latin American musicians. Dancing is encouraged.
Open Wed.-Sat. 12:30 p.m.-5:30 p.m.

Gallery K
2010 R St. NW
• 234-0339

Recently moved from P Street to R Street, Gallery K occupies one of the handsomest new gallery spaces in Washington. Two floors and an outdoor terrace off the second floor are always full of interesting and intriguing art by an international group of young artists. Some of Washington's best young artists also are handled by the gallery. There is a tendency toward surrealism here, and many of Gallery K's artists have a healthy interest in fantasy.
Open Tues.-Sat. 11 a.m.-6 p.m.

Jane Haslem/ Downtown
2025 Hillyer Pl. NW
• 232-4644

Jane Haslem shows a wide range of contemporary work by younger artists. If you're lucky enough to catch her around, you can find out all you want to know about the art of printmaking. Especially good, too, are her periodic drawing shows.
Open Wed.-Sat. noon-6 p.m.

Hom Gallery
2103 0 St. NW
• 466-4076

This gallery is devoted to Old Master and nineteenth- and twentieth-century prints. Hom also has a good selection of American printmakers of the 1930s and 1940s.
Open Tues.-Sat. 11 a.m.-5 p.m., open additional hours by appt. in summer.

Jones Troyer Fitzpatrick Gallery
1614 20th St. NW
• 328-7189

Some of the most exciting galleries in Washington are devoted to photography, and Jones Troyer offers a wide selection of contemporary work by artists who don't mind experimenting with the medium. Here, you're just as likely

to see a photographic collage or painted photographs as a simple black-and-white print. The owners are not afraid to show prints and drawings, either. Always interesting.
Open Wed.-Sat. 11 a.m.-5 p.m.

B. R. Kornblatt Gallery
406 7th St. NW
• 638-7657

There's a major renovation underway on 7th Street NW, the link between the Mall and Gallery Place. When it's completed, it will be one of the handsomest areas in Washington to window-shop and gallery-hop for art. Already one block is known as "Gallery Row," but with so much construction, galleries are coming and leaving at a great pace and the whole area is still in a state of flux. At number 406, Kornblatt shows contemporary painting, sculpture, prints and drawings. At 413, Zenith Gallery (Monday to Friday 10 a.m. to 6 p.m., Saturday 11 a.m. to 6 p.m., Sunday noon to 4 p.m.) specializes in contemporary 3-D works. At number 403, Zygos Gallery (Tuesday to Sunday noon to 5 p.m.) handles contemporary Greek art as well as an international cast of artists.
Open Tues.-Sat. 10:30 a.m.-5:30 p.m.

Marsha Mateyka Gallery
2012 R St. NW
• 328-0088

This gallery has a wide variety of work by artists who have already acquired a reputation in the art world. A show may include prints by Robert Motherwell, William T. Wiley and Howard Hodgkin. If you're in search of a specific work, an inquiry here may well produce the piece in question.
Open Wed.-Sat. 11 a.m.-5 p.m.

Middendorf Gallery
2009 Columbia Rd. NW
• 462-2009

Occupying one of the grand houses that line the avenues north of Dupont Circle, Middendorf Gallery presents modern and contemporary works by well-known artists. Exhibitions focus on major artists of the twentieth century, especially the work of American modernists such as Stuart Davis, Georgia O'Keeffe and Rawlston Crawford, but there is often a good selection of work by younger artists. The third-floor gallery features the work of photographers, with emphasis again on the important modern figures.
Open Tues.-Fri. 11 a.m.-6 p.m., Sat. 11 a.m.-5 p.m.

Osuna Gallery
1919 Q St. NW
• 296-1963

Osuna shows contemporary work, much of it by local artists, but he also indulges his interest in earlier traditions. Often his exhibitions feature eighteenth-century Latin American painting.
Open Tues.-Sat. 10 a.m.-5 p.m.

Tartt Gallery
2017 Q St. NW
• 332-5652

One of the best new galleries to open recently in Washington, the Tartt Gallery consistently shows provocative work by contemporary artists. Exhibitions range from paintings and prints to photography. If you'd like to see the work of a particular "hot" new artist, chances are you can find it here. The gallery space itself has been beautifully designed. Look up as you enter, there's even art on the ceiling. *Open Tues.-Sat. 11 a.m.-5 p.m.*

Wallace Wentworth Gallery
2006 R St. NW
• 387-7152

In the past two years, Dupont Circle has regained its distinction as the center of Washington's art scene. While the artists themselves may have been driven out by high rents and gourmet restaurants, the art galleries have never been better. The best have moved to R Street, and in the space of two blocks, you can sample just about every kind of art Washington has to offer. Wallace Wentworth normally features unusual installations that may offer sound and moving lights along with more traditional paintings and sculpture. *Open by appt. only.*

THE NATIONAL MUSEUMS

SMITHSONIAN INSTITUTION

Arts and Industries Building
900 Jefferson Dr. SW
• 357-2700

Consider this a warm-up museum. It's much smaller than its other Smithsonian counterparts and much more narrow in its focus. Essentially, the museum transports you back to the late eighteenth century, when America was celebrating its 100th birthday at the Centennial Exposition in Philadelphia. In fact, much of the material on display here was first shown at that exposition. America was newly in love with machines back then, and the exhibits show just how much. They highlight the technological wonders of the times—printing presses, steam drills, locomotives, Samuel Morse's telegraph and even an ice-cream maker. To give you a feel for how Americans lived during the Victorian era, there's a large exhibit of period furniture and household items, right down to the desk lamps. Tours available periodically throughout the day. *Open Tues.-Sat. 10 a.m.-5 p.m., Sun. 1 p.m.-5 p.m. Closed Christmas. Admission free.*

National Air and Space Museum

6th St. & Independence Ave. SW

• 357-2700

This is now officially the world's most popular museum, with almost ten million visitors a year. Once inside the revolving doors, it won't take you long to figure out why. A few steps into the main lobby and you're staring into the cramped space capsule that carried John Glenn around the Earth. Nearby is a real moon rock that you can run your fingers over. Up above, suspended from the ceiling, is the actual plane used by the Wright Brothers to get aviation off the ground. Next to it is the *Spirit of St. Louis*, the plane that made Charles Lindbergh an international hero. No scale models here; everywhere you look is another full-size technological wonder. Other museums may have more history, but none has as many icons that have been part of our lives.

But be prepared—the scope of the museum's journey through air travel can be overwhelming. One room is full of World War II aircraft, another focuses on voyages to the moon. Still another covers balloon and zeppelin travel, a fourth, the evolution of the helicopter. There is no shame in deciding you can't see everything, but make a point of working your way over to Space Hall, where you can get as close as you'll ever want to get to a 60-foot Minuteman missile. Check out the Apollo–Soyuz spacecraft that hooked up in space, and personally inspect Skylab Orbital Workshop. If you're one of those people who goes to museums to absorb information, take one of the 90-minute tours; they start at 10:15 a.m. and 1 p.m. daily. Cassette-recorded tours are available in English, French, German, Spanish and Japanese.

Also not to be missed is the Samuel Langley Theater, where you can, through IMAX film projection, experience the sensation of flight, whether it's during a space walk or through the eyes of a glider pilot. The films, shown on a giant, five-story-high screen, include the long-running *To Fly*, a bird's-eye view of America, *The Dream Is Alive*, an exploration of space flight that includes awe-inspiring footage shot by American astronauts and *On the Wing*, an exhilarating look at what humankind has learned from the birds. You may find yourself reaching for a seat belt in midfilm. Each movie is shown continuously during the day; for times and other information, call 357-1686. Your best bet is to buy tickets—$2.25 for adults, $1.25 for children—as soon as you arrive at the museum. Pick a show that begins an hour or so later, so you can do some sightseeing first. *Open daily 10 a.m.-5:30 p.m. Closed Christmas. Admission free.*

National Museum of American History
14th St. & Constitution Ave. NW
• 357-2700

It has appropriately been dubbed "America's Attic," because there's little from the nation's past that does not have a place here. The collection ranges from the truly famous (the actual flag that inspired "The Star-Spangled Banner") to the everyday (the homes of three real-life eighteenth-century families have been re-created). But somehow it all makes American history a lot more fascinating than it ever sounded in school.

What makes the museum particularly appealing is that it isn't just interested in showing visitors artifacts of the rich and famous. Instead, it is dedicated to showing how ordinary people have actually lived in America. So there is a restored pharmacy from the 1890s, a section of America's first self-service restaurant, a nineteenth-century post office and rooms from three centuries of Americans' homes.

And there are galleries full of old clocks and watches, others crammed with vehicles—from a Conestoga wagon to a 280-ton steam locomotive to a 1913 Ford Model T—and machinery from combines to printing presses to sewing machines to dentist's drills. It's hard to find a phase of America's cultural evolution that isn't given its due, be it politics, science, technology, transportation, medicine, sports, communications or home life.

Of course, celebrities aren't exactly ignored. (Even the Smithsonian needs a few big-name draws.) George Washington's false teeth are on display. So are one of Thomas Edison's first phonographs, a chair used by Robert E. Lee at Appomattox, the ruby slippers worn by Judy Garland in *The Wizard of Oz* and Archie Bunker's chair. Another big attraction is the First Ladies Hall on the second floor, where you can not only see how much style some first ladies have had in selecting their inaugural gowns, but also how little taste others have had.

As a general guide, the first floor features science and technology, including the crowd-pleasing Foucault Pendulum, which knocks down pegs as it rotates like the Earth. The second floor focuses on social and political history, and the third floor showcases musical instruments, coins, graphic arts, stamps, photography and communications memorabilia.

Tours are available, but you should call 357-1481 for more information. The museum has a cafeteria on its lower level.

Open daily 10 a.m.-5:30 p.m. Closed Christmas. Admission free.

National Museum of Natural History

10th St. & Constitution Ave. NW
• 357-2700

If you're a sucker for National Geographic specials, this is your kind of museum. It celebrates all living things, though it does so with exhibits that are quite dead—and have been so for quite a long time.

To give you a taste of the natural wonders to come, the largest-known elephant is displayed in the rotunda. The giant African bush elephant stands thirteen feet high and weighed eight tons when killed in 1955. It took two years to stuff. And that's just for starters. Elsewhere is an 80-foot-long dinosaur skeleton, a 92-foot-long blue whale suspended from the ceiling, a 3.5-billion-year-old fossil found in Australia, the 45.5-carat Hope diamond and one of the stone heads from Easter Island.

Not every exhibit is so spectacular, but most are just as intriguing. Name any type of bird or mammal, and it's a good bet you'll find a model of it here. There's a coral reef community living in a large aquarium, oblivious to the voyeurs on the other side of the glass. There are enlightening exhibits on Eskimo and Native American cultures. Perhaps most noteworthy is the Insect Room, where thousands of bugs go through their daily routines; the sight is far more captivating than most prime-time TV shows.

Of course, kids, being the curious creatures that they are, will need to touch something, and the Discovery Room holds endless delights for young (and not-so-young) minds. There they can rub their hands over a crocodile head or a piece of petrified wood, and they can smell and taste herbs they'll never find on a pizza.

Free tours are available at 10:30 a.m. and 1:30 p.m., but for group tours, call 357-2747. There's a cafeteria near the museum shop on the first floor.

Open daily 10 a.m.-5:30 p.m. Closed Christmas. Admission free.

OTHER MUSEUMS

The Capital Children's Museum

800 3rd St. NE
• 543-8600

This relatively new museum—opened in 1979—was designed as a touchy-feely experience for kids. They can write with a quill pen, learn Morse code, play with pulleys and levers, slide down a real fire pole, match wits with a computer or drive a mock bus. They can even have their own pan-cultural experiences by trying on clothes and tasting food from other lands. Some kids have been known to say it's more fun than watching cartoons, if you can believe that. One caution: this museum is in a borderline area, so use care in parking and walking.

Open daily 10 a.m.-5 p.m. Adults & children $5, seniors $2.

Folger Shakespeare Library
201 E. Capitol St. SE
• 544-7077

While it may seem out of place in the midst of so much American history, the Folger is a must-see for anyone whose imagination has been captured by the Bard. The exhibit hall is full of Shakespearean memorabilia—costumes, props, musical scores from his plays, first editions of his works, even knives used by various Hamlets through theater history. But this is no one-man show; Shakespeare's contemporaries are also featured. The hall is designed to reflect the style and tastes of Elizabethan England, as is the small theater next door, where plays are staged regularly. *Open Mon.-Sat. 10 a.m.-4 p.m. Admission free.*

Mount Vernon Plantation
George Washington Pkwy., 17 miles south of Washington in Va.
• (703) 780-2000

The parking lot is crowded, and during peak tourist season, the wait to get in can last more than half an hour, but each day thousands of history buffs make the pilgrimage to the former estate of George Washington. It's been restored to give you a sense of how Washington lived—tables are set in the slave quarters, hams hang in the smokehouse, colonial utensils decorate the kitchen. The mansion itself will never be confused with the homes of European royalty, but it does have its own simple grace. Perhaps most impressive are the grounds, 30 acres garnished with vegetable and flower gardens; they encourage a leisurely stroll to Washington's tomb. If you can break away from the rush of the crowds, take a moment to gaze out on the Potomac River from the front porch. If you drive, try to get there early and tour the mansion before walking through the grounds. Metrobus and Tourmobile tours are available, but if you have the time, you might consider taking a five-hour *Spirit of Washington* boat cruise, which leaves for the plantation from 6th and Water streets SW. Call 554-8000 for information. *Open daily 9 a.m.-5 p.m. Adults $5, seniors $4, children $2.*

National Archives
8th St. & Constitution Ave. NW
• 523-3000

More a storehouse for historical documents and photographs than a museum, the Archives still draw their share of visitors who want to see the original profundities of American political history—the Declaration of Independence, the Bill of Rights and the U.S. Constitution. During the day, they are displayed in the building's rotunda in special vaults filled with helium, and each night, they are lowered into deep concrete vaults. Staring at old documents can lose some magic after a while, so for a little variety you might want to pursue one of the changing exhibits the museum presents in the hall around the rotunda. Usually they focus on an influential American and make use of the Archives's massive collections of photographs.

Primarily, however, the Archives are a gold mine for

researchers, whether you're working on a scholarly paper or tracing family history. If you need research information, call 523-3220. For tour information, call 523-3183. If you're a Watergate buff, don't miss the Nixon memorabilia. *Open daily 10 a.m.-5:30 p.m. Closed Christmas. Admission free.*

LANDMARKS

Arlington National Cemetery
Across Memorial Bridge from Lincoln Memorial, Arlington, Va.
• (703) 692-0931

The long rows of simple, white marble gravestones are a sight both stunning and sobering. More than 60,000 American war veterans are buried here on the Virginia side of the Potomac River, and every day at least a half dozen more are added to their solemn ranks. Some visitors come to pay homage, others to see some of the cemetery's more historic gravesites, the most famous of which is the one belonging to President John F. Kennedy. Marked by an eternal flame and a low wall containing quotations from Kennedy's inaugural address, it is a surprisingly simple memorial, although it does offer a spectacular view of the Washington skyline. Nearby are the graves of his two infant children who died before him and the plot of his brother, Robert F. Kennedy, also the victim of an assassination.

Almost as poignant is the Tomb of the Unknown Soldier, which contains the remains of unidentified victims of World Wars I and II, the Korean War and the Vietnam War. Every half hour during the day, there is an intricate changing-of-the-guard ritual, complete with clicking heels and gun maneuvers, but otherwise done in complete silence. The ceremony is repeated less frequently during the winter and at night.

Since cars are forbidden and the key points of interest are in various sections of the cemetery, consider taking the Tourmobile, which leaves from the Visitors Center. If you have time, stop at the Arlington House—also known as the Custis-Lee House—which belonged to Robert E. Lee before the Federal government confiscated the property and turned it into a military cemetery. The mansion, open from 9:30 a.m. to 6 p.m. during the spring and summer and until 4 p.m. during the fall and winter, has been restored to look as it did when Lee and his wife, Mary Anna Randolph Custis, lived there.

Apr.-Sept.: open daily 8 a.m.-7 p.m. Oct.-Mar.: open daily 8 a.m.-5 p.m. Admission free.

Bureau of Engraving and Printing
14th & C Sts. SW
• 447-0193

Never underestimate the appeal of watching thousands of dollars of fresh money roll by. That's the draw of this otherwise dull-looking government building; this is where all of American's paper currency is printed, not to mention its stamps, treasury notes and invitations to the White House. There aren't any guides, but enter through the main lobby, where you get warmed up for the big show by perusing press plates and the work of counterfeiters. Then it's upstairs, where to the accompaniment of a recorded explanation over the public address system, you witness the creation of a small fortune. Unfortunately, the closest you'll come to leaving with any of it is if you buy one of the bags of shredded bills they sell in the Visitors Center.
Open Mon.-Fri. 9 a.m.-2 p.m. Admission free.

The Capitol
Pennsylvania Ave. & 1st St. SE
• 224-3121

It may not receive quite as much media attention as does the White House, but the Capitol, which will celebrate its 200th birthday in the year 2000, remains a major tourist attraction, and is, of course, the place where Congress works. In truth, much of the real work of Congress is done in the nearby office buildings, where the congressional staffs toil, but this is where the legislative branch of the American government is on display.

You're most likely to see Congress in action if you visit in November or December, when the congresspeople are scrambling to tie up legislative loose ends before the holiday recess. To get into the Visitors' Gallery in either the Senate Chamber or the House Chamber, you'll need to stop by your senator's or representative's office to pick up a pass. To locate the office and also to find out what's on the day's schedule, call 224-3121. *The Washington Post* also runs a daily listing of congressional activities. Foreign visitors can enter the galleries by showing their passports.

Debates can be even livelier at congressional hearings, particularly if television crews are present, and if any presidential candidates are involved. Hearing schedules are also published daily in the *Post*. A visit to the galleries is included in the free tours of the Capitol that leave from the Rotunda every fifteen minutes, but mainly the guides concentrate on the building's rich history. The starting point is the Rotunda, perhaps best remembered as the place where deceased American leaders, from Presidents Lincoln through Johnson, and other political luminaries have lain in state. Almost 180 feet high and 100 feet in diameter, it is the Capitol's most awe-inspiring feature, flavored by the fresco painted in the eye of the dome in 1865 by Italian painter Constantino Brumidi and the monumental historical paintings by John Trumbull that encircle the room. Also featured on the tour are Statuary Hall, where 92 statues of famous Americans, from Robert E. Lee to Will Rogers, are displayed, and the Old Supreme Court Chamber and Old Senate Chamber, which were both restored to their 1860s glory as part of the Bicentennial Celebration in 1976.

The Capitol and the nearby office buildings are rich in historical significance, as the sites of such events as the British burning of the building in 1814, the Watergate hearings in 1973, or the Iran-Contra hearings in 1987, but they are also inexhaustible sources of trivia that can be used to impress your friends. For instance, ask them if they know that the Capitol dome is cast iron repainted to look like marble, and that it takes 600 gallons of paint to repaint it every six or seven years. Or tell them that each day, hundreds of different American flags fly over the Capitol. The reason is that a flag flown over the Capitol has become such a popular souvenir for patriotic visitors—flags are sold at every congressional office for less than $8—that several government workers spend their day running them up and down four flagpoles atop the Capitol. Government works in strange ways.

Open daily 9 a.m.-3:45 p.m. (Rotunda & Statuary Hall open daily 9 a.m.-8 p.m. in summer). Closed Thanksgiving, Christmas & New Year's. Admission free.

Christ Church, Capitol Hill
620 G St. SE
• 547-9300

This Episcopal church—a place of worship for Thomas Jefferson and other early presidents—was built in 1805 according to plans by Benjamin H. Latrobe, whose work also graced the White House and the Capitol. Later emendations make it difficult to pinpoint the oldest work and difficult to determine what this Gothic Revival charmer looked like originally.

Open Sunday for services. Admission free, but donations welcome.

The FBI Building
10th St. & Pennsylvania Ave. NW
• 324-3447

Despite the fact that this building is one of the ugliest in the city, and perhaps in western civilization, the tour of the FBI headquarters still packs in the tourists. Some people may tell you they go to get a deeper understanding of the criminal mind; others might say they stop in to pay homage to J. Edgar Hoover, represented by his old desk and chair. Don't buy it. The real reason most people take the tour is the firearms demonstration, which ends with a submachine-gun flurry that leaves the crowd cheering.

Open Mon.-Fri. 8:45 a.m.-4:15 p.m. Closed holidays. Admission free.

Jefferson Memorial

On the Tidal Basin near
15th St. SW
• 426-6822

Some find this monument neither warm enough nor dramatic enough to truly memorialize Thomas Jefferson, the leading architect of American democracy. Others say it is simple and elegant, a fitting tribute to a dedicated critic of royal bombast. Make up your own mind, although if you visit in late March or early April, when the surrounding cherry trees are in full blossom, you're not likely to be disappointed in any way.

In the middle of the Greek Parthenon–style temple stands Jefferson, all nineteen feet of him. The original plans called for Jefferson to be clad in a toga, but that idea didn't play well with critics, who argued that a great American need not be dressed as a Roman. So instead, the bronze statue shows him in a fur-lined greatcoat. Like the Lincoln Memorial, the Jefferson, opened in 1943, is built on filled-in swampland along the Potomac River. But since it's a bit off the main tourist routes on the Mall, it doesn't draw the crowds the other monuments and museums do. Jefferson would probably like that.

Open daily 8 a.m.-midnight. Admission free.

Library of Congress

1st St. & Independence
Ave. SE
• 707-5000

Most people don't make a point of working a visit to a library into their vacation plans, but before ruling it out, remember: this is not just any library. In terms of documents, records, books and other items, it's the biggest in the world, with 80 million items—almost 400 are added every hour. All this from the starter library Thomas Jefferson sold to the federal government in 1815 after its original collection was destroyed by British soldiers. His private collection at the time contained more than 6,000 volumes.

Despite its rich history, the Library of Congress is primarily geared to research. If you need to track down elusive information, this is the place to do it. Most of the staff is helpful, and trained to do much more than tell you to keep quiet. This is also an excellent place to find out-of-town newspapers from every place you've heard of and some you haven't.

Among the building's rarest treasures are two Bibles produced in Mainz, Germany, in the fifteenth century. One is hand-written in Latin; the other is one of only three Gutenberg Bibles printed on vellum in the world. As impressive as they are, the Reading Room itself is even more breathtaking—a high-ceilinged, ornate octagon that does justice to the pleasure of learning.

The place can be overwhelming, so set aside time for a tour. The tours leave from the orientation desk on the ground floor and for 45 minutes take you behind the scenes of one of the country's most fascinating buildings.

Open Mon.-Fri. 8:30 a.m.-9:30 p.m., Sat. 8:30 a.m.-5 p.m., Sun. 1 p.m.-5 p.m. Closed Christmas & New Year's. Admission free.

Lincoln Memorial

23rd St. off Constitution Ave. NW
• 426-6841

Martin Luther King delivered his "I have a dream" speech from its steps. Opera singer Marian Anderson, banned from singing in the D.A.R. auditorium because of her race, performed from the same steps before 75,000 people. Richard Nixon surprised antiwar protesters with a middle-of-the-night visit in 1970.

This, needless to say, is one heavyweight historical landmark. But despite that, and despite the busloads of tourists who climb its steps every day, the Lincoln Memorial remains one of the most serene spots in Washington. It is a massive, dignified temple that can inspire reflection even in a campaigning politician.

It's a pensive place, from the chiseled words of Lincoln's Gettysburg Address on one wall and his Second Inaugural Address on the other, to the imposing statue of Lincoln himself. The sixteenth president is seated, but he still towers over the room. (He's 19 feet tall; if he were standing, he'd reach a height of 28 feet.) The statue, designed by Daniel Chester French, and dedicated in 1922, is sometimes called the "brooding Lincoln," because of his somber expression. Some claim, however, that Lincoln is simply being ambivalent—that if you stand on his right, he appears to be smiling, while from the left, he seems to be frowning. Another bit of mythology has it that Lincoln's oversized hands are signing the letters "A" and "L."

Even more impressive, perhaps, is the view from the top of the memorial's stairs. Have a seat and take in the grandeur of Washington, the Reflecting Pool stretching 350 feet to the Washington Monument, and, behind that, the splendor of the Capitol's dome. The vista is most striking at night, or during sunset or sunrise. Monument-watching doesn't get any better.

Open daily 8 a.m.-midnight. Admission free.

National Geographic Society Headquarters

17th & M Sts. NW
• 857-7000

It's not the same as making your own expedition to the North Pole, of course, but you and your kids should get some vicarious thrills by taking in the exhibit in Explorers Hall. The hall is now designed with computer screens that talk when touched. You can also zoom in on lizards with a video camera, talk to the resident macaw, Henry, or hop into Earth Station One, a simulated space flight which will

312

embarrass you with your lack of basic geo-info. Recent additions to the hall include Geographica, a wide-screen video that culls from the society's best shots: a frog licking his eye, a shy Moscow maiden, a billowing sea creature, and their revamped largest free-standing globe in the world—eleven feet from pole to pole, 35 feet in circumference. *Open Mon.-Sat. 9 a.m.-5 p.m., Sun. 10 a.m.-5 p.m. Closed Christmas. Admission free.*

National Shrine of the Immaculate Conception
4th St. & Michigan Ave. NE
• 526-8300

A touch more elevation, and this hulking relic of Byzantium would hover above Washington as Sacré-Coeur does above Paris. As with the basilica in Montmartre, this recent Roman Catholic pile is of limited architectural and decorative interest except for its outré nature. To many, in fact, the campanile, of Venetian design, and the dome, which resembles the "mammorial" adornment of a belly dancer, are laughable. The side chapels inside do not fare much better.
Open daily 7 a.m.-7 p.m. (Apr.-Oct.) or 7 a.m.-6 p.m. (Nov.-March). Admission free, but donations welcome.

National Zoological Park
3001 Connecticut Ave. NW
• 673-4800

Kids can stare at motionless museum exhibits for only so long, so give them—and yourself—a break, and take them to the National Zoo. Not only are there plenty of animals (almost 2,500), but most of them also have lots of room to move. This is an open zoo spread over 176 acres, and most of its inhabitants roam in "environment areas"—no pacing back and forth in tiny cages here.

The big draw are Ling-Ling and Hsing-Hsing, the two giant pandas donated to the zoo by the People's Republic of China in 1972. They are outrageously cute, especially when they're eating—feeding times are 11 a.m. and 3 p.m.—but the viewing area in front of their pen is usually crowded and, in truth, they aren't the most lively creatures. That may help explain why, as of this writing, they're having trouble producing offspring.

You'll probably get a much better show at the Monkey House, the Seal Pond or even the Reptile House, and bird-lovers would never forgive themselves if they miss the 90-foot-high Great Flight Cage, which you can walk right into. If that's not enough of a thrill, track down the rare white tigers, striking regal beasts that will make you treat your house cats with a lot more respect.

The zoo has parking for $3, but is also within a relatively short walk of the Zoo–Woodley Park Metro station. Once inside the gates, follow the clearly marked paths to your animals of choice. One last tip: kids can get very cranky if they get to a zoo only to see a bunch of animals sleeping, so try to arrive in the morning or late afternoon, when the inhabitants are a little friskier.

Grounds: open daily 8 a.m.-8 p.m. (May 1-Sept. 15), 8 a.m.-6 p.m. (Sept. 16-Apr. 30). Buildings: open daily 9 a.m.-6 p.m. (May 1-Sept. 15), 9 a.m.-4:30 p.m. (Sept. 16-Apr. 30). Closed Christmas. Admission free.

St. John's Church
16th & H Sts. NW
• 347-8766

Another confection of Benjamin H. Latrobe, sometime architect of the Capitol and the White House (as well as being the parish organist), who donated the plans for this 1816 work. Later additions included some in the 1880s by James Renwick. Pew 54 is, by tradition, reserved for the president, who theoretically could walk across the park, but doesn't, leaving the somewhat precious interior to tourists and well-heeled communicants from the suburbs.

Open Mon.-Sat. 8 a.m.-4 p.m., Sun. 8 a.m.-noon. Admission free, but donations welcome.

Supreme Court
1st & E. Capitol Sts. NE
• 479-3211

One of the places in Washington where you can, with some luck, witness history being made. The Court is in session from the first Monday in October through the end of June, and you can watch hearings (Monday through Wednesday 10 a.m. to noon and 1 p.m. to 3 p.m.), and maybe even hear a precedent-setting case being argued or a major decision being announced. Generally, decisions come down on Mondays. The justice who wrote the opinion usually states the facts of the case and explains the decision. Other members of the Court may announce that they concur or dissent. To see what cases are being reviewed, consult *The Washington Post.*

Seating in the courtroom is limited, however, so you should try to get there by 9 a.m., especially if a newsworthy case is being decided. If there's a big crowd, you may be allowed to stay only a few minutes, so other visitors can get a chance to see the proceedings.

Even if you don't see the justices on the bench, you shouldn't rule out a visit if you're interested in how the judicial branch of the government works. The interior of the building is also quite spectacular. Don't hesitate to grab a meal in the building's cafeteria—it's one of the best government dining spots in the city.

Open Mon.-Fri. 9 a.m.-4:30 p.m. Admission free.

Torpedo Factory

105 N. Union St.,
Alexandria, Va.
• (703) 838-4565

This munitions-factory-turned-art-factory lets you walk through studios and see artists at their best; yanking out hair, holding fingers to their chin in concentration, or sitting moodily in the corner.

More than 150 artists—jewelers, photographers, painters, sculptures, weavers, musical-instrument makers—work in this 1918 steel-and-concrete building, stacked up, one on top of the other, like torpedo cases. All work displayed has been created within its confines. Don't miss the studios with views of the Potomac, or Robert Rosselle's Hieronymus Bosch–like creatures in ceramic spheres on the third floor.

Open daily 10 a.m.-5 p.m. Admission free.

Vietnam Veterans' Memorial

23rd St. at Constitution Ave.
NW

Perhaps no place in Washington evokes more sadness than the Vietnam Veterans' Memorial, located at the west end of the Mall, several hundred yards from the Lincoln Memorial. As you walk down a sloping sidewalk, a polished black marble wall in the shape of a "V" rises beside you, and etched on its face are the names of more than 57,000 Americans who died in the war. It's a moving experience, particularly if you visit after dark and witness the nightly ritual of people holding flickering matches as they search for the name of a loved one. Often, they will leave behind a flower or some other small, personal remembrance which seems that much more poignant in such a public place. Nearby is a statue of three soldiers, erected after critics complained that the memorial did not adequately reflect the heroism of the war victims. But it is the vision of the black marble wall that stays with visitors long after they have walked away.

Open daily noon-midnight. Admission free.

Washington Cathedral

Wisconsin Ave. at Woodley
Rd. NW
• 537-6200

The closest thing in the Federal City to being a national church, this Episcopal cathedral is *the* correct place at which to be memorialized. A testament to doing things right, this huge edifice, also known as the Cathedral of St. Peter and St. Paul, has been under construction for more than 80 years now. When it's finished —the crews working on it are supposedly in the home stretch—the building will be the sixth-largest Gothic-style cathedral in the world. It's a beautiful example of medieval architecture, complete with massive arches and hundreds of carefully sculpted gargoyles. In fact, a documentary on the handful of craftspeople carving the cathedral's stone won an Academy Award in 1986. The 30-minute tour is probably the best way to understand the majesty and history of the building, but if you'd rather go your own way, pick up a copy of the *Guide to the National Cathedral* at the gift shop. While visiting, you might want to make a little brass rubbing, a favorite pastime of many tourists. You'll also find on the nicely kept grounds an Herb Cottage and a plant nursery.

If you're at the cathedral on a Sunday afternoon, frequently there are free organ concerts, which begin at 5 p.m., and experience the edifice in all its glory. *Open daily 10 a.m.-4:30 p.m. Admission free, but donations welcome.*

Washington Monument
14th St. & Constitution Ave. NW

It's no accident that the Washington Monument towers over the city's skyline; building regulations prohibit any taller structure from being built in the District of Columbia. The giant white obelisk stands slightly more than 555 feet high in the middle of the Mall, the center of a cross formed by the Lincoln Memorial and the Capitol in one direction and the White House and the Jefferson Memorial in the other. Ironically, the man who picked the site, Pierre L'Enfant, wouldn't recognize the monument, which was dedicated in 1885. He had wanted to erect a statue with George Washington on horseback, but that idea wasn't considered grand enough.

You once were able to walk the 898 steps to the top, but for safety reasons, you now have to take the 70-second elevator ride to the observation room. (Escorted groups can still walk down.) But it doesn't really matter how you get there, because the view from the top is spectacular enough to justify the time you'll spend waiting in line. *Open daily 9 a.m.-5 p.m. (winter), 8 a.m.-midnight (summer). Admission free.*

The Washington Post
1150 15th St. NW
• 334-6000, 334-7969

It's been sixteen years since Woodward and Bernstein toppled a president. Silent computers have replaced those rip-'em-out-quick typewriters, and power ties have replaced the blue jeans. But the place still can give you the shivers. Bernstein's no longer there, but you might catch a glimpse of Woodward talking on the phone with a source. In any event, you'll get to check out the newsroom on the fifth floor and the gargantuan printing presses down below. *Open for tours Mon. & Thurs. 10 a.m., 11 a.m., 1 p.m. & 2 p.m., by appt. only.*

The White House

1600 Pennsylvania Ave. NW
• 456-7041

First things first. You have no chance of actually seeing the president, or even getting anywhere near the Oval Office during a White House tour. Visitors, except, of course, those invited by the president himself, are kept away from the West Wing, where the work of the White House is done.

That said, almost two million people every year take a tour of the mansion with the most famous address in America. Mainly, it's a chance to spend a few moments in the aura of presidential power and to get a glimpse of how past leaders have lived.

Visitors on the regular tour see five rooms: the Green Room, the Blue Room, the Red Room, the East Room and the State Dining Room. At one time the presidential families spent a lot of time in the first three rooms, but now they are primarily museum exhibits, occasionally used for receptions. Before Jackie Kennedy moved into the White House, these rooms contained a mish-mash of furniture collected by previous First Families. But she had the rooms restored and filled them with antiques that recapture some of the mansion's early atmosphere. The largest room on the tour is the East Room, often used for presidential press conferences and dances. It is a favorite of tourists because it contains the famous Gilbert Stuart painting of George Washington.

To take a tour during the period from Memorial Day through Labor Day (late May through early September), you must personally pick up a ticket in the booth on the Ellipse behind the White House grounds. Be warned that the booth opens at 8 a.m. and that tickets are sometimes gone by 9 a.m. Also be warned that you may have to wait in line for two hours for a tour that lasts about fifteen minutes. Tickets are not required in the off-season between September and May, but visitors should get in line at the East Gate no later than 10 a.m. if they hope to get in.

A better idea is to write your congressman or senator several months ahead of your visit and request a ticket for a VIP tour. Held in the morning before the regular public tours, the VIP tours generally last longer and cover several more rooms.

Open Tues.-Sat. 10 a.m.-2 p.m. (Memorial Day–Labor Day), Tues.-Sat. 10 a.m.-noon (Sept.-May). Admission free.

Wolf Trap Farm Park

1551 Trap Rd.,
Vienna, Va.
• (703) 255-1800

One of the true summer pleasures of Washington, Wolf Trap is a bucolic throwback to the times when the Virginia suburbs weren't one big traffic jam. It's a rolling 117-acre park, the focal point of which is the Filene Center, a comfortable open-air performing arts center. Regulars come prepared with picnic dinners, which they eat on the spacious grounds before the concerts begin, or during the show if they're sitting on the grassy hillside above the auditorium. And Wolf Trap now has its own outdoor restaurant. The entertainment is wide-ranging, from the New York City Opera to Dizzy Gillespie to the Kirov Ballet to Peter, Paul and Mary. Shows can sell out quickly for big-name acts, so buy your tickets in advance.

If you can't get reserved seats inside the Filene Center, don't rule out the lawn seats, which can be delightful, especially for musical events where what you hear is more important than what you see. And if you want to avoid the after-concert traffic jams, you can now take the Metro to Wolf Trap. A shuttle bus runs every twenty minutes on performance nights from the West Falls Church Metrorail station to the Filene Center. The return trip leaves Wolf Trap at 11 p.m. For visitors who miss the summer season, check to see what is playing at the Wolf Trap Barns, a delightful, smallish concert hall that frequently offers excellent musical acts throughout the winter months.
Open June-Sept. Showtimes & ticket prices vary.

PARKS & GARDENS

Constitution Gardens
Constitution Ave. between 17th & 23rd Sts. NW

Shaded by thousands of dogwood, oak, elm and crab apple trees, this 50-acre oasis comes complete with a small lake and a tiny island. Picnickers love it. It is part of the more recent landscaping efforts on the Mall. Once the site of some ramshackle World War I office buildings, it is now a handsomely landscaped part of the Mall.
Open daily noon-midnight. Admission free.

Dumbarton Oaks
31st & R Sts. NW
• 338-8278

It's beautiful, historic and almost magically peaceful in these acres smack in the middle of bustling Georgetown. Maintained, along with museums and libraries, by Harvard University since 1940, when it was donated by its owners, Dumbarton was where wartime plans were made for the new United Nations. About sixteen acres in all, it boasts paths that wind around reflecting pools, under decorative arches and beside lavish fountains. There are benches in solitary corners. Occasional concerts bring crowds, but mostly it's just the sun and the smell of blossoms.
Open daily 2 p.m.-6 p.m. Closed holidays. Admission $2.

Hillwood Museum Gardens

4155 Linnean Ave. NW
• 686-5807

Hillwood is the 25-acre former estate of Marjorie Merriweather Post (of the breakfast cereal). The formal grounds include a Japanese garden and a French parterre and more than 3,500 kinds of plants and trees. Designed by Perry Wheeler, who helped supervise the creation of the White House Rose Garden, its formal gardens blend into the wild on the edge of Rock Creek Park. There's also a greenhouse containing some 5,000 orchids!
Open Mon. & Wed.-Sat. by reservation only. Admission $2 (grounds only), $7 (museum & grounds).

Lady Bird Johnson Park

Across Memorial Bridge, then off George Washington Pkwy., on the Va. side of the Potomac River

This is a fifteen-acre island (literally) of tranquility just beyond the traffic of a major set of commuting thoroughfares. The park boasts azaleas, rhododendron and more than 2,700 dogwoods. It was dedicated to commemorate the former First Lady's national beautification campaign. It provides a pleasant view of the Potomac River and the Washington skyline, and you can walk the length of the island. The LBJ Memorial Grove, where you'll find a mile of hiking and biking trails, is to the south.
Open daily dawn-dusk. Admission free.

Kenilworth Aquatic Gardens

Kenilworth Ave. & Douglas St. NE
• 426-6905

More than a century old, the gardens were begun by a humble civil servant on what was then private property. They're a treasured site now, a haven for waterfowl and other Anacostia River wildlife, and a showplace for more than 100,000 water lilies and other water plants. The best time to visit is summer through early fall.
Open daily 7 a.m.-sunset. Admission free.

National Arboretum

3501 New York Ave. NE
• 475-4815

Although it's a major national research facility, the arboretum, with its more than 70,000 azaleas alone, is also one of the most spectacular of all Washington's attractions. Within its 440 acres are the gorgeous National Bonsai Collection (open daily from 10 a.m. to 2 p.m.) and the National Herb Garden. The Bonsai Collection, representing the Japanese art of growing dwarf plants in shallow pots, is itself worth a trip to Washington. You'll find 53 trees of 34 species, which range in age from 30 to 350 years old. The collection was given to the United States by Japan as a Bicentennial gift and is estimated to be worth close to five million dollars. The best season for the other extraordinary offerings of the arboretum, obviously, is spring—which lasts well into May for the flowering dogwood and moun-

tain laurel—but it's a fine place for a long walk almost anytime through the summer and fall, too.
Open Mon.-Fri. 8 a.m.-5 p.m., Sat.-Sun. 10 a.m.-5 p.m. Closed Christmas. Admission free.

Rock Creek Park
Cathedral Ave. & Rock Creek
Pkwy. NW

It's hard to believe that such a peaceful mecca exists in this busy metropolitan area. Rock Creek Park is one of the largest and finest city parks in the nation. Located in northwest Washington, the park was purchased by Congress in 1890 for the nation. It is four miles long and about one mile wide, and it offers a variety of terrain that can accommodate a wide range of activities, from driving, walking, hiking, bike riding, horseback riding, exploring or throwing a frisbee to just sitting back and enjoying a peaceful picnic lunch. Great stands of near-virgin forest grace the hills and valleys of the park, and Rock Creek itself weaves a peaceful path through the park area. About 70 picnic areas, many with grills or fireplaces, are scattered throughout the park (bring your own fuel), and on Sundays, from 8 a.m. to 6 p.m., Beach Drive between Joyce and Broad Branch roads is closed to motor vehicles and turned into a paradise for bicycle enthusiasts.
Open daily. Admission free.

Tulip Library
Near the Tidal Basin &
Jefferson Memorial

No, you can't "borrow" anything from this collection but, in spring, when the approximately 250,000 tulips are out, and in the summer and fall, when annuals are blooming, it's sufficient to take only the memory home. It's a splash of color and fragrance you won't easily forget.
Open daily. Admission free.

U.S. Botanic Garden
Maryland Ave. & 1st St. SW
• 225-8333

Washingtonians flee to this cavernous greenhouse when snow flies, but the most spectacular time of year is spring when, from March through early April, the azaleas are in breathtaking bloom. But don't miss the world-famous collection of orchids that includes 10,000 plants and at least 500 varieties, 200 of which bloom every week. There are plants from all over the world, and the collection of cycads—plants that date back to prehistoric times—is considered the finest on earth. The Botanic Garden is a strictly decorative facility, with no research section, but gardening and horticultural tips are available in pamphlets. And if you wonder why the plants in the office of your senator or representative look so good, it's because they come courtesy of the Botanic Garden.
Open daily 9 a.m.-5 p.m. Admission free.

SPORTS & LEISURE

PROFESSIONAL & COLLEGE SPORTS

THE MAJOR TEAMS

America's national pastime, baseball, is not played in America's national capital, Washington, nor has it been played on a professional level since 1971, at which time the fortunes of the Senators had sunk to an incredible low.

But although the lack of baseball is something of an affront to diehard fans, many Washingtonians have transfered their fanatic loyalty to the Orioles in Baltimore, living and dying with each win and defeat. In Washington and nearby, football, basketball, rugby, cricket, golf, tennis, hockey, horse racing, sailing, biking, swimming, bowling and other sports are played. Some of it is very, very good. Some of it is much better in other cities around the country.

If Washington has a passion that transcends politics, it is the Redskins, the professional football team which is enjoying great years of glory with no downturn in sight. How big are the Redskins in Washington? Well, it is safe to say that more people know the name of the Redskins' all-pro defensive end, the brilliant and voluble Dexter Manley, than the names of their government officials. When the Redskins won the Super Bowl, more than a million people watched a victory parade they could not see. A torrential downpour forced the players into buses, almost completely obscuring them from the huddled masses.

This immense, near cult worship of the Redskins poses problems for those who want to see them. There are no tickets. Robert F. Kennedy Stadium, a twenty-block straight shot from the Capitol, has been sold out forever for Redskins games, and there are more than 30,000 on the waiting list. Tickets are left to grief-stricken heirs in last wills and testaments and sometimes are part of settlements in divorce cases.

But that does not mean a visitor cannot see the Redskins. There are two ways—one for those with a lot of money, and one for those with no money. Tickets, which normally cost $12 to $25, are sometimes listed for sale in the classified sections of the city's newspapers. But the price asked for a single seat to a playoff game goes as high as $250. The other way to see the Redskins is on television (which most of those who live in Washington do)—either in the quiet of your hotel or motel or in a bar, any bar, in the city. If you venture into a bar for the game, it is risky just to remain silent; extremely hazardous to root for the other team; and probably suicidal to cheer for either the New York Giants or the Dallas Cowboys.

Shoppers take note: The time at which the Redskins play, about three hours on Sundays between the first part of September and at least the middle of December, is considered the best time to go shopping in Washington—the stores are empty.

Boxing, once a big sport in Washington, has virtually disappeared, although bouts are periodically held at the D.C. Armory (546-3337). One of the great champions, Sugar Ray Leonard, lives in the Washington suburbs, but big-name fighters don't box here. Nor, for that matter, do good little-name ones.

To watch professional soccer, you have to go to Baltimore, but 32 teams in Washington compete for the Embassy Cup from mid-May through June. They play near the Reflecting Pool at the Lincoln Memorial, and the teams are mostly from the many embassies in the city. Admission is free.

There are polo matches at West Potomac Park near the Lincoln Memorial on Sundays from May to July and in September and October. Admission also is free.

OTHER PRO TEAMS

Washington's two other major professional teams, the Washington Bullets in the National Basketball Association and the Washington Capitals in the National Hockey League, have yet to develop the loyal following that the Redskins enjoy. The advantage is that tickets are available. Both teams play in the modernistic Capital Centre at Landover, Maryland, about a 25- to 30-minute drive when the road is clear, sometimes much longer when the traffic is heavy.

The Bullets
Capital Centre,
Landover, Md.
• (301) 350-3400

One of the more solid teams in the NBA, the Bullets have the tallest player in the pro ranks. Manute Bol stands seven feet six inches and is a member of the Dinka tribe, the largest and tallest people in the Sudan. Bol, the premier shot-blocker in the league, was once considered about as mobile as the Washington Monument, but experience and special diet have made him stronger and removed all speculation that he is only one very large freak. Phone or check newspapers to see if the Bullets are at home or on the road. *Open in season: Oct.-Apr., later for playoffs. Tickets $7.50-$17.50.*

The Capitals
Capital Centre
Landover, Md.
• (301) 350-3400

The Capitals suffer, to some extent, because Washington is historically a southern city with no tradition of kids growing up playing hockey. Even today, there is little hockey, because it rarely stays cold enough to freeze the Potomac, or even the concrete "lakes" on the Mall. But the Caps, helped by hockey on television and by migrations of people who began life in colder climes, have caught on. They have made runs at the Stanley Cup, which goes to the winner of the NHL, but have fallen short. As with most American teams in the league, the Capitals' players are Canadians, with a sprinkling of Swedes and a few homegrown U.S.A. types. Phone or check newspapers for the schedule. *Open in season: Oct.-Apr. Tickets $11-$23.*

COLLEGE TEAMS

On the college level, the Washington area boasts several top-flight football and basketball teams. There is also baseball, but it is not a big attraction. College football is played from September through early December, and basketball begins in November and runs through March.

Georgetown University Hoyas (basketball)
Capital Centre,
Landover, Md.
• (301) 350-3400

Since Big John Thompson took over as coach, the Georgetown Hoyas have become one of the powers of college basketball; they won the national championship in 1984. The school is white; the basketball teams are black. *Tickets $5-$15.*

The Naval Academy Middies (football)
Navy-Marine Corps
Memorial Stadium,
Annapolis, Md.
• (301) 268-6060

There's major college football at the Naval Academy in Annapolis. It's about an hour's leisurely drive, but the pomp and pageantry are worth the time. *Tickets $15.*

University of Maryland Terrapins (basketball)
Cole Field House,
College Park, Md.
• (301) 454-2121

Maryland basketball is in a rebuilding process, jarred by the tragic death of Len Bias from cocaine abuse on the eve of a promising professional career. The ACC is arguably the toughest college basketball league in the country, with four or five teams in the conference nationally ranked, as Maryland has been in the past and will be again. *Tickets $5-$14.*

University of Maryland Terrapins (football)
Byrd Stadium,
College Park, Md.
• (301) 454-2121

The premier college football team in the area, the Terrapins play just outside the city limits. They are members, and sometimes champions, of the Atlantic Coast Conference. *Tickets $17-$20.*

SPECTATOR & PARTICIPATORY SPORTS

GOLF

The best public courses are in Virginia and Maryland, a healthy jaunt out of town, and to get there, you definitely need a car. They get crowded early, especially in the spring and fall. The area's most famous course, at the Burning Tree Country Club, where premiers, presidents, potentates and power-brokers play, is one of the last all-male bastions and is never open to the public. Women are not permitted except on one day when they can come to the pro shop to buy Christmas presents for their member husbands, boyfriends or lovers. But Washington has three public courses, for those desperate to play. And if you want to see the game as it was intended to be played, try the Kemper Open.

The Kemper Open
**Tournament Players Club at Avenel ,
Potomac, Md.
• (301) 469-3700**

The Kemper, with $700,000 in prize money, is the area's only major pro golf tournament. It was held for years at the Congressional Country Club, but has now moved a short ride away to the Avenel Farms course. Avenel, a new course, was the site in 1986 of holes in one by the legendary Arnold Palmer on the same hole on two successive days in a seniors tournament. The Kemper's format is a pro-am match on Wednesday, with the 72-hole tournament running Thursday through Sunday. Although the Kemper draws many of the top touring pros, some skip the event to get ready for the U.S. Open, one of the four majors, which comes two weeks later.
Open for tournament: week after Memorial Day, Wed.-Sun. Admission $17.50 each round, grounds only, $25 a round, grounds & pavilion.

East Potomac Park
• 554-7660

Langston Golf Course
**26th St. & Benning Rd. NE
• 397-8638**

Rock Creek Park
• 882-7332

East Potomac, Langston and Rock Creek are public courses operated on National Park Service land. None is what can be described as a championship course, and all tend to be very crowded. Rock Creek wins the scenic award hands down. East Potomac, on Hains Point, is flat and dull, but it does offer a driving range with a small ($2) fee. Langston also has a driving range with a $2 fee.
Open daily dawn to dusk. Greens fees: $5 for 9 holes, $8 for 18 holes (weekdays); $6 for 9 holes, $10 for 18 holes (weekends). Senior citizens rates available. No reservations.

HIKING & BIKING

Visitors who are not exhausted by just walking from tourist attraction to tourist attraction will find Washington a great place to go hiking, biking or jogging. Areas in or near the city include Rock Creek Park in upper Northwest, East and West Potomac Parks near the monuments, the C & O Towpath in Georgetown, the Mall behind the White House and the George Washington Parkway from Memorial Bridge south to Mount Vernon. Or, do as Washingtonians do, and jog down the city streets or anywhere the spirit moves you.

Bicycles can be rented at Fletcher's Boat House (244-0461), Canal and Reservoir roads, for $2 an hour (2 hour minimum) or $7 a day; at Metropolis Bike and Scooter (543-8900), 709 8th Street SE, for $15 a day; or at Thompson Boat Center (333-4861), Rock Creek Parkway and Virginia Avenue SW, for $2 an hour or $10 a day. The bike trails are essentially the same as the jogging paths and are all pretty much connected.

Fletcher's and Thompson also rent canoes by the hour or by the day for a little personal exploring of the Potomac. Although the river may look inviting on a hot day, the stretches near the city are not yet considered free enough from pollution to be absolutely safe for swimming.

HORSE RACING

Horse racing is a year-round sport in the Washington area. It is never too hot for the horses and rarely, very rarely, too cold for the noble steeds. There are two premier events on the racing calendar each year—The Preakness at Pimlico and The International at Laurel.

The Preakness, the second jewel in America's Triple Crown, is run the third Saturday in May, two weeks after the Kentucky Derby, and before the third gem, the Belmont. Post time is noon.

The International, run on grass, attracts entries from all over the world, and goes off every first Saturday in November.

Flat-track racing runs at Laurel in nearby Maryland (725-0400) from June 14 to July 25 and September 20 to December 31. Tickets range from $3 to $5; post time is 1 p.m. on weekdays and 12:30 p.m. weekends.

Flat-track racing also runs at Pimlico (301-542-9400) from March 15 to June 13; from July 26 to August 24; and from September 4 to 19. Admission is $3 to $5; post time, except on Preakness Day, is 1 p.m. weekdays and 12:30 p.m. weekends. But Pimlico is in Baltimore, some 50 miles away, and is not worth the trip, except for the Preakness.

The Laurel and Pimlico tracks offer the full range of betting options—the basic win-place-show, daily doubles, exactas (first two finishers), double triples (winners of three races) and other exotic ways to lose money.

Trotters and pacers run at Rosecroft Raceway at night. It is very near Washington and has been known to name a race in honor of an individual if a big enough party comes. The season goes from January 14 to May 17 and from October 6 to December 30, with post time 7:30 p.m. on week nights and 6:30 p.m. on weekends. Admission is $2 to $4.

One of the best steeplechase events in the country, the Virginia Gold Cup, is run the first Saturday in May at Great Meadow Farm, two miles south of I-66 in The Plains, Virginia. General admission for the masses runs $15 to $20 per car, while reserved seating for the elite runs from $150 to $400. And yes, the races are over in time for you to head to a pub and catch that other horse race down in Kentucky.

HORSEBACK RIDING

Rock Creek Park Horse Centre
Military & Glover Rds. NW
• 362-0995

Guided rides on horseback are $15 an hour. *Rides Tues.-Fri. 3 p.m. & 4:30 p.m., Sat.-Sun. noon, 1:30 p.m., 3 p.m. & 4:30 p.m.*

PERSONAL FITNESS

What with the great restaurants, frequent cocktail parties and elaborate dinners that make up Washington life, it's no surprise that exercise is considered essential by so many area residents. Health clubs abound, as do exercise studios. A few of the better known follow.

If the prices seem a bit steep, you might give the D.C. Department of Recreation a call. The city operates nineteen outdoor swimming pools during the months of June, July and August and eleven indoor pools open year round. Admission is free. The D.C. Department of Recreation also sponsors a number of exercise classes around the city. For more information on location and fees, call 673-7661.

Body Design By Gilda
4801 Wisconsin Ave. NW
• 363-4801

Gilda's offers four different levels of aerobic and nonimpact aerobic classes, as well as a stretch-and-firm nonaerobic class. Most classes are an hour long, except for a single 75-minute advanced aerobics session. Both men and women are welcome, and a reservation is required only for the first class. This is primarily an exercise studio with full dressing room and shower facilities, but no other special facilities such as a steam room or sauna. Gilda's offers a series of five classes for $65, ten for $118 or twenty for $225. The series is valid for a year.
Open Mon.-Fri. 7 a.m.-8:30 p.m., Sat. 8 a.m.-5 p.m., Sun. 8 a.m.-12:30 p.m.

Massage Associates
J.W. Marriott Hotel,
1331 Pennsylvania Ave. NW
• 626-6931

If a fast-paced style has you a bit tense, you might give Alan Alper a call. Alper, a master therapist, and his associates work out of the health club at the Marriott, close to the White House, where some of Alper's clients are not unknown. An hour of firm, relaxing, regenerative rubbing runs $50. Half-hour sessions are also available, but who'd want to cut short such bliss? An appointment entitles clients to use the hotel's swimming pool, whirlpool and sauna. The massages get higher marks than the health club here.
Open by appointment only.

The Racquet Club
The Washington Hilton and Towers
1919 Connecticut Ave. NW
• 483-3000

This health club at the Washington Hilton has a wonderful membership program—built around the best outdoor swimming pool in town and three outdoor lighted tennis courts—for Washingtonians who can afford it. Full use of the Olympic-size pool runs $650 for the season, and a combination tennis and swim membership costs $940. The pool is open from May 1 to the end of October, while the tennis courts open in April and close at the end of November. Once you plunk down that hefty fee, you have full access to the Hilton's health club facilities, which include a Jacuzzi, saunas, an exercise room and classes, as well a host of social amenities such as an outdoor restaurant and a bar. The exercise classes are aerobic, the exercise equipment Universal. Two lanes of the pool are reserved for lap swimming. The exercise facilities remain available throughout the year even if the pool and tennis courts are closed, but hours vary during the November-to-April time period. *Open daily 7 a.m.-11 p.m. (Apr.-Nov.).*

Somebodies Exercise Studio
1070 Thomas Jefferson St. NW
• 338-3822

If you are thinking about getting into the exercise routine or if you once exercised but are badly out of shape, Somebodies may be the place for you. The instructors here pride themselves on being particularly sensitive to beginners, and stress individual attention and proper exercise technique. Offering both high- and low-impact aerobics for men and women, Somebodies has classes at the beginning, intermediate and advanced levels. Classes are limited to eleven participants, so reservations are required. Somebodies sells monthly series of classes, asking clients to make that much of a commitment. The idea is that once you begin to see the results, exercise will become a regular activity and—perhaps—a way of life. The first class is free. Then you can opt for one, two, three, four or five workouts a week. Prices start at $48 for one class a week for a month and $77 for two classes a week for a month. Single classes run $13 an hour. There are dressing rooms and showers here, but no other "extras" such as sauna or a steam room.
Open Mon.-Wed. 6:30 a.m.-9 p.m., Tues., Thurs. & Fri. 6:30 a.m.-8 p.m., Sat. 7:30 a.m.-2 p.m.

The Watergate Health Club
2650 Virginia Ave. NW
• 298-4460

Anything that has "Watergate" in its name is bound to be costly, and this health club is certainly no exception. Here you will find an exclusive clientele that enjoys a variety of special services and pampering. There's a 10-by-50-foot swimming pool, a Jacuzzi, a sauna, a steam room and a weight room that has an electronic treadmill, stairmasters and Universal exercise equipment. The highly trained staff conducts exercise classes throughout the day, from a whole range of aerobics to water exercise. Each member receives a full evaluation, and a personal exercise program is designed based on his or her condition. The club also offers Swedish massage and pressure massage for men and women every day including weekends. The locker room, sauna and steam room facilities are separate for men and women, while the rest of the facilities are shared. Year memberships are $925 ($475 initiation fee). You can get a half-year membership—same initiation fee, half the one-year membership fee—or pay $175 for one month. If you are only in town briefly, you can come in and get a one-hour massage for $55 ($30 for half an hour.) Classes are on a first-come, first-served basis, and you may have to wait a bit to join, since the memberships slots are always pretty close to full. *Open Mon.-Fri. 6 a.m.-10 p.m., Sat.-Sun. 9 a.m.-7 p.m.*

Westin Fitness Center
2401 M St. NW
• 429-2400

The fitness center is not affiliated with the Westin Hotel, but is available to hotel guests as well as the guests of three other hotels in the general vicinity—the Grand, the Four Seasons and the Vista—on a daily-fee basis. Otherwise, it's a membership club. The weight room is filled with exotic-looking equipment, and there are squash and racquetball courts, a lap pool, treadmills, exercise bikes and rowing machines. In addition, the club has a steam room, a whirlpool, a sauna, tanning beds and massage services, as well as a sports medicine center, a beauty salon and a juice bar. And there's a complete range of aerobics classes, conducted daily. A full membership runs $1,050 a year (plus a $600 initiation fee), limited-hour membership costs $725 a year ($300 initiation fee). You can also join on a month-by-month basis for $150 per month. The Westin center is particularly known for its cardiovascular fitness programs and offers a full range of personal fitness evaluations as well as nutrition programs and various seminars on lower-back pain and other common ailments. For business people, the Westin center has full reciprocity with the Vista executive fitness center in the World Trade Center in New York. *Open Mon.-Fri. 6 a.m.-10 p.m., Sat.-Sun. 8 a.m.-7 p.m.*

YMCA of Metropolitan Washington
1711 Rhode Island Ave. NW
• 362-9622

A great exercise facility, the YMCA's offers a full line of services to its members, including the best indoor swimming pool in town. A fitness membership that includes the swimming pool and other facilities, but excludes the fancy exercise equipment, steam room and whirlpool, costs a nonrefundable $200 for an initiation fee and $46 a month. The top membership, called the athletic membership, requires a $250 initiation fee and $78 a month. There are two other membership categories, both less expensive, for those who can meet the age or income criteria. This Y will honor other membership cards from other cities, but there is no single-day membership.

Open Mon.-Fri. 6 a.m.-11 p.m., Sat. 8 a.m.-7 p.m., Sun. 11 a.m.-6 p.m.

TENNIS

There are many public tennis courts in Washington, but beware, there are also many tennis players. More than 55 public courts—clay, asphalt, concrete and composition—are operated by the D.C. Department of Recreation, but some are in such obscure places, you could never hope to find them (would you believe 15th and Constitution on the Mall?). If you do, you'll probably have a long wait. One of the most popular public courts—and your best shot at getting on, especially during the week—is Hains Point at East Potomac Park. Hains, operated by the National Park Service, has both clay and concrete courts, and five are under a bubble for year-round play. Indoor rates at Hains range from $10 to $21 an hour, outdoor rates are substantially less. Reservations are not only possible, but required. You must go in person to sign up, with court time available up to a week in advance.

For professional tennis watching, Washington hosts both the Sovran Bank—D.C. National Tennis Classic for men and the Virginia Slims tournament for women.

The Sovran offers touring pros $294,000 in purses but in the past has suffered from two major drawbacks—the slow clay courts and torrid temperatures with humidity to match. The tournament is played at the same time each year—late July to early August—which coincides with Washington's ugliest weather. The big boomers such as Lendl and Becker tend to skip this tournament, although it draws many top-rated pros, especially the clay-court specialists from Latin America and some from Europe. The courts—at the Rock Creek Tennis Center at 16th and Kennedy streets NW—are now hard-surfaced, so one problem is gone, but there is nothing the sponsors can do about the weather. Tickets are from $6 to $21, depending on time and day.

The Virginia Slims tournament, sponsored by the Meritor Savings Bank, is held annually in late March and played indoors at the George Mason Patriots Center (276-3030) in nearby Virginia. This tournament draws the best of the pros, and tickets range from $8 to $18, depending on time and day.

TOURS

Babel Tours
• 386-4900

These tours are standard if-it's-eleven-o'clock-this-must-be-the-Capitol fare, but a bus tour can be just the ticket when time is limited or when you just can't walk one more block. American Coach offers all sorts of tours, but the basic half-day tour touches on virtually anything the visiting tenderfoot might expect to boast about to the folks back home. Alternatively, you can ask for a special full-day tour. It's best to book a day ahead.
Tour times vary; call office for further information.

C & O Canal Tours
• Georgetown barge information, 472-4376; Great Falls barge information, (703) 299-2026

The Chesapeake & Ohio Canal, built in the first half of the nineteenth century, brought Washington most of its coal until the railroads took over. Now it's a National Historic Park, one of the most popular in the nation. From spring through fall, visitors can choose between narrated mule-drawn barge trips starting at Great Falls, Virginia, or at the Georgetown end on 30th Street between M and K streets NW. Either way, Park Service employees in period costume show how the locks work and demonstrate the fine points of getting what will seem like a huge vessel through a narrow ribbon of water. Warning: the Great Falls area is an extremely beautiful, but extremely dangerous, portion of the Potomac River, so use great care in walking, don't try to swim and watch the kids closely. Also, the unmistakable canal odors may take some getting used to.
Tour times vary. Adults $4, seniors $3, children $2.50.

Cruise Ship *Dandy*
• (703) 683-6076

Refined dining it is not, but cruising the Potomac River on the company's air-conditioned riverboat, the *Dandy*, is fun and, in the right circumstances, very romantic. One right circumstance is the dinner cruise, which features after-dinner dancing. There are surprising sights to be seen along the river, even at night, when the major monuments and the Capitol present a floodlit vista of spectacular beauty. Departures are from Prince Street in Alexandria, Virginia.
Cruises 11:30 a.m. & 6:30 p.m. Lunch cruise (bar excluded) $25 (Mon.-Fri.), $27 (Sat.), $29 (Sun.); dinner cruise $47 (Sun.-Thurs.), $50 (Fri.), $55 (Sat.).

Gray Line
• 289-1995

Don't expect anything off the beaten track, obviously, but the driver-guides are experienced, and they know how to maneuver their huge vehicles through Washington's clogged streets. The half-day tour includes most major historic buildings and monuments downtown, plus Arlington Cemetery. The day-long version adds Old Town Alexandria and Mount Vernon, Virginia.

Tours start about 9 a.m. All-day: adults $36, children $25; half day: adults $15-$20, children $7.50-$10. Stops at major downtown hotels.

Old Town Trolley Tours
• 269-3020 (recorded information),
269-3021 (groups & other queries)

Built to resemble old-fashioned trolleys, these cute orange buses travel a two-hour circuit (complete with narrated tour) with thirteen stops, ranging from Capitol Hill and the Smithsonian to Georgetown and its environs. It's an easy way to visit such out-of-the-way marvels as the Washington Cathedral, a splendid modern-day reproduction of Gothic architecture. Buses stop at several major hotels—the Hyatt Regency, J. W. Marriott, Capitol Hilton and the Mayflower among them—and tickets are available at most. The best advice is to use Metrorail. Get off at the Federal Triangle station on the Blue-Orange line. There's a trolley stop and ticket booth across 12th Street NW. A ticket gives you unlimited boarding rights for the day, so you can get on and off as you please. Buses pass by every 25 minutes or so.

Tours & shuttle service daily 9 a.m.-4 p.m. (Labor Day–Memorial Day) or 9 a.m.-7 p.m. (Memorial Day-Labor Day). Adults $12, children $5.

Scandal Tours
1727 Q St. NW
• 387-2253

This is the bus tour that will validate all those nasty things you've muttered under your breath about the capital. Starting from the Ritz-Carlton Hotel on Massachusetts Avenue, Gross National Product (a comedy troup that has made a mint out of satirizing local events) escorts you to where power and sleaze have not only met, but have lain down together. Stops include The Watergate, naturally, the Pentagon, and the Tidal Basin, sight of a famous skinny-dipping spree.

Public tours Sat.-Sun. 1 p.m. & 3 p.m.; $30. Private charters daily; prices vary.

Spirit of Washington Cruises
• 554-8000

Formerly known as Washington Boat Lines, this firm runs a number of Potomac cruises, but the Mount Vernon trip is its star attraction. The fare includes admission to Mount Vernon. A nearly two-hour stop at the plantation is the centerpiece, but the famous river itself, its shores studded with historic sites, is appealing enough on its own. The line also offers lunch cruises three times a week, moonlight dance cruises twice a week and a "city lights" jaunt along the Georgetown and Arlington, Virginia, shores on Sunday evening. Reservations are strongly recommended. Departure from Pier 4 at 6th and Water streets SW.

Mt. Vernon cruise Tues.-Sun. 9 a.m. & 2 p.m. Adults $16.50, children $7.25-$9.25, seniors $14.25. (All prices includes entrance fee).

Tourmobile

• 554-7020, 554-7950 (recorded information), 554-7020 (group tours)

Don't be put off by the cattle-car look: this is a cheap, efficient way to take in the major federal sights without doing irreparable harm to the feet. Tourmobile holds the National Parks Service concession for narrated tours of major monuments, the Mall and Arlington Cemetery. The 90-minute Mall area circuit begins at the East Front of the Capitol, but you can board wherever you find the firm's red-and-white boarding signs. Most are near the major monuments and along the Mall. You can pay at ticket booths or on board. A ticket gives you unlimited use throughout the day. Get off at any of eighteen stops and then reboard later. The odd-looking, open-air buses pass by every twenty minutes. Two-day tickets are also available. The Arlington Cemetery tour alone is $2.50; children $1.25). In addition, Tourmobile offers a scheduled bus tour to George Washington's plantation at Mount Vernon via Old Town Alexandria ($13.50 for adults, $6.25 for children).

Shuttle service daily 9 a.m.-6:30 p.m. (summer) or 9:30 a.m.-4:30 p.m. (winter). Adults $7.50, children $3.75.

OUT OF
WASHINGTON

ANNAPOLIS

It could have been the other way around. Washington could have been the side trip if the Founding Fathers, as they searched for a permanent site for the seat of government for the new Republic, had stayed here—a lovely, thriving seaport on Chesapeake Bay when it served from 1783 to 1784 as the United States capital. Instead, they selected an undeveloped and swampy tract 30 miles farther west. We're not sure we know what got into them.

Fifty years older than Williamsburg and the state capital of Maryland for 300 years, Annapolis today still offers a glimpse of a bygone America with its quaint, narrow streets, brick sidewalks and the greatest concentration of eighteenth-century buildings in the country. But it frames history in twentieth-century aluminum and glass.

As one of the nation's premier yachting centers, Annapolis seems to have more masts than trees. Sailboats are everywhere. Acres of them. The view down Main Street toward the sparkling harbor, spread with sails on a brisk afternoon, can be breathtaking. With its four tidewater creeks, sixteen miles of shoreline and many boatyards, Annapolis is unquestionably a boat-lover's paradise. It is also the home of the U.S. Naval Academy, whose presence is everywhere in evidence—from the ramrod-straight "Middies" always about town to the huge visting naval ships, anchored out in the bay.

During a sailing season that lasts from late March to early December, a parade of boats moves steadily past the City Dock, some sailed by grizzled old salts, some by young racing skippers with all the latest high-tech equipment, others by paunchy middle-aged executives showing off their toys. Oyster and crab boats, skipjacks and other working craft share space with cruise boats, pleasure craft and old sailing ships. Water taxis crisscross the harbor, launches come and go from anchored foreign-flag ships, sailboarders abound. Even in the dead of winter, when the harbor is often filled with patches of ice, Saturday "frost bite" races rouse the seagulls from complacency.

Annapolis boasts at least 50 homes built before the Revolution, many restored and open for inspection or transformed into shops, restaurants and museums. The city is one of the most beautiful of the state capitals, with a harbor that is an integral part of downtown and all the main shops and points of interest within an easy walk. But enjoy it now. The secret is out. *Everyone* has discovered Annapolis. As a result, its character is changing rapidly. Once-sleepy shorelines are yielding to high-rise condominiums and flashy marinas that offer tennis courts, swimming pools and boutiques. Downtown is becoming a Georgetown East, packed with roving teens on Friday and Saturday nights. Moreover, where a staid seafood restaurant and variety shop stood up until a few years ago at a prime waterfront corner address, a large and gaudy Banana Republic store now sprawls. Is nothing sacred?

Annapolis straddles a peninsula where the Severn River flows into Chesapeake Bay (with 5,000 miles of shoreline, one of the largest bodies of water in the United States).

It's an easy drive from Washington, about 40 minutes due east on Route 50 (a.k.a. George Hanson Highway). There is also Greyhound Trailways Bus service.

Puritans "established" the village in 1649, calling it "Providence." (They weren't very original with names, those Puritans.) Of course, there were already Native Americans living there when the Europeans arrived, so a peace treaty of sorts was signed with a local chief in 1652, under a tulip tree that still stands on the campus of St. Johns College. Later, the city was renamed Anne Arundel Town, to honor the wife of the second Lord Baltimore. In 1694, it became the provincial capital of Maryland and was renamed Annapolis, after Princess Anne, who later became Queen Anne.

It soon began to thrive as the major seaport on the Chesapeake, chiefly from tobacco trade with Britain and the Caribbean. Some of the showplace townhouses that still stand were built by the early plantation owners. It is also the site of the first library and theater in the colonies.

From November 1783 to August 1784, Annapolis served as peacetime capital of the United States. The present Maryland State House was the seat of government for the Continental Congress, making Annapolis the oldest state capital in continuous use. In this House, George Washington resigned his commission as commander in chief and the Treaty of Paris was signed. The treaty ended the American Revolution, signaling British recognition of United States independence and providing the name for one of the town's most celebrated latter-day restaurants. As a further concession to that treaty, Annapolis is the only United States city officially to celebrate Bastille Day (July 14).

In the following two centuries, Annapolis gradually lost commercial shipping to Baltimore; however, the city was the center of naval activity during the War of 1812. A nine-acre tract along the Severn River was selected in 1845 as the site for the naval academy. During the Civil War, Union forces used the academy grounds and St. Johns College as a hospital. In 1965, the National Park Service designated the entire downtown area a National Historic District.

The heart of Annapolis is its extensively renovated harbor area—an assortment of boats, restaurants, shops and parking meters. More than half the buildings facing the harbor date from the eighteenth and nineteenth centuries. Bisecting the waterfront is a long, narrow basin containing boat slips for rent by the hour or by the day. During the boating season, there's seldom an empty berth, even on weekdays, so most boats anchor for free just off the docks and come ashore either in their own small dinghies or by summoning one of the two water taxis that ply the harbor.

You don't need to own a boat to take the *Ginny* or *Buck Boat* water taxis. They operate from the City Dock and for $1 a head will ferry you anywhere in the area. A good destination: directly across the harbor to Eastport, which has its own assortment of shops, restaurants and boatyards. A more organized cruise of the harbor may be had for $5 ($3 for children under 12) in one of the four boats that leave every half hour from the City Dock. Longer cruises to St. Michael's and other Bay locations are available as well from Chesapeake Marine Tours (301-268-7600).

Sightseeing cruises operate from the City Dock during the summer. For $5 ($3 for children), you can take a half-hour cruise around the harbor in a double-decked boat that offers a snack bar selling hot sandwiches and alcoholic beverages. The boat weaves in and out among anchored craft, passes the Naval Academy, takes a short trip up the Severn River, then pokes its nose briefly into the Bay—within sight of the impressive, five-mile-long Bay Bridge and, closer by, the network of tall red-and-white radio antennas that link the Pentagon with its fleet of nuclear submarines in the Atlantic. You can get great photographs from the open upper deck.

In July and August, the Naval Academy presents free concerts every Tuesday night. The dock area also hosts an art festival in June and the nation's largest in-the-water sailboat show each October. The boat show is an institution, judging from the crowds that turn out. For a $7.50 admission fee, you can explore hundreds of brand new sailboats, inside and out. Permanent docks are augumented by floating wooden ones that deck over much of the harbor.

Annapolis is also a walker's delight. Everything worth seeing is within six blocks of the State House. In the downtown historic district, streets radiate from two circles: State Circle around the State House and Church Circle at St. Anne's Episcopal Church. Here are two distinct shopping streets—Main Street, a spoke that leads from Church Circle to the waterfront, and brick-paved Maryland Avenue, which leads from State Circle east to the Naval Academy. You should wear comfortable shoes. Those brick sidewalks can be murder on feet. And who knows? An opportunity might arise—if the wind is up—to put aside shopping for a brisk sail around the harbor.

PLACES OF INTEREST

Annapolis Sailing School
601 Sixth St.,
Annapolis
• (301) 267-7205

Two-hour "Try Sailing Adventure" courses are the attraction here. and are offered daily. If you're going to spend time in Annapolis, you should consider doing at least some of it under sail. This is the quickest way to put you behind the tiller. Call ahead for reservations.

Open for courses Sat.-Sun. at noon; Mon.-Fri. at varying times. Cost $25 for course.

Maryland State House
State Circle,
Annapolis
• (301) 974-3400

Construction began on this structure in 1772, making it the oldest state capitol in continuous legislative use. It also claims to have the largest wooden dome in the United States, made from cypress beams and wooden pegs. It served from November 1783 to August 1784 as the nation's capitol. George Washington resigned his commission in the Old Senate Chamber on December 23, 1783, and the Continental Congress met here to ratify the Treaty of Paris, which ended the Revolution. Tours take place from 11 a.m to 4 p.m.

Open daily 9 a.m.-5 p.m. Admission free.

Old Treasury Building
State Circle, next to Maryland State House, Annapolis
• (301) 267-8149

Built in 1735, this is the oldest public building in Maryland. It was restored in 1950 and now houses the Historic Annapolis Foundation, the organization that publicizes the city and also sponsors a two-hour guided walking tour. *Open Mon.-Fri. 9 a.m.-4:30 p.m. Admission free. Walking tour: adults $6, children 6-18, $3.50.*

Paca House & Gardens
186 Prince George St., Annapolis
• (301) 263-5553

William Paca was one of the few forefathers who both signed and voted for the Declaration of Independence. He was also a three-term governor of Maryland during the Revolution. This 37-room colonial mansion, built from 1763 to 1765, was used as a hotel in the early 1900s. Currently, it serves as a conference center for the State Department and as an occasional guest house for foreign visitors. Next door is a fastidiously manicured two-acre garden .
Open Tues.-Sat. 10 a.m.-4 p.m., Sun. noon-4:30 p.m. Adults $5, children ages 6-18, $3.

St. Johns College
College Ave., between St. John's & King George Sts., Annapolis
• (301) 263-2371

When it opened in 1696, it was one of the first public schools in America. The 400-year-old tulip tree on the lawn is purportedly where a peace treaty was signed in 1652 with the Native Americans. During the Civil War, it was used by Union forces as a hospital.
Open (grounds) daily. Admission free.

U.S. Naval Academy
Visitor's Gate, King George St., Annapolis
• (301) 263-6933

The academy, located between the Severn River and downtown, was founded in 1845. Its attractions include the world's largest dormitory, Bancroft Hall, which houses all 4,400 midshipmen; the foremast of the battleship *Maine*, blown up in Havana Harbor in 1898; and the crypt containing the remains of naval hero John Paul ("I have not yet begun to fight") Jones. You can drive or stroll through "The Yard." Enter Gate 1 at the foot of King George Street. The visitor information center is in Ricketts Hall. Guided walking tours leave promptly every half hour from March through November. Commissioning week, the third week in May, offers parades, air shows and a graduation ceremony with flying hats. The academy also houses the Naval Academy Museum, which contains John Paul Jones memorabilia, an extensive model ship exhibit and uniforms worn by famous officers. It is open Monday to Saturday from 9 a.m. to 4:30 p.m. and Sunday from 11 a.m. to 4:30 p.m. For additional museum information, call (301) 267-2108. *Tours 10 a.m.-3 p.m. on the hour (Mar. 1-May 31 & Labor day-Thanksgiving), 9:30 a.m.-4 p.m. (June 1-Labor day). Adults $3, children $1.*

Victualling Warehouse & Maritime Museum
77 Main St.,
Annapolis
• (301) 268-5576

A warehouse on this site during the Revolution stored "victuals," including flour, molasses, salt pork in barrels and other supplies. Now a mini-museum, its displays include views of the waterfront as it appeared over a period of three centuries—the most impressive of which is a three-dimensional model of the dock area in the mid-1700s, when Annapolis was the principal seaport on the Chesapeake. *Open daily 11 a.m.-4:30 p.m. Admission free.*

RESTAURANTS

Café Normandie
195 Main St.,
Annapolis
• (301) 263-3382
FRENCH

12/20

As you walk down Main street in Annapolis, there are innumerable restaurants that you can peek into. This is one you should eat in. It is small, as snug as a ship's galley or a European café, after which it is modeled. The one room seats 35 at most, and that with diners who aren't afraid to rub against each other's knees. What it lacks in space, it provides in flavor, such as the simple, yet strong, soups: a hot crab or a refreshingly balanced Vichyssoise. The entrée of choice is a crêpe. The flagship crêpe, the Annapolis, comes with lobster sauce, shrimp, scallops and mushrooms. The ratatouille crêpe seems to contain every vegetable in the garden, and the chicken-and-mushroom crêpe is an artful example of the basics. There are also a few pasta and seafood dishes, and a portion of quiche that is downright manly. The wine list is short, but the staff is willing to pop open a bottle of Muscadet, just so that you can have one glass. Best bets for dessert are the chocolate or fruit crêpes. The waiters seem to operate as a team; the automatic 15-percent service charge is well earned. Breakfast is also served here. About $60 for two, for dinner with wine. *Open Sun.-Thurs. 8 a.m.-10 p.m., Fri.-Sat. 8 a.m.-10:30 a.m. & 5 p.m.-10 p.m. Cards: AE, MC, V.*

Jimmy Cantler's Riverside Inn
458 Forest Beach Rd.,
Annapolis
• (301) 757-1311
SEAFOOD

10/20

This out-of-the-way crab house once primarily served boaters who pulled in needing food and fuel. Now, even Naval Academy midshipmen, who are supposed to be locked in study halls devoting themselves to the intricacies of the slide rule, have found their way to Cantler's to devote themselves to the pleasures of eating hard crabs. The popularity seems to have had little effect on Cantler's, other than to spruce up the tables on the outdoor deck and to add a satellite dish to boost the reception of the bar TV. We stick to the crabs and fried fish. About $50 for dinner for two, with beer. *Open Mon.-Fri. 11 a.m.-11 p.m., Sat.-Sun. 11 a.m.-midnight. Cards: AE, MC, V.*

Conrad's

849 Baltimore-Annapolis
Blvd.,
Severna Park
• (301) 544-3328
AMERICAN

11/20

Conrad's is a quiet spot, away from the waterside activity of downtown Annapolis. When we spotted it, on a winding country road about twenty minutes north of Annapolis, it looked like somebody's suburban home. It is, in a way. Conrad Lindley is the chef and proprietor of the small, spare restaurant. His training at New York's Culinary Institute of America shows in his dishes: veal paired with shiitake mushrooms, steamed fresh fish, and fresh vegetables, even in the cold months. The breads and spicy honey mustard are must-eats. Desserts are uneven. The serving staff is sometimes overwhelmed. About $70 for dinner for two, with wine.

Open Tues.-Sat. 5.30 p.m.-10 p.m. Cards: AE, MC, V.

O'Leary's Seafood

310 3rd St.,
Annapolis
• (301) 263-0884
SEAFOOD

12/20

Since Annapolis is known as a port city, we like to eat seafood when we are in town. A surefire spot for fish is O'Leary's, in the Eastport section of town. The best way to get there is to take the water taxi across Spa Creek from the Annapolis City Dock. Automobile traffic is an unmitigated mess in Annapolis, and besides, we think it appropriate to arrive at a seafood restaurant via boat. We also like the fact that O'Leary's operates a fresh-fish market as well, just down the quay from the restaurant. This is a pink-tablecloth restaurant, with the most notable decoration being a large wooden carving of, what else, a fish. The menu refers to 30 varieties of fish, counting eel, but chalkboards around the restaurant give an accurate account of the daily fish specials. Moreover, we get to choose which way we want our fish cooked—grilled, poached, sautéed or baked. Start with a smoked bluefish appetizer. It is an excellent treatment of a local fish that—aside from this dish—is more fun to catch than to eat. The tomato crab bisque is also recommended. The crabcake is sautéed in sweet butter and its big lumps are held together more by will power than binder, which is how it should be. Swordfish and even the often overused redfish are cooked correctly. In short, the fish tastes like fish. O'Leary's has two chicken dishes and a mesquite grilled steak. The desserts are homemade; the wine list leans toward California; and the correct after-dinner behavior is to float around the harbor, again, in the water taxi. About $80 for dinner for two, with wine.

Open Sun.-Thurs. 5. p.m.-10 p.m., Fri.-Sat. 5 p.m.-11 p.m. Cards: AE, V, MC.

QUICK BITES

Cantina Mama Lucia
150 H. Jennifer Rd.,
Annapolis
• (301) 266-1666

Good Italian food is featured here, in an unconventional setting. It is located in a shopping center and has a fast-food style of service. This is authentic fare—such as homemade manicotti and lasagne—served on plates, not cardboard. We walk up to the counter, order pasta and mussels marinara, scoop up a glass of Italian wine, and wait for our order to be called. Around us are tables with groups of men and women speaking Italian. The food arrives, fragrant, hot, served with crusty bread. We are impressed. We are also told to try the pizza next time.
Open Mon-Sat. 11 a.m.-10 p.m., Sun. 11 a.m.-9 p.m. No cards.

Chick and Ruth's Delly
165 Main St.,
Annapolis
• (301) 269-6737

While eateries come and go like the tide in Annapolis, Chick and Ruth's is the town's Rock of Gibraltar. It is a Main Street delicatessen where residents go to grab a thick sandwich and the latest news. Reporters frequent it because they can always get a quote there, either from those hard-to-find actual Annapolis residents, or from the government legislators and staffers who wander over from the nearby state office-buildings. The deli even names sandwiches after politicians. The sandwiches are generous, which is more than can be said of their namesakes. We love the toasted bagels.
Open daily 24 hours. No cards.

Market House
City Dock,
Annapolis
• No phone

Whenever we are in a hurry and want to slurp some raw oysters, or grab a sandwich, we stop at the market in downtown Annapolis. There has been a market on this site since 1784; the present one dates from 1950. It is an indoor market housing a variety of retail businesses—a fish market, a raw-seafood bar (serving oysters, shrimp and the like), a delicatessen, a fruit-and-vegetable store, a bakery, a fried-chicken stand, a cheese outlet, a sandwich bar and a yogurt shop. On nice days, we carry lunch outside to the small park at the head of the boat channel. There, we sit on one of the benches, and watch the promenade of boats and boaters vying for attention.
Open Mon. & Wed.-Sat. 9 a.m.-6 p.m., Sun. 10 a.m.-6 p.m.

Truffles
50 West St.,
Annapolis
• (301) 626-1038

As firm believers in the philosophy of eating a light lunch and heavy dessert, we feel at home at Truffles. There are the obligatory salads, pastas and quiches, but the real reason we come here is for the desserts, plural: the carrot cake, the nut cake, the Derby pie. These we eat by the forkful, with good coffee or Champagne by the glass. The dessert plate, a sampling of five desserts for $8.75, is our usual choice. This is an excellent place to reward yourself after hours of historic sightseeing.

Open Mon.-Wed. 11 a.m.-4 p.m., Thurs. 11 a.m.-9 p.m., Fri.-Sat. 11 a.m.-10 p.m., Sun. 10 a.m.-2 p.m. Cards: MC, V.

SHOPS

Annapolis Country Store
53 Maryland Ave., Annapolis
• (301) 269-6773

One of those cluttered, comfortable old emporiums that seems as if it once must have had a little of everything, this place now carries mostly candles, wicker baskets and fancy soaps. The Country Store boasts that it is the oldest and largest wicker outlet in Maryland. Lots of pottery, too, along with fancy soaps.

Open Mon.-Sat. 10 a.m.-6 p.m., Sun. noon-5 p.m.

Easy Street
8 Francis St., Annapolis
• (301) 263-5556

Easy Street is an extensive and often whimsical collection of feather masks, elaborate kaleidoscopes and porcelain figurines, many of delicately crafted animals. You'll find it an amusing place to browse.

Open daily 10 a.m.-6 p.m. (hours may vary).

Fawcett's
110 Compromise St., Annapolis
• (301) 267-8681

This waterfront chandlery offers a full line of boating supplies and boat clothes and footwear, so you can look like a sailor even if you don't know a jib from a jig. It calls itself the "Tiffany's of Annapolis," but we're not sure exactly why—unless it applies to the prices on some of the designer sailing togs. Despite the name of the street (isn't it wonderful?), there's no compromising here. It's full-price city. Still, Fawcett's is crammed with interesting boating gear, from teak and brass goodies to a well-stocked book area, full of nautical lore.

Open Mon-Sat. 8:30 a.m.-5:30 p.m., Sun. 11 a.m.-4 p.m.

Mills Wine & Spirit Market
87 Main St., Annapolis
• (301) 263-2888

Yes, you can buy booze in Maryland on Sundays. At Mills, there is an excellent, wide selection of wines, from $2 bottles to splendid French Bordeaux in the $100-a-bottle range. There are crates and crates, with much of the best stuff in a separate back room. The staff is knowledgeable about wine, and helpful.

Open Mon.-Thurs. 9 a.m.-7 p.m, Fri. 9 a.m.-7:30 p.m., Sat. 8:30 a.m.-7:30 p.m., Sun. 11 a.m.-5 p.m.

Pendragon Gallery
155 Main St.,
Annapolis
• (301) 263-4277

This is a fantasy shop, starring art about witches, dragons, wizards, giants, ogres and other magical and frightening beasts. Painted chests, offbeat oil paintings, carvings and originals of book covers are also featured.
Open Mon.-Sat. 10 a.m.-5:30 p.m., Sun. noon-5:30 p.m.

The Ship & Soldier Shop
55 Maryland Ave.,
Annapolis
• (301) 268-1141

Toy soldiers and large-scale electric trains, boat models, old-fashioned heavyweight metal toys for children, grown-up and otherwise, are featured here.
Open Mon.-Sat. 10 a.m.-5:30 p.m., Sun. noon-5:30 p.m.

BALTIMORE

If Washington, with all its sights and intensity, is getting to be a little too much, you might consider a short excursion down the Baltimore–Washington Parkway to Baltimore, the city of Babe Ruth, H. L. Mencken, clipper ships and steamed crabs. Developed around a natural harbor on the Chesapeake Bay, Baltimore grew prosperous as a port of trade, served as a key point between North and South during the Civil War and, more recently, rescued itself from the effects of urban decay partly by turning its inner harbor into a nationally known showplace.

A mere 40 miles from Washington, Baltimore is an easy 60-minute drive or a pleasant 40-minute train ride (you have just enough time to read a newspaper) from the District. Drivers should use the Baltimore–Washington Parkway, a tree-lined highway, where no heavy trucks are allowed. The Amtrak option leaves from Union Station in Washington and arrives at Pennsylvania Station in Baltimore, a quick cab or bus ride from the Inner Harbor. Trains leave every hour, with the one-way fare for the trip $13.50 and the round-trip fare $20.50.

Baltimore is a real city, with plenty of ethnic diversity and a blue-collar heart. Babe Ruth swatted home runs here; columnist Mencken penned his acid commentaries here; jazz singer Billie Holiday was born here; Edgar Allan Poe wrote poetry here; and Francis Scott Key was inspired to write the national anthem while watching the British attempt to bomb the city.

Founded in 1729 as Baltimore Town, the city soon turned its attentions from growing tobacco and shipping it on a small-scale basis, to milling and exporting flour on a grand scale. Baltimore prospered as a port and quickly became a successful shipbuilding town. Much of its reputation stemmed from the successes of the "Baltimore clipper," a sleek vessel that slipped through blockades, outran gunboats and kept a profitable overseas trade going even in times of war.

During the Revolutionary War, the Baltimore clippers extracted a substantial toll from the British, capturing vessels and seizing treasures. The losses were never forgotten, and during the War of 1812, Britain made Baltimore a special target for destruction.

The British decided to blockade the Atlantic Coast and teach the former colonies a lesson about who ruled the seas. One fleet was stationed in the Chesapeake Bay to watch over the unruly Baltimoreans, while British troops marched toward Washington.

On September 11, 1814, the British fleet moved to the entrance of Baltimore Harbor, but the city was ready for the attack. The British began firing on Fort McHenry, but were too far out in the bay to hit anything. They fired all night, making a lot of noise and providing quite a fireworks display, but the only thing of importance that they struck was a poetic chord in Francis Scott Key. He was so moved by the sight of the bombs bursting in air and the American flag atop Fort McHenry, that he wrote a poem, "The Star-Spangled Banner." Soon, it was put to the tune of a drinking song, and it became the national anthem in 1931.

Baltimore was friend and financier to many Southern plantation owners, so when the Civil War broke out, the city had strong Southern sympathies despite its Northern location. This caused great concern to the Union Army, and to make sure the city stayed in line, Federal troops occupied Federal Hill overlooking the city and kept cannons pointed at the heart of Baltimore throughout the war. Federal Hill, at Warren Avenue and Key Highway, offers the best free view of the harbor now, and is a great picnic place.

When the war ended, the merchants of Baltimore played an important role in getting the South back on its feet economically. Newly freed Southern slaves migrated to Baltimore by the thousands in search of work in the North.

Disaster struck the business district in 1904, when fire devastated the downtown area, but a new city emerged from the ashes.

Baltimore fell victim to the same urban rioting in 1968 that struck many major cities, and the riots, coupled with white flight to the suburbs, posed the biggest challenge to the city since Revolutionary War days. For its solution, once again, Baltimore turned to its greatest resource—the harbor—as the inspiration that would revitalize downtown. Baltimore's now-famous Harborplace, a glistening gem on the waterfront, is the city's major tourist attraction. More than 130 restaurants, shops, food stands and market stalls can be found in two stunning glass pavilions on the harbor. Outside, long, broad walkways are perfect for strolling and watching the ships that range from paddle boats and yachts to an eighteenth-century frigate.

Also nearby is another treat, the Lexington Market. A Baltimore landmark, it celebrated its 200th birthday in 1982, and is a favorite of locals as well as tourists. You can shop for produce and fish here, stop at Faidley's Raw Bar for oysters and beer or eat your way happily through food stalls. Located at Lexington and Paca streets in downtown Baltimore, the market is so popular that some people come to Baltimore just to visit it.

In the neighborhoods, Baltimore remains a town of row houses, small shops and great ethnic diversity. Among the ethnic neighborhoods that remain well defined are Little Italy and the Polish section. The ethnic heritage is clearly reflected in the food you can find in local restaurants. Little Italy, just east of the Inner Harbor, is full of small restaurants and big treats. One of the city's most popular crab houses, Obrycki's, is located further east in Fells Point, along with an assortment of bars and restaurants that are not fancy but are full of character.

Baltimore has an excellent bus system ($1), but unless you're at the train station or on Charles Street, the main drag through downtown, it may be hard to find a cab. If you're only traveling downtown and around the harbor, you might try the 25-cent trolley. If you're driving, there are metered parking areas around the harbor, and street parking downtown except during rush hours.

Several companies run tours of the city. Good ones are About Town Tours (301-592-7770), Baltimore Good Time Tours (301-539-3330) and Baltimore Rent-a-Tour (301-653-2998). Walking tours are also conducted by the Women's Civic League and the Citizen's Planning and Housing Association. For more information, contact the Baltimore Visitors Information Center (837-4636 or 800-282-6632).

If you're a boat buff, there are great harbor tours that range from a 90-minute spin on the *Baltimore Patriot* (301-685-4288) to lunch and dinner cruises aboard the elegant *Bay Lady* and *Lady Baltimore* (301-727-3113).

Visitors to Baltimore also can see Babe Ruth's birthplace, Mencken's row house, Poe's home and burial place and Fort McHenry. Then again, you can forget all that history and head straight for the steamed crabs, harvested from the bay and served up hot and spicy. Or go directly to the ball park, where the fans are frequently as colorful and exciting as the Orioles baseball team. Whether you decide to go the historic route or opt for just plain fun, Baltimore has a lot to keep you busy.

PLACES OF INTEREST

HARBORPLACE & VICINITY

The centerpieces of the Inner Harbor development are two glass pavilions at the corner of Light and Pratt streets, just south of downtown. They are designed for dining, snacking, shopping or strolling. You can grab a quick crabcake sandwich, oysters on the half-shell or countless varieties of junk food, and enjoy your treat on the many benches indoors and outdoors. The pavilions are open Monday through Friday, from 10 a.m. to 9:30 p.m. On the weekend, Light Street and Pratt Street Pavilions are open from 10 a.m. to 8 p.m. The restaurants with separate entrances are all open later.

The National Aquarium and the World Trade Center are on the same side of the harbor as the Pratt Street Pavilion; the Maryland Science Center is on the same side as the Light Street Pavilion. The Rusty Scupper restaurant, with a great view of the water, is on the south side. Federal Hill is within walking distance—or a short trolley or water-taxi ride—across the highway and directly above the harbor.

Maryland Science Center
601 Light St.,
Baltimore
• (301) 685-2370

Operated by the Maryland Academy of Sciences, the Center features films, displays and a fine planetarium.
Open Mon.-Fri. 10 a.m.-5 p.m., Sat. 10 a.m.-6 p.m., Sun. noon-6 p.m. Adults $4.50; children under 12 $3.

Fort McHenry National Monument & Historic Shrine
E. Fort Ave. (at the end)
Baltimore
• (301) 962-4299

Fort McHenry is at the foot of East Fort Avenue in South Baltimore, a short drive from Harborplace. This is the fort that successfully defended Baltimore against the British in the War of 1812. On a boat anchored nearby, Francis Scott Key wrote the national anthem.
Open daily 8 a.m.-5 p.m. (winter), 9 a.m.-6 p.m. (summer). Adults ages 17-61 $1; others free.

National Aquarium
501 E. Pratt St.,
Baltimore
• (301) 576-3800

This high-rise aquarium took the title "national" away from a little aquarium in Washington because Baltimore's exhibit is such a superior attraction. Its five-story marine display tank boasts more than 5,000 creatures, including hammerhead sharks, manta rays and giant turtles.
Open Mon.-Thurs. 9 a.m.-5 p.m., Fri.-Sun. 9 a.m.-8 p.m. (mid-May to mid-Sept.); Mon.-Thurs. 10 a.m.-5 p.m., Fri. 10 a.m.-8 p.m., Sat.-Sun. 10 a.m.-5 p.m. (mid-Sept.–mid-May). Adults $7.75, children ages 12-18 $6, children ages 3-12 $4.75, discount for seniors, children under 3 free.

Top of the World
Baltimore World Trade Center,
Baltimore
• (301) 837-4515

This observatory on the 27th floor of the World Trade Center offers the best view of the city's skyline and the Inner Harbor activity. You'll also find exhibits on Baltimore's history and neighborhoods.
Open Mon.-Fri. 10 a.m.-4:30 p.m., Sat. 10 a.m.-6:30 p.m., Sun. 11 a.m.-5:30 p.m. (summer), Mon.-Sat. 10 a.m.-4:30 p.m., Sun. noon-4:30 p.m. (winter). Adults $2; seniors & children ages 5-15 $1; children under 5 free.

U.S. Frigate *Constellation*
Pier 1 & Pratt St.,
Baltimore
• (301) 539-1797

This restored frigate was the first ship commissioned by the U.S. Navy. It was launched from Fells Point on September 7, 1797, and served until 1945. It's moored at Harborplace; its decks are open to the public; and there's a souvenir shop and museum on the dock.
Open daily 10 a.m.-8 p.m. (June 15-Labor Day); 10 a.m.-6 p.m. (day after Labor Day-Oct. 15 & May 1-June 14); 10 a.m.-4 p.m. (Oct. 16-May 15). Adults $2.75, children ages 6-15 $1.55, children under 6 free, seniors $2, active military $1.

THE ORIOLES AND OTHER ATTRACTIONS

B & O Railroad Museum
901 W. Pratt at Poppleton St., Baltimore
• (301) 237-2387

The site of the nation's first passenger and freight train station, this museum is a must for railroad buffs. It has the most extensive collection of railroad memorabilia in the United States and the second-largest train exhibit in the world.
Open Wed.-Sun. 10 a.m.-4 p.m. Adults $4; seniors and children over 6 $3.

Baltimore Orioles
33rd St. & Ellerslie Ave., Baltimore
• (301) 243-9800

In good times and bad, the Orioles in their orange-and-black uniforms are a colorful and delightful diversion. Memorial Stadium, where the Birds hold forth, is about a fifteen-minute drive from the Harbor. There are also buses that will take you within a few blocks of the stadium. Grab a hotdog, a Polish sausage or a bag of peanuts and enjoy the game. Be forewarned—opening day tickets usually sell out well in advance. The team is scheduled to move to a new downtown stadium in 1992.
Open during baseball season. Tickets from $4.75 for general admission seating to $11 for box seats.

The H. L. Mencken House
1524 Hollins St., W. Baltimore
• (301) 396-7997

Another treat for literary types is the home where Mencken, the acid-penned critic and social commentator for *The Baltimore Sun*, lived for 70 of his 75 years.
Open Wed.-Sun. 10 a.m.-4 p.m. & by appointment. Adults $1.75, seniors $1.25, children 75 cents.

Edgar Allan Poe House
203 N. Amity St., Baltimore
• (301) 396-7932

This is the tiny house where Poe lived from 1832 to 1835, the early years of his writing career. But since morbid subjects were more to Poe's liking, you might prefer to visit his gravesite in the western burial ground of Westminster Church. The graveyard is always open, and there's a midnight tour every Halloween. Or you might wish to try to find the solution to one of the literary world's little mysteries. Every year since 1949, a mysterious stranger has left roses and a good bottle of Cognac on Poe's grave on January 19, his birthday. All the bottles of Cognac have been saved—unopened—and are on display at the Poe house.
Open Wed.-Sat. noon-3:45 p.m. (April–mid-Dec.). Adults $2; children under 12 $1.

The Babe Ruth House
216 Emory St.,
Baltimore
• (301) 727-1539

This is the twelve-foot-wide row house where George Herman Ruth, the legendary "sultan of swat," was born on February 6, 1895. In addition, this house is the home of the Maryland Baseball Hall of Fame. There are displays documenting Babe Ruth's life, including pictures of him playing ball at the tender age of 3, plus lots of Orioles memorabilia.

Apr.-Oct:. open daily 10 a.m.-5 p.m.; Nov.-Mar.: open daily 10 a.m.-4 p.m. Adults $3, seniors $2, children $1.50.

RESTAURANTS

L'Auberge
505 S. Broadway St.,
Baltimore
• (301) 732-1151
FRENCH

12/20

Tucked in among some unlikely neighbors—a dimestore, a paint shop, an exotic-underwear store—this warm little restaurant is a find. L'Auberge is often compared to a French country inn, as its name indicates, and the comparison holds (if you overlook the underwear shop). We walk in past the kitchen, are greeted by the proprietor's wife, and sit at a linen-covered table. We have the pâté, the soup, the snails, the lamb or the chateaubriand. All the while, we're eyeing the sideboard that is groaning with homemade genoise and fruit tarts. While there are two dining rooms, the downstairs is the better. When the crowds are slack, this is a charming, secretive spot. However, when the restaurant fills, we can unwittingly share in the conversation, and sometimes the cigarette smoke, of nearby diners. About $80 for dinner for two person, plus wine.

Open Mon.-Thurs. 5:30 p.m.-10 p.m.; Fri.-Sat. 5:30 p.m.-11 p.m. Cards: AE, MC, V.

Dalesio's
829 Eastern Ave.,
Baltimore
• (301) 539-1965
ITALIAN

12/20

A relatively new kid in Baltimore's Little Italy neighborhood, Dalesio's does things differently. Surrounded by restaurants known for huge portions and seas of sauce, Dalesio's stresses herbs and fresh vegetables. The fetuccine is whole-wheat, the tuna grilled, the tomatoes sun-dried. Some dishes have their fat content and calorie count printed on the menu. The restaurant calls itself "spa Italian"; others think the food hails more from Venice, California than Venice, Italy. But whatever its origin, we find food here to have clean and satisfying flavors. The wine list is a functional selection of Italian and Califorian wines, with a few correct bows to Maryland vineyards. The desserts worth noting are the old-style, cream-and-pastry offerings, imported from a nearby neighborhood bakery. About $70 for dinner for two, with wine.

Gunning's

3901 S. Hanover St.,
Baltimore
• (301) 354-0085
SEAFOOD

11/20

Baltimore's quintessential crab house, Gunning's is a corner bar and restaurant, a fixture in the South Baltimore neighborhood about a five-minute cab ride from downtown. Gunning's still cooks its hard-shell crabs the old-fashioned way, steaming them over pots of boiling water flavored with beer. The spicy crabs are served nightly at dinner and are a must for anyone who wants to eat like a local. Enjoying hard crabs requires a willingness to eat with your fingers, and some knowledge of crab-ordering lingo. When the waitress says "the crabs are running twenty, twenty-four and twenty-eight," it means that the price ranges from $20 a dozen for smaller crabs to $28 a dozen for jumbos. Since freeing the crab meat from the shell entails a fair amount of effort, buying bigger crabs is the correct labor-saving approach. If you want crab meat without all that work, then Gunning's crabcake, acclaimed in *Esquire* magazine, is the answer. Our favorite is the soft-crab sandwich: an entire fried crab served on toast. For dessert, try the deep-fried green pepper rings sprinkled with powdered sugar. About $50 for dinner for two, with beer.
Open daily 11 a.m.-10 p.m. Cards: AE, MC, V.

Hampton's

Harbor Court Hotel,
550 Light St.,
Baltimore
• (301) 234-0550
AMERICAN

Arguably the city's best and most expensive restaurant, Hampton's features New American cuisine at new-age prices (blackened buffalo at $32, for example). Hampton's is a sumptuous, 74-seat restaurant in a new harborside hotel that caters to the barons and baronesses of traveling America. The oversize chairs are made for diners to settle in for a two- or three-hour meal. A typical appetizer is black bass wrapped in potatoes. The potatoes are sliced thin, wrapped around a fillet of bass, then baked quickly and served in a citron sauce with passionfruit. The entrées are equally labor-intensive—duck stuffed with venison and mushrooms or smoked quail in a sage glaze. The steak tournedos topped with blue-cheese croutons are the result of the chef's experimentation on his backyard grill. The wine list of some 200 names is remarkable; the wine steward delights in steering diners to wines they haven't heard of before. There is also a wide selection of ports to cap off the evening, and the desserts reflect the pastry chef's belief that chocolate should be decadent and bittersweet. This is not simple food, and a slight misstep can take the edge off what is supposed to be perfection. When Hampton's is on—and its batting average is high—it makes for an impressive evening. About $150 for dinner for two, plus wine.
Open Tues.-Sat. 5:30 p.m.-11 p.m., Sun. 10 a.m.-3 p.m. All major cards.

Maison Marconi

106 W. Saratoga St.,
Baltimore
• (301) 727-9522
SEAFOOD

12/20

Not only does Marconi's look like the kind of restaurant H. L. Mencken frequented, it seems likely that he ordered from the same menu. This place is vintage Baltimore, both in architecture and attitude. Located in a downtown rowhouse, it has white tablecloths, waiters in tuxedos, uneven tile floors, faded wallpaper and excellent, straightforward food. The only thing the kitchen freezes is the ice cream. Aficionados feast on the calf's liver; there is sole and lobster cardinal; and in the summer, sautéed soft crab. In the months, when the oysters are plump, oysters Pauline are served on Fridays. These are oysters in a lobster and Mornay sauce, flavored with Parmesan cheese and baked and served in the oyster shells. It is worth planning your trip around. The creamed spinach could pass for dessert; we always order the sundae, which employs a heavenly, warm, homemade chocolate sauce. Marconi's is comfortably set in its ways, and one of its ways is that it closes early, around 8 p.m. Another is that it doesn't take reservations, and doesn't have a bar. Mencken dined here, and according to the restaurant's habituées, liked the lamb chops. Dinner for two, with wine, costs $80.
Open Tues.-Sat. noon-3 p.m. & 5 p.m.-8 p.m. Cards: MC, V.

Milton Inn

14833 York Rd.,
Sparks
• (301) 771-4366
FRENCH

Long known as an exceptionally romantic place with so-so food, the Milton Inn has recently brought the dining up to the level of its scenery. An old fieldstone mansion that once served as a boy's school, training among others John Wilkes Booth, the Inn has since attracted a better class of people. It is nestled among the tall trees and rolling fields of northern Baltimore County where, when people ask if you "ride," they mean horses, not bicycles. The food is as upper-crust as some of the old families. Caviar-stuffed potatoes and morel, shiitake and chanterelle mushrooms are found everywhere: in soups, on salads, flavoring veal. The dish we die for is the soft-shell crabs. The crabs are sautéed, then served in a whole-grain mustard sauce, which is several months in the making. Every spring, when the first local soft-shell crabs arrive from the Chesapeake Bay, we make it a point to greet them, fork in hand, at the Milton Inn. The desserts are made on the premises and we have never been able to say no to the chocolate-walnut cake with caramel topping. It's a 30-minute drive from downtown, and worth the trip. Dinner for two is $130, with wine.
Open Mon.-Thurs. 11:30 a.m.-2:30 p.m. & 5:30 p.m.-9 p.m., Fri.-Sat. 5:30 p.m.-9:30 p.m., Sun. 5 p.m.-8 p.m. All major cards.

Obrycki's
1727 Pratt St.,
Baltimore
• (301) 732-6399
SEAFOOD

10/20

An institution among Baltimore crab houses, Obrycki's stayed in its old East Baltimore neighborhood, but recently moved down the street from its former rowhouse setting into more spacious, if modern, digs. Obviously, we go there for the steamed crabs, but the steamed shrimp is not to be overlooked. The deviled crab, a spicy version of the crabcake, is our favorite. About $50 for dinner for two, with beer. Closes during winter months
April-Nov.: open Mon.-Fri. 11:30 a.m.-11 p.m., Sat. 4 p.m.-11 p.m., Sun. 4 p.m.-9:30 p.m. Sept.-Nov.: open Mon.-Fri. 11:30 a.m.-10 p.m., Sat. 4 p.m.-11 p.m., Sun. 4 p.m.-9:30 p.m. All major cards.

The Prime Rib
1101 N. Calvert St.,
Baltimore
• (301) 539-1804
STEAKHOUSE

12/20

The Prime Rib has the best piece of beef in the city. The entrance to the restaurant is surprising: a ramp around the corner from a downtown apartment building. But once inside, you are awash in elegant darkness. Like a little black dress, this restaurant is tasteful, never extreme. The obligatory appetizer is the fried potato skins, which the restaurant claims to have invented. For entrées, there is one preferred choice, the plate-covering hunk of prime rib. All the beef is aged, Midwestern, grain-fed and cooked to order. The lamb dishes, like the lamb ribs with Cajun spices, are very good, in part because this restaurant respects the taste of meat. The seafood is handled similarly, no daring-do, just respectable flavors. Desserts, sadly, are not up to the rest of the meal. One of the nicest touches of the Prime Rib is the pianist. One of the drawbacks is that it, like most Baltimore restaurants, doesn't have separate smoking and nonsmoking sections. About $130 for dinner for two, with wine
Open Mon.-Sat. 5 p.m.-midnight, Sun. 5 p.m.-11 p.m. All major cards.

Tio Pepe
10 E. Franklin St.,
Baltimore
• (301) 539-4675
SPANISH

13/20

Every serious diner in Baltimore has an opinion about Tio's. Some swear by it, some at it. Let's start with the drawbacks. Service can be cool; getting a seat can be very difficult, especially on weekends. Some say it is noisy. We have heard all this, and experienced some of it. We still like Tio's—a lot. Instead of a noisy basement, we see white walls, candlelight and think of it as a festive, Spanish treasure cave. Moreover, we like the food. The shrimp, swimming in garlic, arrives, sizzling, minutes after it is ordered. The crab-meat-in-champagne-sauce appetizer is perfect, as is the red snapper with clams and mussels, again laced with garlic. The roast suckling pig, served with earthy black beans, is so popular that often the restaurant runs out of it.

To guard against this, get there early on a Sunday night. Don't miss the extensive list of Spanish wines, or the pine-nut cake. About $100 for dinner for two, with wine. *Open Mon.-Thurs. 11:30 a.m.-2:30 p.m. & 5 p.m.-10.30 p.m., Fri. 11:30 a.m.-2:30 p.m. & 5 p.m.-11:30 p.m., Sat. 5 p.m.-11:30 p.m., Sun. 4 p.m.-10:30 p.m. Cards: AE, MC, V.*

QUICK BITES

The Crazy Carrot
Village of Cross Keys,
5100 Falls Rd.,
Baltimore
• (301) 435-1435

The Crazy Carrot is a natural food grocery with a counter in the back. Blessed both with a good cook and a good location, it sits in a pleasant upscale mix of shops and condominiums. The vegetable soup is a meal and garden in itself, the muffins substantial, the chicken free-range, the carrot cake too good to be healthy. Even the catsup is "natural." This is an excellent place for breakfast or lunch. About $20 for two, with juice.
Open Mon.-Fri. 9 a.m.-8 p.m., Sat. 9 a.m-6 p.m. Cards: AE, MC, V.

JaFe
Brookshire Hotel,
120 E. Lombard St.,
Baltimore
• (301) 727-0062

East meets West and they get along, even if the pairing is not always perfect. We order the cucumber and miso soups, the fried shrimp in pastry triangles, the grilled salmon and the California-roll sushi. For desserts, we look to the West for profiteroles with pistachio ice cream, and fruit tarts. Located on the the tenth floor of the hotel, the restaurant has a pleasant, but endangered, view of the Baltimore harbor. (Across the street, construction is beginning on a taller office building.) In true Eastern style, future diners will have to look inward, rather than outward. About $70 for dinner for two, with wine.
Open Mon.-Thurs. 11:30 a.m-2:30 p.m. & 5:30 p.m.-10:30 p.m., Fri. 11:30 a.m.-2:30 p.m. & 5:30 p.m.-11 p.m., Sat. 5:30 p.m.-11 p.m., Sun. 5:30 p.m.-10 p.m. All major cards.

Sisson's
36 E.Cross St.,
Baltimore
• (301) 539-2093

In addition to being a good Cajun restaurant and a friendly bar, Sisson's recently added the distinction of being the first pub in Baltimore to brew its own beer. The kettles are right next to the new dining room, and here the Sisson family brews its own dark and light ales and porter; all are smooth and well made. Sisson's is right across the street from the Cross Street Market, the city's best indoor market. The place is small, so reservations are recommended for weekend dining. About $50 for dinner for two, with beer.
Open Mon.-Fri. 11:30-3 p.m & 5 p.m.-11 p.m., Sat.-Sun. 5 p.m.-11 p.m. Cards: MC, V.

Women's Industrial Exchange
333 N. Charles St.,
Baltimore
• (301) 685-4388

This is the kind of place where you can still get eggs over easy, homemade biscuits and a sliced-chicken sandwich with lettuce and mayonnaise. Little old ladies are fond of this place, and so do downtown moguls hungry for a meal like Mom used to make. Be sure to stop at the gift shop, where the items on sale are handmade, and not by the hands of young urban professionals. Actress Ruth Gordon likes it so much, she has her own favorite waitress.
Open Mon.-Fri. 7 a.m.-2:30 p.m. No cards.

PLEASANT DRIVES

BEYOND MOUNT VERNON

Remnants of colonial life worth visiting dot the northern Virginia countryside. Close at hand, and historically related to George Washington, are three edifices worth a day trip.

Gunston Hall
4 miles E. of U.S. 1 on
Gunston Rd.
• (703) 550-9220

Plain on the outside and elegant within, this was originally the house of George Mason, who wrote, among other things, the Declaration of Independence. He also had pretty good taste, picking architect William Buckland to design this Georgian country seat. A superb stand of boxwood is at the rear.
Open daily 9:30 a.m.-5 p.m. (last full tour 4 p.m.). Adults $3; seniors $2.50; children ages 6-15 $1.

Pohick Church
U.S. 1, 12 miles south of
Alexandria, Va.
• (703) 339-6572

A quintessential Episcopal church from the colonial period (built 1769-1774), with liturgical practices as rectilinear as the design (by Washington himself, apparently a bit of admiring plagiarism from James Wren's Christ Church in Alexandria, Virginia). Washington may have slept here, say, during a soporific sermon in the summer, but he definitely surveyed the site and was on the vestry.
Open daily 9 a.m.-4 p.m. Admission free.

Woodlawn Plantation

U.S. 1, 7.8 miles south of Alexandria, Va., or 3 miles west of Mt. Vernon, Va., where the George Washington Pkwy. dead-ends into U.S. 1
• (703) 780-4000

A design of William Thornton, the original architect of the Capitol, this elegant hilltop "farmhouse" was a wedding gift of the Washingtons to General Laurence Lewis, Washington's nephew, and Nellie Custis, Martha Washington's granddaughter from her earlier marriage. The house dates from 1800 to 1805, and some of the roses that overrun the gardens in May are said to be of the same vintage. But all on the grounds is not antique: a small Frank Lloyd Wright design from the 1940s, Pope-Leighey House, was moved to an unobtrusive, but not unsympathetic, spot on the grounds in 1964.

Open daily 9:30 a.m.-4:30 p.m. (last tour at 4 p.m.). Adults $5, seniors & students $3.50.

CIVIL WAR SAMPLER

A day-long trip through the Maryland, West Virginia and Virginia countryside can provide a glimpse of what the soldiers in the American Civil War saw more than 120 years ago.

Antietam National Battlefield

Sharpsburg, Va.
From Washington, take I-270 to I-70, then Md. 65.
• (301) 432-5124

About 70 miles northwest of Washington lies one of the best-preserved Civil War battlefields, where, on September 17, 1862, more than 120,000 men of the Blue and Gray ranged over the rolling hills of Washington County in the war's bloodiest single day of fighting. President Lincoln sent a wire to General George McClellan instructing him to "destroy the rebel army," which was plunging across the nearby Potomac in a serious attempt at invasion of the North. The Southern leaders expected nothing less than victory of General Robert E. Lee. By the end of the day, more than 20,000 soldiers were dead, and the battle was a draw.

The residents of Sharpsburg, many of whose ancestors fled to caves along the Potomac during the fighting, commemorate the battle at least twice a year—near Memorial Day and around the anniversary of the battle itself. There are special programs on soldiering and related topics throughout the year.

An orientation stop at the visitor's center gives an overview of the battlefield, which can then be explored on foot or by car. Memorials to Union units in the fighting dot the landscape as well as the cemetery. Confederate dead were buried in Hagerstown, Maryland, thirteen miles north.

Park: open daily dawn to dusk. Visitor's center: open daily 8:30 a.m.-5 p.m., summer (Memorial Day-Labor Day) 8 a.m.-5 p.m. Adults $1.

Harpers Ferry National Historical Park

Harpers Ferry, W. Va.
From Sharpsburg, take Md. 34 to Boonsboro, Md.; then 67 to Potomac River; follow signs briefly through Va. into W. Va. and the park.
• (304) 535-6371

A finger of land at the confluence of the Potomac and Shenandoah rivers seemed destined to play a pivotal role in a conflict between North and South. Even before the Civil War began, this dramatic setting was the scene of an incident that galvanized both the fears of the slave-holding South and the determination of the abolition-minded North. On October 16, 1859, John Brown, with a murderous raid on Southern settlers in Missouri under his belt, attacked the Federal arsenal at Harpers Ferry. He intended to use the weapons he would seize to arm a slave rebellion. Instead, he was captured by Federal troops—led, ironically, by Robert E. Lee—convicted, tried and hanged before the year was out. Brown was accompanied on his exploit by fewer than two dozen raiders, ten of whom were killed, including two of his sons. Early in the war, Union forces abandoned Harpers Ferry (then still in Virginia, as the pro-Union state of West Virginia was not formed until later in the conflict) and burned the armory, depriving the Confederacy of a principal rifle-making site. Parts of the old town, stretching from the rivers up the bluff, have been restored or reconstructed in a fairly evocative style. The most scenic return to Washington is through the Virginia Hunt Country: Loudon Country Road 671 to Virginia 9 (through charming Leesburg) to Virginia 7, which intersects with major freeways in the Washington suburbs.

Open daily 8 a.m.-5 p.m. Admission $5 per auto; $2 per pedestrian or bike rider.

CITYLORE

CITY OF DUALITIES

Washington is a city founded on contradictions, not the least of which is the fact that in planning the American capital, Pierre L'Enfant carved its few score of square miles from the holdings of the adjoining states of Maryland and Virginia. L'Enfant envisioned the new town as a square balanced on one tip, ten miles to an edge, but political reality forced its southwestern perimeter to hug the Potomac River's meandering shoreline. Hence, L'Enfant's perfection exists only as a Washington of the mind—a useful metaphor in this or any capital, where perceptions about the seat of government depend greatly on the eye of the beholder.

Elsewhere, the Frenchman's plan survives: Washington's streets pass through four quadrants (Northeast, Northwest, Southeast and Southwest) organized in precise alpha-numerical order. So exacting was L'Enfant's eye that on streets running north—south, the shadows of streetlight poles converge in a single line at high noon, unerringly arrayed toward true north. Even though much of Washington's initial growth came toward the end of the nineteenth century, the street-naming system remained intact; with each succeeding alphabet of names is one syllable longer than the one preceeding—except where they aren't, or where they collide with another L'Enfantian device: the traffic circle. Plopped into major intersections, the good major reasoned, circles would provide an excellent means of defense against attacking armies, especially when coupled with the extra-wide roadbeds of the avenues that crisscross the city in every direction.

However, the only hordes that invade Washington do so on semifriendly terms— whether daily as commuters who ought to know better, or seasonally as tourists who've had no advance warning. In either case, the city's circles dutifully perform as L'Enfant intended, slowing the rush of traffic and throwing the unwary into confusion. No sight strikes more terror and hilarity in a native's heart than to stand by at rush hour and watch a recreational vehicle from a distant state attempting to navigate a circle. The spectacle inevitably brings to mind a whale struggling not to beach itself among the pilot fish and small sharks that make up much of workaday, auto-borne Washington.

OLD VERSUS NEW

In transplanting Europe's traditional roundabout and overwide avenue to America's capital, L'Enfant imported old-world touches that have survived into the present, sometimes standing pleasantly at odds with America's national adolescence and with the energetic development that has characterized the city's downtown since the mid-1970s. For example, along with a wide roadbed and a circle—Dupont—the stretch of Connecticut Avenue north of Farragut Square is packed edge-to-edge with samples from every era in recent architectural memory: Empire adjacent to Victorian, down the street from beaux arts, hard by art deco beside modern next to postmodern alongside neo-Victorian, pressed together in an amiable jumble that has survived—so far—because of revived interest in historic preservation.

Other districts of downtown have not been as fortunate, or as well-watched. Sometimes an unfortunate accident involving flammable substances or moonlight bulldozing takes out an old building located in a highly desirable location, particularly along the path of the still-growing Metro subway system. Sometimes, the forces of preservation intent on retaining a block's character must settle for facadectomy, in which the barest shell of an original property is retained, jacked onto pilings like the skeleton of an enormous insect, then filled in behind with new everything else, preserving the building's profile but eliminating its soul. In the acres north of Pennsylvania Avenue between 5th and 13th streets, whole blocks of historically undistinguished, but undeniably human-scale, buildings are coming down, to be replaced by monoliths and slabs and sheets of reinforced glass. In the meantime, though, the aging stock of buildings is home to a revolving cast of bohemian entrepreneurs, including those who have made the 900 block of F Street NW an impromptu nightclub zone—at least until the wreckers arrive.

But history persists amid the amputations, even in a town where the power structure can re-invent itself as often as every four years. Though not always writ large or marked well, the real Washington can lurch into view when least expected. True, the city has monuments and museums by the carload, but it also offers tiny epiphanies.

In the 1300 block of New York Avenue NW, someone pulling into a parking space beside a red-brick church and opening the passenger-side door can nearly trip over the hitching post that Abraham Lincoln used to secure his horse and carriage on Sunday mornings when attending services.

The public restroom in the shadow of the Washington Monument at 17th Street and Constitution Avenue NW began life as a lockhouse at the eastern terminus of the Chesapeake and Ohio Canal, which still stretches 190 miles along the north bank of the Potomac to Cumberland, Maryland. The canal offers an almost instant escape from the cares of living in Washington or the twentieth century, or both.

The front parlor of a row house on 13th Street NW contains a baby grand piano played by little James Edward Ellington, long before he got the nickname "Duke."

COMPANY TOWN

Like Hollywood, Washington has one main industry—some would say the *same* industry, if the illusions that coalesce in the corridors of power can be compared with those preserved on film or videotape—but the shadowplay at that industry's periphery is the stuff of which thousands of careers are made.

Entire law firms toil for decades in the vineyard fertilized by warring perspectives on a single federal rule. Trade associations spring up overnight, spurred into being by the discovery of a new technology, or by the discovery that an existing trade group doesn't quite fit the bill for a disgruntled faction of former members. Arcane newsletters and journals of every imaginable stripe—and many stripes unimaginable elsewhere—flourish, their scribes providing a guide for each of the minuscule tribes whose fates they interpret and predict. It's not unusual to find that an otherwise normal colleague includes on his résumé a stint writing a quarterly report on the progress of a single railroad bankruptcy—circulation, 50 readers, each of whom pay $3,600 a year for the news. A neighbor might reveal that the source of his income is a learned interest in the laws and regulations affecting the manufacture of pasta, or potato chips, or penny candy, or condoms or any of a myriad of products. The Reagan Revolution of the 1980s may have claimed to slim the bureaucracy, but officialdom has a way of restoring itself and branching far beyond the point to which it was earlier trimmed, no matter how fiercely the clippers are wielded.

BLACK & WHITE
& A FEW OTHER COLORS

Ah, the dualities! Official Washington consists mostly of white people, many of whom work in white buildings; but most of the city's population is black, and lives in buildings made of dark-red, native brick. With rare exception—the city's own government being the main one—the precincts in which political muscle is flexed approximate Johannesburg in the racial division of labor and responsibility.

But no matter what their color, native Washingtonians usually are as invisible to the official city as it is to them. For example, in a 1989 episode that was illuminating on several levels, President Bush punctuated a national speech on drug abuse by displaying a bag of crack cocaine. He noted that federal agents had bought the drug not a hundred yards from the White House, in the middle of Lafayette Square. But a week later, the *Washington Post* revealed that to make the buy, the agents had had to give the teenage dealer everything but a hand-drawn map. Told where the transaction would take place, he asked, "Where the ____ is that? Oh, you mean where Reagan lives?"

The quality of relations between the races varies. Washington's essential Southernness—desegregation came in the schools and public accommodations only in the mid-1950s—also has meant that blacks and whites sometimes come to know one another on terms personal enough to defuse the tensions that mark race relations in cities where a member of one race must travel miles to encounter a member of another. Some Washington neighborhoods fit either side of that equation, but in many districts—particularly those at the city's residential core—there is, if not harmony, at least wary acceptance.

A word about all that "Murder Capital, U.S.A." propaganda: relax. It's true that some neighborhoods resemble combat zones, complete with bullet nicks on the balconies and Kevlar vests on the police, and it's true that a staggering number of people are shot and killed in Washington, but the cruel truth is that the killings usually involve competitors or clients in the admittedly dangerous world of illicit drugs. Sure, if you come to the capital, you won't be in Kansas anymore, but the chances of a villain plugging Toto with an Uzi are extremely small, unless Toto goes sniffing around where he shouldn't.

But black and white aren't the only shades on Washington's spectrum. One running joke among the city's restaurant-goers is that every time there's a revolution somewhere in the world, Washingtonians acquire another stratum of excellent eating, usually along 18th Street NW in Adams Morgan, the city's polyglot entertainment zone, or in a nearby suburb. For example, the fall of South Vietnam in 1975 triggered an influx of refugees, who made Wilson Boulevard in Arlington, Virginia their home base, opening stores, restaurants, even nightclubs in their image. Today, development is pushing the Vietnamese farther out, but spring rolls and caramel beef and pho, the pungent Vietnamese noodle soup, are now staples of area cuisine. Upheavals in Ethiopia and Cambodia and Afghanistan have similarly enriched the vocabulary of Washington gourmets. Suburban strip malls that once strained to support a pizzeria now sport ethnic restaurants of nearly every persuasion.

Along with its culinary impact, the internationalization that has engulfed Washington in the past 40 years has been accompanied by a blossoming of music, theater and art. Washington has always had its share of splendid galleries and concert halls; in recent years, however, the list of places to see and hear material worth seeing and hearing has lengthened considerably.

Though race is a factor—perhaps *the* factor—in the city's politics, Washingtonians of all colors enjoy considerably less than the full perquisites of U.S. citizenship. Residents of the "capital of the free world" didn't get to vote in presidential elections until 1968, and any law passed by the city council is subject to veto by the Congress, where Washingtonians' voice is that of a single (nonvoting) delegate in the House of Representatives. Small wonder that there is an active movement on behalf of statehood, or that the message "D.C.: Last Colony" remains popular on the bumpers of resident vehicles.

THRIVING ON SURVIVAL

Washington sometimes seems to survive in spite of itself. Its elm trees by the dozen are dying of blight; its air sometimes is as brown as the tip of a well-worn spark plug; its highways and streets appear in certain seasons to be nothing more than a harvest of potholes. The scandalous reputations of its local politicians are overshadowed only by those of the solons who gather here in the House and Senate. The real estate prices are nightmarish, and the taxes concomitant.

And yet on a wet night at the center of the city, with the rain gleaming on the pillars of the buildings where the government resides, with the streetlights illuminating the statuary in the parks, with the pink crepuscular glow rising into the mist over the rooftops leading toward the Capitol, Washington seems a new city. Every time you look at it, the city seems glazed with promises that don't erase the stains, but that take on the illusory glow of a patina, rich and optimistic and waiting for the next rising of the sun.

MEMOIRS & MEMENTO MORI

Interested in further reading about the political intrigues of this great city? A rash of books has been written in the past few years, about what really went on behind the capital's stately facade during the Reagan era. Among the more recent are *For the Record,* by former Reagan chief of staff Donald Reagan; *Speaking Out,* by former Reagan press secretary Larry Speakes; *Behind the Scenes,* by Reagan's former deputy chief of staff Michael Deaver; Nancy Reagan's *My Turn;* and *What I Saw at the Revolution,* by former Reagan speechwriter Peggy Noonan.

BASICS

ARRIVING

To the uninitiated, Washington will seem, well, a tad incomplete. Freeways dwindle pathetically into ordinary two-lane streets. The ultramodern subway, just into its second decade of service, isn't quite extensive enough yet to get everyone everywhere. Taxis, although cheap and seemingly plentiful, can be as scarce as congresspeople in August, depending on the time and neighborhood. If you have the misfortune of arriving amid a rare winter storm, even a small one, nearly everything you've planned will have been canceled, closed or postponed. And, in the District itself, your hotel room probably won't have cable. Some fun.

Still, forewarned is forearmed, and if you've done your homework—with this book and a good map—even a first-time visitor can quickly adapt to Washington's idiosyncrasies. Plan ahead. Don't wait for the first gas station inside the Beltway—especially if you're not quite sure just what the Beltway is. Let's begin with that, the monster ring road called the Capital Beltway which, if you're arriving on wheels, will be your first taste of Washington's manic side.

BY BUS

The main intercity bus terminal is in an area that is hardly picturesque but nonetheless convenient enough to major hotels and other services. The Greyhound Trailways terminal is at at 1005 1st Street NE; 565-2662.

BY CAR

First, note that the Beltway is hardly ever marked as such, and instead is known as 495. This is a huge—more than 60 miles long—interstate highway that circles the city and connects Washington, through numerous spin-off highways and traffic arteries, to the surrounding suburban areas in Montgomery and Prince George's Counties, Maryland, and Fairfax County, Virginia. Just getting on 495 is not enough, unless you don't care where you're going. The Beltway has a northern part and a southern part, and although one could conceivably get where one was going by just driving on, who wants to drive 55 miles, say, if five miles will do the trick? By and large, if you are seeking destinations in Maryland, take 495 North (look for Silver Spring or Baltimore signs). Virginia locations (look for Northern Virginia or Richmond signs) will be 495 South.

The Beltway can be a terrifying experience for the uninitiated. Lanes and lanes of traffic, moving at sinfully fast speeds, leave little room for error or tolerance for a tourist driver. Or, if you make the mistake of trying to use the Beltway during morning or evening rush hours, you could end up sitting in traffic jams for hours. Study the map in advance and know which of the many roads into Washington you want to take. If you miss your exit, go to the next one. *Never, never* try to back up on this or any other major Washington traffic artery.

In addition to 495, you'll find an I-95, an I-395 and an I-295, all of which funnel commuters in and out of the District.

If you're arriving from the northeast, you'll probably want to come into Washington on New York Avenue. That's marked clearly enough, but, near downtown, it deteriorates abruptly into a quagmire of construction-related detours. Luckily, you can't help but land on one major street or another at that point. If you arrive from the north, perhaps by way of I-83 or I-270, you have a number of choices, including Connecticut Avenue, Wisconsin Avenue or 16th Street NW, any of which will get you within asking distance of the city center.

From the Virginia side, Routes 66 or 50 will get you across the Potomac and into Washington's heart. Route 395, which branches off from the Beltway far to the South, will take you right across the 14th Street Bridge to the central downtown area, or you can spin off to the right for the Maine Avenue waterfront or Capitol Hill. If you do much exploring or shopping in the nearby Virginia suburbs, 395 will become a close friend.

BY PLANE

There are three airports in all, one of them discouragingly far away and another—if you watch Arlington's office towers slip by during the approach—unnervingly close.

National Airport, the closest, is like a commuter port gone berserk. It's a hodgepodge of new and old terminals strung haphazardly along the Potomac River. Convenience is what sustains it. For years, residents along its flight paths have tried to argue its removal—but a fifteen-minute limousine ride to Capitol Hill is nothing to sneeze at for busy members of Congress, who defend it as their own. There's even a large parking area beside the main terminal especially set aside for the city's powerful—legislators, diplomats and judges.

For those of less rarefied calling, National still is the most convenient major airport in the United States. The fastest escape is via the Metrorail subway system which, for 85 cents (non-rush-hour), will take you into the heart of the city in minutes. Taxis are reasonably cheap, too, and the White House, for instance, is just three miles away. Typical taxi fare to downtown is $8 plus tip. It will do you no good, farewise, to share a cab with someone also heading into the city. Unless passengers are picked up and discharged together, each is charged individually. An airport pick-up fee is normally added to your taxi fare, and you may be charged more for extra luggage. (But more about taxis later.)

In addition, Washington Flyer's buses leave on the half hour on weekdays (hourly on weekends) from the Capitol Hilton Hotel at 16th and K streets for the National terminals; from the airport, the same buses will deliver you to the Capitol Hilton, the Washington Hilton, the Washington Sheraton, the Mayflower or the Omni Shoreham. The fare is $5 each way; call 685-1400 for more details.

Washington-Dulles International Airport, 28 miles east of the city in Virginia, is a lovely, uncomplicated place and, thanks to airline deregulation, is among the fastest-growing airports in the nation. This is the airport where most international flights arrive and where passengers get to and from their planes in little people-mover buses.

The distances in Washington pose the main problem for travelers. It can easily take 30 to 45 minutes to get into the city, longer if there are traffic problems. There are on-again, off-again proposals for a mass-transit link, but until that happens, the choice is between bus and taxi. Washington Flyer holds the main bus concession and, for $12 each way, departs on the half hour from the Capitol Hilton for Dulles. Washington Flyer (685-1400) also runs buses that connect Dulles to National. For $8 to $15 (depending on your destination), Washington Flyer will deliver you from Dulles to selected hotels in Virginia, D.C. and Maryland. You'll pay three times that for a cab to or from Dulles.

Farther away still is Baltimore-Washington International Airport, which is closer to Baltimore than it is to Washington. BWI is, nonetheless, a frequent arrival and departure point for international flights. (Note that the only international flights into National Airport are from Canadian points with U.S. Customs and immigration preclearance facilities.) But BWI boasts a relatively convenient rail link. A free shuttle bus connects with Amtrak's southbound trains. The seven daily trains run from 7:18 a.m. to 7:17 p.m. (800-USA-RAIL); it's a half-hour trip, and the fare is $10.50 one way, $16 to $21 round trip.

Bus service is also available to National and Dulles airports. Taxi service is available but, at about $45, quite pricey.

BY TRAIN

The newly renovated Union Station is worth a trip by itself, in fact it's where many Washingtonians now go for a night out. The millions spent by the city and federal governments show up in the form of brass ticket counters, marble columns, and soaring gilt ceilings. Passengers hop off the train into a maze of food stalls, elegant shops and top-notch restaurants. Many schedule extra time to grab a bench and stare at the splendor of it all. One step on the escalator leads to the Metrorail or you can hail a cab for a short ride to any of the major hotels.

AT YOUR SERVICE

IS IT SAFE?

Well, look, it's not Bismarck, North Dakota. But neither is it a war zone. Washington has its crime problems, its dangerous sections and its share of unpredictability in the streets. But few visitors encounter anything more worrisome than the hordes of partying teens that flood affluent Georgetown every Friday and Saturday night. (Even the raucous kids seem sometimes to be all but outnumbered by police.) A few relatively obvious precautions: stay out of parks after dusk; if a cab won't take you someplace, find out why not; and if you simply must go there anyway, phone a radio cab to get home, even if it means waiting indoors a little longer. Follow your instincts. There's just no point in ambling down a dark and vacant street at 2 a.m. Anywhere. Even in Bethesda. The good news is that the subways are well-patrolled and safe at all hours.

FOREIGN EXCHANGE

There is a bank here that calls itself the most important bank in the most important city in the world, but life still won't be easy if you hope to exchange your sterling for dollars on a Sunday. In fact, it can't be done anywhere in the city, unless your hotel cashier can oblige. During weekday office hours, a number of major banks, but by no means all of them, will accept foreign currency. Several private agencies also exist, including Deak International (872-1427) at 1800 K Street NW, and Reusch International (887-0990) at 1140 19th Street NW.

Traveler's checks denominated in U.S. dollars are acceptable almost anywhere, but don't be surprised if you're asked to produce identification. Out-of-town bank checks, again payable only in U.S. currency, are accepted by some, but not all, merchants.

Think about your currency situation before you head out onto the streets. Although Americans may get upset when they can't use their dollars outside the country, there's no such courtesy afforded to foreign tourists here. It's dollars or credit cards or nothing.

ACCESS FOR THE HANDICAPPED

Washington is one of those rare cities where it's easy to get around if you have a disability. The street intersections are all designed with cut-out curbs and ramps for wheelchairs, and often, the building elevators have numbers in braille and a special tone system for the deaf. All public buildings have special access and restroom facilities for the handicapped.

There are elevators in all subway stations, and some municipal buses are equipped with special lifts (call 962-1825 for bus information). Subway information for the hearing-impaired is 638-3780, TDD.

TELEPHONE NUMBERS

The area code for Washington is 202. Nearby Maryland suburbs have a 301 area code, and Northern Virginia has a 703 area code. However, no area code need be dialed for Virginia or Maryland numbers from the metropolitan area.

The telephone directory information number for Washington and surrounding suburbs is 411. Be aware that Washington has experienced some serious response-delay problems with its 911 emergency number, as have many large cities. At this writing, the system is under review but remains the sole option for critical medical emergencies.

AAA Road Service, 222-5000
Access for the Handicapped, 547-8081
Animal Bites, 576-6664
Better Business Bureau of Metropolitan Washington, 393-8000
Capital Reservations (handles about 70 area hotels), (800) VISIT-DC
Deaf Emergency (TTY/TDD), 727-9334
Dental Referral Service, 547-7615
Dial-a-Park (day's events), 485-7275
Doctor Referral, 362-8677
Emergency (police, fire, ambulance), 911
FBI, 324-3000
Fire and Ambulance (nonemergency), 462-1762
Harbor Police, 727-4582
Poison Control Center, 625-3333
Police (nonemergency), 727-1010
Rape Crisis Center, 333-7273
Sports Update (*Washington Post*), 334-9000
Suicide Prevention, 561-7000
Time of Day, 844-1111
Tourist Information, 737-8866
Traveler's Aid, 347-0101, 684-3472
U.S. Capitol, 224-3121
U.S. Customs, 566-8195
U.S. Passport Office, 647-0518
U.S. Supreme Court, 479-3000
Visa Inquiries, 663-1895
Washington, D.C. Convention & Visitors Association, 789-7000
Weather, 936-1111
White House, 456-1414

SALES TAXES

Some visitors find them steep (at 6 percent in Washington stores), but you can avoid some of the sting by having goods shipped home. Unfortunately, meals, which can't very well be mailed, are subject to a 9-percent tax. The sales tax in Virginia is 4 percent, and the sales tax in Maryland is 5 percent.

TIPPING

Now don't go into tourist shock, but the old 10-percent rule (for tips other than in restaurants) doesn't hold here at all. A standard tip in Washington is no less than 15 percent, with tips of 20 percent not all that uncommon, especially if you benefit from good service. You can probably get by with a lesser tip if you're just sitting at a bar but not if you're engaging in a drink-a-thon, especially at a more fashionable watering hole. Taxi drivers usually get some tip, also. Frequently, it amounts to a logical rounding off of the fare. A $2.10 trip, for instance, usually would be $2.50 with tip included.

GETTING AROUND

Even before you decide how to get there, find out *exactly* where you're going. Usually, that's not difficult, once you absorb the unusual layout of the city and accept that such navigational concepts as north, south, east and west may seem completely impossible to use.

Remember that the Capitol is where everything starts, the dividing point for the four quadrants splayed out from it. The basic grid begins with numbered streets running north and south and alphabetized streets running east and west. Be particularly aware of the the quadrant design of the city, since every street address carries a designation—NW, NE, SW or SE. Make sure you have that designation before you head out, since the same address could be in as many as four different places.

There are a few other quirks, even at this basic stage. I Street is frequently spelled "Eye," for instance. And, since "I" and "J" were used interchangeably when the city was being planned, there is no J Street now. Neither will you find a "B," "X," "Y" or "Z" street.

Beyond the lettered streets are two-syllable street names, also in alphabetical order (Adams, Bryant, and so on). Then the city moves into three-syllable street names, beginning with Albemarle and Brandywine.

Now the hard part. The nice logic of everything thus far turns practically whimsical when it comes to the avenues. These are usually broad streets that run diagonal to the numbered and alphabetically named streets. All named after states, the avenues swoop through the grid, taking unsuspecting motorists on trips to nowhere. What's more, they are linked by traffic circles, the most fiendishly terrifying system of traffic interchanges known to humanity. This is where such niceties as yielding to the right simply collapse in chaos. For navigational purposes, it's wise to ask for the nearest intersection.

Although Washington bowed to federal pressure and finally approved the concept of "right turn on red," it did so only grudgingly. As a result, the city has done the bare minimum it can in that regard. Right turns are allowed on red lights *if* you see no sign, but those intersections are a tiny minority. More frequently—and for absolutely no reason in most cases—you will find right turns on red expressly prohibited or allowed only between 7 p.m. and 7 a.m.

Quite frequently, you will also find intersections where turns are allowed only when a green arrow tells you to proceed. And, if all that hasn't discouraged you from driving, consider that during morning and evening rush hours, perfectly normal streets suddenly become one-way in or out of the city. As a result, you could be driving along bothering no one and suddenly, the clock will strike 4 o'clock and a rush of traffic will be coming directly at you—on your side of the street, no less. The only suggestion is the obvious one: get out of the way, quickly!

Also, the District, Virginia and Maryland are particularly hard on drunk drivers. If you've had a few too many, do yourself a favor and don't drive.

Do not venture out without a map of the city. You can get one free at the Visitors Center, which can be found on the first floor of the Department of Commerce at 15th and E streets NW. The map also shows the subway (Metrorail) routes.

METRORAIL & METROBUS

Destination determined, Washington's glitzy subway system is often the best way to go. Even with one of its lines, the Green Line, still under construction, the Metro is remarkably efficient, and it challenges the likes of Montreal and Moscow for cleanliness and sheer beauty.

Don't be dismayed by the high-tech gadgetry. Like Boston and San Francisco, Washington uses a farecard system. That can mean negotiating long rush-hour lines in front of frequently balky fare machines. Best to load up in advance, depositing as much as you might reasonably need in the days ahead. Most machines accept $1 and $5 bills, as well as silver, and make change. Do not, whatever you do, deposit $5 and then ask for $4.20 back. You'll need an armored car for the resulting torrent of nickels.

The basic fare is 85 cents, but it increases during rush hours (morning and evening) and with distance traveled. The most a rush-hour trip will cost you in Washington is $2.55, while the most a non-rush-hour trip will cost is $1.25. If you take the subway beyond the city limits, you will pay more. If you need to add to your farecard, there are "addfare" machines at each exit. They look like ordinary fare machines. Just slip your card in and pay the additional amount indicated.

The subway system operates from 5:30 a.m. to midnight Monday through Friday, from 8 a.m. to midnight on Saturday and from 10 a.m. to midnight on Sunday. On holidays, the subways operate on Sunday schedules.

Route and schedule information, and—if you provide your destination, even the exact fare you will need to pay—can be obtained by phoning 637-7000.

Bicycle lockers are available at some stations. Permits are required for bikes taken on board. Call 962-1116 for information.

There are limitations to Metrorail. One is that is closes at midnight; another is that several major neighborhoods, including the Georgetown and Adams Morgan restaurant districts, are not directly served.

Municipal buses help fill Metrorail's gaps, trundling along about 400 routes around the clock. There's nothing quite as awful as finding oneself trapped inside a hermetically sealed Metrobus on a blazing day in mid-July, with the air conditioning not working. But the Transit Authority claims things have been improving lately. In any event, the buses are a useful adjunct to the subway system.

If you need to go from subway to bus, obtain a bus transfer from machines just after you pass through the subway turnstile. (The transfers from buses, however, work only on buses and are not accepted on the subway.)

The basic bus fare is 85 cents in the District—and more in the suburbs at rush hour. Bus drivers don't make change, but if you have only a $1 bill, they'll accept it.

If you are planning well in advance, the Transit Authority will send you specific bus timetables by mail; phone 637-7000. Route information and bus tokens can be obtained at a number of locations, and Metro Information at 637-7000 will happily provide you with the proper bus to take—and where to catch it—if you tell the operator where you are and where you wish to go.

PARKING

Whether done legally or illegally, parking in Washington is expensive. A downtown parking garage can cost $8.50 a day or more. And a parking ticket can cost $20 at a minimum. However, you can find the occasional lot in a decent area that charges as (relatively) low as $7.50 a day.

If you're staying with friends in a residential area with restricted parking, your best bet is a visitor's parking permit, available at police stations. That will allow you to park in the neighborhood without risking a parking-zone violation. Or you can park at special Metrorail parking areas, near the outskirts, and take the subway into the city.

There are also numerous streets in the city where metered parking is allowed. But check carefully to determine the hours for the meters. Before 9:30 a.m. and after 4 p.m. are frequently "no parking" times, and your car *will* be towed away. Liberating it will cost a cool $50, to say nothing of the hassle, and the traffic division doesn't afford any special privileges to folks with out-of-state license plates. If your car is gone, look at the sign you ignored in the first place for instructions.

If you choose the parking-meter route, load your pockets with quarters. The going rate is 25 cents for 20 minutes. Often, meters are good only for one hour, and sometimes only 30 minutes. Washington also uses the charming Denver Boot—a nasty device that completely immobilizes your car—to crack down on folk who don't pay their traffic tickets. You win this prize with three unpaid tickets. (For information, call 727-5000.)

TAXIS

Big changes may be afoot for Washington's taxi industry, if reports from City Hall are to be believed. For the moment, however, Washington is stuck with the dingiest, oldest—but most convenient and, by big-city standards, cheapest—cab fleet in the country. In its current, unreformed state, the average taxi may, just may, get you to your destination without getting lost. If so, you'll have had a transportation bargain.

Here is how it works. You can flag a cab down on the street, have a hotel doorperson whistle one down or you can summon a cab by phone ($1 will be added to fare) through any of the major cab companies (try the Yellow Pages). Once inside, you'll notice that District cabs don't have meters. They operate on a zone system. Driving within one zone costs a flat $2.65 for one person, plus a surcharge for extra passengers. It should be noted that one can travel from Capitol Hill to virtually every tourist attraction and many downtown locations for a one-zone fare. The speculation is that Zone 1 is so large because Capitol Hill types swing a lot of influence and don't cotton to paying a higher fare for their city travels.

There's also a $1 additional charge during evening rush hour, from 4 p.m. to 6:30 p.m. That rush-hour charge is applicable only for trips that originate at 4 p.m. or after. Do not allow a fast-talking cabbie to bill you for rush hour just because you arrive at your destination after 4 p.m. If the city declares a "snow emergency," your taxi fares will rise dramatically.

Now, here is how it *doesn't* work. You will find vast armadas of cabs waiting idly outside major hotels at times when not one is available at Union Station. Or, if it rains, you can wave for all you are worth, and the taxis will simply glide on by, drivers' eyes fixed determinedly at some point in the middle distance. Or, if you wish to go to some less affluent section, the driver may simply refuse. District rules prohibit a cab driver from refusing to take you to where you want to go once you are inside the cab. But it's legal—and, unfortunately, practiced all too often—to grill a passenger who is standing on the street as to his or her destination before agreeing to the fare.

There are many fine cab drivers in the city, honest men and women who play by the rules and who aren't out to bilk or abuse the passenger. But there are also some real losers driving the streets in cabs. Of late, it seems that cab driving has become the job of choice for recent arrivals to this country. Often, they don't speak English all that well and frequently don't have a hint of where they're going (we're talking the Capitol and the Supreme Court, not some obscure residential address). Sadly, some of these drivers are not licensed to be operating a cab in the District.

The first clue that you're being taken for a ride is the absence of anything resembling an official sanction for the operation of the cab itself or the driver in it. Do you see, prominently displayed, the driver's "face," or license, with photo? Does the driver have a clipboard on which to record the address where you were picked you up, your destination and the fare? Does the cab have a legible and updated zone map or a poster explaining your rights as a passenger? If the answer to these questions is no, you might want to get out of the cab right then and flag down another. If the cabbie gives you any grief about nonpayment, you might wish to suggest that he or she take you directly to a police station.

Complaints may be pursued with the city, but the complainant must be present for a later hearing. For the visitor, the more practical course may be a call to the cab company. Either way, be sure to have particulars. You can get the driver's identification number from his "face," or record the number of the cab or its license plate.

Remember, too, drivers may, with your permission, pick up other riders. It won't affect your fare one way or the other. But if the additional passenger is going out of your way, you must be taken to your destination first. If you don't want company, say so. That's your right.

GOINGS-ON

In addition to ongoing exhibits, events and attractions, the Washington area also offers special seasonal activities. Exact dates and times of these listings vary, so it's wise to check in advance with the Visitor Information Center (789-7000) or the National Park Service.

JANUARY

- Congress formally opens (first week).
- Presidential Inauguration, January 20, every fourth year (1993 is next), on the steps of the Capitol. A parade follows down Pennsylvania Ave.
- Martin Luther King Jr.'s birthday is celebrated, third Monday, with events throughout the metropolitan area; 755-1005.
- Robert E. Lee's (and his father, Light-Horse Harry Lee's) birthday observances, Jan. 28, Lee home, 607 Oronoco St., Alexandria, Va.; (703) 838-4200. Arlington House celebration, (703) 557-0613.

FEBRUARY

- Chinese New Year's Festival, early Feb., Chinatown. Parade on Chinese New Year, and special holiday menus at area restaurants.
- Abraham Lincoln's birthday observed, Feb. 12, Lincoln Memorial; 485-9666.
- George Washington's birthday parade, Feb. 19, down Washington St. in Old Town Alexandria, Va. Free. (703) 838-4200.
- Washington's birthday observed, Feb. 22, Washington Monument, at Mount Vernon, Va.
- Washington International Boat Show, Convention Center, 900 9th St. NW, date varies; 789-1600.
- World of Wheels Custom Auto Show, Convention Center, date varies; 371-4200 or 789-1600.

MARCH

- St. Patrick's Day Parade down Constitution Ave., Mar. 11, with floats, military bands, Irish dancers and bagpipers; 424-2200.
- Smithsonian Kite Festival, Mar. 17, Washington Monument grounds; free; 357-3030.

APRIL

- Cherry Blossom Festival, late Mar. or early Apr., week-long festivities; 737-2599 or 789-7000.
- Easter Sunrise Services, late Mar. or early Apr., Arlington National Cemetery; 692-0931.
- Easter Egg Roll, Easter Mon., late Mar. or early Apr., White House lawn; 456-7041.
- Georgetown House and Garden Tour, mid-Apr.; 333-4953.
- Gross National Parade, mid-Apr., unorthodox parade along Pennsylvania Ave. from the White House to Georgetown to benefit Police Boys and Girls Club; 686-3051.
- Jefferson's birthday observed, Apr. 13, Jefferson Memorial; 485-9666.
- Old Town Alexandria, Va., house tour, late Apr.; (703) 329-1737.
- Shakespeare's Birthday celebration, Sat. closest to Apr. 23, Folger Shakespeare Library; 544-7077.

- Washington Craft Show, late Apr., jury-selected offerings of 100 artists from across the country. Dedicated to crafts as fine art; 357-2700.
- White House Spring Garden Tour, mid-Apr., featuring the Rose Garden and West Lawn, the White House grounds; 456-7041.
- White House Easter Egg Roll, Apr. 16, for children 8 and under (accompanied by an adult); free; (202) 456-2200
- Spring Design for Living Show, Convention Center, date varies; 798-1600 or 371-4200.
- White House News Photographers Assoc. show, Library of Congress; 707-5000.

MAY

- Washington Cathedral Outdoor Fair, first weekend in May.; 537-6200.
- Greek Spring Festival, mid-May, Saints Constantine and Helen Greek Orthodox Church, 4415 16th St. NW; 829-2910.
- Memorial Day, last Mon., services at Tomb of the Unknown Soldier, Arlington National Cemetery, 692-0931; services at the Vietnam Veterans Memorial, 485-9666; free concert by National Symphony on Capitol grounds, no phone.

JUNE

- Outdoor stages open for the season at Wolf Trap, Merriweather Post Pavilion and Carter Baron Amphitheater, late May or early June; check *Washington Post* for schedules.
- Civil War Pageant, Alexandria, Va.; (703) 838-4200.
- Potomac River Fest, early June, various sites along the river; 387-8292.

JULY

- Bastille Day Race, July 13. Waiters race 12 blocks down Pennsylvania Ave. balancing Champagne and glasses for free trip to Paris, starting at Dominique Restaurant, 20th St. & Pennsylvania Ave. NW; 452-1132.
- Highland Games, Alexandria, Va., two-day Celtic Festival; (703) 838-4200.
- Independence Day Celebration, July 4, music performances and evening fireworks display, Washington Monument grounds and Mall; free concert by the National Symphony on the Capitol grounds; 485-9666.

- Smithsonian's Annual Folk Life Festival, late June or early July, the Mall; 357-2700.

AUGUST

- Hispanic Festival, Adams Morgan & Mount Pleasant districts, date varies; no phone.
- Arlington County Fair, mid-Aug.; Thomas Jefferson Center, 3501 S. 2nd St., Arlington, Va.; free; (703) 358-6400.
- DC Blues Festival, Aug. 27, Anacostia Park; 483-0871.

SEPTEMBER

- Adams Morgan Day, mid-Sept., 18th St. & Columbia Rd. NW; 332-3292.
- Labor Day concert, first Mon., National Symphony, Capitol grounds; free; 785-1800.
- Rock Creek Park Day, birthday celebration for the park, last Sat. in month; 426-6832.
- Washington Redskins football season opens, early Sept., RFK Stadium; 546-2222.
- Open House Arts Festival, mid-Sept., Kennedy Center, free; 254-3600.
- Kalorama House Tour, mid-Sept., The Woodrow Wilson House Museum, 2340 S St. NW; 387-4062.
- Oktoberfest, end of Sept., Pavillon at the Old Post Office; 289-4224.

OCTOBER

- Colonial Craft Fair, Decatur House; 842-0920.
- Columbus Day, second Mon., wreath laying at Columbus Memorial, Union Station; 638-0220.
- Supreme Court opening ceremony, first Mon.; 479-3000.
- Washington International Horse Show, Oct. 21-28, Capital Centre, Largo, Md.; (301) 840-0281.
- White House Fall Garden Tour, mid-Oct., White House grounds; 426-6700 or 472-3669.

NOVEMBER

- Marine Corps Marathon, early Nov., 26.2-mile course, beginning at the Iwo Jima Statue; 690-3431.
- Veteran's Day service, Nov. 11, Arlington National Cemetery amphitheater; 692-0931.
- Vietnam Veteran's Day Salute, Nov. 11, Vietnam Veterans Memorial; 485-9666.
- Washington Bullets basketball season opens, late Nov., Capital Center, Landover, Md.; (301) 350-3400.

DECEMBER

- Festival of Music and Lights, Nov. 30-Jan. 1; Mormon Temple, Kensington, Md.. Concerts evenings 7:30 p.m.; free; (301) 587-0144.
- Christmas Candlelight Tour through famous old homes of Alexandria, Va., second weekend of the month; (703) 549-0205.
- Christmas Tree Lighting, mid-Dec., Capitol; 224-3069.
- National Capital Area Auto Show, date varies, Convention Center; 371-4200 or 789-1600.
- Pearl Harbor Day observance, Dec. 7, Iwo Jima Memorial; 433-4173.
- Pageant of Peace/Lighting of the National Christmas Tree, early to mid-Dec., the Ellipse near the White House; 426-7041.
- Scottish Christmas Walk, early Dec., Old Town Alexandria, Va.; (703) 838-4200
- White House Christmas Candlelight tours, Dec. 27-28; free; 456-2200.
- New Year's Eve Celebration, Dec. 31, Old Post Office Pavilion, 1100 Pennsylvania Ave. NW; 289-4224.

MAPS

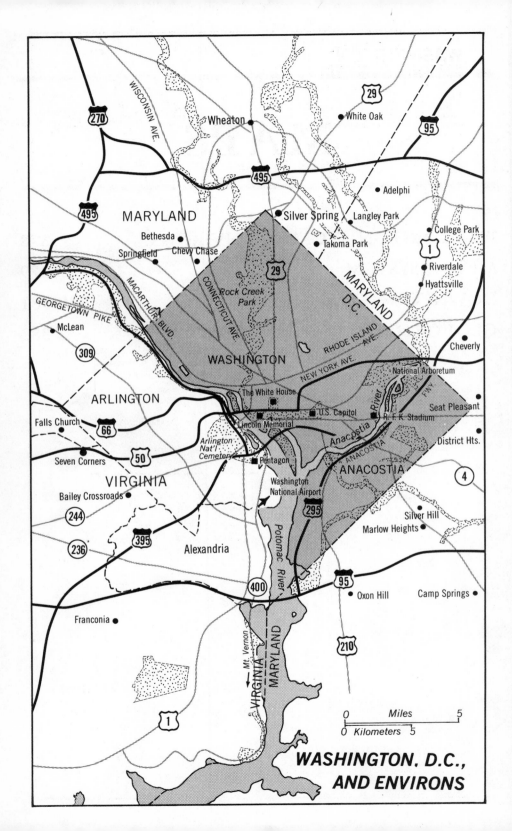

**WASHINGTON, D.C.,
AND ENVIRONS**

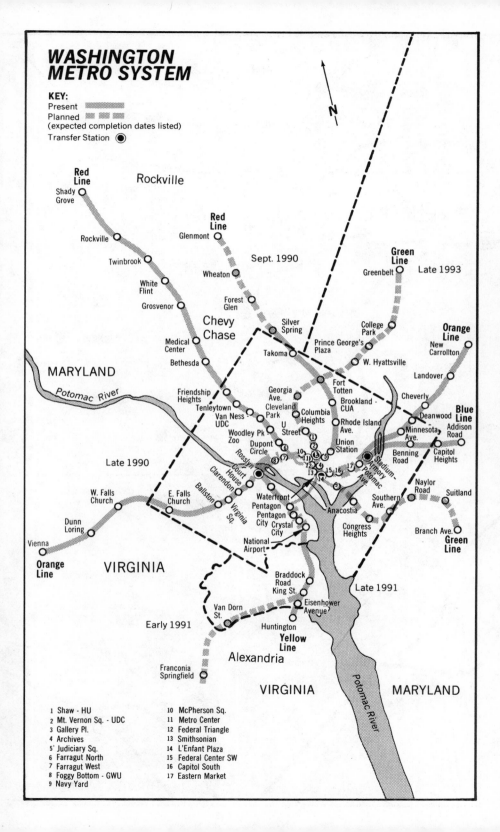

WASHINGTON METRO SYSTEM

KEY:
Present
Planned
(expected completion dates listed)
Transfer Station ◉

Red Line
Shady Grove
Rockville
Twinbrook
White Flint
Grosvenor
Medical Center
Bethesda

Rockville

Red Line
Glenmont
Sept. 1990
Wheaton
Forest Glen
Chevy Chase

MARYLAND
Potomac River

Green Line
Greenbelt
Late 1993
College Park
Prince George's Plaza
W. Hyattsville

Orange Line
New Carrollton
Landover
Cheverly

Silver Spring
Takoma

Friendship Heights
Tenleytown
Van Ness - UDC
Woodley Pk Zoo
Georgia Ave.
Cleveland Park
Columbia Heights
U Street
Dupont Circle
Fort Totten
Brookland - CUA
Rhode Island Ave.
Union Station

Deanwood
Minnesota Ave.
Benning Road

Blue Line
Addison Road
Capitol Heights

Late 1990
Rosslyn
Court House
Clarendon
Ballston
Virginia Sq.
E. Falls Church
W. Falls Church
Dunn Loring
Vienna

Orange Line

VIRGINIA

Waterfront
Pentagon
Pentagon City
Crystal City
National Airport

Braddock Road
King St.
Van Dorn St.
Early 1991
Huntington
Franconia Springfield

Eisenhower Avenue
Late 1991

Yellow Line
Alexandria

VIRGINIA

Stadium - Armory
Potomac Ave.

Naylor Road
Suitland
Southern Ave.
Anacostia
Congress Heights
Branch Ave.
Green Line

Potomac River

MARYLAND

1 Shaw - HU
2 Mt. Vernon Sq. - UDC
3 Gallery Pl.
4 Archives
5 Judiciary Sq.
6 Farragut North
7 Farragut West
8 Foggy Bottom - GWU
9 Navy Yard
10 McPherson Sq.
11 Metro Center
12 Federal Triangle
13 Smithsonian
14 L'Enfant Plaza
15 Federal Center SW
16 Capitol South
17 Eastern Market

N

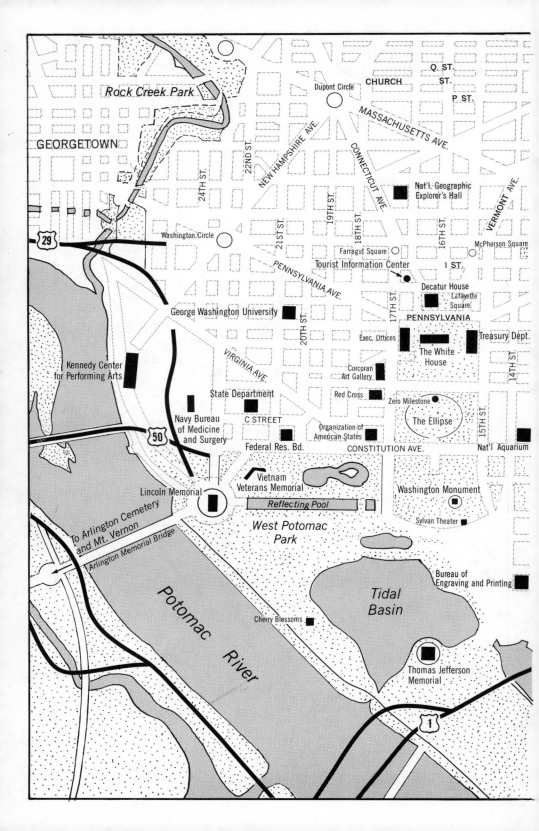

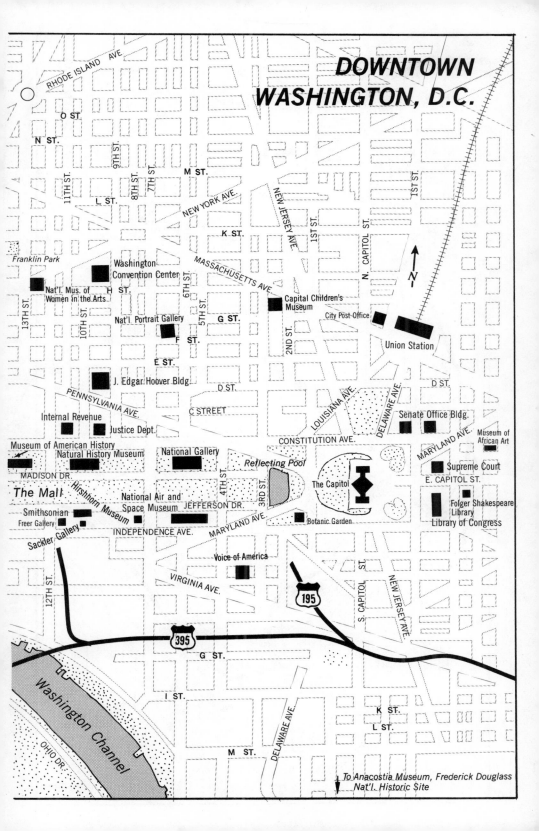

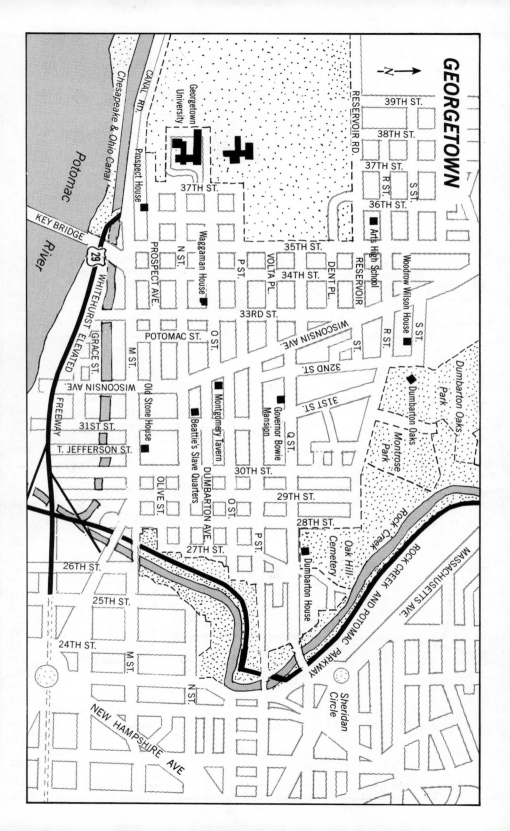

INDEX

QUESTIONNAIRE

The Gault Millau series of guidebooks reflects your demand for insightful, incisive reporting on the best (and worst) that the world's most exciting destinations have to offer. To help us make our books even better, please take a moment to fill out this anonymous (if you wish) questionnaire. Return it to:

Gault Millau Inc.
P.O. Box 361144
Los Angeles, CA 90036

1. How did you hear about Gault Millau guides: bookstore, newspaper, magazine, radio, friends or other ? (please specify) _____
_____

2. What cities (and/or countries) are you most interested in seeing covered in a Gault Millau guide? Please list in order of preference:_____
_____
_____

3. Do you refer to Gault Millau guides only on your travels, or do you use the Gault Millau guide for your own city, too?

☐ Travels   ☐ Own city   ☐ Both

4. What are the three features you like most about Gault Millau guides?
   1._____
   2._____
   3._____

5. What are the features, if any, you dislike about Gault Millau guides?
_____
_____
_____

6. Please list any features you would like to see added to Gault Millau guides.
_____
_____
_____

Please turn over →

7. Do you use any other travel guides in addition to Gault Millau? If so, please list:_____

_____

_____

8. If you use another guidebook series, please list the features you enjoy most or find most useful about it:_____

_____

_____

9. How many trips do you take per year?

Business trips: Domestic _____   International _____

Pleasure trips: Domestic _____   International _____

10. Please check the category that reflects your annual household income:

☐ $20,000–$39,000   ☐ $80,000–99,000
☐ $40,000–$59,000   ☐ $100,000–$120,000
☐ $60,000–$79,000   ☐ Other (please specify)_____
                                                      _____

11. We thank you for your interest in Gault Millau guides, and we welcome your remarks and recommendations about restaurants, hotels, nightlife, shops and services around the world.

   If you have any comments on Gault Millau guides in general, please list them in the space below.

André Gayot's
TASTES
with the Best of Gault Millau

THE WORLD DINING & TRAVEL CONNECTION

P.O. Box 361144, Los Angeles, CA 90036

- ♦ All you'll ever need to know about the beds and tables (and under the tables) of the world.
- ♦ The best—and other—restaurants, hotels, nightlife, shopping, fashion.
- ♦ What's hot, lukewarm and cold fromHollywood to Hong Kong via Paris.

☐ **YES,** please enter/renew my subscription for 6 bimonthly issues at the rate of $30. (Outside U.S. and Canada, $35.)

Name_____

Address_____

City_____State _____

Zip_____Country _____

☐ **ALSO,** please send a gift subscription to: *

Name_____

Address_____

City_____State _____

Zip_____Country _____

Gift from_____
(We will notify recipient of your gift)

* With the purchase of a gift subscription or a second subscription, you will receive, **FREE,** the **Gault Millau guidebook of your choice**—a $17 value. (See preceding order form for a complete list of Gault Millau guides.)

☐ CHECK ENCLOSED FOR $ _____.
☐ PLEASE SEND ME, **FREE,** THE GAULT MILLAU GUIDE OF MY CHOICE: _____

304/90

MORE GAULT MILLAU "BEST" GUIDES

Now the guidebook series known throughout Europe for its wit and savvy reveals the best of major U.S., European and Asian destinations. Gault Millau books include full details on the best of everything that makes these places special: the restaurants, diversions, nightlife, hotels, shops, arts. The guides also offer practical information on getting around and enjoying each area. Perfect for visitors and residents alike.

Please send me the books checked below:

☐ The Best of Chicago $15.95
☐ The Best of London $16.95
☐ The Best of Los Angeles $16.95
☐ The Best of New England $15.95
☐ The Best of New York $16.95
☐ The Best of Paris $16.95
☐ The Best of San Francisco $16.95
☐ The Best of Washington, D.C. $16.95
☐ The Best of France $16.95
☐ The Best of Italy $16.95
☐ The Best of Hong Kong $16.95

PRENTICE HALL TRADE DIVISION
Order Department—Travel Books
200 Old Tappan Road
Old Tappan, NJ 07675

In the U.S., include $2 (UPS shipping charge) for the first book, and $1 for each additional book. Outside the U.S., $3 and $1 respectively.

Enclosed is my check or money order made out to Prentice Hall Trade Division, for $ _____

NAME_____

ADDRESS_____

CITY _____STATE _____

ZIP_____COUNTRY _____